AF606890

Sea of Ink ∽ Forest of Pens

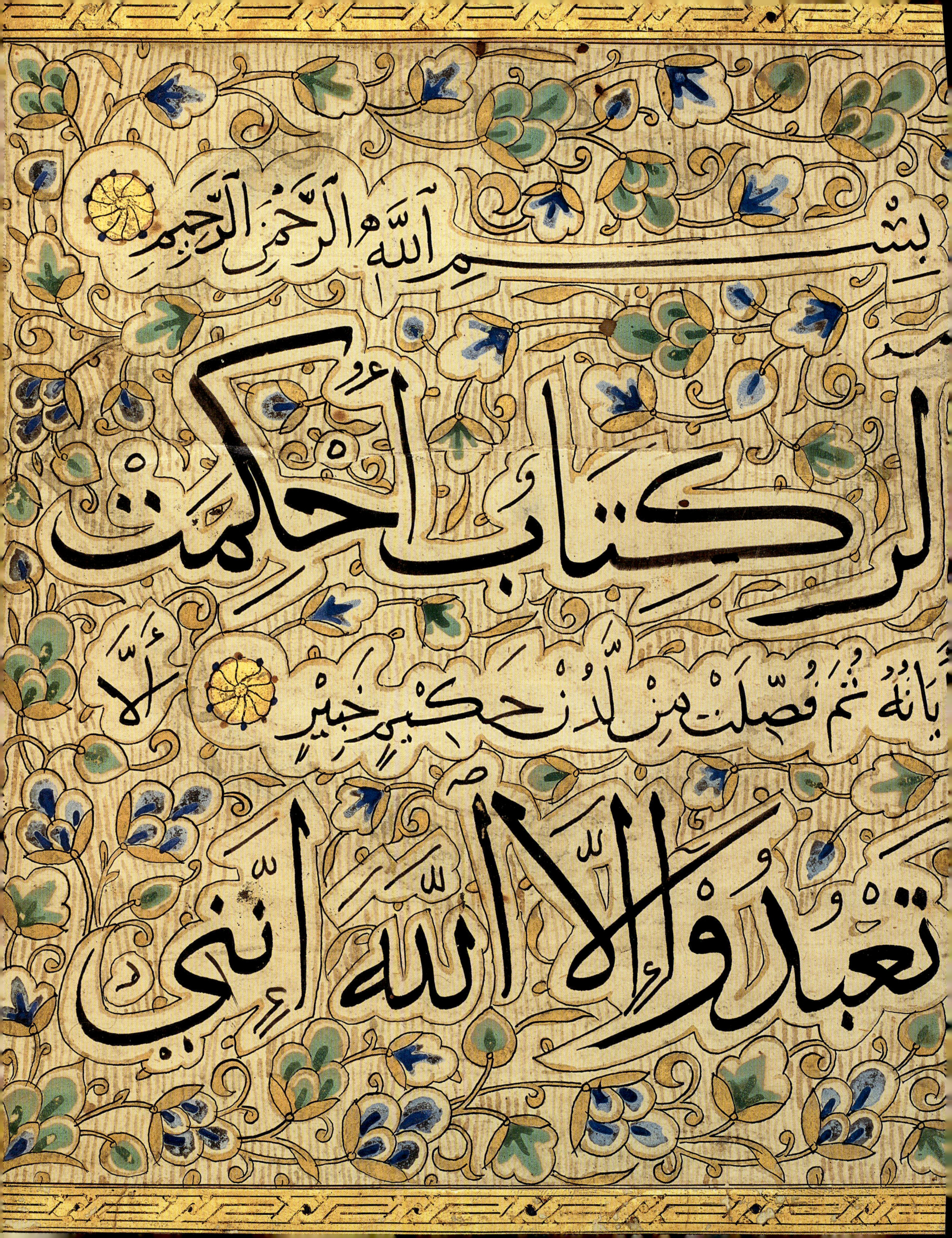

بسم الله الرحمن الرحيم
الر كتاب أحكمت
آياته ثم فصلت من لدن حكيم خبير
ألا
تعبدوا إلا الله إنني

Sea of Ink ∽ Forest of Pens

The Art of the Qur'an in the Hossein Afshar Collection

By David J. Roxburgh
Edited by Aimée Froom

The Museum of Fine Arts, Houston

Distributed by Yale University Press
New Haven and London

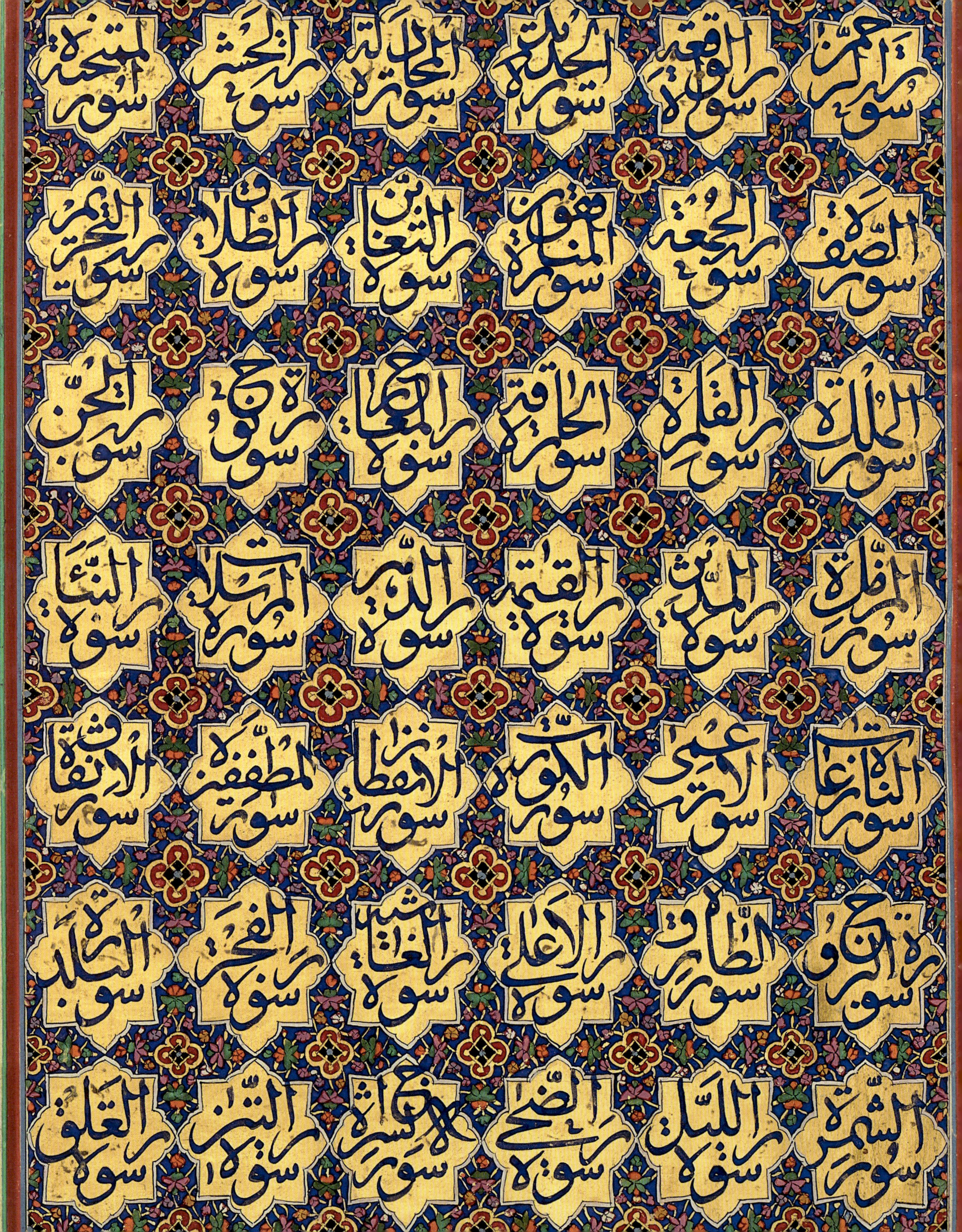
سورة الرحمن
سورة الواقعة
سورة الحديد
سورة المجادلة
سورة الحشر
سورة الممتحنة
سورة الصف
سورة الجمعة
سورة المنافقون
سورة التغابن
سورة الطلاق
سورة التحريم
سورة الملك
سورة القلم
سورة الحاقة
سورة المعارج
سورة نوح
سورة الجن
سورة المزمل
سورة المدثر
سورة القيمة
سورة الدهر
سورة المرسلات
سورة النبأ
سورة النازعات
سورة عبس
سورة التكوير
سورة الانفطار
سورة المطففين
سورة الانشقاق
سورة البروج
سورة الطارق
سورة الاعلى
سورة الغاشية
سورة الفجر
سورة البلد
سورة الشمس
سورة الليل
سورة الضحى
سورة الانشراح
سورة التين
سورة العلق

Contents

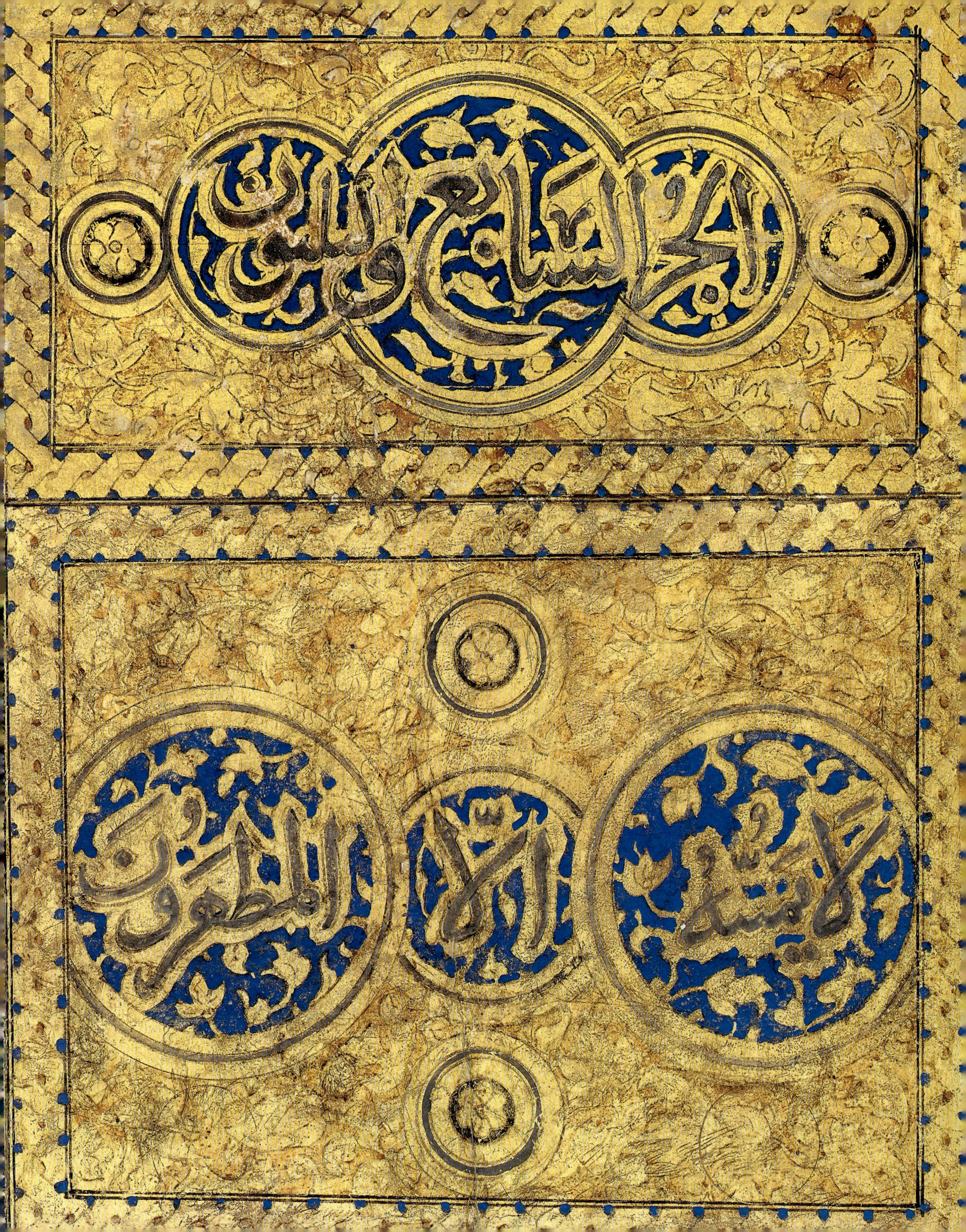
لا يمسه إلا المطهرون

If all the trees of the earth were pens and the oceans ink,
with many more oceans for replenishing them,
the colloquy of God would never come to end.
He is indeed all mighty and all wise.

QUR'AN 31:27

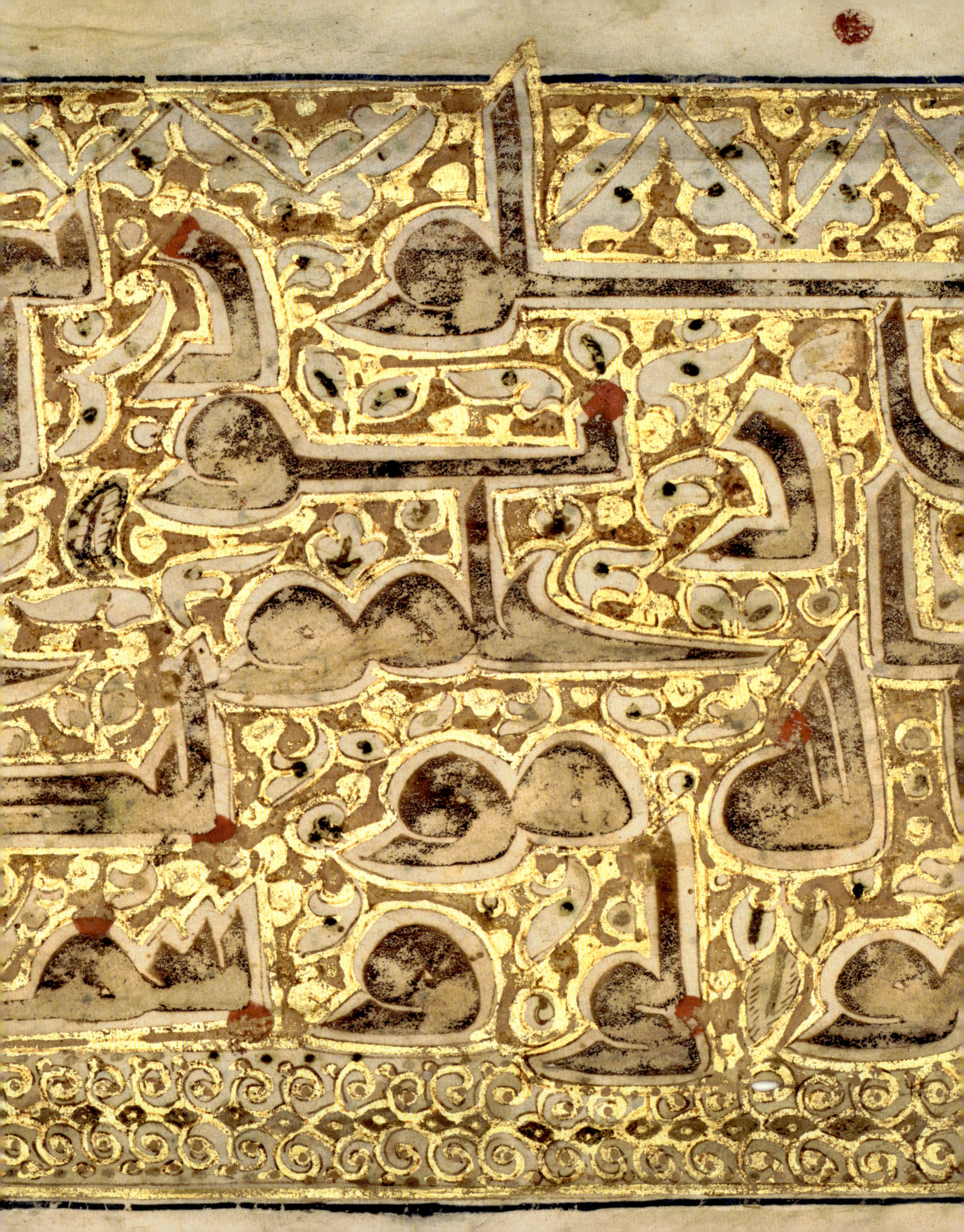

Foreword

The opening of the new galleries for Art of the Islamic Worlds at the Museum of Fine Arts, Houston, on March 5, 2023, marked a milestone for this initiative which began in 2007. It was made possible largely because of the generosity of Mr. Hossein Afshar, for whom the galleries are named. In addition to his financial support, we are privileged to have on long-term loan his collection, which is one of the greatest collections of the arts of Iran in private hands, built carefully over the last fifty years. This partnership began in 2017 with an inaugural exhibition and catalogue, *Bestowing Beauty: Masterpieces from Persian Lands – Selections from the Hossein Afshar Collection*, which featured masterpieces of Iranian visual culture from the sixth to the nineteenth century, including metalwork, ceramics, paintings, textiles, and lacquer work. Most of these works are now on view with the Museum's permanent collection in nearly six thousand square feet of space in the new Hossein Afshar Galleries for Art of the Islamic Worlds.

The present catalogue is a focused publication that delves deeply into a specific area of artistic expression and demonstrates Mr. Afshar's dedication to preserving for future generations the artistic and cultural heritage of Iranian civilization, as well as that of the Islamic lands more broadly. Calligraphy, or "beautiful writing," is the most highly regarded art form in Islamic cultures. The Qur'an, the book of God's revelations to the Prophet Muhammad, was copied in Arabic over the centuries using a range of distinctive and extraordinary scripts.

Focusing on extraordinary examples from Mr. Afshar's collection—from folios featuring the earliest scripts developed in central Islamic lands to nineteenth-century Qajar Qur'an manuscripts with highly illuminated borders and bindings—and masterfully written by David J. Roxburgh, Prince Alwaleed Bin Talal Professor of Islamic Art History, Harvard University, this book celebrates and thoughtfully explores this exquisite art form pursued in the service of copying the Qur'an.

We are grateful for Mr. Afshar's generosity to the Museum and for his support of our mission to collect, exhibit, and interpret art of the Islamic worlds. To him, we extend our deepest thanks and dedicate this publication that celebrates the most esteemed visual and textual form of expression in Islamic lands.

Gary Tinterow
Director
The Margaret Alkek Williams Chair
The Museum of Fine Arts, Houston

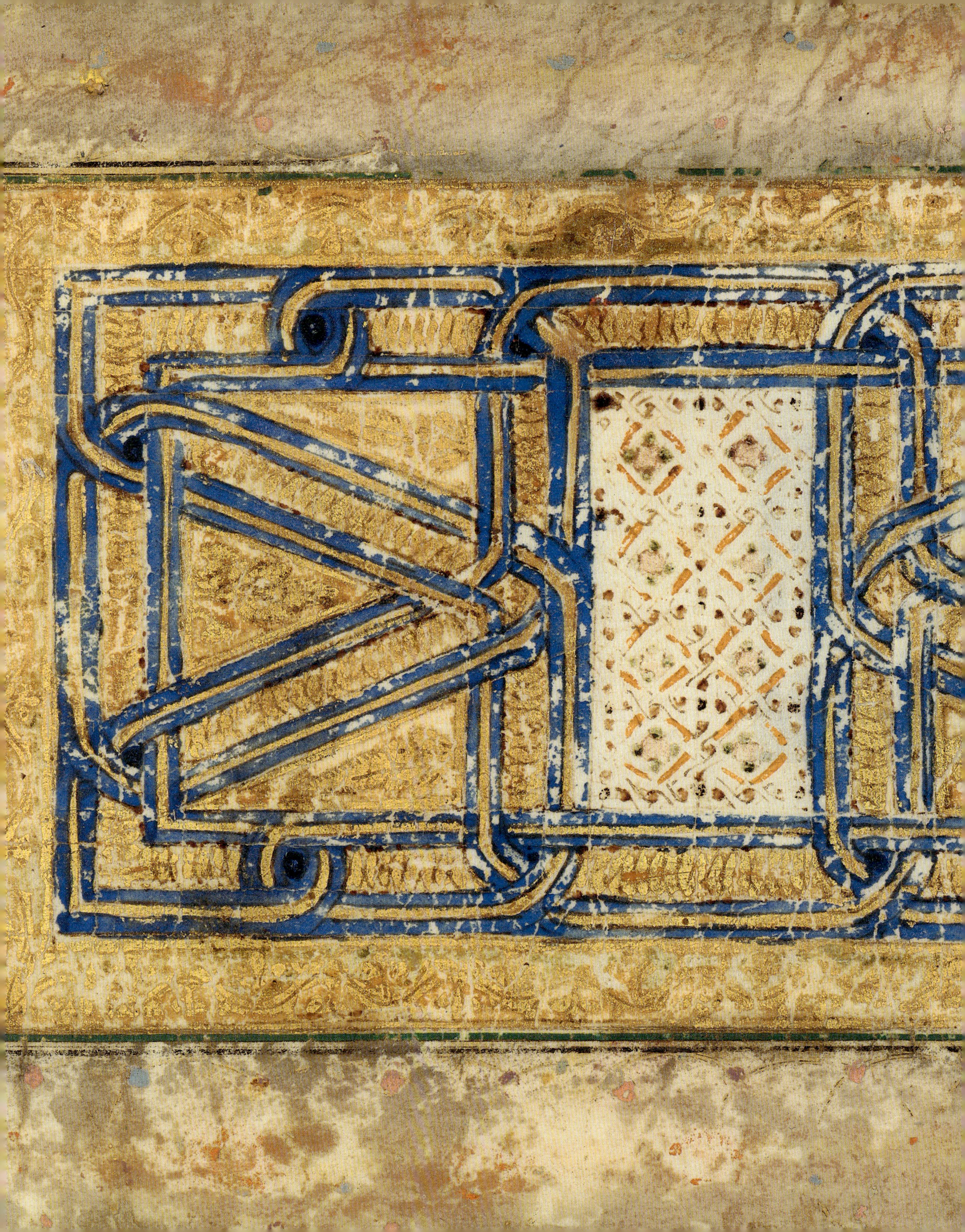

Acknowledgments

It is with deep gratitude and admiration that I acknowledge those who made this publication possible. First and foremost, I would like to thank Mr. Hossein Afshar for his commitment to preserving the artistic heritage of greater Iranian and Islamic lands and for his generosity to share these works publicly through traveling exhibitions and the Hossein Afshar Galleries for Art of the Islamic Worlds at the Museum of Fine Arts, Houston.

I would also like to express my sincere thanks to Gary Tinterow, director and the Margaret Alkek Williams Chair of the Museum of Fine Arts, Houston, for his extraordinary leadership of the multifaceted engagement with the Hossein Afshar Collection and for his dedication to the Art of the Islamic Worlds initiative. This initiative was begun in 2007 as a museum-community partnership and continues to thrive today thanks to the important patronage of our Art of the Islamic Worlds Subcommittee and local communities in Houston.

It is a joy, as ever, to collaborate with author Dr. David J. Roxburgh, Prince Alwaleed Bin Talal Professor of Islamic Art History, Harvard University. His scholarship expertly sheds new light on our understanding of the development of Qur'an manuscripts and Qur'anic materials from their earliest period to the nineteenth century through the lens of Mr. Afshar's collection.

For their significant contributions to the contents and elegant design of this publication, it is my pleasure to acknowledge editor Melina Kervandjian; translators Will Kwiatkowski, Margaret Squires, and Etienne Muller; glossary author Anushka Hosain; book designers Rita Jules and Miko McGinty of Miko McGinty, Inc.; and photographer Neil Greentree.

This publication was also made possible by the efforts and contributions of current and former members of the Art of the Islamic Worlds department, notably Anushka Hosain, curatorial assistant, and Margaret Squires and Shireen Shah, former curatorial assistants; Vivian Nguyen, administrative assistant, Sara Craig, former administrative assistant, and Hannah Kemal-Hyden, postdoctoral curatorial fellow. Colleagues across numerous departments throughout the Museum gave generously of their time and expertise, including Tina Tan, senior works on paper conservator; Heather Brand, publisher in chief; Jason Dibley, collections manager; Marcia (Marty) Stein, manager, and Cynthia Odell, image projects and rights coordinator, in the photographic and imaging services department; Julie Bakke, chief registrar, and Kim Pashko, collections registrar.

Aimée Froom
Curator, Art of the Islamic Worlds

الَّذِينَ فِي قُلُوبِهِمْ

آنان را که در دلهاشان

مَرَضٌ يُسَارِعُونَ

بیماری است می‌شتابند

فِيهِمْ يَقُولُونَ نَخْشَى

Note to the Reader

Transliteration of Arabic words includes the letters *'ayn* and *hamza* and omits diacriticals and long vowels. Dates are in the Islamic (AH) and or Gregorian (CE) calendars. For consistency and clarity, the spelling of certain terms quoted from previously published materials have in a few instances been modified to reflect the style adopted for the present volume.

Translated titles of chapters (suras) of the Qur'an follow those in Ali 1990. Identifications of verses for each folio (or bifolio) do not indicate the specific point in the verse(s) as they begin or end on the folio.

A bifolio is a piece of paper or vellum folded in the middle, creating two folios. Bifolios can be either conjoint or non-conjoint, and they are the basic units comprising gatherings, which are nestled together at their spineblocks to create the text block of a manuscript. (For more on the composition of bifolios, consult the website islamicmanuscriptconservation.org.)

Arabic texts are read from right to left. In the present volume, in almost all cases folios and bifolios have been displayed to reflect their visual orientation within their respective original Qur'an manuscripts, with the left sides of folios (or bifolios) positioned on the left pages, and the right sides on the facing, or right pages. The letter designations "A" and "B" have been employed to further signal the position of a page within the original manuscript, with "side A" indicating that the page is from the left, and "side B," indicating the right side.

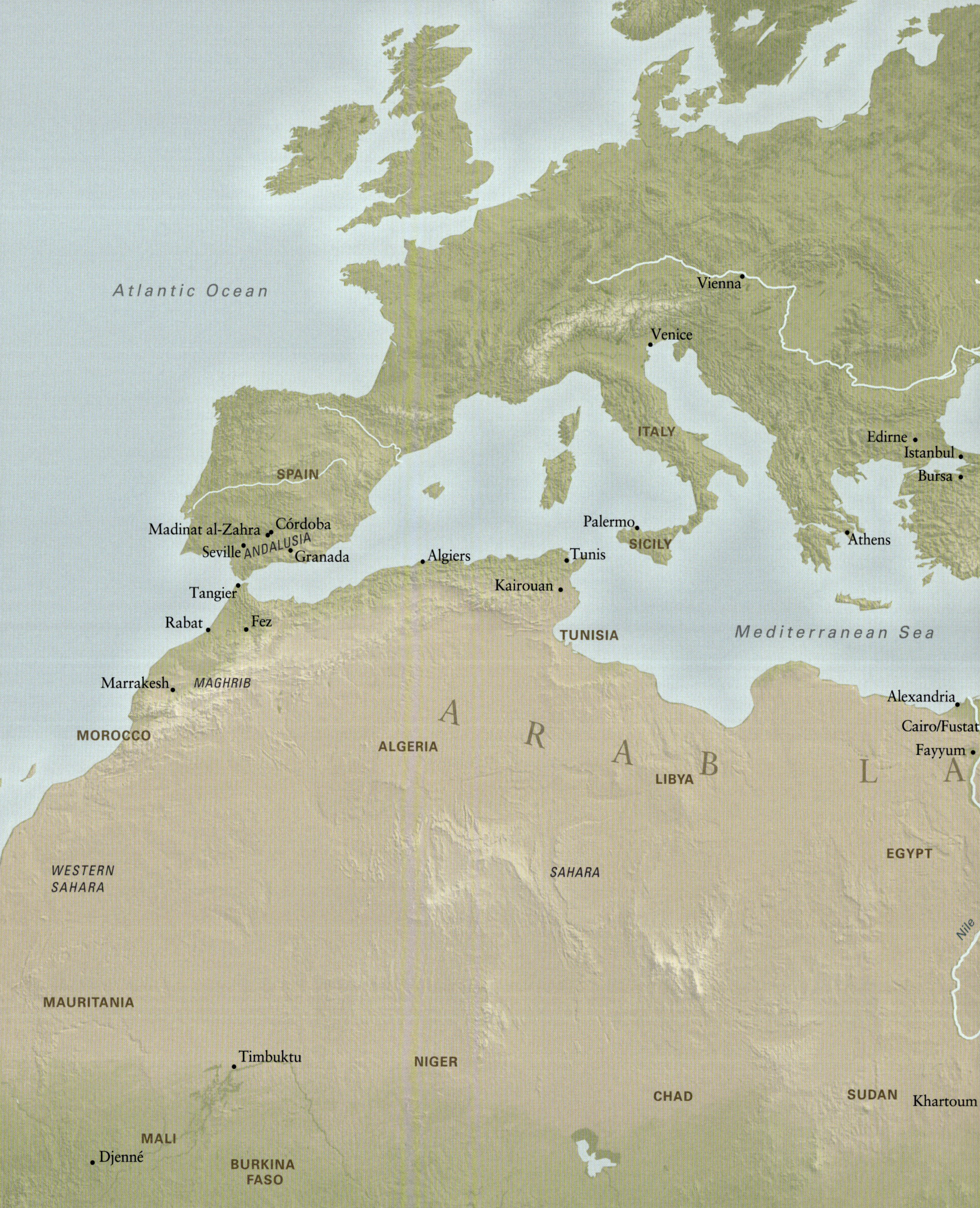
Atlantic Ocean
Vienna
Venice
ITALY
Edirne
Istanbul
Bursa
SPAIN
Madinat al-Zahra
Córdoba
Seville
ANDALUSIA
Granada
Palermo
SICILY
Athens
Algiers
Tunis
Kairouan
Tangier
Rabat
Fez
TUNISIA
Mediterranean Sea
Marrakesh
MAGHRIB
MOROCCO
ALGERIA
A R A B I A
LIBYA
Alexandria
Cairo/Fustat
Fayyum
EGYPT
WESTERN SAHARA
SAHARA
Nile
MAURITANIA
Timbuktu
NIGER
CHAD
SUDAN
Khartoum
MALI
Djenné
BURKINA FASO

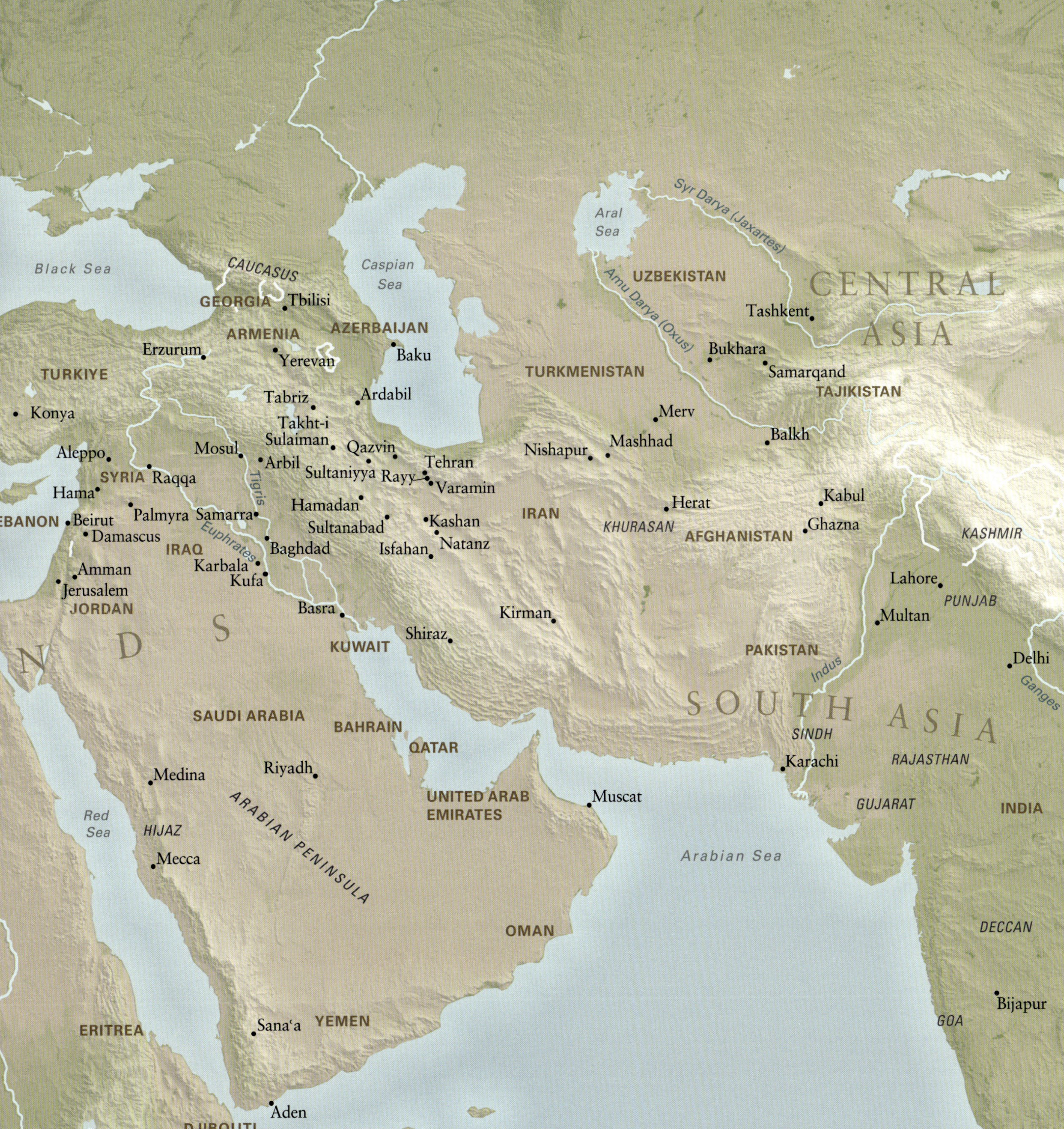

CENTRAL ASIA
SOUTH ASIA
Black Sea
Caspian Sea
Aral Sea
Syr Darya (Jaxartes)
Amu Darya (Oxus)
CAUCASUS
GEORGIA
Tbilisi
ARMENIA
AZERBAIJAN
Yerevan
Baku
Erzurum
TURKIYE
Konya
Aleppo
SYRIA
Raqqa
Hama
EBANON
Beirut
Damascus
Palmyra
Amman
Jerusalem
JORDAN
Mosul
Arbil
Tigris
Euphrates
Samarra
Baghdad
IRAQ
Karbala
Kufa
Basra
KUWAIT
Tabriz
Ardabil
Takht-i Sulaiman
Qazvin
Sultaniyya
Tehran
Rayy
Varamin
Hamadan
Sultanabad
Kashan
Natanz
Isfahan
IRAN
Shiraz
Kirman
UZBEKISTAN
Tashkent
Bukhara
Samarqand
TAJIKISTAN
TURKMENISTAN
Merv
Nishapur
Mashhad
Balkh
Herat
KHURASAN
AFGHANISTAN
Kabul
Ghazna
KASHMIR
Lahore
PUNJAB
Multan
PAKISTAN
Indus
Delhi
Ganges
SINDH
Karachi
RAJASTHAN
GUJARAT
INDIA
DECCAN
Bijapur
GOA
SAUDI ARABIA
BAHRAIN
QATAR
Riyadh
Medina
HIJAZ
Mecca
Red Sea
ARABIAN PENINSULA
UNITED ARAB EMIRATES
Muscat
Arabian Sea
OMAN
YEMEN
Sana'a
Aden
ERITREA
DJIBOUTI

الخبايث انهم كانوا قوم سوء فاسقين

وادخلناه في رحمتنا انه من الصالحين

ونوحا اذ نادى من قبل فاستجبنا

له فنجيناه واهله من الكرب العظيم

ونصرناه من القوم الذين كذبوا

Embodiments of Divine Speech
Qur'ans and Qur'anic Materials, 7th–19th Century

DAVID J. ROXBURGH

If all the trees of the earth were pens and the oceans ink,
with many more oceans for replenishing them,
the colloquy of God would never come to end.
He is indeed all mighty and all wise (Qur'an 31:27)

Say: "Surely if men and jinns get together to produce the like of this [Qur'an],
they will not be able to produce the like of it,
however they might assist one another" (Qur'an 17:88)

Say: "If the ocean turned to ink for writing down the colloquy of my Lord,
the ocean itself would be exhausted ere the words [and wonders] of my Lord come to end,
even if we brought another like it for replenishment" (Qur'an 18:109)[1]

These three verses (Ar. sing. *aya*; pl. *ayat*), selected from more than 6,000 making up the Qur'an, form an epigraphic program for a gilded and stamped leather binding made to protect the sacred text (fig. 1).[2] In their sequence the verses are extratextual—they do not follow the arrangement of the 114 chapters (*suras*) according to length—and they are bracketed by two phrases, the first Qur'anic, the *basmala* ("In the name of God, most benevolent, ever merciful" [*bism Allah al-rahman al-rahim*]), the second non-Qur'anic, "the almighty God speaks the truth" (*sadaqa Allah al-'azim*), a formula used to indicate Qur'anic quotation.[3] Brought out from the interior contents of the Qur'an to the exterior surfaces of the binding, the verses proclaim the unparalleled, unique, inimitable nature of God's colloquy recorded in the Qur'an, a collection of utterances conveyed by God through the angel Gabriel to the Prophet Muhammad (d. 632 CE), which closed the cycle of monotheistic revelation given to earlier messengers—Moses, Abraham, David, John the Baptist, and Jesus—and embodied in other books, scrolls, and scriptures, principally the Torah, Psalms, and Evangel. The revelations of "the book" (*al-kitab*) sent down (in Arabic) to the Prophet Muhammad began in Mecca in 610, continued in Medina between 620 (the year of the "exile" [*hijra*]) and 630 CE, and were concluded in Mecca 630–32 CE. Issued to the Prophet Muhammad as the "seal of the prophets" (*khatam al-nabiyyin*), the Qur'an closed the cycle of revelation. It was the messenger's most important "evidentiary miracle," particularly so since the Prophet Muhammad was illiterate.[4]

The verses selected for the binding assert that even if the resources of the world's trees and oceans were to be transformed into pens (pl. *aqlam*; sing. *qalam*) and ink (*midad*) to make writing—and multiplied many times beyond their terrestrial scope and temporal existence—they could never exhaust God's divine speech and His capacity for producing

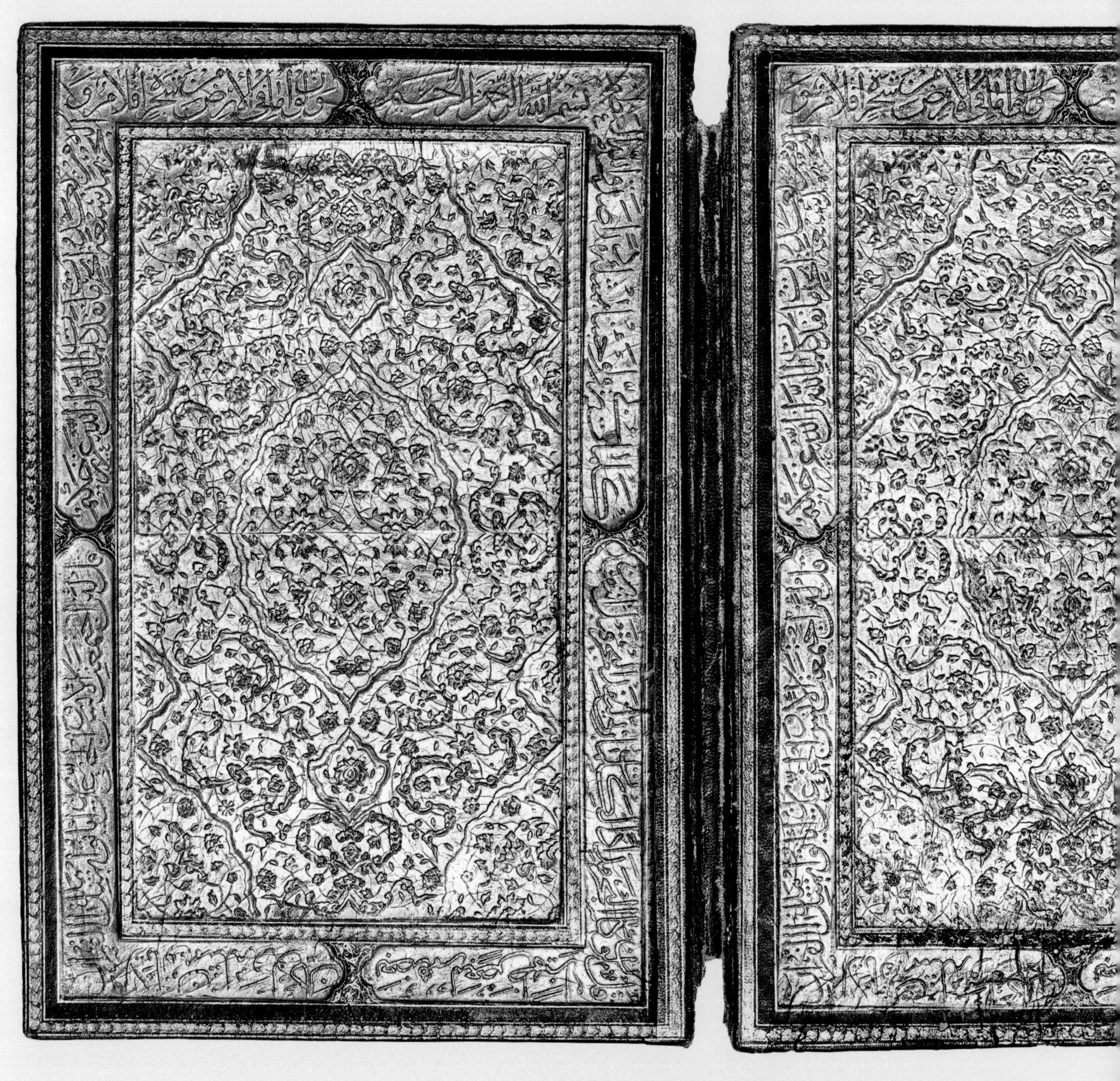

"words" (*kalimat*). These and other verses assert that while the Qur'an might be finite, God's speech was infinite. And even if humans were to collaborate with jinns—intelligent beings created from the "white-hot flame of fire" (Qur'an 55:15) and renowned for their capacity for grueling labor and abilities outstripping humankind's—the "likes" (*mithl*) of the Qur'an would still exceed their collective reach.[5] These potent statements signify God's radical singularity, the ways in which He was absolutely dissimilar in His creative capacities—and in all attributes of being and action—to created things. Such statements are made—in these and many other Qur'anic verses—to assert God's creative power and prerogatives through a language and epistemology comprehensible to humans and jinns, while simultaneously establishing an insuperable difference between them and the eternally transcendent God. God's capacities were untainted by any association

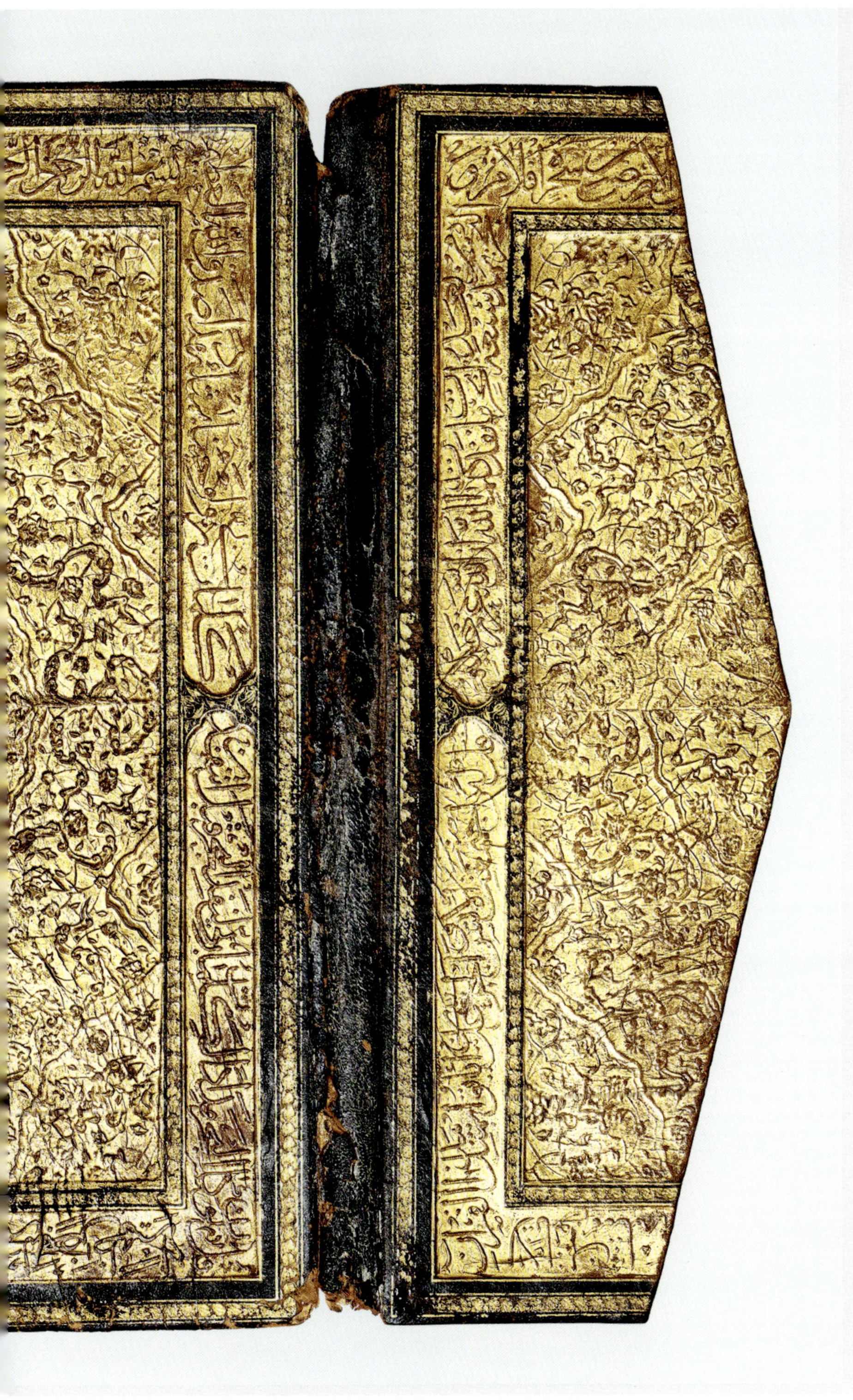

Fig. 1. **Bookbinding for a Qur'an** (*cat. 63*), Iran, c. 1525–50.

with created things, unaffected by any kind of limitation, agency, or contingency of the sort experienced by man and jinn. These and other verses contend with the problem of anthropomorphism, of "likening" (*tamthil*) and "assimilating/comparing" (*tashbih*) God to His creatures, by qualifying, negating, or abrogating their statements, and by imposing two ontologies—the first nature of being applying to God, the second to all created things. The doctrinal concept of *tashbih* was paired with that of *tanzih*, which signified God's transcendence.[6]

One can readily understand the several ontological questions presented by the Qur'an, particularly in its materialization, that is, the rendering of God's "divine speech" and His revelations into sensually perceptible and comprehensible things, either as something recited (oral) and heard (auditory)—reiterative, performative, and evanescent in nature—as well as something written and read (seen and also touched by hands)—and permanently fixed in a physical form.[7] Multiple verses in the Qur'an use the verbal noun *qur'an*—derived from the verb *qara'a* (to recite, read aloud)—to denote recitation, a passage of revelation given to the Prophet Muhammad, or to intimate the whole revelation sent down by God.[8] In one verse (9:111), the word *qur'an* appears alongside the Torah (*al-tawra*) and Evangel (*al-injil*), suggesting their interrelation as books of revelation, but since the Qur'an was at that time an ongoing, unfolding revelation, its reference here could not denote a "closed codex."[9] Throughout these verses, the oral-auditory dimension of the Qur'an retains its primacy. Other terms used to reference the revelation of the Qur'an include the noun *kitab* (a scripture, book, or writing), whose increased incidence in the dynamic, diachronic cycle of revelations issued to the Prophet Muhammad between 610 and 632 CE appears to prefigure the Qur'an as a totality and in the form of a material book.[10] Yet other internal references to revelation in the verses of the Qur'an mention the "mother of the book" (*umm al-kitab*) and "the well-guarded tablet" (*al-lawh al-mahfuz*)—often understood as synonyms for each other—whose meaning came to be understood as a primordial written record of the totality of creation of which the separate revelations to the "people of the book" (*ahl al-kitab*) constituted only a part, or, in narrower terms, that "the well-guarded tablet" was the divine prototype of the Qur'an.[11]

The Qur'an's proper modality of transmission by oral-aural (recitative-auditory) and/or visual (seen through graphical representation) means was an immediate and ongoing concern among Muslim theologians, as were other fundamental questions, such as the nature of divine speech and its relation to human speech and writing, the createdness or uncreatedness of the Qur'an, and relatedly whether it stood inside or outside time.[12] To maintain God's transcendence and eternality, the doctrine of the "uncreation" (*ghayr makhluq*) of the Qur'an achieved the majority opinion in Sunni Muslim theology stemming from the schools of Abu Hasan al-Ash'ari (d. 936 CE) and Abu Mansur al-Maturidi (d. 944 CE). Counter to the heretical view of the Qur'an as created (*khalq al-qur'an*)—an opinion promulgated by the caliph al-Ma'mun (r. 813–33 CE), of the Abbasid dynasty, and Mu'tazili theology—the orthodox Sunni view asserted the relation between God's divine speech and the Qur'an to be one of concordance, with God's attribute of speech as eternal and the temporal form through which it was communicated—oral, visual—as created. The uncreated and the created were linked only by their meaning.[13] The created forms of the physical Qur'an—recited and written—were an "expression" (*'ibara*) and "imitation" (*hikaya*) of God's divine speech, metaphorically and not literally related to the latter.[14]

The complete, fixed, finite form of the physical Qur'an (*mushaf*) as we know it today descends from the consonantal text realized during the reign of 'Uthman (r. 644–56 CE), the third caliph to succeed the Prophet Muhammad as leader of the Muslim community. 'Uthman acted out of concern for the capacity of a purely oral transmission to secure the Qur'an's accurate reproduction across generations of Qur'an readers (*qurra'*) who had memorized the revelation. The frailty of human memory and resulting incidences of error had already become clear through variations in recitations of the revelation during communal prayers.[15] 'Uthman's authorized recension, which secured the codex as a vehicle for the Qur'an, was met with opposition, as had been the case in earlier attempts staged under the caliphs Abu Bakr (r. 632–34 CE) and 'Umar (r. 634–44 CE).[16] This was not simply a matter of resistance among the Qur'an readers amid a culture that privileged the sense of hearing over sight—and that favored the oral transmission of knowledge—but also in light of ongoing concerns about how the revelation should be recorded in the *mushaf*, if at all.[17] Anything extraneous to the created concordance of divine speech—verse markers and counters, divisions of text, chapter headings and titles, embellishments of any kind on the folios enclosing text—could be questioned, as well as the addition of vocalization (*tashkil*) and letter-pointing (*nuqat*) and the kinds of materials used.[18] Indeed, some Qur'anic verses caution against written scripture, including 2:79, "But woe to them who fake the Scriptures and say: 'This is from God,' so that they might earn some profit thereby; and woe to them for what they fake, and woe to them for what they earn from it!;" and the second half of 6:91, "Ask them: 'Who then revealed the Book that Moses brought, —a guidance and light for men, —which you treat as sheafs of paper, which you display, yet conceal a great deal, though through it you were taught things you did not know before, nor even your fathers knew?'"[19] These verses highlight questions about payment for copying Qur'ans and the risks of confusing the *mushaf* for divine speech, conflating the earthly created copy and the heavenly uncreated original.[20]

Notwithstanding different concerns, resistances, and reluctances, which changed over time and continuously varied among a spectrum of liberal and more strictly orthodox Muslim thinkers, the Qur'an established itself as a concrete object and steadily developed consistent, one might even say *insistently*, material forms of embodiment as a book. Despite being a fixed text and a closed corpus governed by normative habits of textual sequence, internal division, and arrangement, the *mushaf* offered an incredibly fertile vehicle for ongoing creativity, for material, artistic, and aesthetic development. The status of the written text as earthly exemplar was sufficient to warrant artistic treatments and responses

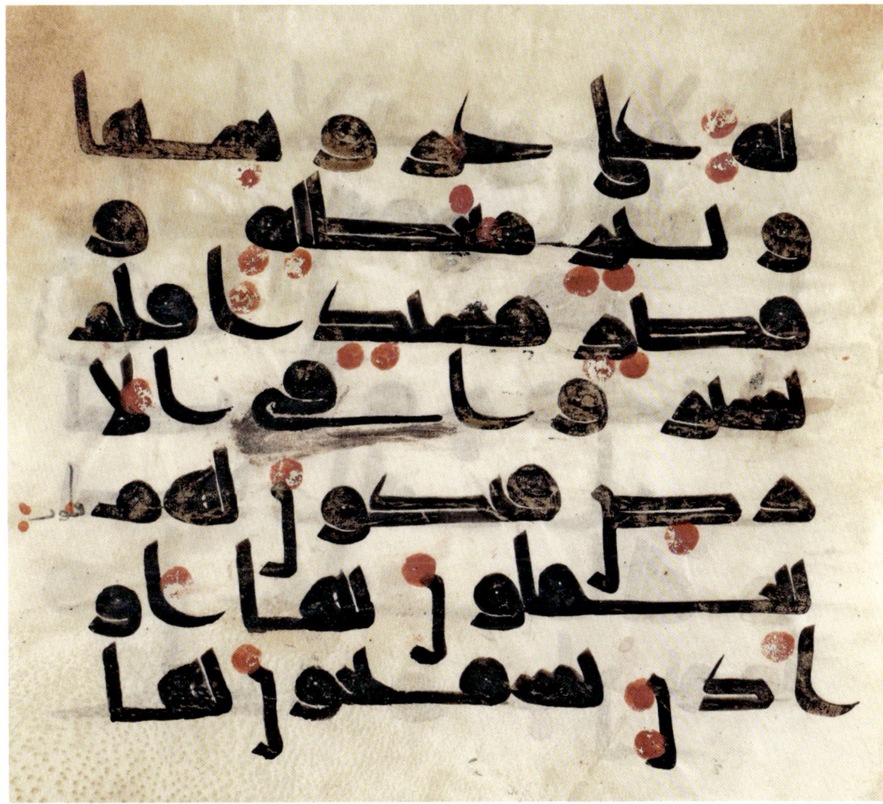

Fig. 2. **Folio from a Qur'an Manuscript** (*detail, cat. 21*), Iran or North Africa, 9th–10th century.

that secured the *mushaf* as something distinctly not mundane despite its created nature and existence in this world.[21] We will return to some of the implications of this observation at the end of this essay. What follows now is an overview of selected structural, material, formal, and aesthetic developments in the Qur'an through examples spanning the seventh through the nineteenth centuries. Materiality, medium, and technique, and their effects, are topics of focused interest, discussed alongside a selection of written sources.

STRUCTURE: DIVISION, SEQUENCE, ARRANGEMENT

The consonantal recension of the Qur'an achieved through caliph ʿUthman's direction secured the organization of the 114 chapters in a sequence of longest to shortest with the exception of sura 1, *al-Fatiha* (The Prologue), a prayer of seven verses. Each chapter is made up of a different number of verses, from 3 to 287, with individual verses ranging considerably in length.[22] Without exception, the Qur'anic prose is arranged in a single column whose rectangular shape follows the horizontal or vertical orientation of the folio (wider than high, higher than wide, respectively). While the earliest Qur'ans copied in Hijazi script adopted a vertically oriented format, those in the Kufic script switched to a horizontal one, with the vertical format restored in the late tenth century coincident with a new repertoire of cursive scripts (refer to the Illustrated Glossary for examples of these scripts). Although the number of lines written on the side of each folio differs—odd or even but always fixed within each manuscript—the text is "justified," giving the impression that the surface area of writing conforms to an invisible perimeter on four sides (fig. 2). Achieving this effect of alignment required that spaces be left between words, and between letters that are not connected to the following letter (*alif*, *dal*, *dhal*, *ra'*, *za'*, and *waw*), in addition to the feature of the varied horizontal extension (*madd*, *mashq*) or contraction (*jamʿ*, *qasr*) of ligatures interconnecting letters. Furthermore, the lines of text construct an orderly appearance by also being arranged parallel to each other and by being evenly spaced, and the relation between the text area to the margins is proportional following a ratio.[23] As a preliminary to copying, a guideline was applied to each folio indicating the position of the lines of text and sometimes also of the outer borders.[24]

One of the main differences between early and later copies of the Qur'an is in the ways in which words are spaced and either broken between successive lines or composed in

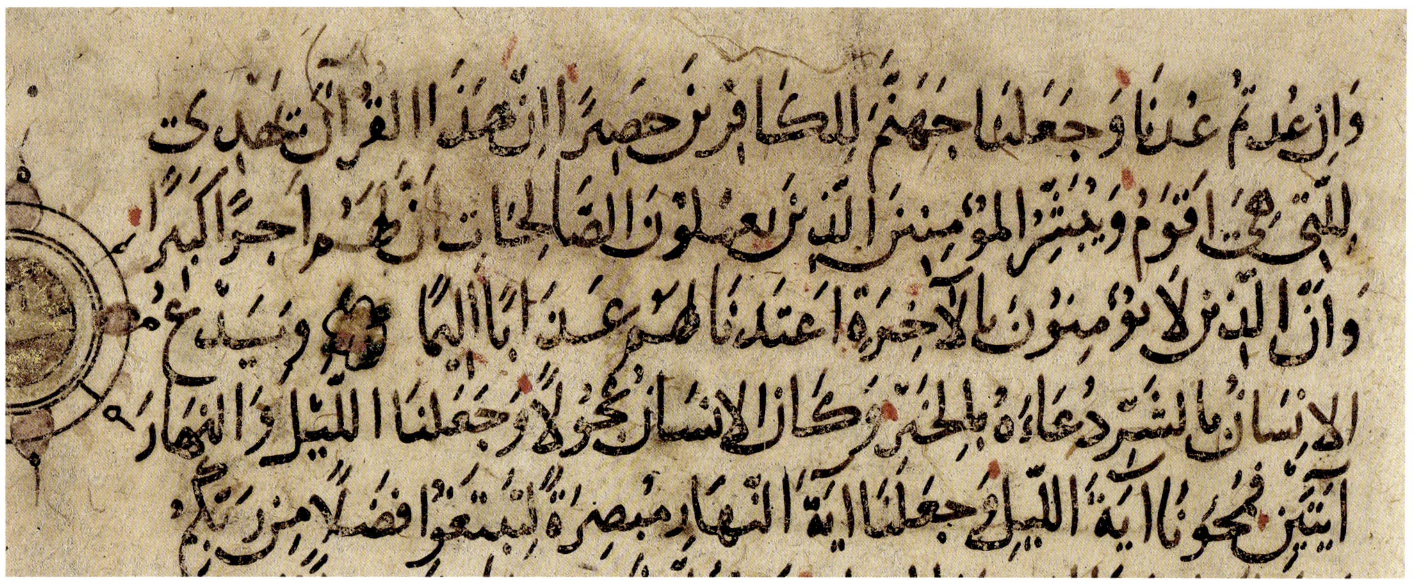

Fig. 3. **Bifolio from a Qur'an Manuscript** (*detail, cat. 32*), Iran or Iraq, 12th–13th century.

a manner that preserves their lexical unity within the span of a single line, as shown in the contrast between figures 2 and 3.[25] The spacing of writing on each line, so that it both conforms to a justified format and maintains the unity of each word, was significantly enhanced by the capacity to change the length of the ligatures, which were connecting lines joining one letter to another: the calligrapher could vary the distribution of joined letters by either stretching or contracting the ligatures, as noted above.[26] Flexibility in spacing was also facilitated in the cursive scripts, adopted from the tenth century onward (comprising the "six scripts," Eastern Kufic/New Style and Maghribi) by the expansion of the area within which the line of text sat, now extending above and below the central line often in equal measure according to the script type (and distinct from the mostly more compacted Kufic characterized by vertical expansion above the line of seating but not much below it) (fig. 3). This last feature also enabled words to be partially nested inside each other (with the final letter of a word extending below the initial letter of the next word).

In addition to these habits of arranging text on the page—which were normative within their particular historical cultures and bookmaking practices—divisions between separate chapters and individual verses could be signaled by an apparatus of forms and motifs, which included chapter headings, verse markers, and marginal verse counters (of five [*khamsa*] and ten [*'ashara*]). These differed in their type and level of elaboration, affecting, perhaps most significantly, their relative visibility. In Qur'ans made up as sets of multiple parts (pl. *ajza'*, sing. *juz'*)—e.g., of two, of seven for reading in one week, of thirty for reading over one month—the beginnings and endings of the parts could be marked by illuminations. There were other divisions to the Qur'an marked on the folio, including the *hizb* (two to each *juz'*, sixty sections in all), *manzil* (a seven-part division for reading the Qur'an in one week), and points which required prostration (*sajda*). These different kinds of divisions—into sets of bound volumes, as verse markers and counters on the page, and written annotations of *hizb* and *manzil*, and so forth—amounted to materializations of time, manifesting the temporal frameworks of the Qur'an's recitative and ritual usage.

Beyond these modalities of textual structuring and arrangement—which had the compounding and cumulative effect of differentiating the Qur'an from other texts in terms of both content and nature—was the inherent rhythmic pattern of the revelation. The language of the Qur'an establishes repetitive patterns through its highly rhythmical prose, which in some instances might suggest meter, as well as recurrences of speech forms, phrases, and formulas.[27] Rhyme, assonance, and repetition are experienced in hearing recitation and are also seen through the graphic representation of writing by two kinds of attentive looking: first, beholding writing as a patterned array; (with or without) second, the sequential reading of words forming lines of text, from right to left, top to bottom.[28] One need not be able to read Arabic to apprehend these visual patterns on cats. 12, folio 1 side A, folio 1 side B–folio 2 side A, folio 2 side B, or on another example, cat. 17, folio 2, side B.

The first mode of seeing, with an eye to gauging and assessing calligraphic form, is one that finds expression in the critical literature, which engages topics related to the making, evaluation, and etiquette of writing. For example, in his *Risala fi 'ilm al-kitaba* (Treatise on the Science of Writing) Abu

Hayyan al-Tawhidi (died after 1009–10 CE) quotes a saying attributed to al-Fadl b. Yahya: "A bad handwriting is one of the two kinds of stammering, even as it has been said: A good handwriting is one of the two kinds of eloquence."[29] Al-Fadl b. Yahya's statement connotes the perceived defects of oral speech with its written cognate, a "bad" writing—perhaps broken, hesitant, repetitive, precipitous, marked by pauses—that corresponded to faltering, incompletely formed speech.[30] Other comments attributed to connoisseurs of fine writing home in on the precise features of letters, including Ibn al-Musharraf al-Baghdadi's assertion that the writing of caliph al-Ma'mun's secretary Ahmad b. Abi Khalid possessed "upright and straight" *lam*s and *alif*s with the only "blemish . . . in the connected *waw*s and unconnected *ya'*s."[31] While al-Tawhidi presents several commentaries on the value of letter-pointing (diacritical marks), in one of them ʿAbd Allah b. Tahir opines that the scribe's only deficiency had been to use "too many diacritical points," which perhaps formed visual clutter disruptive to the apprehension of letter composition.[32]

Still other sayings offered by al-Tawhidi focus on the challenge of connecting letters. In one, which encapsulates several key elements of writing, al-Tawhidi reports something he heard al-Zuhri say:

> He who has acquired a thorough knowledge of the unconnected letters and then has learned to connect two letters, then three, then four, and so on, to the ultimate number of connected letters that are found in words, such as, for instance, *fa-sa-yukfīkahum*, and who has further become acquainted with words which contain combinations of letters that are similar to each other, such as *ḥaṭaṭtu* . . . and the great number of similar cases, can in my opinion be expected to reach the highest summit of calligraphy. He said: The decisive factor is the ability to keep the ends of the lines straight, to make even the beginnings of the letters, to preserve order and arrangement, to avoid precipitation, to show forcefulness while letting oneself go, and to let one's hand go while using a forcefully compact writing.[33]

Before offering a collection of wise sayings about writing, al-Tawhidi opens his treatise with a description of basic principles, the forms and characteristics of good writing, "giving a distinct shape to all letters . . . those which are not connected and those which are, with their long strokes and their short strokes, their apertures and curvatures" which "concerns all the letters together."[34] He comments on individual letters "making eyeballs," which references the inner area of letters (such as *ha'*, *kha'*, and *jim*), "rounding front, middle, and tail of the *waw*, *fa'*, and *kaf*," "piercing" or "keeping open the loops of the *ha'*, *ʿayn*, *ghayn*, and similar letters" whether standing alone or connected to other letters, "bringing out the *nun* and *ya'* . . . at the ends of words . . . so that it is as if they were woven on a single loom," and he also mentions several other categories devoted to proportion, equilibrium, neatness, keeping lines straight, exactness, and spacing.[35] While these are offered to the calligrapher as fundamental principles of shaping, connecting, and arranging letters and words, they also amount to a highly developed nomenclature of description, akin to an anatomy lesson on graphic forms, through which the quality of calligraphy could also be assessed. They record a way of seeing writing beyond its primary communicative function.

MATERIALS, MEDIUMS, AND TECHNIQUES

Acacia; Almond; Aloeswood; Alum; Ambergris; Anemone; Arsenic (red and yellow); Bitumen; Camphor; Carbon; Cardamom; Cat hair; Celandine; Chalk; Charcoal; Cinnabar; Citron; Clove; Coconut oil; Collyrium; Copper; Coriander; Ebony; Egg white; Fennel; Gold; Gallnuts; Glass; Glue, of fish and snail; Grape; Gum Arabic; Honey; Indian white tin; Indigo; Iron filings; Ivory; Lac; Lapis Lazuli; Laudanum; Lead (red and white); Leather; Lemon; Lime; Mercury; Milk; Myrtle; Mulberry; Musk; Nutmeg; Oak; Olive; Onyx; Opium; Parchment of cows, sheep, goats, and gazelle; Pine sap; Pistachio; Pomegranate; Pumice; Quills; Rags of linen, hemp, and flax; Reeds; Rice; Rosewater; Safflower; Saffron; Sal Ammoniac; Saliva; Salt; Sandarac; Sandalwood; Sapanwood; Silver; Soap; Soda; Squirrel tail; Starch; Sulfur; Talc; Tamarisk; Tar soot; Tin; Tragacanth; Turquoise; Verdigris; Vinegar; Vitriol; Walnut; Water; Weasel's hair; Wool; Yogurt.

This list of organic and inorganic materials is extracted from the treatise written by al-Muʿizz ibn Badis (1008–1062 CE), the *Kitab ʿumdat al-kuttab wa ʿuddat dhawi al-albab* (Book of the Staff of the Scribes and Implements of the Discerning, c. 1025 CE).[36] Though the preceding list of ingredients might be long, it does not exhaust the inventory enumerated by Ibn Badis and by other authors, who recorded their technical knowledge of the art of bookmaking and penmanship in treatises spanning the centuries.[37] Across its separate chapters, Ibn Badis's treatise offers detailed instructions on the preparation and application of the materials necessary for the art of fashioning books of parchment and paper—encompassing calligraphy, illumination, and binding—and in the craft of making tools—implements such as reed pens, quill pens, and hairbrushes—and on how best to use them, while also describing other kinds of equipment.[38]

Sourced from land and sea, the repertoire of materials encompasses the full scope of the Islamic lands, extending beyond their frontiers into Africa and across Asia. The material ecology of the Qur'an, and other aesthetically elaborated manuscripts, enfolded the created world. It was with these materials that makers of books produced their supports, inks, paints, metallic leaf, binders, mordants, adhesives, starches, and leathers. Once mined, harvested, and gathered, these many materials were subjected to procedures whose steps included drying, grinding, pulverizing, crushing, powdering, pressing, washing, filtering, settling, squeezing, soaking, sieving, dissolving, cooking, heating, cooling, evaporating, ripening, beating, kneading, agitating, stirring, mixing, rubbing, dyeing, tinting, and tanning. These actions—differing from material to material in the making of mediums—occurred across manifold scales of time and shifted according to season and meteorological conditions.

With these materials, calligraphers, illuminators, and binders—and many other specialized practitioners—produced physically and visually appealing Qur'ans that withstood repeated use, travel, and the effects of climate and time. Although information about the places and conditions of manuscript production—culled from colophons and a gamut of written sources—are not equally rich for all periods, Qur'ans were clearly made in diverse settings. Throughout the history of the Islamic lands, they were copied in different religious institutions, including mosques and madrasas, in libraries and palaces and the workshops/scriptoria attached to them, and even in private homes. The most lavish Qur'ans required extensive resources, of both materials and skilled people, and a degree of sustained financial support possible only at the most privileged societal levels. There is also evidence, however, that less well-to-do individuals could also acquire copies of the Qur'an that were made through modes of speculative production. Highly involved, labor intensive, and thus expensive, copies of Qur'ans were commissioned by elite patrons—caliphs, sultans, princes, and princesses—as well as by members of the military, clerical, and bureaucratic elites, and offered as endowed gifts to mosques, madrasas, tombs, and khanqahs (Sufi centers for religious instruction and devotion). In these buildings, collections of Qur'ans were stored in libraries (*bayt al-kutub*, *kitabkhana*) and treasuries (*khizana*, *bayt al-mal*) and made available for use and for study by resident communities and visitors, including pilgrims.[39] The Qur'ans deposited there could also be made available for the purposes of copying. Such vibrant social centers were thus simultaneously places for learning, religious practice and devotion, and the further dissemination of knowledge.

CALLIGRAPHY

> Beautiful writing gives to truth more clarity. It demonstrates that when the pens are good, the books smile. (Saying attributed to the Prophet Muhammad, Ibn Badis)[40]
>
> I heard al-ʿAsjadi say: "The embroidered cloth of handwriting is its evenness. Its design is its shape. Its coloring is the well measured arrangement of the black [writing] on the white [paper of the page]. Its elegance is the individual components in the composition of the whole." (al-Tawhidi)[41]
>
> Al-Kindi said, "I do not know of any other form of writing in which the letters undergo so much beautifying and refining as they do in Arabic writing." (Ibn al-Nadim)[42]

Culled from a vast corpus of sources on writing in Islamic cultures, these three quotations highlight the power of "beautiful writing," its capacity to enhance the inherent meaning of language in its graphic form, and its essential formal and compositional features. Writing in the early Islamic period, the philosopher Yaʿqub b. Ishaq al-Kindi (d. 873 CE) could already remark on the focused attention given to calligraphy, pointing to its ongoing development, restless innovation, and the wealth of its aesthetic outcomes. Calligraphy (*khatt*) continued to occupy a central place within Islamic societies in later historical periods when calligraphers developed the resource of an alphabet in manifold ways and for diverse purposes. Apart from the infinite permutations afforded by an alphabet of twenty-eight letters—which each had initial, medial, final, and isolated forms—choices always needed to be made with respect to: distribution, arrangement, and size; scope of use of connecting ligatures (*mashq/madd*); size of script relative to script (large, *jalil*; small, *khafif*) and to folio-producing effects of scale; the adoption of a predominantly monochrome or polychrome palette; the functional purposes of different scripts (for the main text, titles, etc.); and permutations in the combinations of scripts. No writing existed without these material and formal choices being made.[43] Each choice had an impact on appearance, effect and affect, and meaning beyond what the graphic form communicated as language. Though recovering the full range of these meanings exceeds our capacity due to the limitations of evidence, what is undeniably clear is the sense of history conveyed by calligraphy and its scripts. A diachronic history, expressed through the endless self-referentiality of writing (not to mention the self-referentiality of the Qur'an as a text), is embedded in every occurrence of writing as calligraphers simultaneously worked within the parameters of established orthographic and aesthetic norms and proposed new directions. Calligraphers also emulated the practice of esteemed master calligraphers of the Islamic tradition, achieved through direct pedagogy or by studying examples of their writing.[44]

SUPPORTS

Parchment (*jild*, *raqq/riqq*) and paper (*kaghad*) became the primary supports used for manuscripts of the Qur'an, with papyrus (*bardi*, *qirtas*) always more circumscribed in its geographical scope.[45] These materials formed the bifolios that together made up the gatherings—usually as quinions, groups of five sheets, folded and stacked—collated and sewn together to form a textblock that was set into a binding making the completed codex.[46] Complex processes of preparation of animal skins (cattle, sheep, goat, wild gazelle) for parchment, and of textile waste fibers (rags of linen, hemp, flax, jute, cotton) for paper, yielded supple, durable, and smooth surfaces for writing and illumination.[47] The natural off-white hues of parchment and paper offered an ideal contrast to the dark inks, enhancing legibility. In the preparation of some Qur'ans, the supports were further enhanced with dyes used to color both parchment and paper. Dyes were most commonly surface applications, put on in successive layers resembling a paint or by dipping the sheet in a vat.[48] Careful processes were applied to both parchment and paper—smoothing, whitening, starching/glazing, and burnishing—to strengthen them and produce surfaces onto which inks and paints would not only adhere but also hold their shape without bleeding into the material of the support—collagen in parchment and cellulose fibers in paper. Finishing treatments of parchment and paper preserved the capacity of a liquid medium to sit on the support, penetrating its upper surface and preserving its crisp, sharp outlines as it dried (fig. 4).

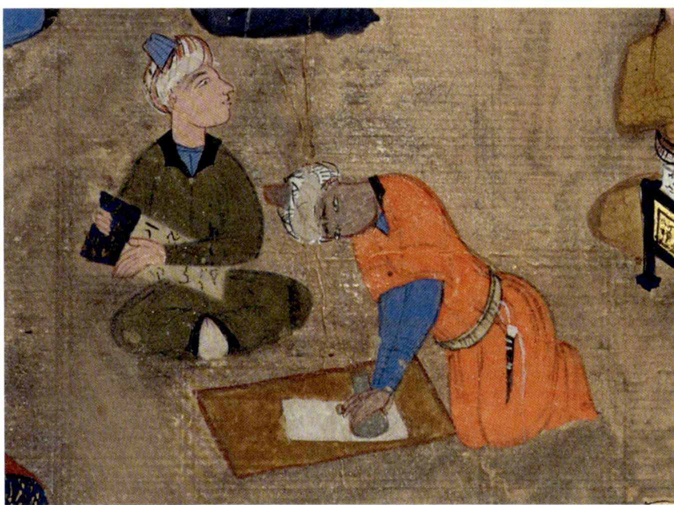

Fig. 4. **"The Severity of a Teacher Is Better than the Love of a Father," folio from a *Gulistan* of Sa'di** (*detail*), signed by Mahmud Muzahhib, Uzbekistan, c. 1545–60, ink, opaque watercolor, and gold on paper, the Hossein Afshar Collection at the Museum of Fine Arts, Houston, TR:979-2015.

BLACK AND BROWNISH-BLACK INKS AND WRITING INSTRUMENTS

In his treatise, Ibn Badis divides his recipes for black inks into two chapters, the first on soot (carbon) inks (*midad*), the second on gallnut (tannate) inks (*hibr*).[49] His recipes for soot inks, several of which Ibn Badis names after regions of the world, combine the carbon procured from chiefly botanical sources with gum arabic (the resin of the Acacia tree) and water.[50] He mentions other ingredients, including salt, yogurt, and vinegar, that had the effect of inhibiting mold formation. While soot ink was characterized by an intense blackness, which made it desirable, it could easily be washed off its support and was not recommended for use on parchment.

Inks of gallnut are the second main type described by Ibn Badis.[51] Processed through pulverization or fermentation, the tannins (tannic acid) from the gallnuts were combined with vitriol (a salt obtained mostly from alum) and gum arabic.[52] While the vitriol controlled the density of the resulting ink, the gum arabic enhanced thickness, viscosity, and luster. Since gallnut inks fused with their supports, penetrating the upper layer of the paper and parchment matrix, they were indelible. If not made properly, however, these inks could be corrosive. Different types of ink, including mixed inks and other variants, are described in the expansive treatise literature across the history of the Islamic lands.[53]

These inks, as well as colored inks (described later), were applied to the support using a pen (*qalam*) made from reeds (*qasab*).[54] Other kinds of materials used as writing instruments included quills (*rish*), wood (*khashab*), and bamboo (*khayzaran*). Ibn Badis recommends that the quill pen be sourced from "the part of the wings of eagles, thick with feathers. . . . From it, the hard thick place is chosen and the quill plucked."[55] Pens fashioned from wood and bamboo—for large-scale calligraphy—resolved the inherent dimensional limitations of reeds and quills. Brushes were also used to apply inks and paints to manuscripts of the Qur'an. Ibn Badis provides a detailed explanation on the manufacture of the "brush pen" made from the hair of weasel, cat, or squirrel's tail mounted at the tip of a handle fashioned from aloeswood, sandalwood, ivory, or ebony. The thinnest brushes comprised four hairs. He further recommends that "it is necessary to prepare two pens for every dye, thick and fine;

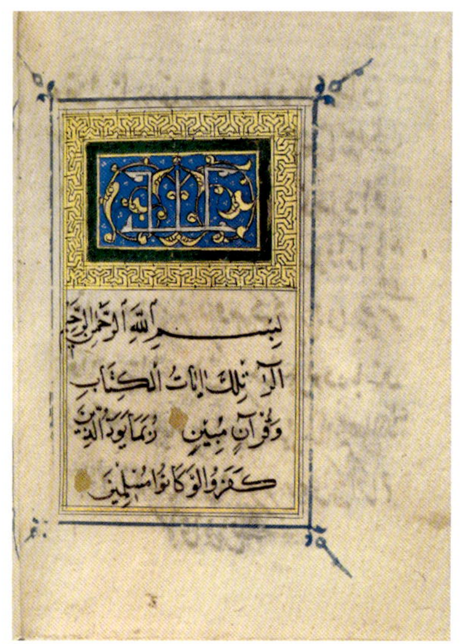

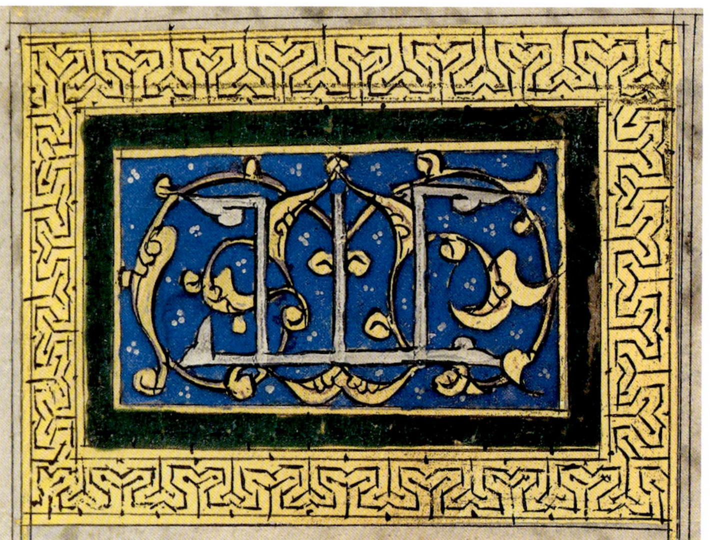

Fig. 5. **Fourteenth Part (*Juz'*) of a Qur'an Manuscript** (*actual size on left and detail on right, cat. 55*), Iran, mid-15th–mid-16th century.

for black, five of them, four for thin and one between thick and thin."[56] Pens and brushes of different sizes could produce writing at different scales; when large and small implements were combined, a contrast could be realized between the written text and the annotation of vocalization and letter-pointing. The variation in the size of Qur'ans made between the seventh and nineteenth centuries is striking: while the largest were limited by the size of the support—parchment or paper—and the physical capacity of the calligrapher to produce writing scaled to those formats, the very smallest were constrained by human vision unaided by magnification (fig. 5).[57]

Following the careful preparation of the pen, seasoning and hardening the reed, paring the sides and core, trimming and cutting the point, and splitting or opening the nib, the calligrapher was ready to apply ink to the support in a series of controlled, measured movements.[58] Different kinds of nib shaping were suited to angular and curvilinear scripts. Although a proscriptive stroke sequence is not articulated in technical treatises, the movement of the pen generally began from top to bottom and passed from right to left. Shifting the orientation and inclination of the pen's nib and varying pressure against the surface produced straight and rounded forms and thicker or thinner lines, respectively.[59] By these means ink was deposited on the surface of the support. The sequence of movements forming letters and words is directly addressed in one of al-Tawhidi's statements where he criticizes the overuse of *mashq*, the interconnection of letters through ligatures: "The constant application of *mashq* means an uninterrupted movement with a disregard for the right proportions. This causes disorder, which results from the hand being tired."[60] Here he cautions against a continuous movement since it can result in poorly formed letters. The regular lifting of the pen away from the support is recommended.

While Qur'ans on paper are typically characterized by a uniform density of black and brownish-black inks—which effectively conceal the process of writing—those on parchment often reveal the segmented nature of letter production, the calligrapher's process of returning pen to inkwell to replenish its load of ink.[61] Through this process, letter forms were built from a succession of strokes that together constructed the grapheme and its connections to other graphemes. The movement of the pen from top down is especially apparent on one Qur'anic folio of the early eighth century (fig. 6) where the ink is denser in the lower sections of the letters than it is in the upper, a pooling that perhaps resulted from the inclination of the folio during the process of copying as well as from the lifting of the pen away from the support.[62] The same phenomenon is seen on another example from the ninth to the tenth century (cat. 12, folio 1, side A, not illustrated). The letters on this folio also offer evidence of the pen retracing letter forms to increase ink density, as well as the sharpening of edges by using a thinner pen than that used to copy the script. The first word at the top right, composed of letters *kaf*, *lam*, *waw*, and *alif*, shows an inscribed outline on the letters *lam* and *waw*, while the letter *ha'* immediately below it (second line, at right) demonstrates the effect of reinking the grapheme through successive layers of ink. Examples of the same reinking process can be found on figure 7—where the edges of letters are outlined and hooks added with a smaller pen (especially the *lam* and *alif* terminating the word *wakilan* [at the end of verse 81])—

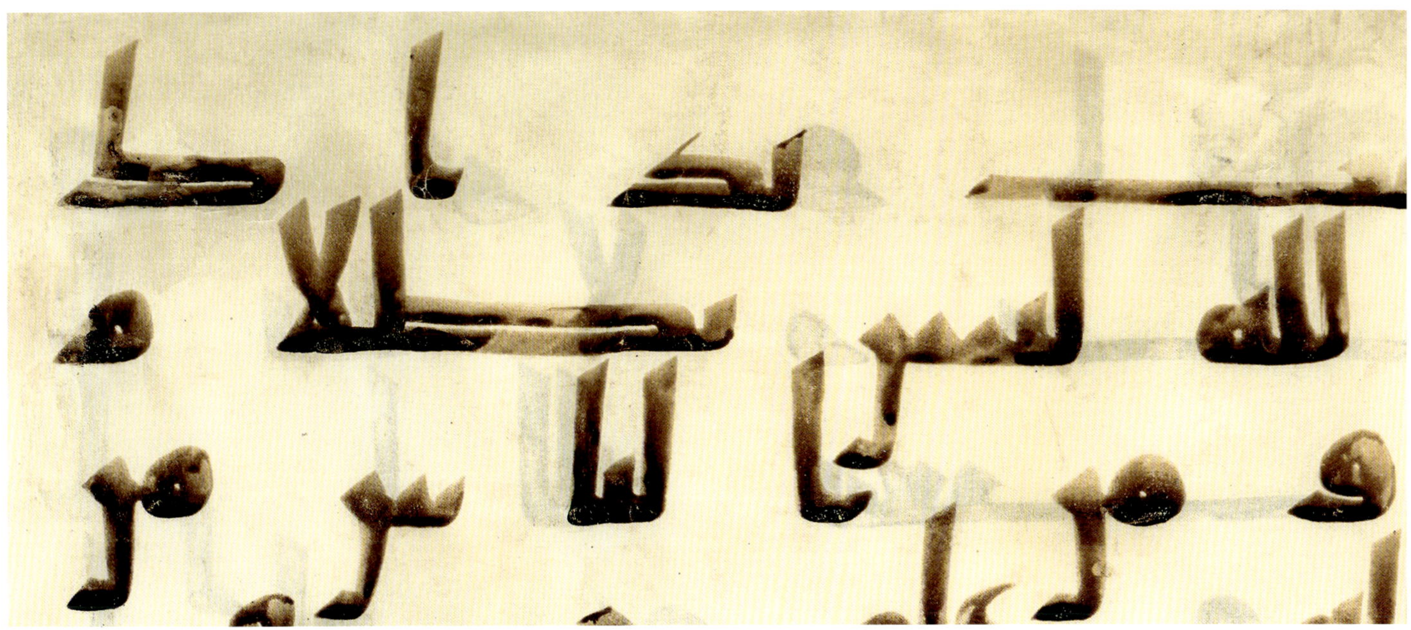

Fig. 6. **Folio from a Qur'an Manuscript** (*detail, cat. 2*), North Africa, early 8th century.

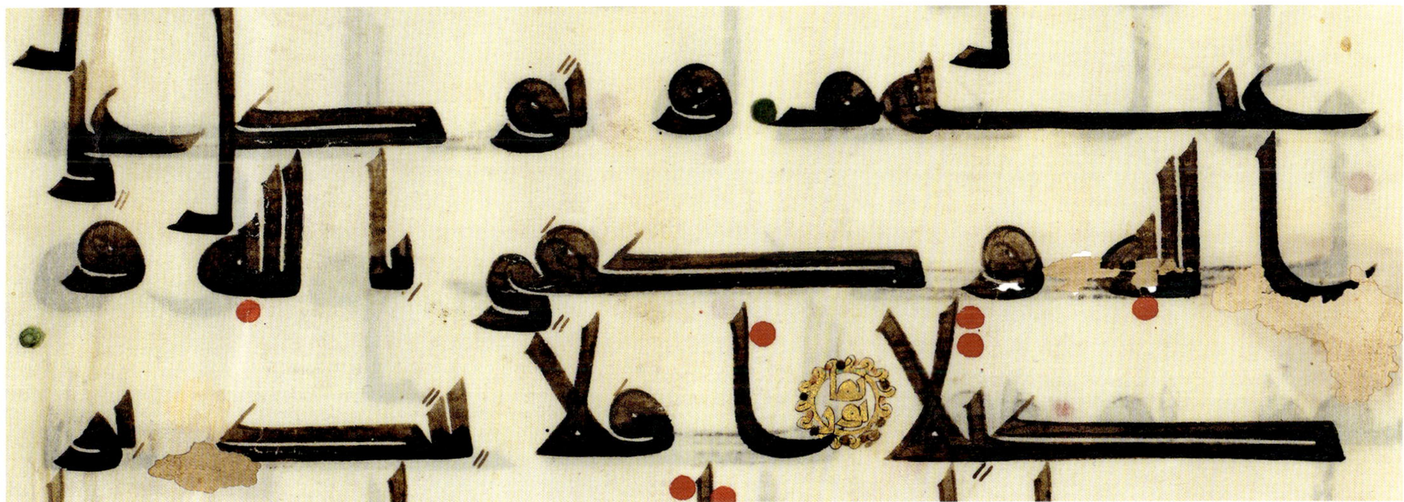

Fig. 7. **Folio from a Qur'an Manuscript** (*detail, cat. 18*), Tunisia, 9th–10th century.

and on another folio (see fig. 8) where the tightly shaped "eyes" of letters *fa'*, *qaf*, *mim*, *waw*, and *ha'* have often been produced by reinking or by adding a circular line to inscribe the outline of the void (as in the first word of the top line, *fa-mathaluhu*). Some of these forms of writing are more closely analogous to the technique of painting.[63] In the process of painting, the surface is built up by succeeding applications of medium over time (as compared to a predominantly single movement of pen loaded with ink); further, in painting there is a far more varied relationship between the shape of the instrument, the brush, and the mark made. Further, the brush has the capacity to produce graphic marks that simulate the effects of the reed or quill pen.

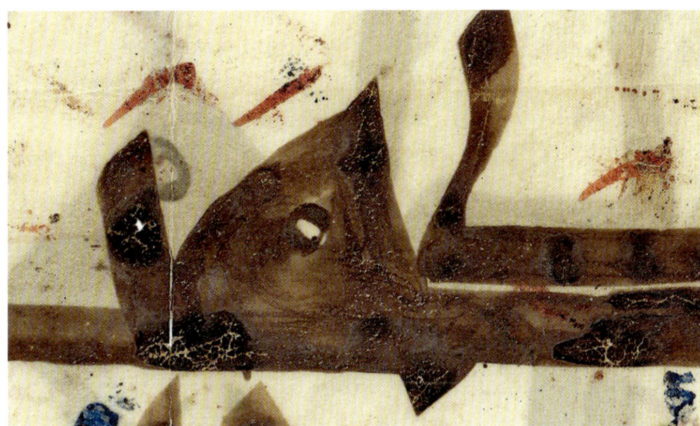

Fig. 8. **Folio from the Nurse's Qur'an (*Mushaf al-Hadina*)** (*detail, cat. 23*), Tunisia, Kairouan, AH 410/1019–1020 CE.

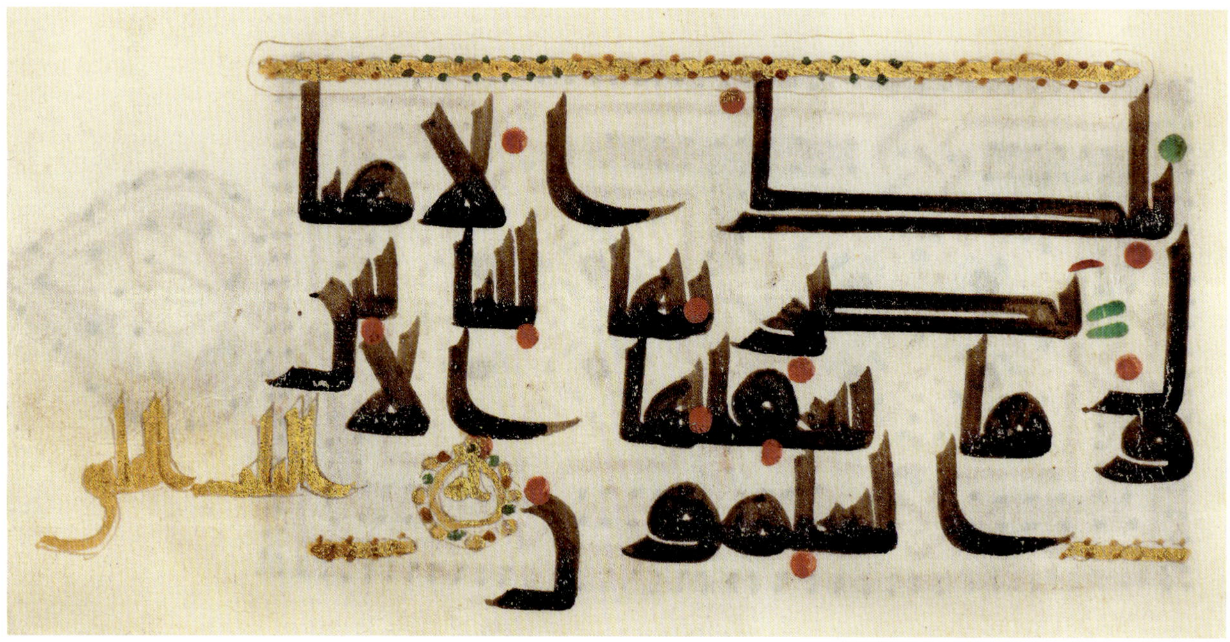

Fig. 9. **Folio from the Twentieth Part (*Juz'*) of a Qur'an Manuscript** (*detail, cat. 8*), North Africa or Central Islamic Lands, 9th century.

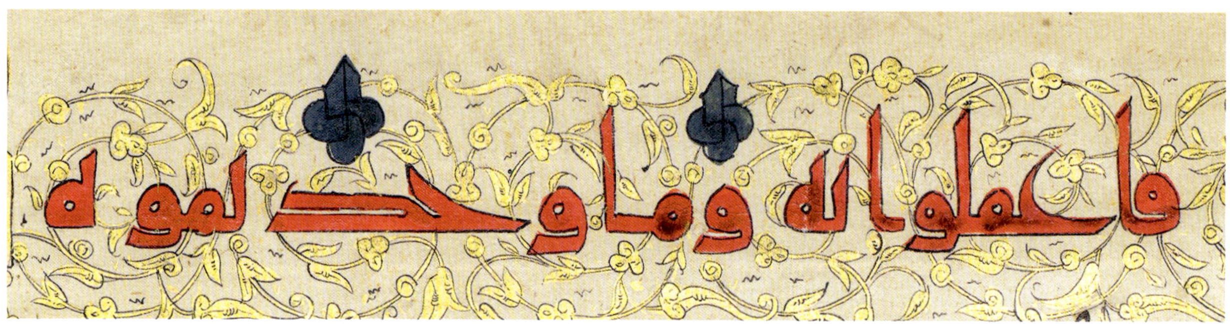

Fig. 10. **Folio from a Thirty-Part Qur'an Manuscript** (*detail, cat. 37*), Anatolia, Iran, or Central Asia, early to mid-14th century.

COLORED INKS

While the vast majority of Qur'ans across the centuries were copied in black or brownish-black ink, this palette was augmented by the addition of colored inks. Ibn Badis provides numerous recipes for making polychrome inks, which he divides into two chapters, those for application with a brush and those for a *liq*—the piece of wool or felt in the inkwell that held the liquid medium—to be used with a reed pen.[64] The essential content of recipes for colored inks across these two categories is much the same, each comprising a pigment (mostly extracted from botanical or mineral sources), a binding agent (gum arabic or glair), and water. Gum arabic and glair held the particles of pigment in suspension, adhered them to the support, and provided a shiny finish when dry. In his presentation of colored inks, Ibn Badis begins with red, yellow, and green, and continues with recipes for peacock-blue, rose, pistachio, purple, ruby, basil, sumac, gold, and white inks. His repertoire of colored *liq*s—for use with a reed pen—is even greater with recipes for several reds, yellows, greens, and blues, as well as for pomegranate, pistachio, white, gold, silver, rose, violet, and verdigris.

In the two chapters devoted to colored inks, Ibn Badis provides recipes for inks that give the appearance of being made with gold, but he does not mention whether these are occasioned by economic limitations or religious factors.[65] One, for parchment, was made from red arsenic and saffron, which "comes out like pure red gold;" another made from lead combined with vitriol and water of gallnut "when polished, . . . comes out a very good golden color;" and a third made from the "male goat's gall" was for writing on paper.[66]

Colored inks were used for letter-pointing and/or vocalization (cats. 3, 11, 51, and fig. 9), rubrics in chapter headings, and for marginal texts (fig. 10). A full palette of colored inks was particularly valuable in texts with developed commentaries, such as that found in a late thirteenth–early fourteenth century Qurʾan from Egypt (see fig. 20). The carefully composed marginal texts, copied in red, black, and blue inks—with titles in gold outlined in black—present commentaries on aspects of interpretation, including the topics of grammar, meaning, and reading.[67] Black and colored inks are used to signify distinct orders and categories of text.

Colored inks could also be used for writing the main text of the Qurʾan. Ibn Badis has a separate chapter devoted to the "writing art with gold, silver, copper, tin, and their substitutes," within which the first four recipes are all for a shell gold, an ink made from pulverized gold whose particles were suspended in various combinations of water of alum, vitriol, vinegar, and water of tragacanth (a water-soluble gum extracted from legumes).[68] In one example of a mid-fourteenth-century Qurʾan copied entirely in shell gold, the size of its *muhaqqaq* (one of the "six scripts") alternates large to small between successive lines and is scribed in gold outlined in black (fig. 11).[69] The vocalization is supplied with red and blue inks and the letter-pointing executed in gold outlined in black but with a smaller implement than that used for the main text. Close study of the gold ink *muhaqqaq* reveals passages where the density of particles lessens, providing reduced coverage, and the use of the black outline to correct and tighten letter shapes, provide detail, and suggest the movement of the pen stroke. As is often the case, the illumination is applied as a gold leaf and not as shell gold.

A still more striking example of writing in gold ink is found in an example attributed to the calligrapher Ahmad b. al-Shaykh al-Suhrawardi al-Bakri (d. 1320/21 CE), a student of the celebrated Yaqut al-Mustaʿsimi (died c. 1298 CE) (fig. 12). These two fragments once formed a folio making up a thirty-part Qurʾan commissioned by the Ilkhanid Mongol

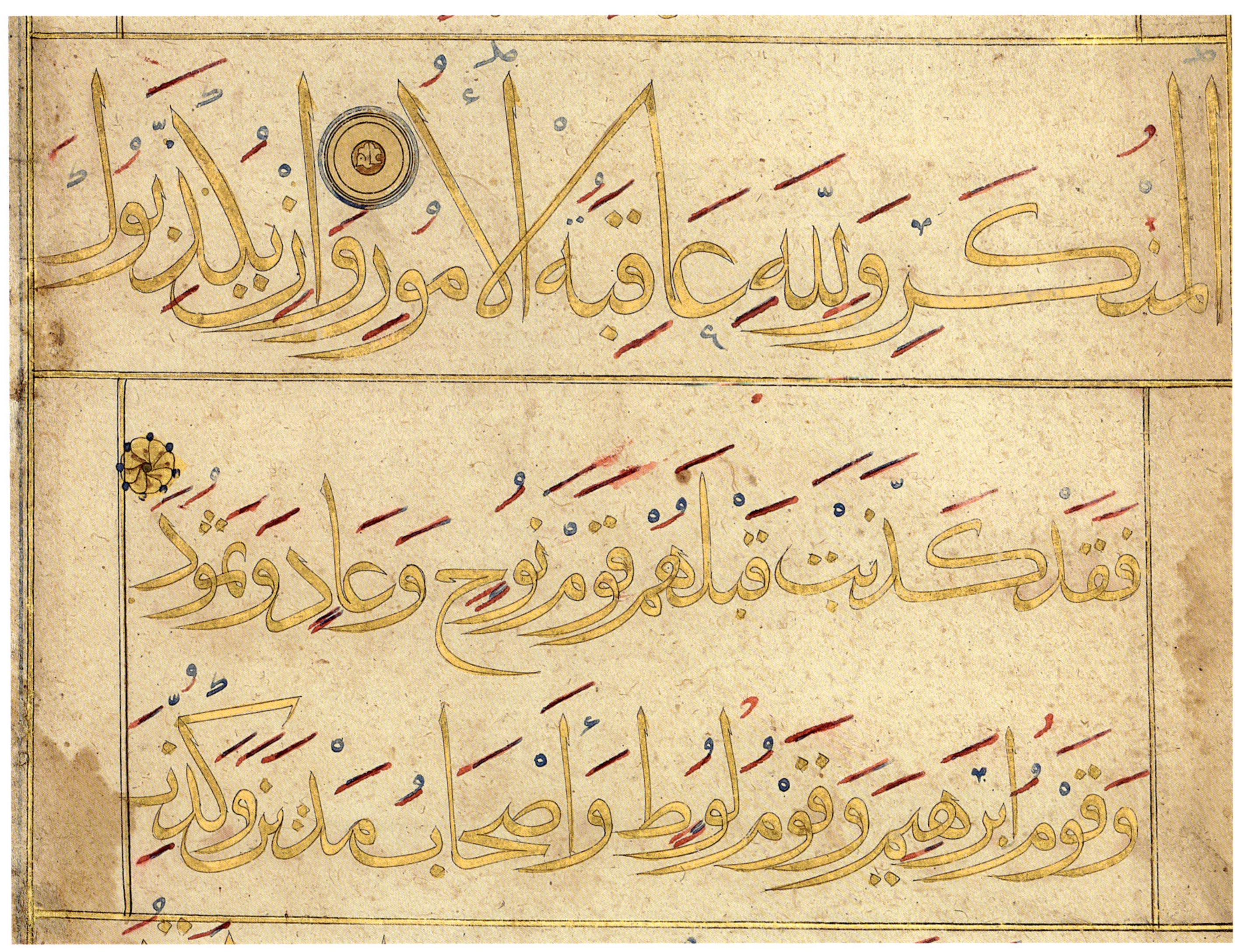

Fig. 11. **Bifolio from a Qurʾan Manuscript** (*detail, cat. 39*), Iran, probably Shiraz, mid-14th century.

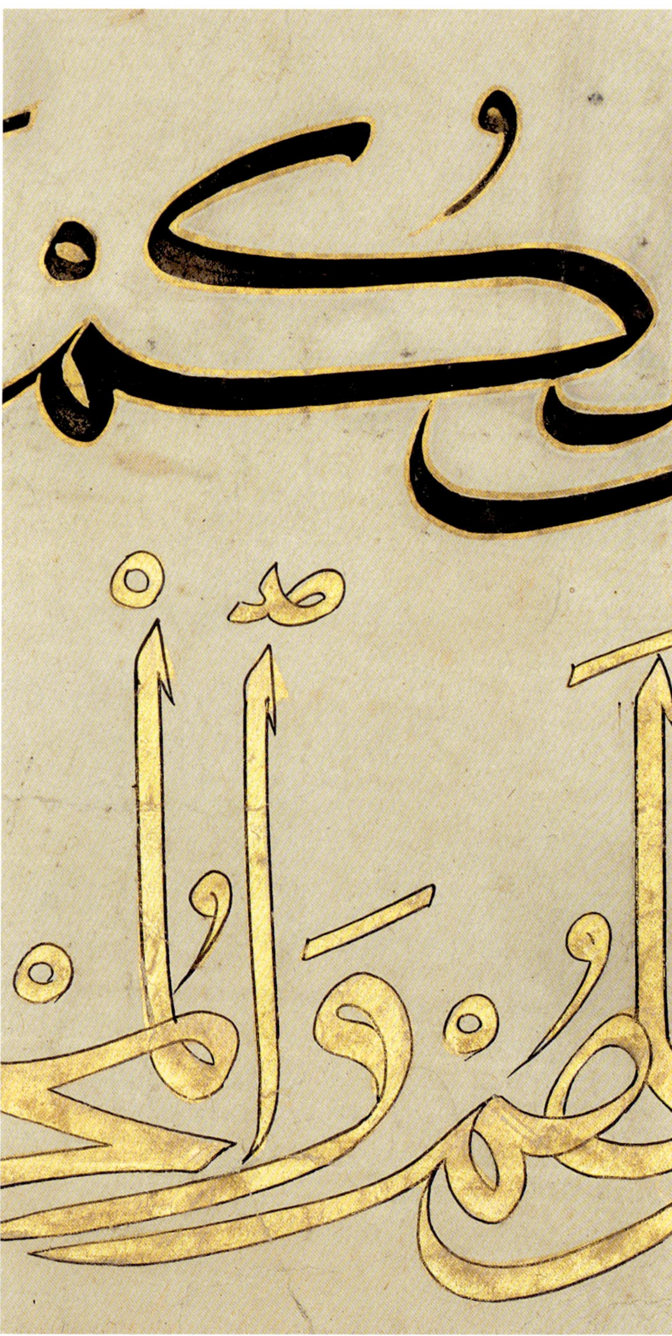

Fig. 12. Calligraphy attributed to Ahmad b. al-Shaykh al-Suhrawardi al-Bakri (d. 1320/21 CE), **Lines from a Qur'an Manuscript** *(detail, cat. 38)*, Iraq, Baghdad, probably AH 707 / 1307–1308 CE.

ruler Uljaytu between 1307 and 1313.[70] Its lines of text are written in *muhaqqaq*, alternating gold outlined in black, black outlined in gold, with matching vocalization and letter-pointing. Close study reveals that while the black outlining sits over the edge of the gold, the gold outlining hews close to the outer edge of the black inked letters but sometimes leaves small gaps between letter and outline.[71] A feature shared by the outlining is its way of suggesting the stroke sequence that formed the letters, adding an illusion of overlapping and hence depth.

A group of Qur'anic folios datable to the fourteenth century, whose text is also composed in lines of alternating colors of ink, evidences a different process (figs. 13 and 14, and cats. 40 and 42). In them, the text on each page is arranged in five lines of *naskh* script that changes from line to line, from blue outlined in gold, to gold outlined in blue. These colors contrast nicely against ivory, pale blue, and pinkish-buff toned papers.[72] The letters carry vocalization and letter-pointing in matching color pairings. While the illuminated verse markers are fashioned from squares of gold leaf over-inked in black to articulate the petals of flowers, punctuated with dots of blue and red, the writing is by contrast applied as a gold ink (shell gold). The blue pigment, somewhat coarse in appearance, is lapis lazuli but not of the finest quality. As in figure 12, the method of applying outlines in blue and gold to the writing lends it a dimensionality. The outline in black around gold can be used to convey the stroke sequence of the pen charged with ink, as it moves from top down and from right to left (this is especially true of the letters *lam* and *alif* in combination, medial letters *'ayn* and *ha'*, and final letter *waw* as either a stand-alone letter or connected to the letter preceding it). Outlining renders visible something otherwise unseen when working with materials characterized by uniform saturation: by marking the edges of the overlapping stroke, the black line shows how the pen crosses over the line formed by an immediately preceding stroke. Hence, the outlining provides a representation of the passage of the pen—something extra, and completely unnecessary—recording a gesture made by the pen held in hand, using overlapping to create a spatial illusion of above and below. The same technique was not applied to the blue script outlined in gold, perhaps because of the challenge of covering lapis lazuli with a thin gold line.

Another remarkable technical aspect of these folios is that the lines of gold and blue script are recessed (see fig. 14). Areas of paper where writing would appear were first depressed by applying pressure to, and/or removing fibers from, the surface. These steps formed shallow, recessed beds into which the writing would be applied in ink and completed through outlining. Such a process is comparable to inlaid metalwork or to the lapidary arts, where the surfaces of supporting materials—brass, bronze, semiprecious stones—were excavated to provide space for the inlay material. These steps may have been necessary given the choice to copy the Qur'an in alternating blue and gold throughout; while shell gold is negligible in its thickness, the same is not true of lapis lazuli. Without these steps the Qur'an would have become excessively thick, potentially distorting the textblock.[73]

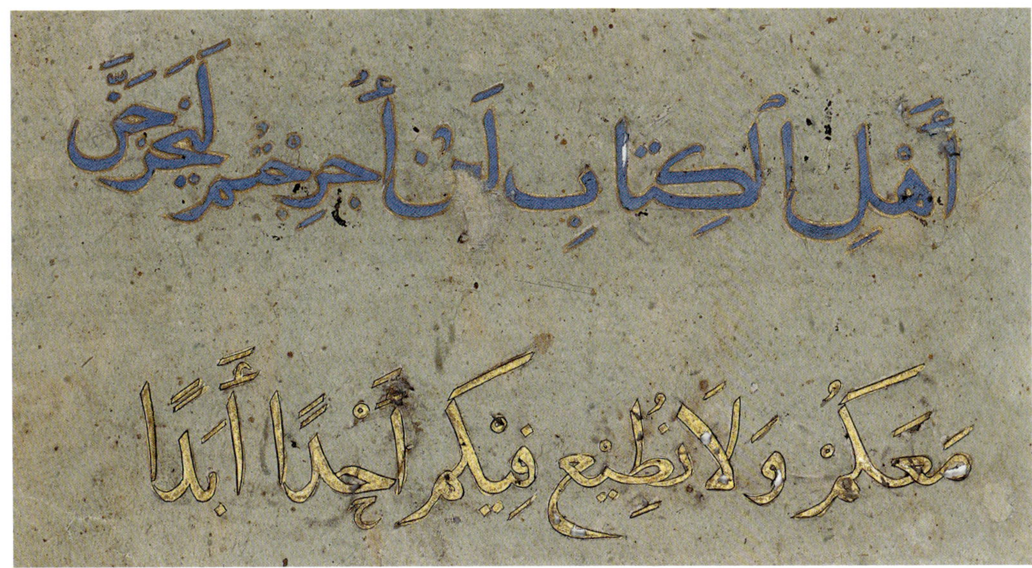

Fig. 13. **Folio from a Qur'an Manuscript** (*detail, cat. 40*), Central Islamic Lands, 14th century.

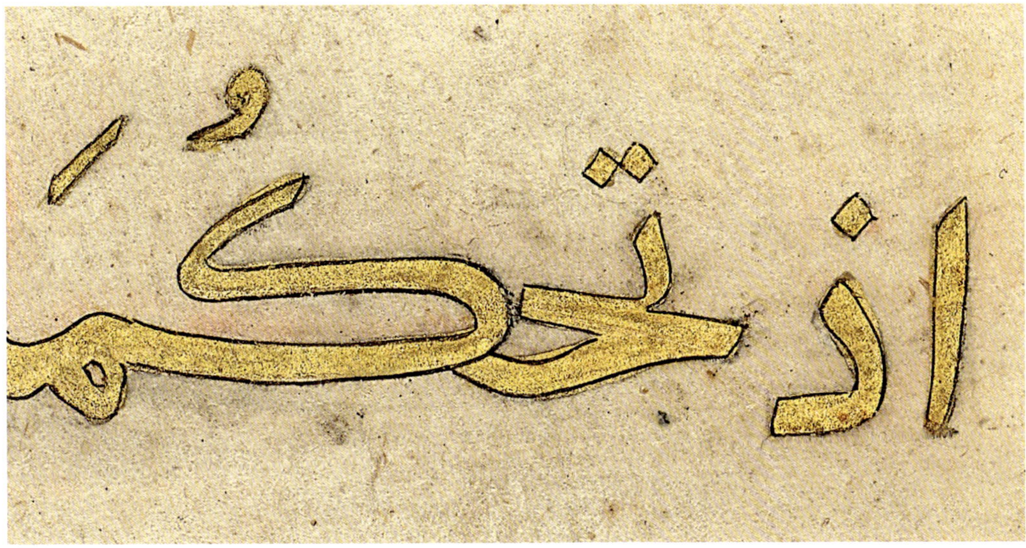

Fig. 14. **Folio from a Qur'an Manuscript** (*detail, cat. 42*), Central Islamic Lands, 14th century.

GOLD LEAF

When gold leaf was used to produce Arabic script, as distinct from shell gold, a completely different set of operations was entailed. Applied rarely to the full text of Qur'ans due to expense—and perhaps because of proscriptions cautioning against the use of precious metals—gold writing (Greek, *chrysographia*) makes the most conspicuous display of costly materials but also of the intensive labor and skills that it required.[74]

Among the most striking examples is a ninth-century Qur'an made in North Africa or the central Islamic lands (see fig. 9 and see fig. 17 and cats. 5, 6, and 7). Its folios, originally divided between two volumes, are each composed of fifteen lines of Kufic outlined in reddish-brown ink set inside borders composed of interlacing motifs, which change from opening to opening, with a motif resembling a tassel, biomorphic in its composite elements, extending into the outer margin at either side.[75] In its overall composition, each Qur'an opening is reminiscent of the *tabula ansata* (Latin, "tablet with handles"), a form used as an epigraphic frame, predominantly for Latin votive or donor inscriptions in classical antiquity.[76]

As in most other calligraphic treatments, gold writing first required the preparation of the sheet—parchment or paper—with a sequence of equally spaced lines produced with a hardpoint which served as a guide for the seating of

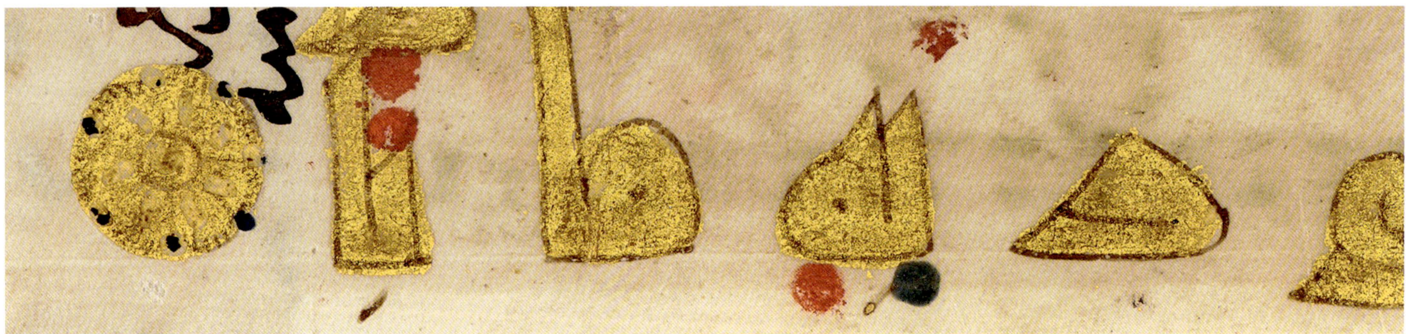

Fig. 15. **Folio from a Qur'an Manuscript** (*detail, cat. 19*), North Africa, possibly Tunisia, Kairouan, 9th–10th century.

the letters.[77] These guidelines, visible in raking light, are still perceptible on another folio from a gold Kufic Qur'an of the ninth to tenth century made in North Africa (fig. 15).[78] The next step is uncertain, namely whether or not the shapes of the letters making up each line of text were outlined on the support, following the structure provided by the lightly incised lines, as an additional guidance that would demarcate the outlines of letters. (The result of subsequent processes has been to obscure this possible step). Regardless of whether an intermediary process occurred, the next known step was to apply to the support a liquid adhesive glue made from fish or desert snails.[79] The application of this viscous glue, subject to a limited timeframe to maintain its adhesive capacity, could be conducted in a manner analogous to the fluidity of writing in ink. Once the glue had been applied to the parchment or paper, sheets of gold leaf were laid over the adhesive, and once attached the segments of unglued leaf were brushed away.[80] Following this stage in the multistep process, the golden letter forms were adhered to the support and could then be completed through a process of outlining in ink that would provide clear edges to the script, a vital tightening that sharpened external contours and marked the interior details of letters (such as the "eyes" of the letters *'ayn*, *ghayn*, *mim*, *qaf*, *fa'*, *ha'*, and *waw*).[81] External and internal applications of ink to letters in leaf can readily be seen on a folio from the third part (*juz'*) of a Qur'an from the late tenth to twelfth century (fig. 16). Here, as elsewhere, lines of ink emend areas of leaf that are too thick or too thin—extending beyond or falling inside the proper boundaries of letter shapes—as well as edges that have insufficient curvature, articulate the internal configurations of letters such as *dal*, *dhal*, *sad*, *kaf*, the "eyes" of others (listed above), and provide the diagonal slants at the upper ends of the letters *alif* and *lam*.

In his treatise, Ibn Badis describes two kinds of glues used in the application of gold to paper and parchment, one made from white fish, the other from desert snails. Adhesive made from desert snails was "the best glue without which the

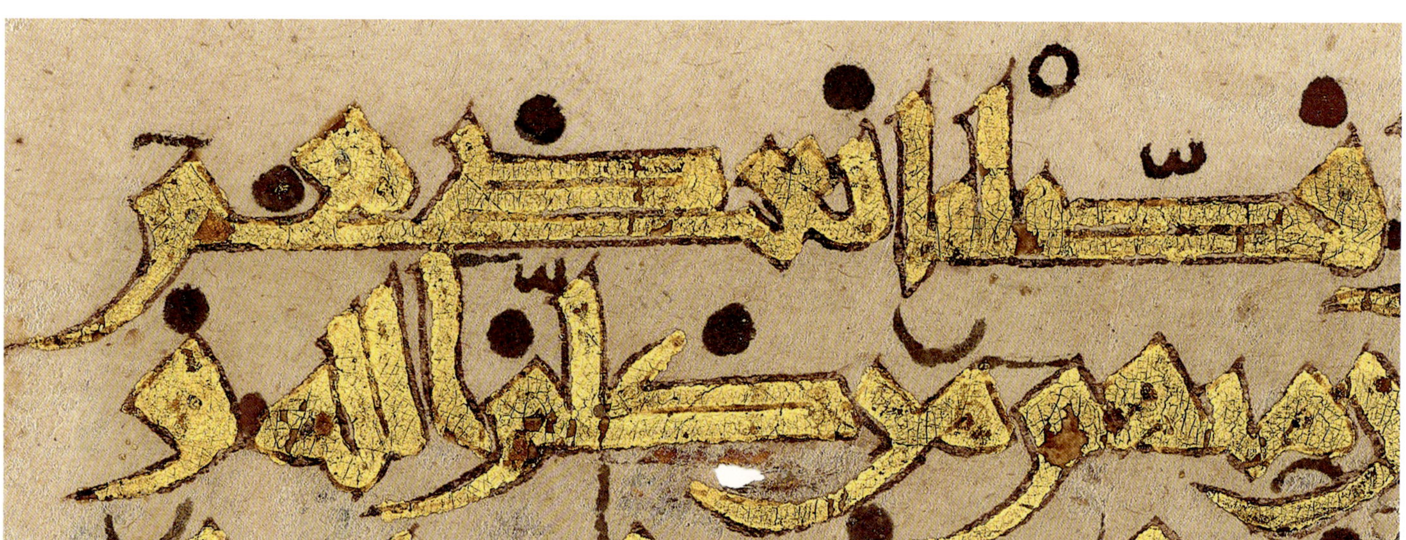

Fig. 16. **Folio from a Qur'an Manuscript** (*detail, cat. 51*), North Africa, Tunisia, or Western Islamic Lands, Sicily, late 10th–12th century.

best work of gold on paper cannot be accomplished."[82] In his second recipe, made from fish glue, he does not specify its use for either parchment or paper. After soaking and moistening cut-up pieces of fish glue in water—to soften it—the glue was dissolved in "sweet water" over a low heat, at which point "a little pulverized saffron is added in a quantity that changes its color." Ibn Badis continues:

> When the weather is hot or cold, a fire should be present since it solidifies quickly. When it is thickened, it is placed on the fire until it melts. When you write with it whatever is desired, the excessively red, beaten Ibriz gold leaf is pressed on that glue a day. It is not delayed more than that. If the gold does not stick properly with the glue, then the gold is heated on the fire and the alum shaken from it so that the whiteness cannot change. When it is pressed, it is left for two days and polished with a stone. Then *kuḥl* is put on it.[83]

This description highlights the temporal limitations and challenges of working in glue—no more than a day should pass between writing in glue and applying the gold leaf—and offers solutions in the event that the adhesive property is diminished. Burnishing can only take place after two days, and the finishing of the letters—their internal and external outlining—in ink comes last. Yet another aspect of Ibn Badis's description is the addition of saffron to the glue, sufficient to "change its color." Saffron is an ingredient of many inks. Its addition to the glue would have rendered a translucent medium more visible on parchment or paper, facilitating the application of gold leaf.[84]

Rendering letters in gold leaf was clearly a complex and highly mediated process. Perhaps guided by an outline of the writing, the process involved the application of the liquid glue—comparable both temporally and physically to writing in ink—followed by the attaching of leaf but within a finite span of time. Any deficiencies in the leaf were corrected with black ink, but also in brown ink, often of a distinctive reddish-brown hue, which enhanced the warmth of the gold (fig. 17 and cats. 5, 6, 19, and 51).[85] Though partially related to calligraphy produced through pen and ink (chiefly in the application of glue), script in leaf cannot properly be considered writing, which as an act is characterized by the comparatively faster production of letters and in a less mediated fashion. Producing writing in leaf comprises steps that are multi-temporal and particularly painstaking, and that involve the disaggregation of surface, instrument, medium, and hand—elements inextricably connected in the act of direct writing with pen (or brush) and ink.[86] Furthermore, the processes of outlining—simultaneously emending and defining—entailed

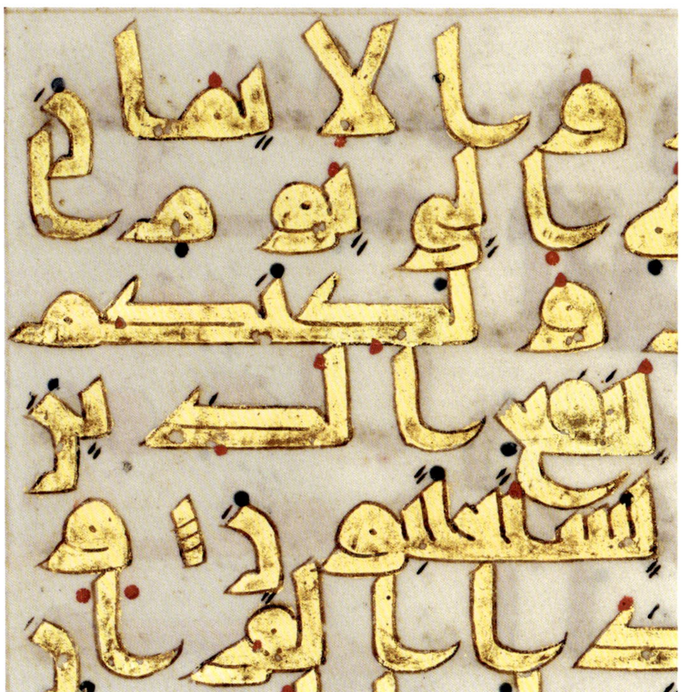

Fig. 17. **Bifolio from a Qur'an** (*detail, cat. 7*), North Africa or Central Islamic Lands, 9th century.

a mental image of letters, as independent or interconnected forms, a way of thinking about writing as an image, as something distinct from acts of writing spontaneously generated by a sequence of bodily movements, a series of gestures (formed through practice and repetition), albeit controlled by limitations of instruments (how much ink the pen could carry before being recharged), canons of proportion, and other norms.[87]

ILLUMINATION

The execution of illumination typically followed the scribing of text. This sequence entailed various levels of coordination, especially when the labor of copying and illuminating was divided between different people.[88] While many *mushaf*s required complex planning to realize highly developed and ambitious programs of illumination, less elaborated manuscripts required only a shared understanding of the scope and nature of the illumination that would populate the folios.[89] Working from this understanding, the calligrapher simply left spaces between consecutive chapters and verses within the text field (*matn*) wherever they were required for headings and markers. Located in the margins (*hashiyya*), other elements—such as verse counters and framing borders—presented less of a planning challenge to the calligrapher as he wrote.

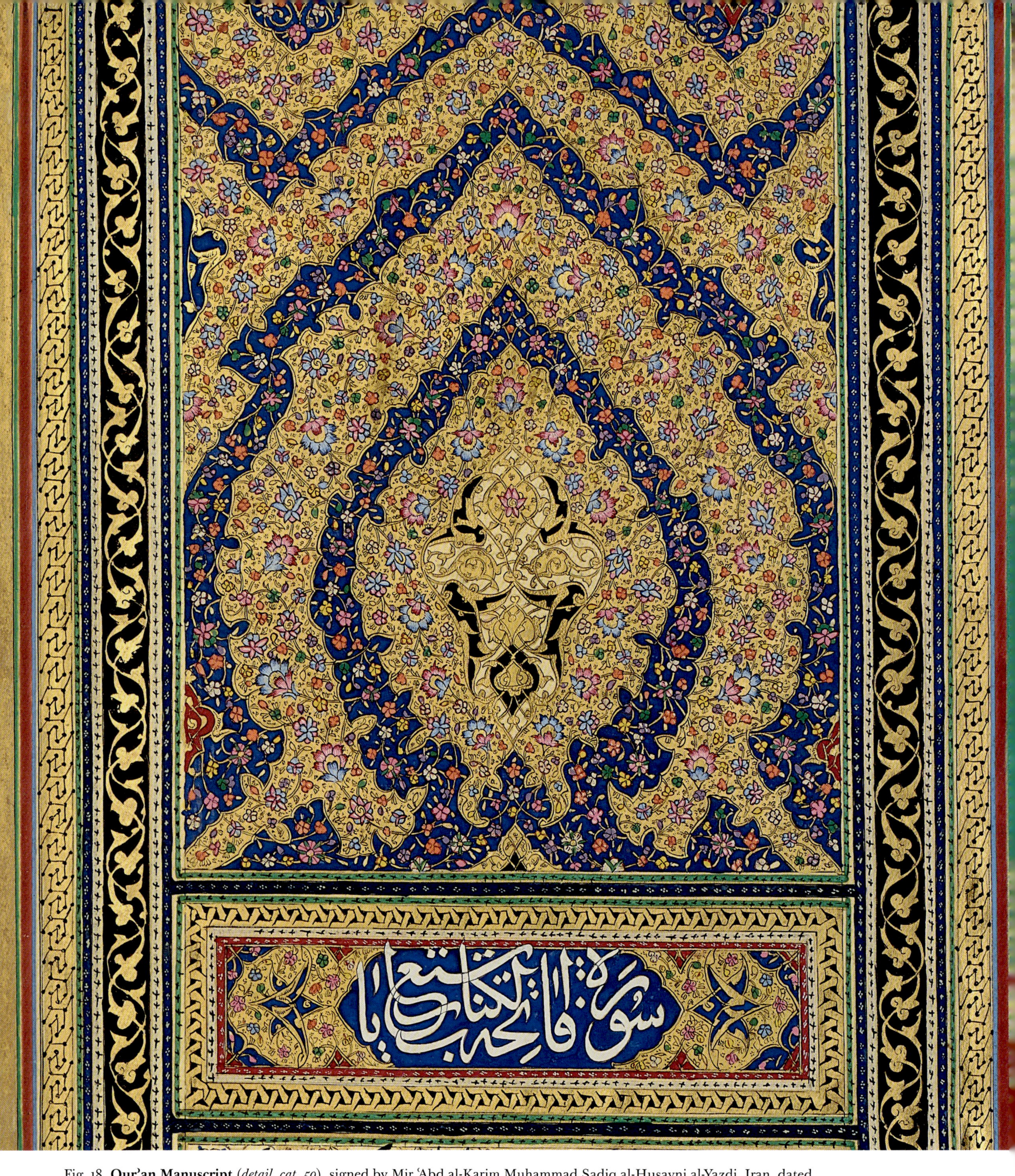

Fig. 18. **Qur'an Manuscript** (*detail, cat. 59*), signed by Mir ʿAbd al-Karim Muhammad Sadiq al-Husayni al-Yazdi, Iran, dated AH 1260/1844–45 CE.

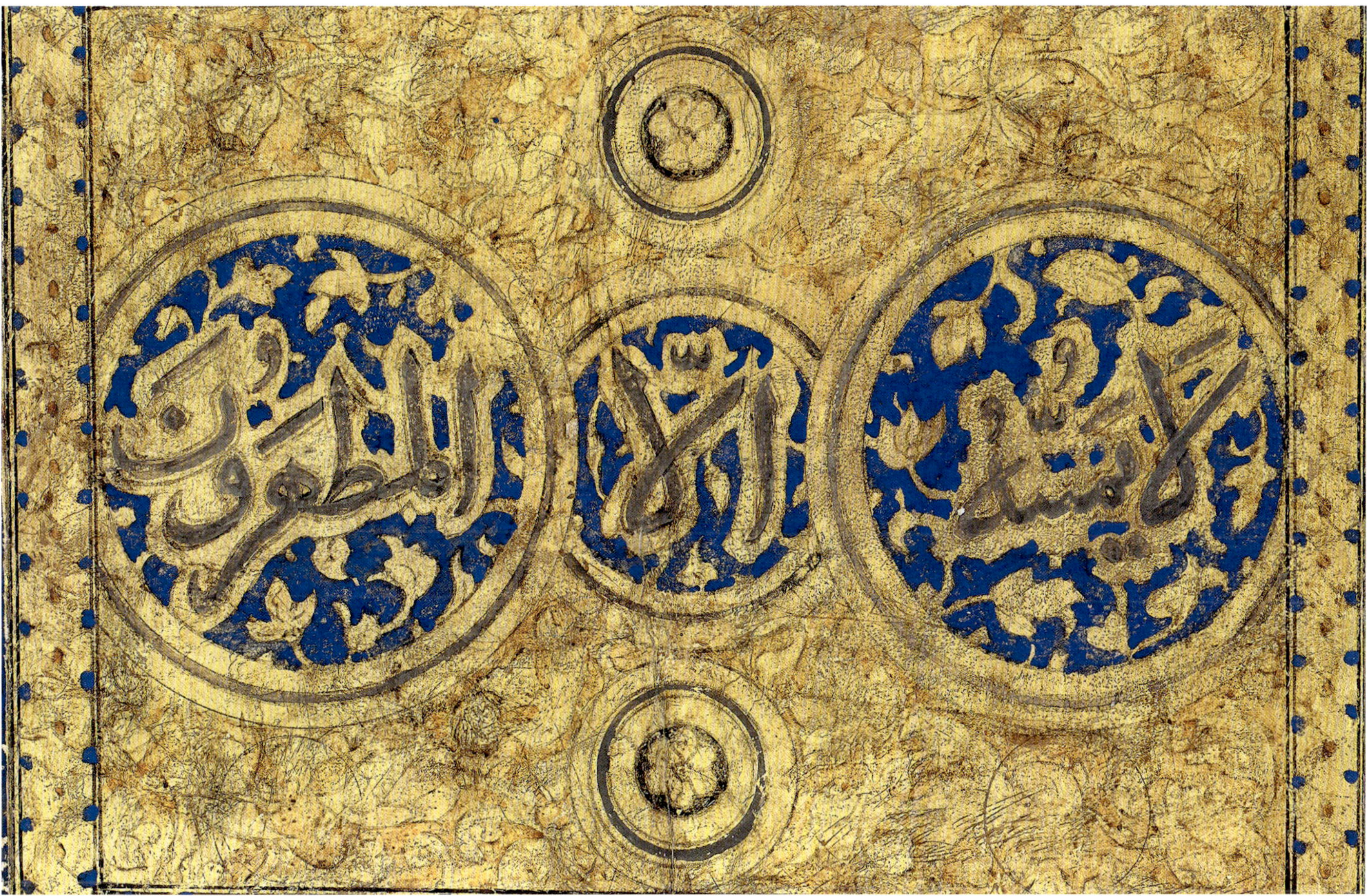

Fig. 19. **Folio from the Nineteenth Part (*Juz'*) of a Qur'an Manuscript** (*detail, cat. 52*), Egypt or Iraq, 14th century.

The greatest change between the seventh and nineteenth centuries lay in the expansion of the palette of opaque watercolor pigments used to decorate the Qur'an, especially under the Mamluk and Ilkhanid Mongol dynasties and after (fig. 18 and cat. 53). Qur'ans of earlier historical periods tend to have more circumscribed palettes even though a broader range of colors was available. Throughout the period between the seventh and nineteenth centuries, illuminated designs and their motifs corresponded to prevailing artistic norms and aesthetic values. This is especially apparent in biomorphic motifs—vegetal and floral forms, sometimes conceived as hybrid species not occurring in the natural world—which reflect the continuity and adaptation of a late antique repertoire up to the thirteenth century, transforming after increased exposure to East Asian art after the Mongols had established their rule over Iran.

Before applying black and colored inks, opaque watercolor, and metal leaf, the illuminator first laid out the shapes of the design using a hardpoint, straight edge, and compass. This network of incised lines may or may not have been completed with an underdrawing. In one example, the frontispiece to the nineteenth part of a thirty-part Qur'an, the composition is arranged as two stacked rectangular panels which each contain intersecting, or overlapping, circles carrying the title of the volume and 56:79, "only they can reach it who are clean [of mind]," in silver *thuluth* script (fig. 19).[90] Of the "six scripts," *thuluth* was the most commonly used for titles. Although the hardpoint ruling is covered by pigment, gold, and ink, the pierced compass point at the center of each circle remains visible. Frameworks of lightly scored lines would have established guidelines for many other illuminations in Qur'ans, configured either as basic geometric shapes with or without more complex figures produced through intersection (fig. 20). These range from chapter headings to single-page or double-page frontispieces or finispieces, with or without text (fig. 21).

A guide for the illuminator could also be drawn in a faint ink or with the reddish-brown medium prepared from safflower. The illuminated borders of the group of Qur'an folios in chrysography, discussed previously (see fig. 17 and cats. 5, 6, 7, 19, and 51), feature this reddish-brown material in their finished border designs as well as in the enriched background of sura headings (cat. 5). Study under magnification reveals that the borders framing the panels of revelation

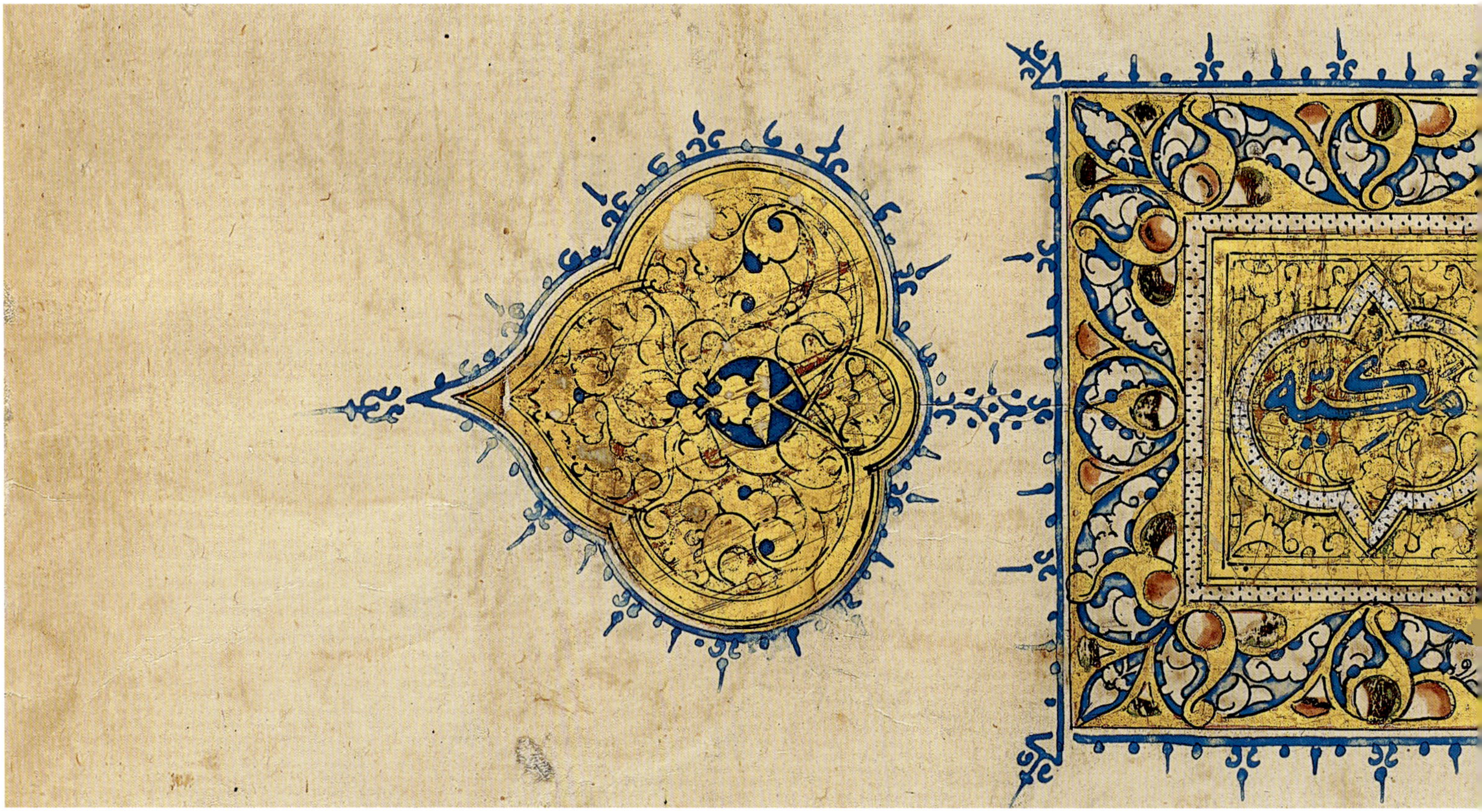

Fig. 20. **Folio from a Qur'an Manuscript** (*detail, cat. 35*), Egypt, probably Cairo, late 13th–early 14th century.

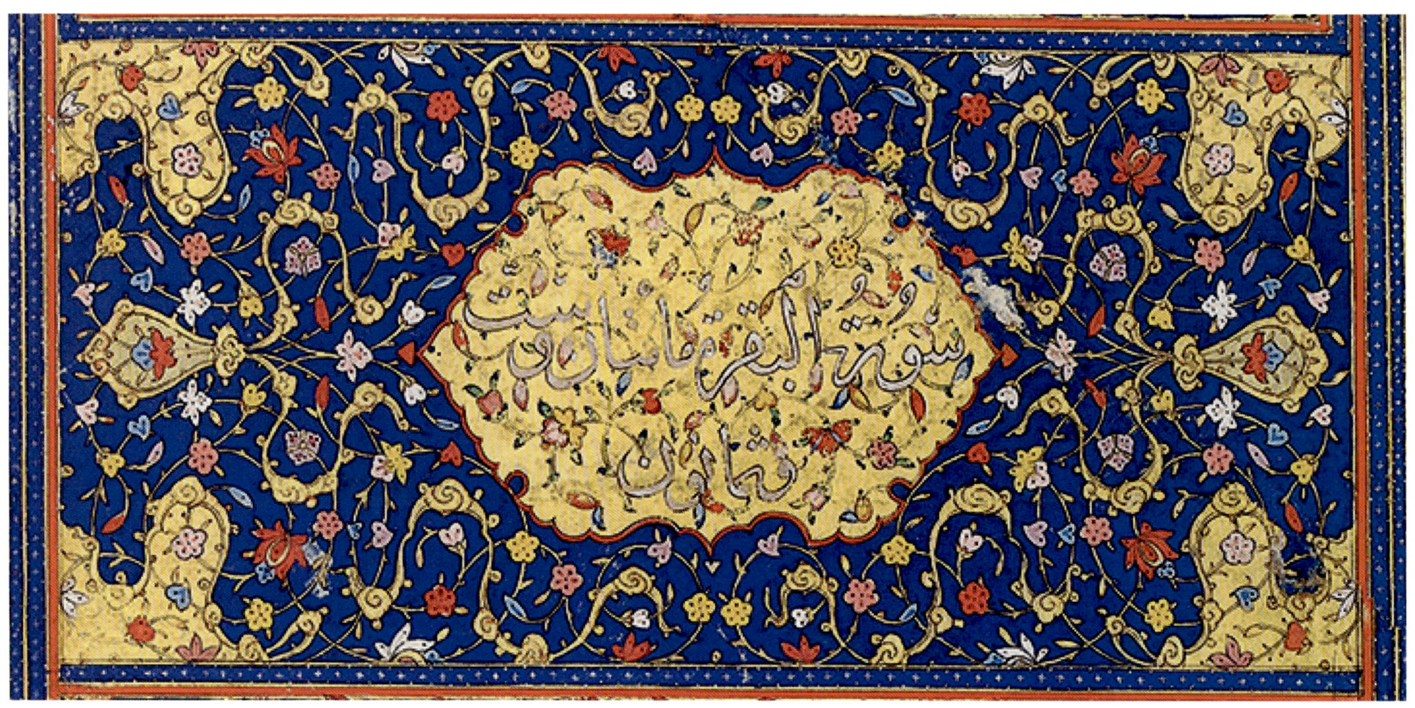

Fig. 21. **Qur'an Manuscript** (*detail, cat. 57*), signed by Husayn al-Shirazi al-Fakhkhar (active 16th century), Iran, possibly Shiraz, AH 961/1553–54 CE.

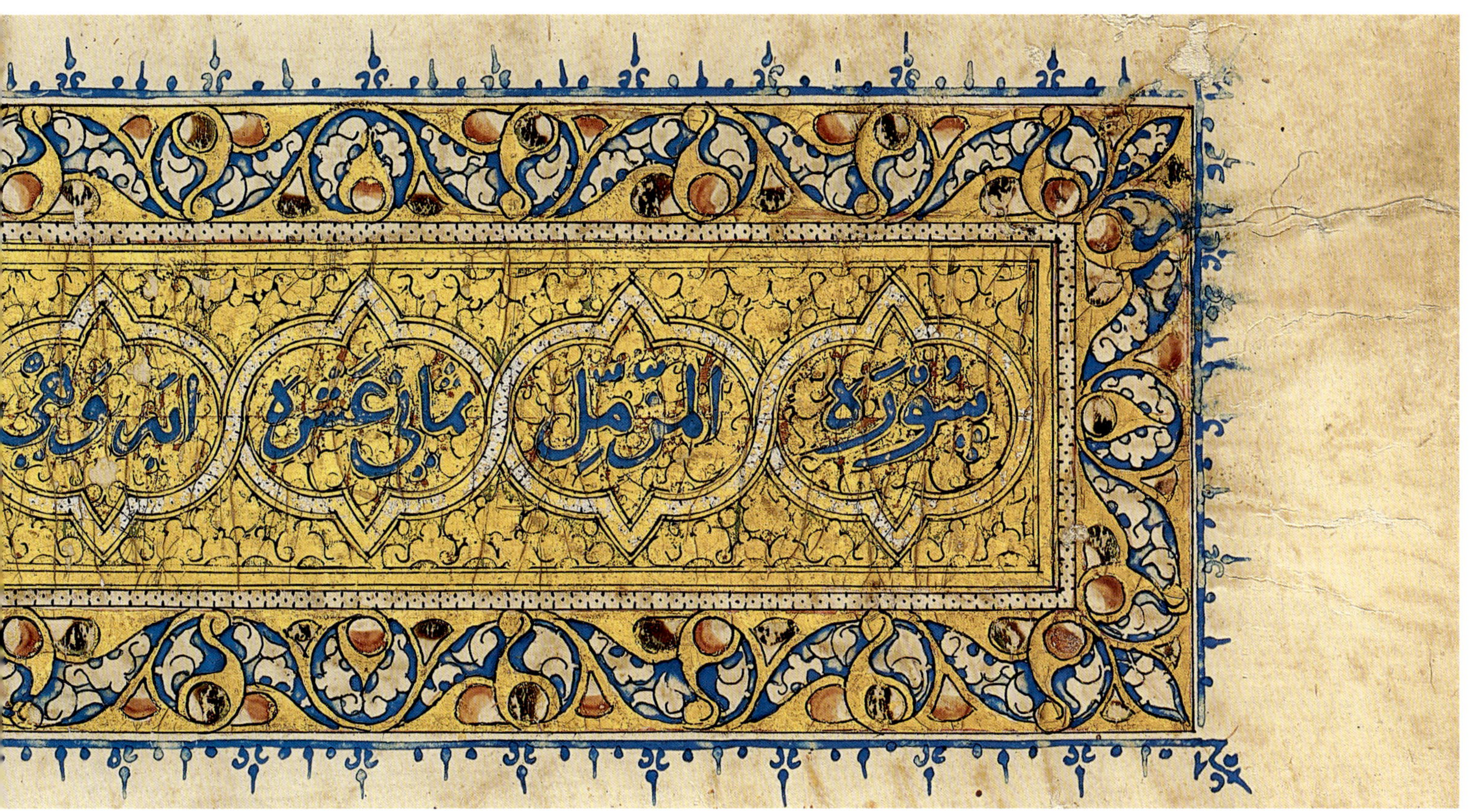

were first drawn in the reddish-brown medium, with specks of red and blue or green added to create the impression of flowers, or perhaps a brocaded textile, and the gold elements between them (circles and lozenges) applied last as small pieces of gold leaf. The reddish-brown medium was also used to outline letters fashioned from leaf and as an overlay to larger surfaces of leaf where it gives the impression of a glaze and provides a warming contrastive color to the cooler plain gold (see fig. 19). Manipulating the hue of gold was a recurring feature of illumination across the centuries, an effect achieved by either using golds with different amounts of silver or copper in them or by overpainting gold with opaque watercolor.

Illumination could also be created by a more organic, fluid process than those structured through geometric frameworks. This is especially true of embellished surfaces around and between lines of text, a form of drawn and painted decoration for which the illuminator would also have been responsible. The last folio of the twenty-sixth part (*juz'*) of a fourteenth-century Qurʾan from Egypt sets its closing verse in a cloudband over an arabesque of winding, arcing stalks and juicy split palmettes. These are configured in a way that suggests their continuity behind the cloudband, drawn in black line, with a more distant plane signaled by hatching in pale brown. The opening folios in the twelfth part of a thirty-part Qurʾan evidence a similar treatment (fig. 22). Set in cloudbands of reserved paper, the script is surrounded by a lively arabesque of blue-white and blue-green flowers with golden leaves and stalks set over a striped ground. The floral field enclosing writing is framed by a golden border of overlapping, interwoven lines, and surmounted by the chapter title in white *thuluth* that floats on a gold arabesque and lapis lazuli ground. The facture of the pigment on this folio indicates the potential range between absolute opacity and the modulated effects achieved through layers of wash.

A third example of an embellished ground is a finispiece to the ninth part of a thirty-part Qurʾan (fig. 23). In this example, the decorated ground produced with gold leaf, shell gold, reddish-brown pigment, and reserved parchment is formed in response to the outlines of the five lines of Kufic. No attempt is made to suggest the illusion of writing floating over a continuous ground behind it; it appears, rather, as a field of vegetal forms shaped according to the interstitial spaces of writing. The vegetation is responsive to the writing, conditioned and generated by its outlines. The upper and lower spaces are treated differently, as a zigzagging line that

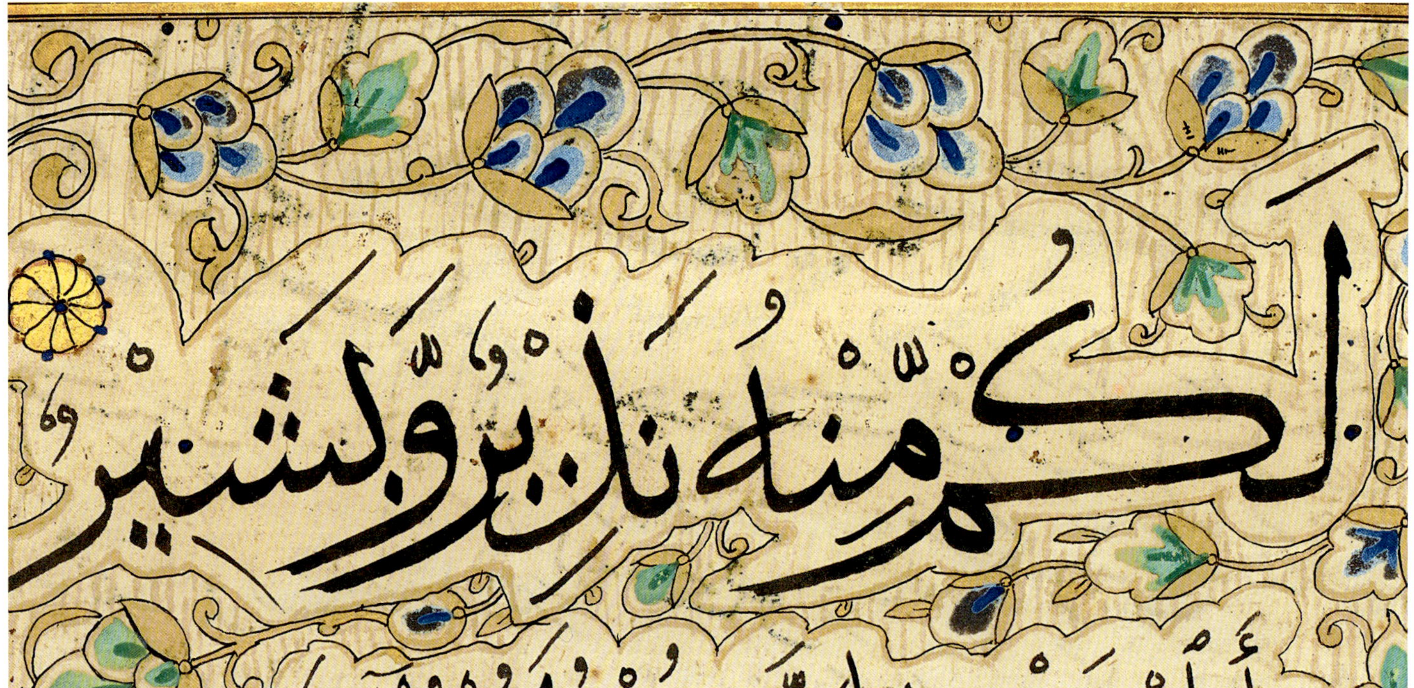

Fig. 22. **Twelfth Part (*Juz'*) of a Qur'an Manuscript** (*detail, cat. 45*), signed by Ahmad al-Isfahani, Cairo, dated 10 Dhu al-Hijja AH 789/ December 22, 1387 CE.

makes a triangular pattern and as a scrolling plant form composed of curling stalks, respectively. To these are added one verse marker, a disk (at upper left), a marginal verse counter of ten (at lower left), and a pendant biomorphic form extending from the rectangular panel of text. The finial is also conceived as a hybrid. Its symmetrical composition is formed from vines and leaves and other elements which reference the natural world. Here, too, reddish-brown and dark brown pigments modulate the visual character of the gold.

The main purpose of illumination was functional, providing a visible structure to the sequence of verses and chapters, marking the beginnings and endings of single-volumes or those of multipart Qur'ans, emphasizing key sections and transitions in the revelation, and providing an annotation for use in recitation and ritual, whether experienced communally by auditory means or individually by reading. These different elements emphasized the organization of the revelation, which was also expressed through the highly legible calligraphic mise-en-page. With the predominant subject matters based on geometry and biomorphic forms—the two often combined within a unified matrix—illumination also offered the opportunity to embellish and exalt the earthly concordance of divine speech by augmenting the materiality of the *mushaf*. Illuminations enhanced the spectrum of color occurring across the pages of the *mushaf*, as well as the sense of texture, effects of transparency and opacity, pattern (which played on the tension between similarity and dissimilarity), the illusion of depth (by overlapping, knotting, and layering), and the reflection of light. They activated the senses of sight and touch, producing effects that changed according to the ways in which light interacted with the surface of the parchment or paper, to viewing distance, and shifts of attention and focus (the broad contrast between glancing and gazing).[91] There can be no doubt that illumination, beautifying and structuring the *mushaf*, always also carried the

Fig. 23. **Folio from the Ninth Part (*Juz'*) of a Qur'an Manuscript** (*detail, cat. 48*), North Africa or Central Islamic Lands, 9th–10th century.

general symbolism of spiritual illumination—signifying knowledge and wisdom—with the physical radiance of light operating semiotically as analogue to written revelation.[92] Illumination lit up the text while the text brought light to humankind. Some illuminated motifs also express this concept literally, for example, through the medallion form of the *shamsa* ("sun"), which resembles a burst of light.

Several examples of illuminated panels made as frontispieces or finispieces to *juz'* share the same basic form as rectangular panels with marginal pendants. But they also exhibit the illuminators' capacity for invention as well as the several formal aspects and effects of illumination described above. In a concluding folio to a twentieth-part of a thirty-part Qur'an, side A sets the four lines of Kufic between two borders of gold studded with red and blue, which resemble a rope, while side B is given over to a rectangular panel with a marginal pendant (see fig. 9).[93] The outer borders take the form of those found on side A and frame two squares whose enclosing borders intersect by being interwoven. Gold, blue, red, and the unpainted parchment make up the palette for a geometric scheme whose tessellated pattern resembles a wall mosaic or perhaps stone inlay on a floor or architectural interior. The tear-shaped pendant contains a vegetal form. A closely related palette and scheme is found in another example, where the central rectangular panel is composed of four interwoven quatrefoils with palmette-like vegetation in the interstices (see cat. 51).

Two further examples echo several of the motifs, compositions, and effects of the preceding folios. The first is dominated by a complex interwoven line in lapis lazuli set over a gold ground of scrolling plant forms, modulated with reddish-brown wash and brown inked lines, with a patterned panel at the center composed of rotated squares (fig. 24). Its visual associations with textiles are pronounced. The second example features the geometry of a circle set amid a rectangular panel and framing border, each one interlinked through knotted and overlapping borders (fig. 25). The interstitial fields are filled with patterns based on the grid—

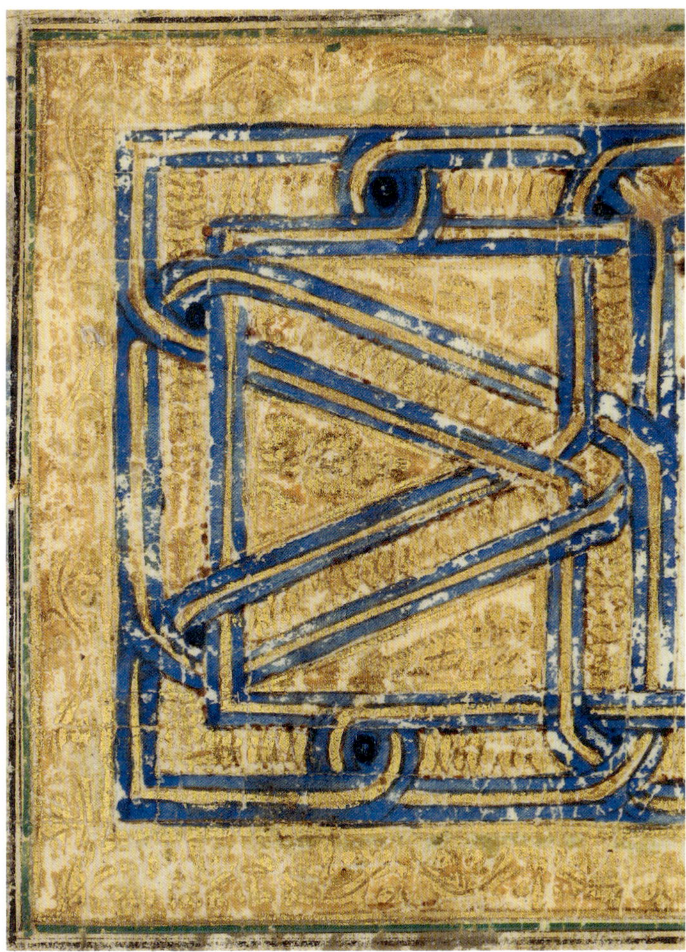

Fig. 24. **Illuminated Panel, Folio from a Qur'an Manuscript** (*detail, cat. 49*), North Africa or Central Islamic Lands, 9th–10th century.

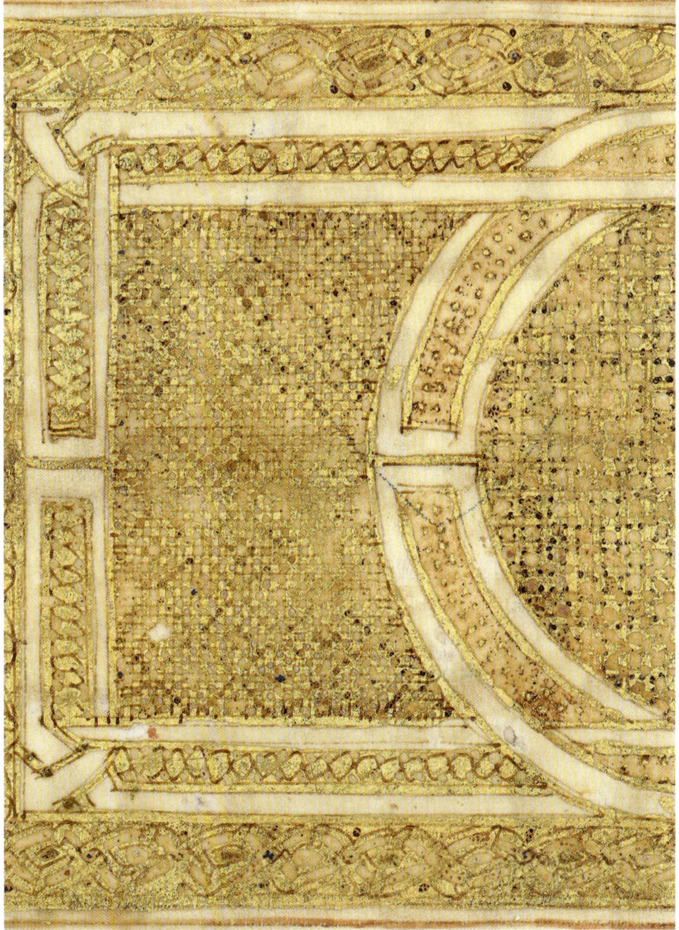

Fig. 25. **Illuminated Panel, Folio from a Qur'an Manuscript** (*detail, cat. 50*), North Africa or Central Islamic Lands, 9th–10th century.

resembling mesh or checkerboard—, a lattice, and rope-like patterns executed in a restricted palette of gold, brown, reddish-brown, and lapis lazuli. The design forms many kinds of contrasts, especially that between movement and stasis, figure and ground. The gridded and lattice designs simulate the technique of weaving and resemble textiles.

Throughout these and other examples spanning the centuries, illuminations in Qurʾans referenced many other mediums and contexts (contemporary to their production), ranging from woven and embroidered cloth and mosaic or stone inlay, to carved stuccoes and wood, and inlaid metalwork. This degree of isomorphism is not unexpected given the high propensity toward intermedial relations in Islamic art and the influence of a repertoire of motifs and habits of composition (panels, frames, finials, pendants, medallions, structured through geometric matrices, etc.) that were shared across multiple mediums. But despite these conditions of artistic conception and production, such associations—formed in the mind of the beholder—brought the Qurʾan into dialogue with other types of objects and physical contexts.[94] Intermedial comparisons are a common element in writings about calligraphy. Al-Tawhidi, for example, cites several sayings in which their speakers liken handwriting to "embroidered cloth," "fine woven cloth," "a finished piece of jewelry," a "filigree of pure gold," and "the garden of knowledge;" describe the pen as a "weaver of fine cloth;" and compare script supplied with diacritical points to "a garden in bloom" contrasted against the "barren soil" of a script lacking these features.[95] Though applied specifically to writing, these and other comparisons, while emphasizing craft—the expression and cultivation of mastery—extend into media comparisons that were made present in the *mushaf* through the techniques, formal properties, and subject matters of illumination. In effect, illumination dressed calligraphy and the Qurʾan while also spatializing them, invoking associations perhaps to a well-tended garden or to architecture that were comparative (the organization of the page and the *mushaf* as a whole) or associative (through motifs and compositions found also in architectural ornament).[96]

CODA TO THE CODEX

Once completed, the calligraphed and illuminated textblock—its quires collated, checked for accuracy, and stitched together—was attached to a binding. While all bindings served a protective purpose—functioning as an outer layer that maintained the physical integrity of the *mushaf*—and were fashioned from diverse materials (leathers, boards of wood and paper, cloth, lacquer) and types of ornament, they could be relatively simple or complex, manifesting pronounced concentrations of labor, resources, and skill (see figs. 1 and 26). The binding was the first thing to be seen, the first point of contact, a threshold and transfer between the world and the text-object it contained, which constituted an earthly trace of the divine, a mediation between God and humankind.[97] And while these materials and forms could signal what the reader would find among the folios of the open *mushaf* through formal affinities, as yet another manifestation of the inherent self-referentiality constructed through the textual Qurʾan, bindings might also include epigraphic programs culled from the language of the revelation itself.[98] These carefully chosen verses often addressed the meaning, significance, and agency of the Qurʾan. Touched and held, the surfaces of bindings were made all the more physical by processes of dyeing and tanning, alternating the colors of outer leather covers and inner doublures, patterning achieved by stamping and blind-tooling (the process of impressing designs on leather without the addition of gold), and textures heightened through the use of larger engraved metal stamps pressed in leather and finished off with gold leaf and paint. The use of filigree—made of colored leathers or papers—laid over painted grounds extended the polychromatic effects of bindings, impressions of difference in size and scale, and heightened tactile properties.

The Qurʾans studied in this essay and catalogue evince an incredible diversity of outcomes and seemingly infinite physical permutations in the treatment of a static text. They were realized through the transformation of commonplace and precious materials, sourced from local and transregional networks, and made into materials and mediums that were used by skilled calligraphers, illuminators, binders, and other specialist craftsmen. These artisans applied their craft with absolute diligence, painstaking work, and innovation. There can be no doubt that the special status of the physical Qurʾan, the *mushaf*, as the created concordance of uncreated divine speech prompted such accumulations of resources, which were deployed in ways that collectively differenced the Muslim scripture from all other books.[99] But it is also true that in the most materially spare of *mushaf*s habits of writing still produced visual effects of harmony and proportionality—making them clearly distinct from ordinary writing—and, moreover, that the inherent structure and cadence of the Qurʾan's language made it immediately recognizable. No other text was ordered in a comparable fashion, especially after the practice of marking individual verses and chapters became firmly established. Any other features of embellishment were a surplus. One might even understand the extraordinary wealth of artistry and diversity of aesthetic features of the *mushaf* over time as rejoinders to the infinite nature of God's speech undertaken through an unending human desire for its exaltation and as expressions of piety.

Constantly holding the aural and visual together, and facilitating both recitation and reading, the *mushaf* engaged the senses of hearing, sight, and touch. While the Qurʾan's miraculous rhythmic Arabic language and shifting cadence—said to have the power alone to convert listeners to Islam or to induce a state of ecstasy as it fell upon their ears—intoned by the reciters or silently read, the material and formal properties of the *mushaf* engaged all those who experienced it through vision and touch.[100] The *mushaf*'s manifold forms constituted objects of worldly beauty, glorifying the word and serving as signs and relays to the place from whence the Qurʾan was sent down. Though addressing the sense of hearing primarily, the hadith "Nobody can escape the pleasure of the Qurʾan" is equally applicable to the visual and physical traits of the several *mushaf*s presented here.[101]

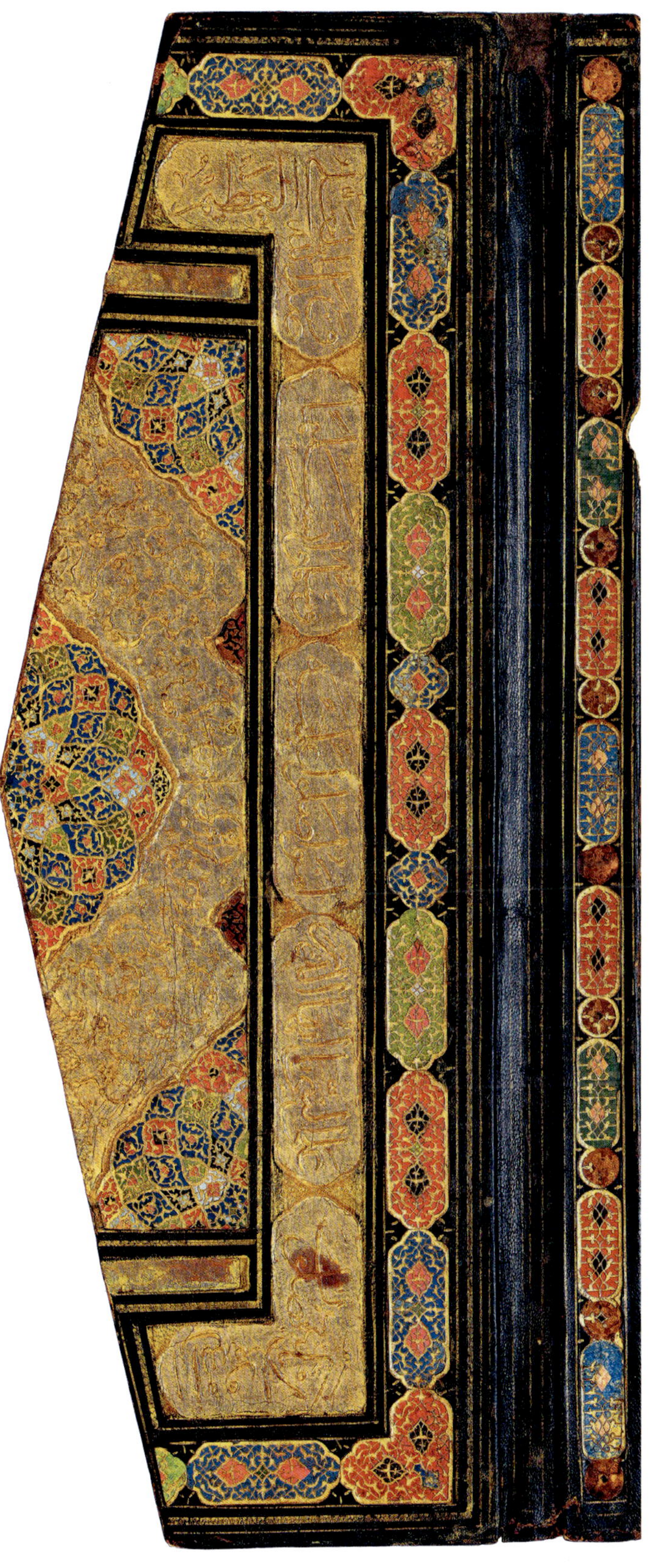

Fig. 26. **Bookbinding Flap (Envelope Flap with Fore-Edge Flap)** (*detail, cat. 60*), Iran, c. 1550–1600.

AUTHOR'S NOTE

I would like to thank Dr. Aimée Froom, curator, Art of the Islamic Worlds, for the invitation to work on this project and for her collegiality and kindness; and Shireen Shah, curatorial assistant, for logistical support during my visits to the Museum of Fine Arts, Houston (MFAH). Jason Dibley, collections manager, provided seamless access to objects in storage. It was a treat to spend time in the conservation lab where Tina Tan, senior works on paper conservator, generously shared her insights and expertise. It has been a pleasure to reprise an author-editor relationship with Heather Brand, publisher in chief at the MFAH, and editor Melina Kervandjian. A special debt of gratitude is also owed to Kirsten Burke, Rachel Hirsch, and Rebecca Selch for their many expressions of *bon courage* as well as conversations about calligraphy in the summer of 2023.

NOTES

1 Translations of the Qur'an are from Ali 1990. Qur'anic references are identified by chapter and verse, e.g., 31:27.

2 Published in Froom 2019, 79–81.

3 Opinions varied about whether the *basmala* was integral to the revelation. See *EI2*, s.v. "Al-Kur'ān" (A. T. Welch et al.), "Structure, 4c."

4 *EI3*, s.v. "Canon and Canonization of the Qur'ān" (Aziz Al-Azmeh). On the miraculous language of the Qur'an and its effects on listeners, see Behrens-Abouseif 1999, 17–19, and *EI3*, s.v. "Aesthetics" (Doris Behrens-Abouseif).

5 Several references are made to the jinn in the Qur'an. In Qur'an 15:14–15, we learn that "He [God] created man of fermented clay dried tinkling hard like earthenware/ And created jinns from the white-hot flame of fire," and in 15:27, "As We fashioned jinns before from intense radiated heat." For other Qur'anic verses and sources on the jinn, see *EI2*, s.v. "Djinn" (D. B. Macdonald).

6 See *EI2*, s.v. "Tashbih wa-Tanzih" (J. van Ess).

7 Harvey 2021, 191, states the problem thus: "Yet how to unite the immanence of an Arabic scripture that can be recited, heard, written and read with the transcendence appropriate to God is one of the oldest problems of Islamic theology."

8 Graham 1984, 362–69.

9 Graham 1984, 373.

10 Schoeler 2010a, 200.

11 See Ory 2000, 367, *EI2*, s.v. "Umm al-Kitāb" (E. Geoffroy and F. Daftary), *EI2*, s.v. "Lawḥ" (A. J. Wensinck and C. E. Bosworth), and Zadeh 2008, 51.

12 Other concerns related to recitation included whether or not the Qur'an must be recited verbatim, if its reciters could offer synopses of its meaning (*ma'na*) and use synonyms, and the legitimacy of translation from Arabic into other languages. See Schoeler 1997, 431–32. For overviews of debates about the difference between divine and human speech, the created and uncreated Qur'an, and the relation between orality and the written, see Watt 1950, Berque 1995, Schoeler 1997, Zadeh 2008, Zahrani 2009, and Harvey 2021, 191–221.

13 For detailed discussions about these doctrines and the views of their major theologians, see Harvey 2021, 191–221, and Watt 1950.

14 Harvey 2021, 206, and Watt 1950, 96. There were of course other viewpoints which continued to be espoused. Ibn Qutayba (d. 889 CE), for example, considered the *mushaf* to be "veritably one and the same as the divine, uncreated Qur'an, and not just an indication (*dalil*) of it" (Zadeh 2008, 52).

15 Berque 1995, 19. The history of the Qur'an's production in written form is summarized in *EI3*, s.v. "Canon and Canonization of the Qur'ān" (Aziz Al-Azmeh), and *EI2*, s.v. "Al-Kur'ān" (A. T. Welch, R. Paret, and J. D. Pearson). Copies of 'Uthman's recension were sent to Basra, Damascus, Kufa, Mecca, and Medina with preceding copies destroyed. Various arguments about the history of canonization, based also on material evidence, are reviewed in Whelan 1998.

16 A source of opposition came from the Qur'an readers. 'Uthman's recension disrupted their normative habits of transmission. See Schoeler 1997, 431–32, and Zahrani 2009, 429.

17 On the privileging of hearing over seeing, see Zahrani 2009, 437–48. Zahrani argues for the dominance of the "audiocentric" contrasted against the recessive "ocularcentric" (ibid., 437–38). Forms of knowledge transmission and the relation between literacy, memory, and writing in the early Islamic period are discussed in Schoeler 1997, Schoeler 2010a, and Schoeler 2010b.

18 Vocalization annotated the consonantal text, which manifest only the long vowels (a [*alif*], i [*ya'*], u [*waw*]). Letter-pointing provided the phonetic value to letters whose shape was shared by other letters of the alphabet since the Arabic alphabet comprises twenty-eight phonemes but only eighteen graphemes. See Gacek 2006, 230, 238, 241–42, and 245. Gacek's study draws from Ibn Abi Da'ud al-Sijistani's *Kitab al-masahif* and provides references to the Arabic edition published by Jeffery 1937. Ibn Abi Da'ud's text addresses numerous topics on the usage of the Qur'an, including whether it should be placed before the qibla in mosques, traveling with the Qur'an to infidel lands, infidels handling Qur'ans, Muslims touching Qur'ans when not in a state of ritual purity (without performing ablutions), and laying the Qur'an on the ground. See Jeffery 1937, 179–83, 185–87, and 189. For an expanded discussion of the *mushaf* and the "system of ritual purity," see Zadeh 2009, 445–52.

19 These and other verses are discussed by Zahrani 2009, 428–29, amid a broader argument about the uses of writing in Islam's early period.

20 On the question of payment, see Gacek 2006, 239–40. The "sacrality" of the *mushaf* as created analogue of uncreated divine speech is most clearly understood through the category of ritual. As Zadeh 2009, 453, notes "in the form of a physical object, the Qur'an enters into the realm of material existence, itself bound to and defined by a larger system of ritual purity," hence questions on its proper handling and use. For views on other issues and conditions related to handling, including menstruation, see Zadeh 2008, 52.

21 Several scholars have discussed historical/regional variations in *mushafs*, attempting to connect their features to prevailing theological debates, general beliefs, and attitudes, as responses to different kinds of concern including proper handling. See Tabbaa 1992, passim, George 2009, 103–4, George 2010, 91–93 and 143–45, George 2017, 123, Flood 2012, 267, Flood 2019, passim, and Gacek 2006, 246. That God issued His revelation in the Arabic language to the Prophet Muhammad lent a special status to the language and its written forms. While no other book matched the Qur'an in importance, one might say that all books and the art of writing partook of its importance. For example, see Behrens-Abouseif 1999, 138–41, and *EI3*, s.v. "Aesthetics" (Doris Behrens-Abouseif).

On the perceived sacrality of copies of the Qur'an, see Ory 2000, 368, and Zadeh 2009, 463. The merits of the Qur'an became a literary genre of their own, the so-called *Fada'il al-Qur'an*. See Zadeh 2008, passim. In attempting to understand the treatment of the Qur'an as a sacred text and its ontology, some scholars have employed the concept of "inlibration," which is seen in parallel to the Christian doctrine of the incarnation, of Jesus as *logos*. This idea has been met with some skepticism. For the debate around its applicability, see Ganz 2019, 6, Harvey 2021, 191, and Zadeh 2008, passim.

22 A detailed analysis of structure is presented in *EI2*, s.v. "Al-Kur'ān" (A. T. Welch, R. Paret, and J. D. Pearson), "Structure 4a–b."

23 Study of early Qur'ans has shown that the surface area of the text was in a proportional relation to the border/margin. See Déroche

1992, 20, and George 2003, 5–6. George developed several of the ideas first offered in his 2003 study of the Amajur Qur'an (dated 876 CE) through a larger corpus while also advancing our understanding of the geometry and proportionality of Kufic script. See George 2010, 56–60 and 95–114. He describes these proportional relations, which lent the early Qur'ans visual harmony and order, as an "architecture of the page" (ibid., 95). The same form of study has not been applied to copies of the Qur'an from the tenth century onward, though their chief scripts—the "six scripts"—are themselves governed by fixed proportional relations and ratios, a "regulated" script attributed to the Abbasid vizier Ibn Muqla (d. 940 CE).

24 This framework, sometimes referenced as the mise-en-page or as lineation—described by George 2003 as a "template grid"—was marked on the support by either a line made with a hardpoint—such as a stylus—which left a line visible in raking light, or by the application, common in later manuscripts, of the *mistara*. The latter was a cardboard strung with threads corresponding to the grid (*mastar*) of text. This framework was registered on the support by pressing it against the *mistara*, a process that left faint marks on the surface of the prepared folio/bifolio. George 2003, passim, offers many useful observations about the evidence for, and use of, the "template grid" in early Qur'ans. For a study of the *mastar* in non-Qur'anic manuscripts of the Mongol and post-Mongol periods, see Porter Y 2003.

25 The gaps between discrete words have been called "intratext spaces." Commenting on the habits of spacing in the Amajur Qur'an, Blair 2008 argues that its intention was to "slow down reading, for the text was not meant to be read, but rather to be recited by someone who had already committed it to memory. . . . The Amajur Qur'an was a document designed for oral recitation" (ibid., 78).

26 One of the most striking observations about the calligrapher's skill in arranging script is made in an album preface composed by Dust Muhammad in 1544–45 CE. Among the traits of calligraphy by ʿAli b. Abi Talib was that "wherever letters are parallel to each other on the front and back of a page, black is on black and white on white." Trans. Thackston 2001, 7. For Dust Muhammad's preface, see Roxburgh 2001, passim.

27 The impression of meter is "caused by the repetition of certain grammatical forms and not by an effort to carry through a strict metre of either syllables or stresses." The verses also end in "an irregular line or assonance." The recurrence of verses and formulas, described as "schematic form," is a distinctive characteristic of the Qur'an wherein "certain verses, or formulas . . . are woven into the narrative in a regular pattern in different stories presented together as a group" (*EI2*, s.v. "Al-Kur'ān" [A. T. Welch, R. Paret, and J. D. Pearson], "Structure 4b"). On these traits, and their effects, also see Berque 1995, 23.

28 Berque 1995, 25–26, has also commented on the visual patterns of script.

29 Trans. Rosenthal 1947, 14. Rosenthal offers an annotated translation of the treatise. For further information about al-Tawhidi and the Baghdad milieu in which he worked, see Necipoğlu 1995, 189, 197, and 204. A related version of this aphorism is recorded in Ibn al-Nadim 1970, 1:20, with the second half opining, "It is also said that bad handwriting is, in connection with culture, a disease. It is further said that ugly penmanship is sterility of culture."

30 Al-Tawhidi's treatise, and many other texts about writing, comment on the relation between thought, speech, writing, and the body. For some aphorisms on these topics, see Rosenthal 1947, 11. I have taken up these issues, and the topic of the senses and the body, in Roxburgh 2008.

31 Rosenthal 1947, 9.

32 Rosenthal 1947, 17. For sayings on diacritical points, see Rosenthal 1947, 17–19.

33 Rosenthal 1947, 8. Al-Tawhidi also offers commentary on the kinds of physical activity which the calligrapher should avoid, quoting ʿAli b. Jaʿfar, about the risk that "the movements assimilate themselves to the letters and the letters get buried in the movements, the essential traits of the forms of the handwriting and of the shape of the letters will be safeguarded only inasmuch as they have become filled with them, and their bodies will be protected only inasmuch as they have been put in relation to them. He said: Recently, I lifted a whip with my hand several times and cracked it over the head of my mount. As a result my handwriting was changed for a while" (ibid., 7).

34 Rosenthal 1947, 5.

35 Rosenthal 1947, 5–6.

36 Ibn Badis (r. 1016–1062 CE) was fourth ruler of the Zirid dynasty of Ifriqiyya (North Africa). His treatise continued to circulate in the fifteenth and sixteenth centuries, as evidenced by its partial translation in Persian. See Porter Y 1989. For the Arabic manuscripts, see Levey 1962, 6.

37 For 148 treatises/texts by 124 authors spanning the ninth and twentieth century composed in Arabic (manuscripts, editions, and translations), see Gacek 2004.

38 Levey 1962, 11, provides a list of the apparatus mentioned by Ibn Badis.

39 There are also examples of buildings specifically dedicated to collections of Qur'ans, as in the Khuda Khana, or Bayt al-Mashaf, of the Masjid-i Atiq, Shiraz, built in 1351. See James 1988, 164.

40 Levey 1962, 13.

41 Rosenthal 1947, 8–9.

42 Ibn al-Nadim 1970, 1:19.

43 Déroche 1990–91, 64, points out that even in the simplest forms of writing, a sparse, distributed text over many more folios than necessary produces a lavish effect.

44 For studies of transmission and emulation, see Roxburgh 2003 and Roxburgh 2008.

45 Papyrus, made from the plant *Cyperus papyrus*, was largely supplanted in Egypt by paper in the late tenth century. See *EI2*, s.v. "Papyrus" (R. G. Khoury). The technology transfer to paper, as well as histories of other supports, is presented in detail in Bloom 2001. Of all the regions of the Islamic lands, it was in western North Africa and the Iberian Peninsula where parchment continued to be used for copies of the Qur'an centuries after the adoption of paper for this purpose in other regions.

46 In early Qur'ans, the quinions could be composed entirely of bifolios (folded sheets of four pages each) or as a combination of bifolios and single folios. See Déroche 1992, 18–19.

47 The best source on Islamic paper, its making and physical characteristics, remains Loveday 2001. For parchment, see *EI2*, s.v. "Rakk" (R. G. Khoury and J. J. Witkam).

48 The best-known example is the "Blue Qur'an," which has been the subject of intensive scholarship with different arguments about its

date and place of production around the Mediterranean and in Iraq. Its indigo-dyed blue parchment folios carry Kufic in gold leaf, the letters outlined in red ink, with silver verse markers. For recent arguments about its context of production, see George 2009 and Fraser 2017. A comprehensive analysis of its materials was published in Porter 2018. Through experimentation, Porter determined that the disadvantages of dipping—reducing suppleness and altering shape—did not affect parchment made from sheep skin (Porter 2018, 579–80). On paper dyeing, see Loveday 2001, 51–52.

49 Levey 1962, 7, and Levey, Krek, Haddad 1956, 242–43, offer analyses of the black inks described by Ibn Badis. For overviews of Islamic inks, see Blair 2006, 61–65, and Schopen 2006. Ink production and technical treatises are taken up in Fani 2021; attempts to make inks from medieval recipes are described in Colini 2021.

50 Levey 1962, 15–18.

51 Levey 1962, 18–21.

52 Vitriols were salts procured from Egypt, Iran, and Cyprus (Levey 1962, 7), either iron or zinc sulfate. Another type of iron gall ink was made with iron filings instead of vitriol. See Colini 2021, 143–47.

53 For mixed inks, see Colini 2021, 148–51.

54 The reed pen is the object of intense attention in Islamic culture with diverse literary genres addressing its function, use, preparation, status and significance. For some of these, see McWilliams and Roxburgh 2007, 12–13, and Roxburgh 2008, 275.

55 Levey 1962, 38.

56 Levey 1962, 38–39.

57 While the size of a sheet of parchment was limited by the animal which supplied the skin, paper was constrained by its technique of production, especially lifting the mesh frame holding the pulp from the vat. Large-format Qur'ans were preferred in the early Islamic period as testified by Ibn Abi Da'ud's *Kitab al-masahif* (Jeffery 1937, 135–36). One of the most monumental Qur'ans ever produced is discussed in Farhad and Rettig 2016, 222–25, and Roxburgh 2007, 49–51.

58 The process of preparing pens is described by al-Tawhidi (Rosenthal 1947, 4–5) and Ibn Badis (Levey 1962, 14–15) and many other writers of treatises. For other texts that transmitted knowledge of calligraphy—especially those attributed to Ibn Muqla (d. 940 CE) and Ibn al-Bawwab (d. 1022)—and the different means of transmission—by direct study of the calligrapher, by textual description in prose and poetry, study of physical specimens, or preserved pens—see Roxburgh 2003. A useful overview of the pen is provided in Blair 2006, 57–61.

59 For a discussion of the curvilinear ductus and rectilinear ductus, based on Mamluk sources, and their classification according to script type, see Gacek 1989.

60 Rosenthal 1947, 7.

61 For an uncommon study of evidence of reinking and direction of movement, see Atanasiu 2000. Also see Blair 2006, 60, who counts the number of strokes required to form certain examples of letters.

62 Blair 2006, 60, accounts for the latter by a change in surface tension.

63 For further thoughts on these aspects of Islamic calligraphy, particularly questions of expressiveness, indexicality, and the relation between writing and body, see Roxburgh 2008, passim.

64 Levey 1962, 8 and 21–29.

65 Levey 1962, 22–29.

66 Levey 1962, 22 and 25.

67 Other folios from the same manuscript are published in Fraser and Kwiatkowski 2006, 96–101. They propose that such a fine manuscript with a commentary would have been used as a teaching copy, perhaps as a gift from an elite patron to a renowned scholar or commissioned by a scholar of means for personal use.

68 Levey 1962, 32–35.

69 A folio from the same manuscript is published in James 1992b, 140–41. The catalogue of James 1992b contains several examples of Qur'ans copied in gold, which became more common after 1000 CE, but especially in the Mongol and Mamluk periods.

70 See Lings 1978, 69–70, James 1988, 92–98, Farhad and Rettig 2016, 196–201, and Blair 2023.

71 Blair 2023, 100–101, describes the production of the calligraphy, suggesting the number of pens that were necessary, highlighting its labor intensiveness, and suggesting that the outlining (*tazmik*) was performed by an illuminator and not the calligrapher. James 1980, 10, suggests that an apprentice, someone other than the main calligrapher of the Qur'an, executed the outlining in some manuscripts. He also notes that vocalization was "often added by another person, who sometimes recorded this in a note."

72 The blue papers of cats. 40 and 41 appear to carry the pigment within their fibers; the pinkish-buff color is a surface application applied as a tint (and appears on one side each of cats. 42 and 43, with the other sides ivory-toned).

73 Two other folios related to this set—cats. 44 and 52—have the same dimensions and feature alternating lines in gold and blue script except that the lapis lazuli is much thinner and none of the writing is set in "beds" formed by depressed paper.

74 Written sources indicate that chrysography in Qur'ans was in use by the early eighth century (Déroche 1992, 67, citing Ibn al-Nadim's *Fihrist*). After an early copyist of Qur'ans, Khalid b. Abi al-Hayyaj, had designed a gold inscription for the mihrab of the Mosque of the Prophet in Medina, caliph ʿUmar II requested that he "transcribe a Qur'an for me like this model." Given its expense, the caliph returned the Qur'an (Ibn al-Nadim 1970, 1:11). Concerns about the use of precious metals in the early Islamic period are discussed in Juynboll 1986 (drawing from hadith) and Flood 2019, 54–64.

75 Folios and bifolios in private and public collections are connected to a Qur'an made up as two volumes of which the first is now held in the Nuruosmaniye Library, Istanbul. See Déroche 1992, 90–91, and Fraser and Kwiatkowski 2006, 30–33.

76 For its use in Islamic period contexts, see Herzfeld 1915, and Bsees 2019, 119–120; for the history of the form in classical antiquity, see Leatherbury 2019.

77 In his discussion of the "Blue Qur'an," Fraser 2017, 207, describes the use of the hardpoint as uncommon in Qur'ans but "standard in Christian manuscripts of the period." Its use has been discussed by George 2003, 4–7, George 2009, 77, and Déroche 1992, 20.

78 The folio is published in Fendall 2003, 22–23, accompanied by a list of locations of other folios and sections from the same Qur'an. Also see Déroche 1992, 67.

79 Glues are discussed in Levey 1962, 9, and Levey, Krek, Haddad 1956, 9.

80 The several steps of working in gold leaf are described in Fraser and Kwiatkowski 2006, 30, Porter 2018, 581, and Porter 2021, 260–61. Porter lists several adhesives used for gold leaf, "gum, glair, or plant and animal adhesive such as fig sap, glue made from parchment shavings, or fish collagen" (Porter 2018, 581).

81 Porter identifies these inks as either "metal tannate (*hibr*) or carbon black (*midad*), and possibly a mixture of both" (Porter 2021, 261).

82 Levey 1962, 37.

83 Levey 1962, 37. Levey glosses "*Ibriz*" gold as "a very pure gold" and notes that *kuhl* was mostly antimony trisulfide used as a cosmetic. Ibn Badis's reference to *kuhl* is intriguing: it makes sense only as a shorthand for "outlining," which is likened to the application of makeup.

84 Invisibility is a category taken up by Ibn Badis in his eighth chapter "On recording secrets." Here he describes invisible inks made from white vitriol with water of gallnut, sal ammoniac, milk, and seed of the prune, each ink revealed by the addition of another material to the surface of the sheet (Levey 1962, 35). Such transformations would be catalyzed by the recipient of the secret correspondence.

85 This reddish-brown ink, used in outlining letters in gold leaf and also over gold leaf in illuminations (where it resembles a glaze), has been described by Porter as a "sticky-toffee" colored red. Porter's analysis revealed it to be safflower (Latin, *Carthamus tinctorius*; Arabic, *ʿasfur*) native to the Islamic lands and India. As she notes, the preparation of a red ink using safflower is one of the recipes described by Ibn Badis, who prescribes its use the same day as it is mixed with vinegar and water of gum, "Its color comes out well. Nothing else mixes with it. It can be applied to gold, silver, and tin. . . . When used on paper or parchment, it comes out a wonderful red color" (Porter 2011, 215–18, and Levey 1962, 31).

86 Contrasting working in leaf versus working with gold and silver paint, Porter describes leaf as a "two-step interrupted process" distinct from the "fluid forms" possible in paint (Porter 2021, 266). She also notes that "At first thought, the idea of 'writing' in leaf form seems strange," but without commenting further on the implications (Porter 2021, 261).

87 The mediated production of writing is better understood in later historical periods through such processes as cut paper (decoupage) or by the production of "facsimiles" of calligraphy—generally "originals" made by master calligraphers—translated into other mediums including simple outlining or illumination. See Roxburgh 2005, chaps. 4 and 6. For earlier periods of Islamic art, George has observed the difference between "the inscription of a text onto a template surface, whether engraved on stone, on wood or set in mosaic . . . from the craft of scribes working with ink and pen" and notes the occasional relationship between such mediums and "manuscript calligraphy" (George 2009, 86). Such intermedial relationships and the technical processes that might account for them would provide fruitful ground for further study.

88 There is ample evidence for both, for example in the division of work between calligraphers and illuminators and calligraphers who were also responsible for illumination. Both are recorded in notations provided in copies of the *mushaf*, in colophons or as signatures. The best-known example of a calligrapher/illuminator is Ibn al-Bawwab and a Qurʾan produced by him in 1000–1 CE. See Blair 2008, 84 and n42. For repeated pairings of calligraphers and illuminators who made Mamluk Qurʾans, see James 1988, 160. For information on the sequential production of calligraphy and illumination, see Blair 2008, 90.

89 The materials published in Lings 1978 and Baker 2007 provide a good understanding of how illumination changed across this lengthy period. Other resources include Déroche 1992, James 1992a, James 1992b, and Bayani et al. 1999.

90 This verse is commonly found on Qurʾan bindings, including cats. 60, 61, and 62. It is sometimes paired with the "Throne Verse" from sura 2, *al-Baqara* (The Cow), verses 255–57, as in cat. 61. As one of the most commonly quoted suras, the "Throne Verse" can be paired with other verses on bindings, e.g., cat. 59, where it is joined by the equally famous sura 24, *al-Nur* (Light), verses 35–36. For another example, see James 1980, 82.

91 Porter 2021, 262, has observed the distinct ways in which leaf, as opposed to shell gold, reflects light.

92 See Behrens-Abouseif 1999, 31–34, and George 2009, 106–8. For a broader analysis of light and beauty, and their relationship to knowledge, see Necipoğlu 1995, esp. chap. 10. One of the most potent expressions of light is in sura 24, *al-Nur* (Light), verses 35–36, which begins "God is the light of the heavens and the earth. The semblance of His light is that of a niche in which is a lamp, the flame within a glass, the glass a glittering star as it were." These verses often appear on bindings, as in cat. 59.

93 Published in Fendall 2003, 20–21.

94 On the relations between the Qurʾan, architecture and other media, for example, see George 2010, 60–89. Also see Flood 2019, passim, and Ganz 2019, esp. 9–12.

95 Rosenthal 1947, 8, 13, 14, and 18.

96 The relation between textile and scripture is discussed in Ganz 2019, 24–25, and in Flood 2019, esp. 54–56, with an emphasis on ornamentation and the categories of jewelry and dress. Ganz 2019, 9–12, also explores aspects of books as "spatial configurations."

97 These aspects of the Qurʾan—as "receptacle for the word of God," as "vessel of revelation"—are discussed in Zadeh 2008, passim. On the worlds of absence and presence, and the respective senses which could access them, see Zahrani 2009, 440–50.

98 For the Qurʾan's "awareness of itself as a scripture," see Zadeh 2008, 50, and the cited references to key studies by William Graham and Daniel Madigan.

99 On this point, see Ganz 2019, esp. 2–22.

100 For the Qurʾan's auditory powers, see Behrens-Abouseif 1999, 18–19.

101 Cited and discussed in Behrens-Abouseif 1999, 18.

يٰأَيُّهَا ٱلْمُزَّمِّلُ قُمِ ٱللَّيْلَ إِلَّا قَلِيلًا نِصْفَ

أَوْ زِدْ عَلَيْهِ وَرَتِّلِ ٱلْقُرْآنَ تَرْتِيلًا إِنَّا سَ

إِنَّ نَاشِئَةَ ٱللَّيْلِ هِيَ أَشَدُّ وَطْئًا وَأَقْوَمُ قِ

سَبْحًا طَوِيلًا وَٱذْكُرِ ا رَبِّ

الاحكام والنسخ

قوله تعالى يا ايها المزمل قم الليل الا قليلا نصفه
هذا حكم نزل على النبي عليه السلام واصحا
اخر السورة ... الناسخ
فرض نسخ به فرض وكان
نافلة له الاية ... وقال
ومنهم من قال هو فرض
فريضة على كل
ابن عباس
النبي عليه

صلاة الفريضة

ابن عباس ومجاهد وغيرهما
ابن عمر وعلي هي ما بين
الحسن وغيره هي العشا
الى الصبح
موقعا

QUR'ANS AND QUR'ANIC MATERIALS

THE HOSSEIN AFSHAR COLLECTION

DAVID J. ROXBURGH

نوبهم وأنشأنا من بعدهم قرنا
كتبا في قرطس فلمسوه بأيد
ان هذا إلا سحر مبين ۝ وقا
ملك ولو أنزلنا ملكا لقضي الأ
وجعلنه ملكا لجعلنه رجلا و
ون ۝ ولقد استهزئ برسل من
وا منهم ما كانوا به يستهـ
الأرض ثم انظروا كيف كا
لمن ما في السموت والأر
نفسه الرحمة ليجمعنكم إلى يـ
فيه الذين خسروا أنفسهم ف
سكن في الليل والنهار وهو
غير الله أتخذ وليا فاطر السـ
يطعم ولا يطعم قل إني أمـ
أسلم ولا تكونن من المشر

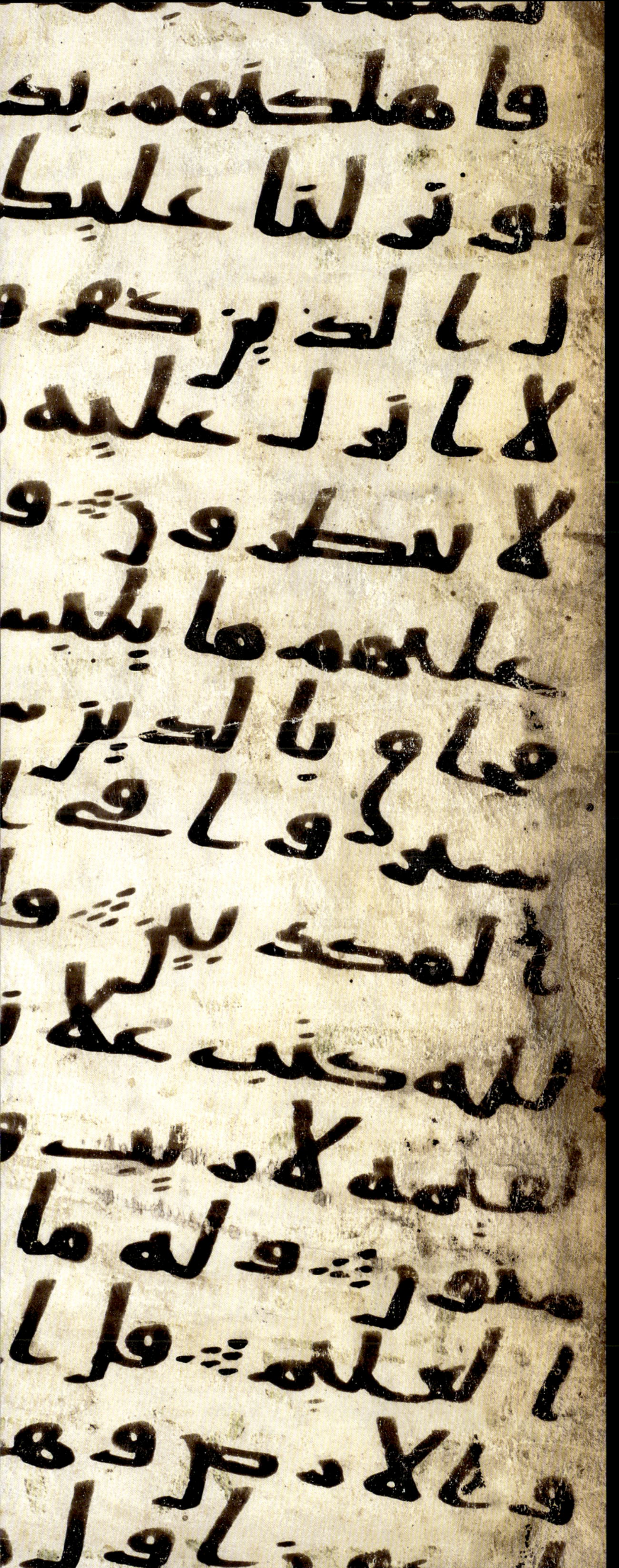

THE EARLIEST RECORDINGS

~

7TH–8TH CENTURY

THE EARLIEST RECORDINGS, 7TH–8TH CENTURY

Reports on the early transcription of the Qur'an—from the orally transmitted and recited word of God to a complete written copy (*mushaf*)—suggest that it was attempted but unrealized by the Prophet Muhammad (d. 632 CE). Other narratives record that the Prophet Muhammad's successor and first caliph Abu Bakr (r. 632–634 CE), urged by 'Umar, tasked Zayd b. Thabit (d. c. 666 CE)—the personal scribe to the famously illiterate Prophet—with the responsibility of collecting revelations that had been inscribed on different materials (papyrus, wood, bones, and palm leaves) and others that had been preserved through memory. During his reign, 'Umar (r. 634–644 CE) obtained these sheets and gave them to his daughter Hafsa, a widow of the Prophet Muhammad. Most commonly accepted is that the codification of the Qur'an took place during the rule of the third caliph, 'Uthman (r. 644–656 CE), whose objective was to produce a definitive version of the Qur'an—in consonantal form—and to have this canonical edition replace all other existing copies of the text.[1] These efforts would secure a fully accurate and authorized Qur'an for further copying and distribution. Codification of the vocalized 'Uthmanic codex was not achieved until the tenth century when Abu Bakr Mujahid (d. 936 CE) asserted that "seven" Qur'an teachers of the eighth century held divine authority. These "seven" readings were the accepted vowelized recitations of the Qur'an.[2]

The earliest extant evidence of physical copies of the Qur'an comprises a small corpus of parchment folios and fragments in the Hijazi script, the vast majority of which lack variant readings and are hence thought to represent the edition sponsored by 'Uthman. This spare, vertically attenuated, and slightly inclined script (the tall vertical strokes lean backward) takes its name from the region of the Hijaz, enclosing Mecca and Medina, the two most important centers of the early history of Islam and both homes to the Prophet Muhammad. There is no reason to believe that the Hijazi script was confined to this region of the western Arabian Peninsula; and despite the coherence inferred from the script's naming, there is sufficient variation among examples to suggest the coexistence of variant types throughout the seventh and eighth centuries.[3] Evidence also suggests that although the Hijazi script continued to be used into the eighth century, it was being replaced by Kufic script from the late seventh century onward. The scope of variation and scribal flexibility found across the corpus of Hijazi folios and fragments has prompted comparisons to handwriting, a form of written notation distinct from the codified and regimented practice of Islamic calligraphy that developed in other script types in subsequent historical periods.[4] The Hijazi leaves, as witnesses to the formative first century of the Islamic calendar, are characterized by striking vertically oriented folios, the arrangement of text in multiple lines formed as single columns, and their potent austerity. With scarcely any complex embellishments to their folios (e.g., illuminated chapter headings), perhaps in response to concerns about the physical nature of the *mushaf* and visually subtle functional elements such as verse markers, their monumentality is enlivened by a script copied in brown and brownish black ink over the various natural hues of parchment.

1

Folio from a Qur'an Manuscript

Saudi Arabia, possibly Medina, mid-7th century
Ink and opaque watercolor on parchment
14 1/4 × 11 1/8 inches (36.2 × 28.3 cm); 28 lines
Side A: sura 5, *al-Ma'ida* (The Feast), verse 111–sura 6, *al-An'am* (The Cattle), verses 1–2
Side B: sura 6, *al-An'am* (The Cattle), verses 3–19
Text copied in Hijazi script in black ink; ending of suras indicated by clusters of black dots; disks of blue and red mark groups of ten verses.
TR:703-2015

وهو الله في السموت وفي الارض يعلم سركم
وجهركم ويعلم ما تكسبون ⁖ وما تاتيهم من اية من
ايت ربهم الا كانوا عنها معرضين ⁖ فقد كذبوا
بالحق لما جاءهم فسوف ياتيهم انبؤا ما كانوا
به يستهزءون ⁖ الم يروا كم اهلكنا من قبلهم من
قرن مكنهم في الارض ما لم نمكن لكم وارسلنا ا
لسما عليهم مدررا وجعلنا الانهر تجري من تحتهم
فاهلكنهم بذنوبهم وانشانا من بعدهم قرنا اخرين ⁖
ولو نزلنا عليك كتبا في قرطس فلمسوه بايديهم لقا
ل الذين كفروا ان هذا الا سحر مبين ⁖ وقالوا لو
لا انزل عليه ملك ولو انزلنا ملكا لقضي الامر ثم
لا ينظرون ⁖ ولو جعلنه ملكا لجعلنه رجلا وللبسنا
عليهم ما يلبسون ⁖ ولقد استهزئ برسل من قبلك
فحاق بالذين سخروا منهم ما كانوا به يستهزءون ⁖ قل
سيروا في الارض ثم انظروا كيف كان عقبة
المكذبين ⁖ قل لمن ما في السموت والارض قل
لله كتب على نفسه الرحمة ليجمعنكم الى يوم ا
لقيمة لا ريب فيه الذين خسروا انفسهم فهم لا يو
منون ⁖ وله ما سكن في اليل والنهار وهو السميع
العليم ⁖ قل اغير الله اتخذ وليا فاطر السموت
والارض وهو يطعم ولا يطعم قل اني امرت ان
اكون اول من اسلم ولا تكونن من المشركين ⁖
قل اني اخاف ان عصيت ربي عذاب يوم عظيم ⁖
من يصرف عنه يومئذ فقد رحمه وذلك الفوز ا
لمبين ⁖ وان يمسسك الله بضر فلا كاشف له الا هو
وان يمسسك بخير فهو على كل شيء قدير ⁖ وهو ا
لقاهر فوق عباده وهو الحكيم الخبير ⁖ قل اي شيء ا
كبر شهدة قل الله شهيد بيني وبينكم واوحي الي

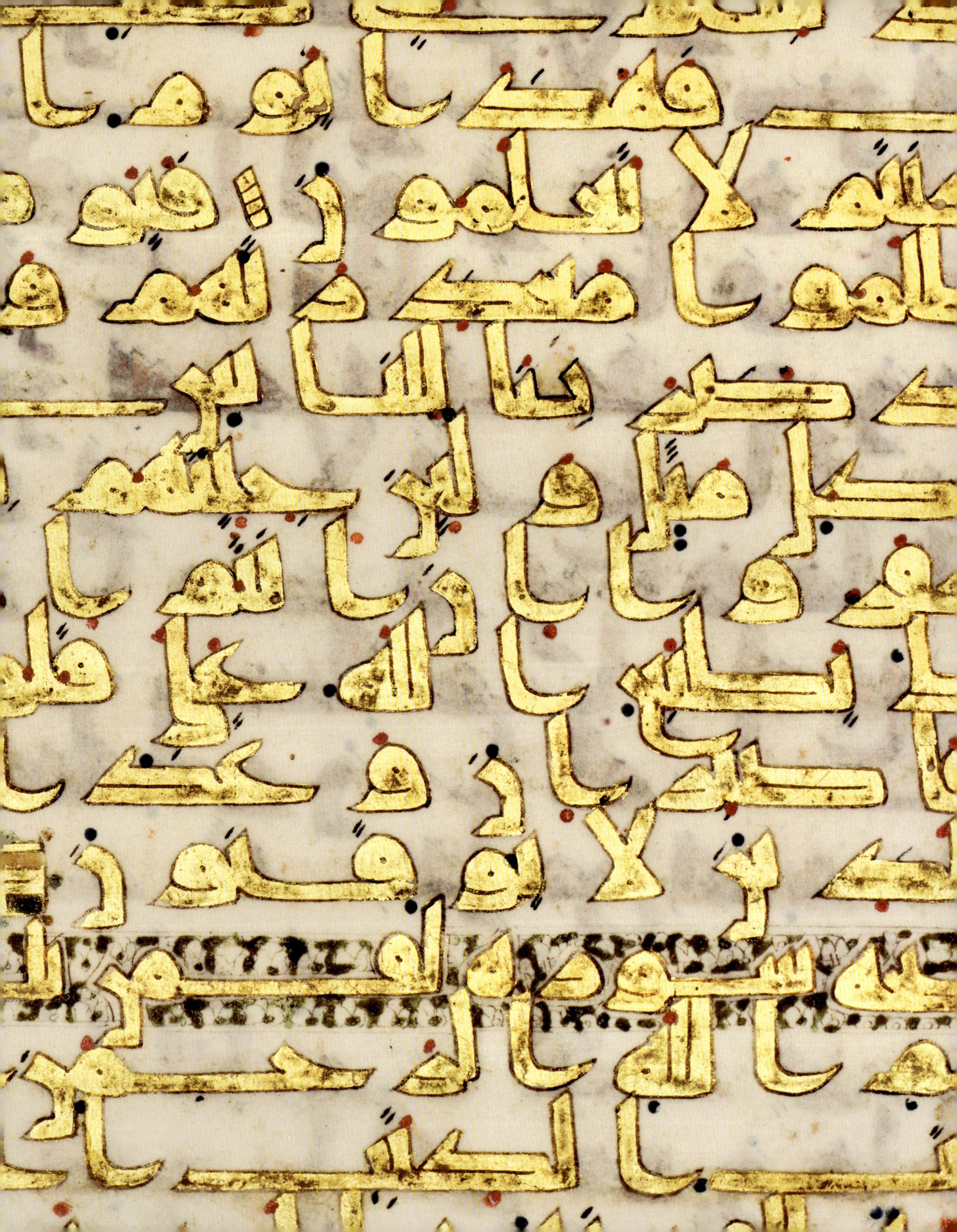

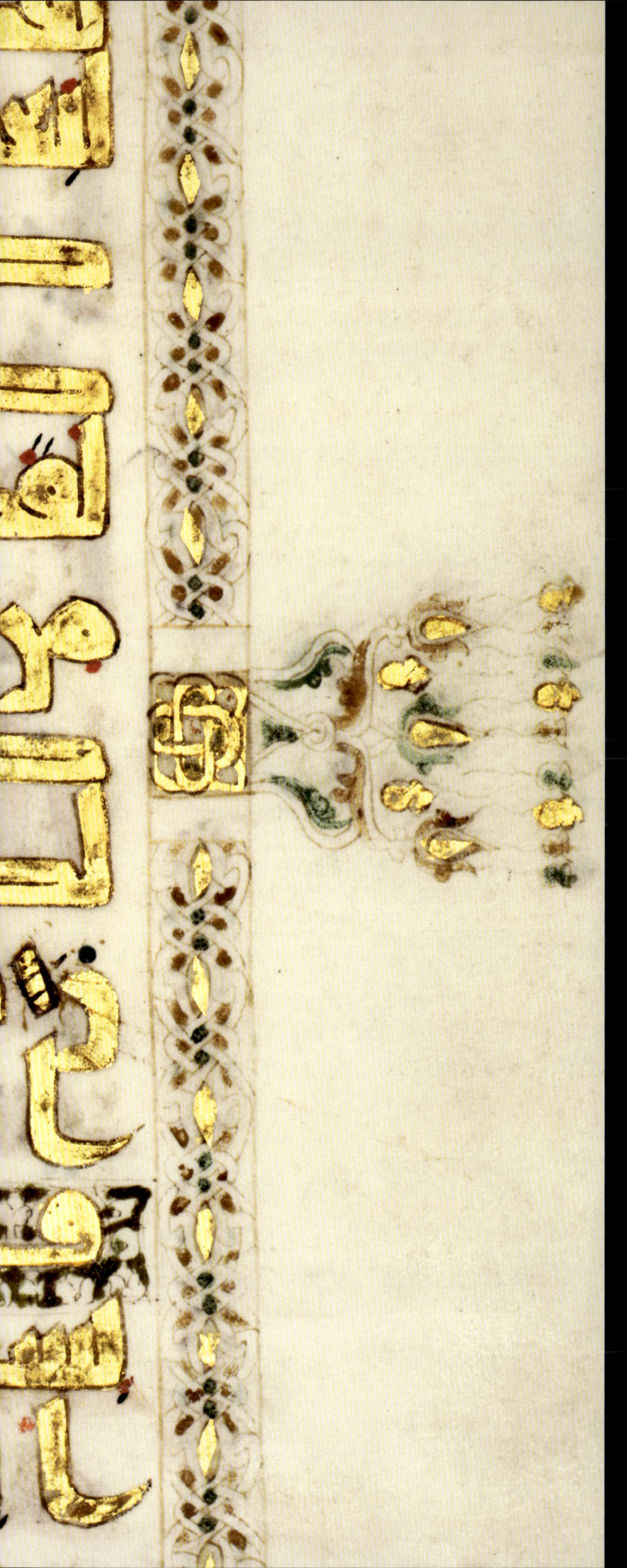

A NEW AESTHETIC

∽

8TH–10TH CENTURY

A NEW AESTHETIC, 8TH–10TH CENTURY

In the seventh century a new script emerged and became the preeminent form used for copying the Qur'an until the tenth century. Kufic script (*al-khatt al-kufi*), named after Kufa in southern Iraq, comprises about seventeen styles divided into six families.[5] The variation among these styles and families is to be contrasted against the diverseness of Hijazi script specimens. From its inception, Kufic was governed by rigid conventions of scribal practice that had the effect of consistently defining letter shapes—whether initial, medial, final, or stand-alone—the proportion of folios overall in relation to the area occupied by text (which was arranged as rigidly parallel and evenly spaced lines), and a uniform number of lines of text per folio in each codex. (Some Qur'ans were divided into separate parts [*juz'*], most commonly of seven and thirty). The number of lines written on each side of a folio differs considerably with fewer lines (especially on larger folios), consequently requiring more sheets of parchment and causing greater expense. Other differences emerged with the rise of Kufic: thicker strokes for the letters, pronounced angularity, horizontal emphasis, and the new horizontal orientation of the support for the writing.[6] To enhance legibility, various systems were developed—and applied intermittently (and sometimes in contexts that were post-production)—to address the inherent ambiguity of the Arabic alphabet. For its twenty-eight letters (phonemes), there are eighteen letter forms (graphemes). Systems of annotation were developed to identify the specific phoneme registered by the letter form when that letter form was shared by other letters of the alphabet (letter-pointing/diacriticals) and to mark the short vowels "a," "i," and "u" (vocalization) among other orthographic symbols.[7] The absence of uniform and complete vocalization and letter-pointing has been understood to reflect a context in which *mushaf*s (the physical Qur'an) functioned as aides-mémoires to reciters who had memorized the text.[8]

The striking effect of Kufic script manuscripts was enlivened by the means through which calligraphers arranged the text across the lines, employing extensions (of interconnected letters) and intervals between letters or groups of connected letters to manipulate the visual cadence of writing. Though practices of arranging words in Kufic script differed considerably from conventions of ensuing scripts—of breaking words between lines, for example—the matrix of text was insistently aligned down the right and left sides. The endings of individual suras, and groups of five and ten verses, were often marked through a variety of forms. Sura headings became normative as well as illuminated components marking frontispieces and finispieces of multipart Qur'ans. Augmenting the material and aesthetic dimensions of Qur'ans copied in the Kufic script were the options, when sufficient resources were available, to produce effects of greater luxury through gold (chrysography) writing, an exceptionally labor- and time-intensive process, and treatments to tint or dye parchment in different colors, including blues, purples, and pinks. Programs of illumination and other material enhancements opened the way to establishing new kinds of cultural meanings for the Qur'an as a material object, especially when they evoked other mediums and objects that ran the gamut from monumental architecture to patterned textiles and carved stuccoes or wood.

2

Folio from a Qur'an Manuscript

North Africa, early 8th century
Ink and opaque watercolor on parchment
21 1/2 × 27 1/2 inches (54.6 × 69.9 cm); 12 lines
Side A: sura 22, *al-Hajj* (The Pilgrimage), verses 6–10
Side B: sura 22, *al-Hajj* (The Pilgrimage), verses 10–12
Text copied in Kufic script in dark-brown ink; verse markers take the form of closely drawn horizontal lines in dark-brown ink; floriated star motif set inside a square in blue, red, and green marks end of verse 10 (on the side B).
TR:850-2015

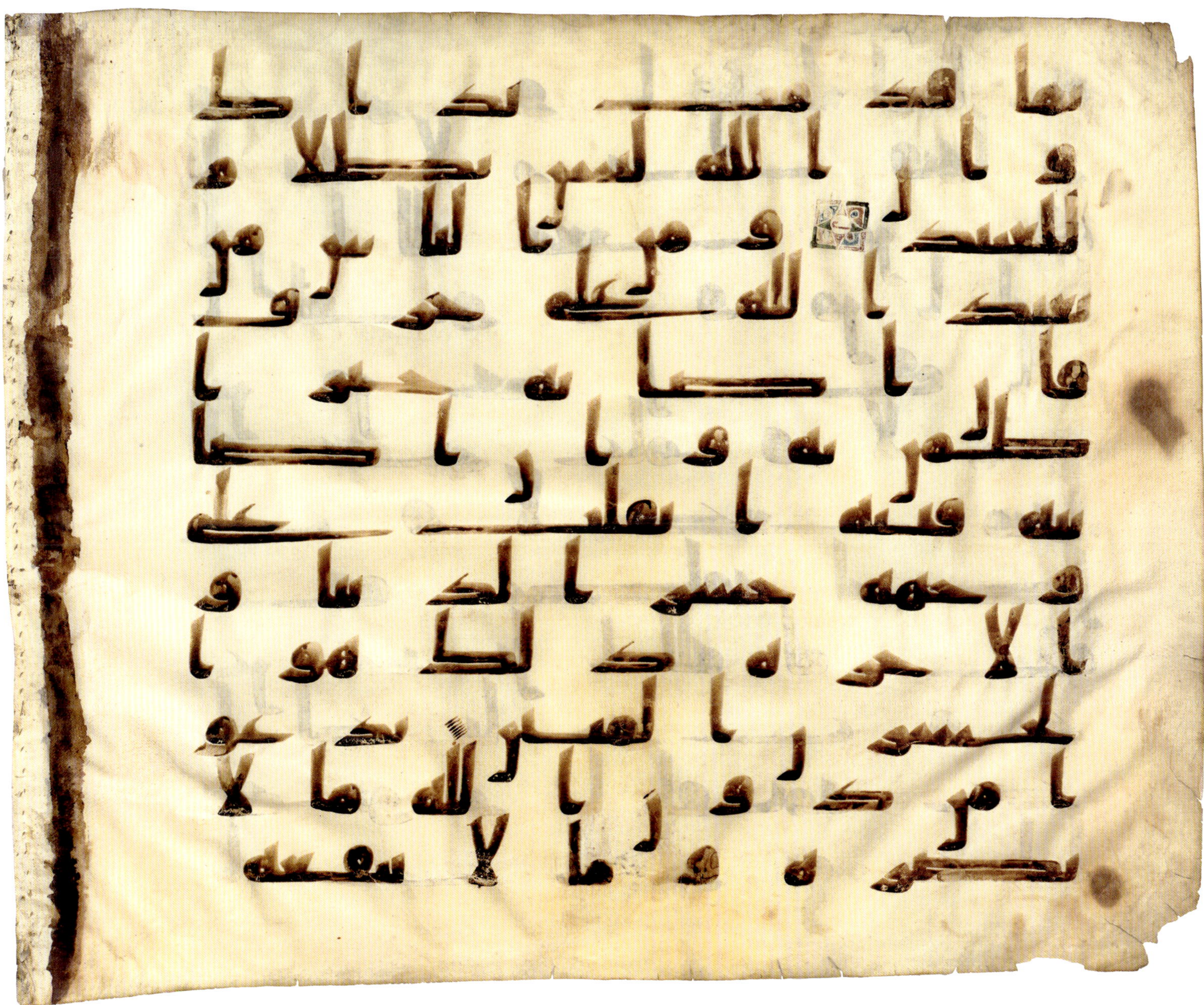

Side B

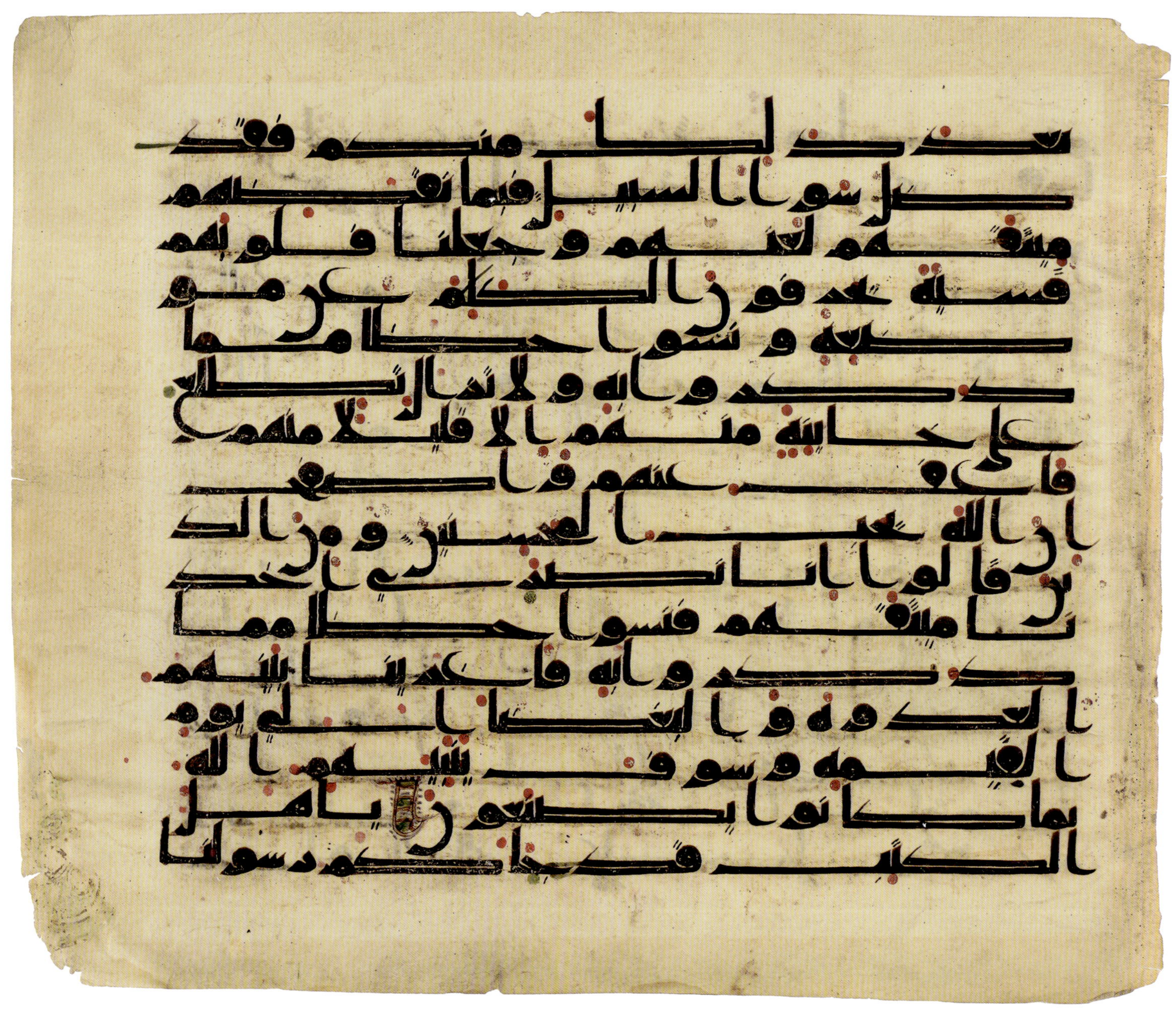

Side A

3

Folio from a Qur'an Manuscript

North Africa or Central Islamic Lands, possibly 8th century
Ink, opaque watercolor, and gold on parchment
Overall: 12 13/16 × 15 1/2 inches (32.5 × 39.3 cm); 16 lines
Side A: sura 5, *al-Ma'ida* (The Feast), verses 12–15
Side B: sura 5, *al-Ma'ida* (The Feast), verses 15–17
Text copied in Kufic script in black ink; vocalization in red and green dots; letter-pointing of single or double diagonal black lines; one verse marker (between verses 14 and 15) in red, green, and gold in the form of a thick letter *alif*.
TR:297-2015

4

Folio from a Qur'an Manuscript

North Africa or Central Islamic Lands, 8th–9th century
Ink, opaque watercolor, and gold on parchment
Overall: 9 13/16 × 13 1/8 inches (25 × 33.3 cm); 5 lines
Side A: sura 20, *Ta' Ha'* (Ta Ha), verses 131–133
Side B: sura 20, *Ta' Ha'* (Ta Ha), verses 133–134
Text copied in Kufic script in brown-black ink; vocalization in red dots; letter-pointing in single and double diagonal black lines; verse marker (between verses 133 and 134) composed of a green disk enclosed by a border of gold disks (the text inside reads "verse 130"); the upper and lower edges of text on the side B are flanked above and below by a border resembling a rope in gold outlined in black studded with brown dots.
TR:500-2017

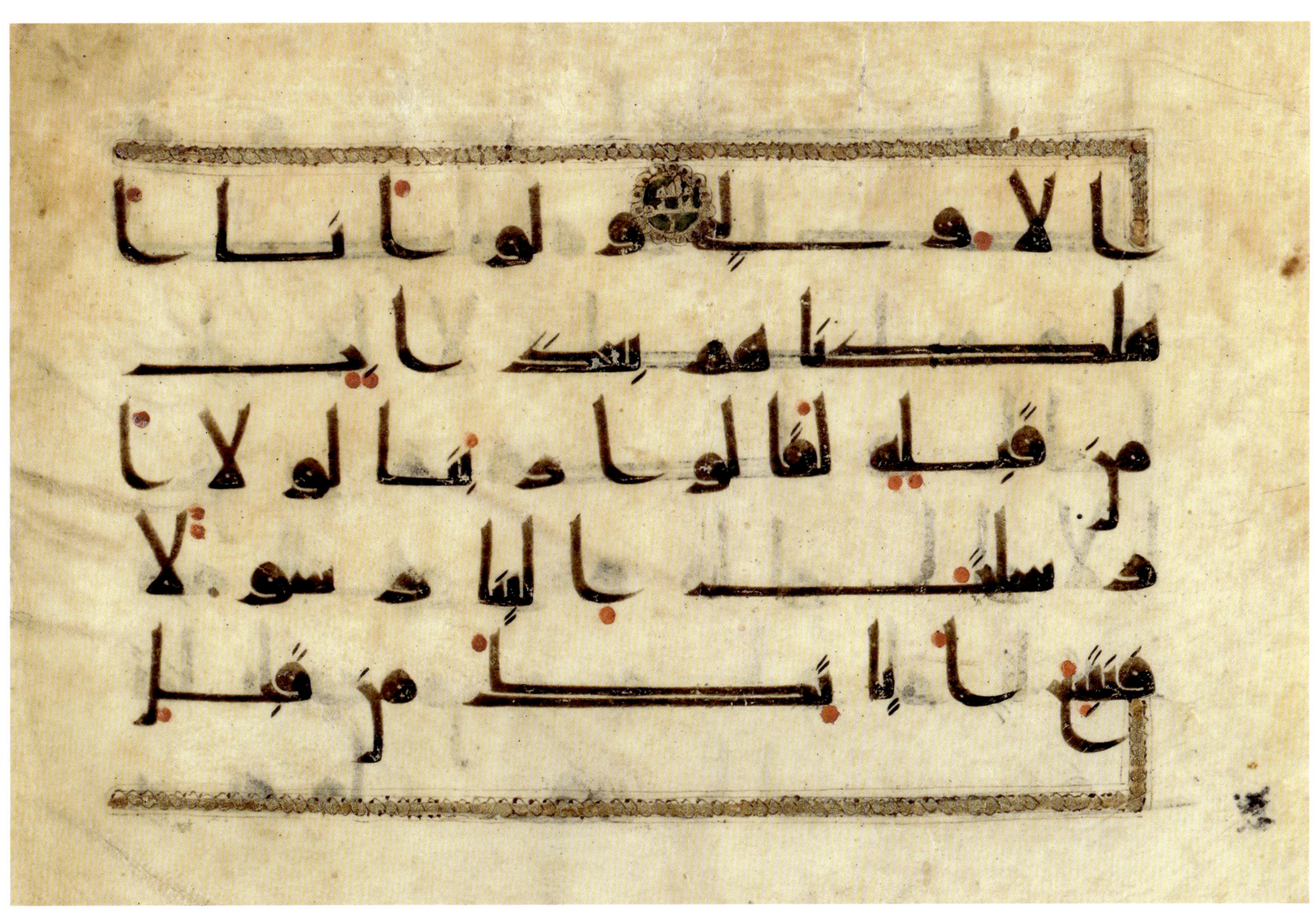

Side B

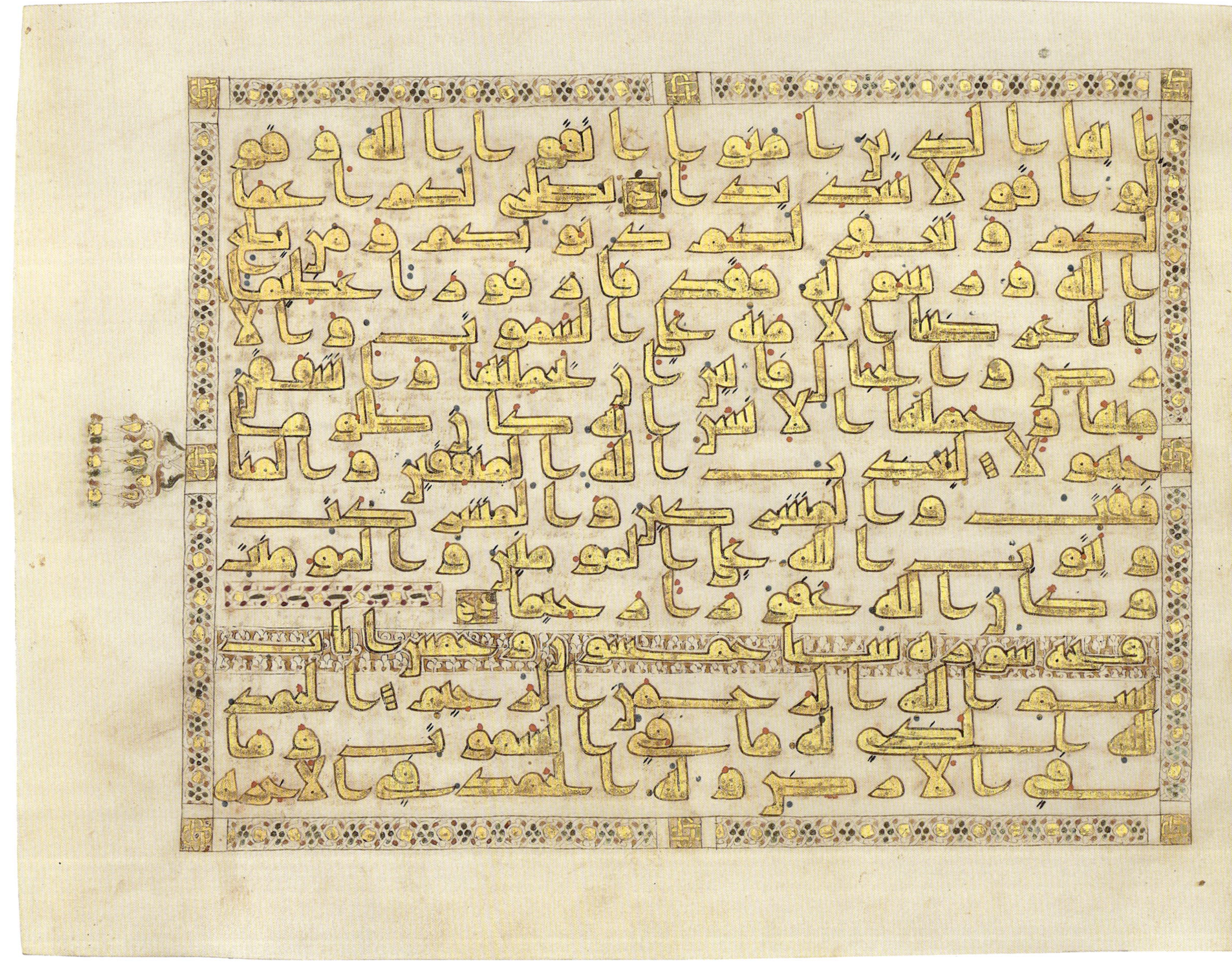

Folio 1, side A

5

Bifolio from a Qur'an Manuscript

North Africa or Central Islamic Lands, 9th century
Ink, opaque watercolor, and gold on parchment
Open: 10 13/16 × 29 3/16 inches (27.5 × 74.1 cm); 15 lines
Closed: 10 13/16 × 14 9/16 inches (27.5 × 37 cm)
Folio 1, side A: sura 33, *al-Ahzab* (The Allied Troops), verses 70–73–sura 34, *Saba* (Sheba), verse 1
Folio 1, side B: sura 34, *Saba* (Sheba), verses 1–7
Folio 2, side A: sura 34, *Saba* (Sheba), verses 51–54–sura 35, *Fatir* (The Originator), verses 1–3
Folio 2, side B: sura 35, *Fatir* (The Originator), verses 3–8
Text in gold Kufic script outlined in brown ink; vocalization in red and blue dots; letter-pointing in single and double diagonal brown lines; verse markers composed of a diagonal gold line; verse counters of five are registered by the letter *ha'* (in gold Kufic script) set in a circle, and counters of ten as square boxes containing an Arabic letter corresponding to their numerical value in the *abjad* system; text panels are framed by borders composed of gold disks or alternating ovals and lozenges—which mirror each other across openings—set amid an interlacing band studded with dots in red and green with knotted motifs at the centers and corners all done in gold outlined in brown; the outer margin features a finial resembling a fluttering tassel done in the same materials as the framing border; the chapter titles are enclosed within a floriate border over a brown or dark green ground.
TR:289-2015

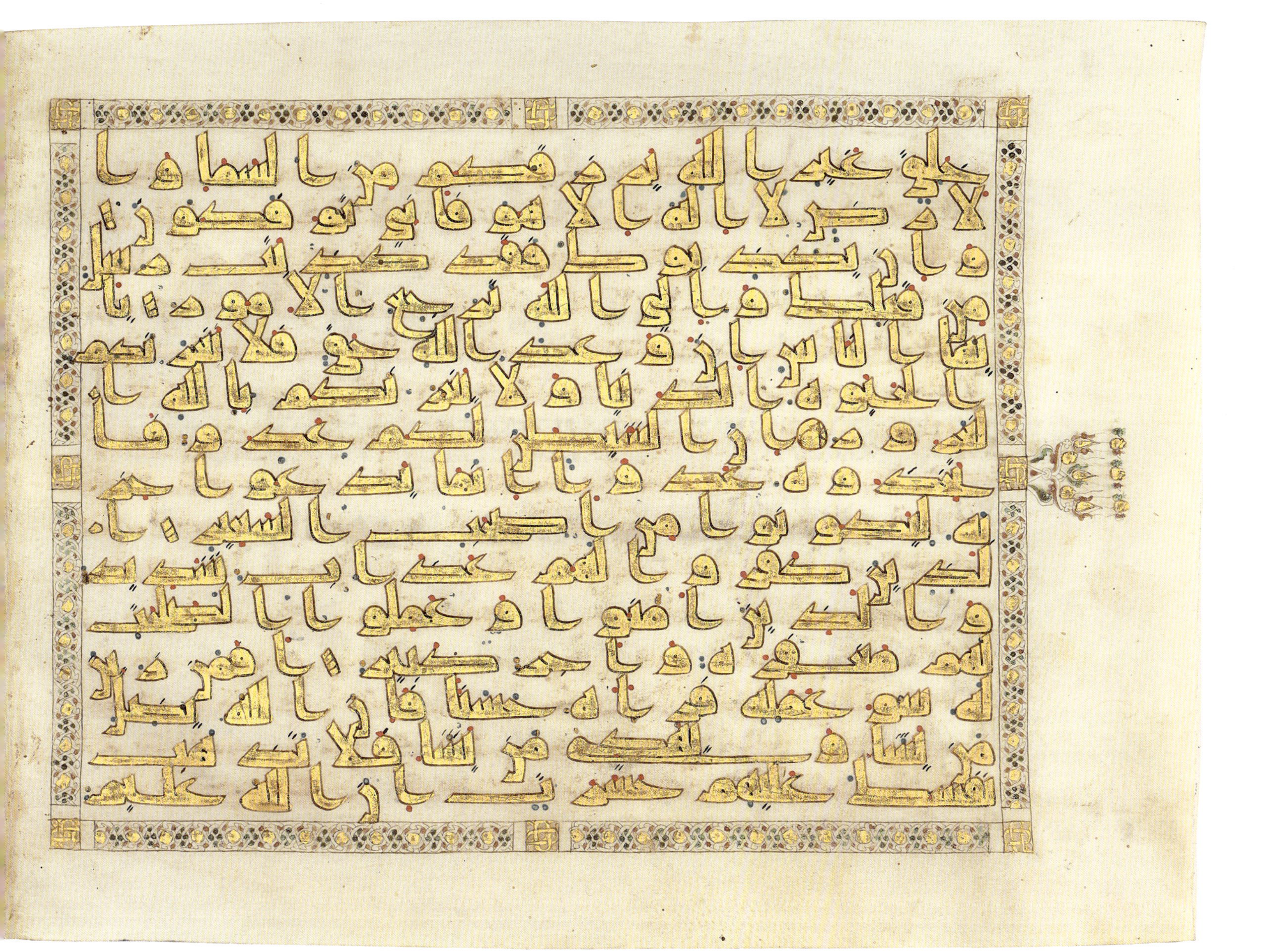

Folio 2, side B

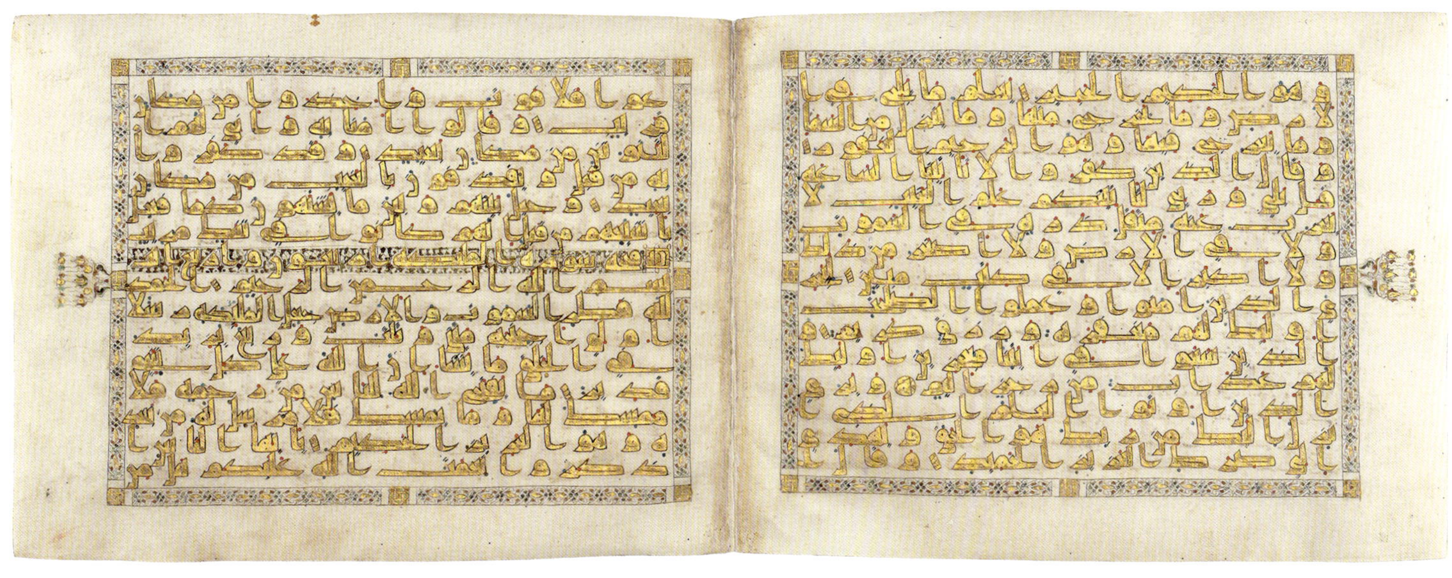

Folio 2, side A

Folio 1, side B

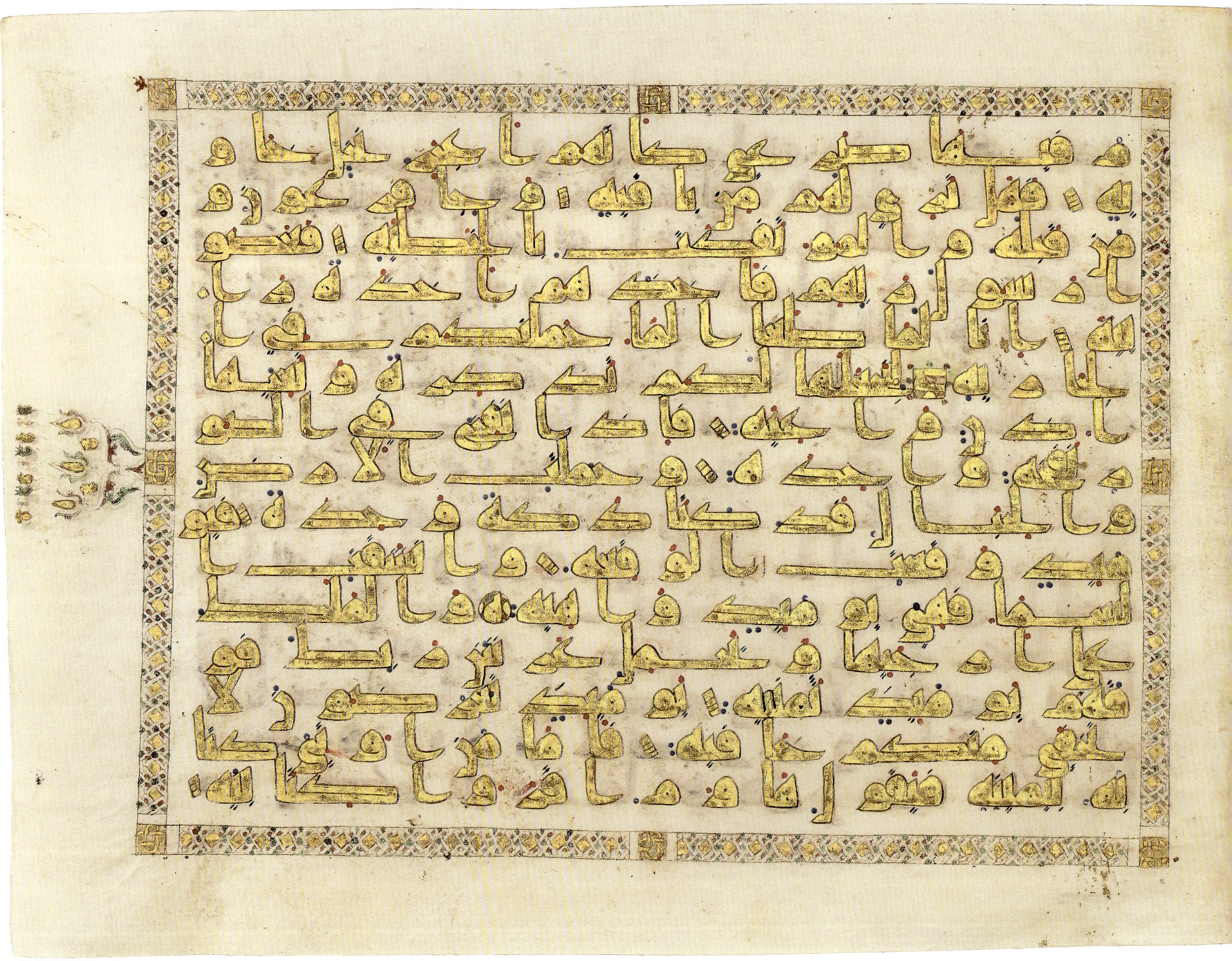

Folio 1, side A

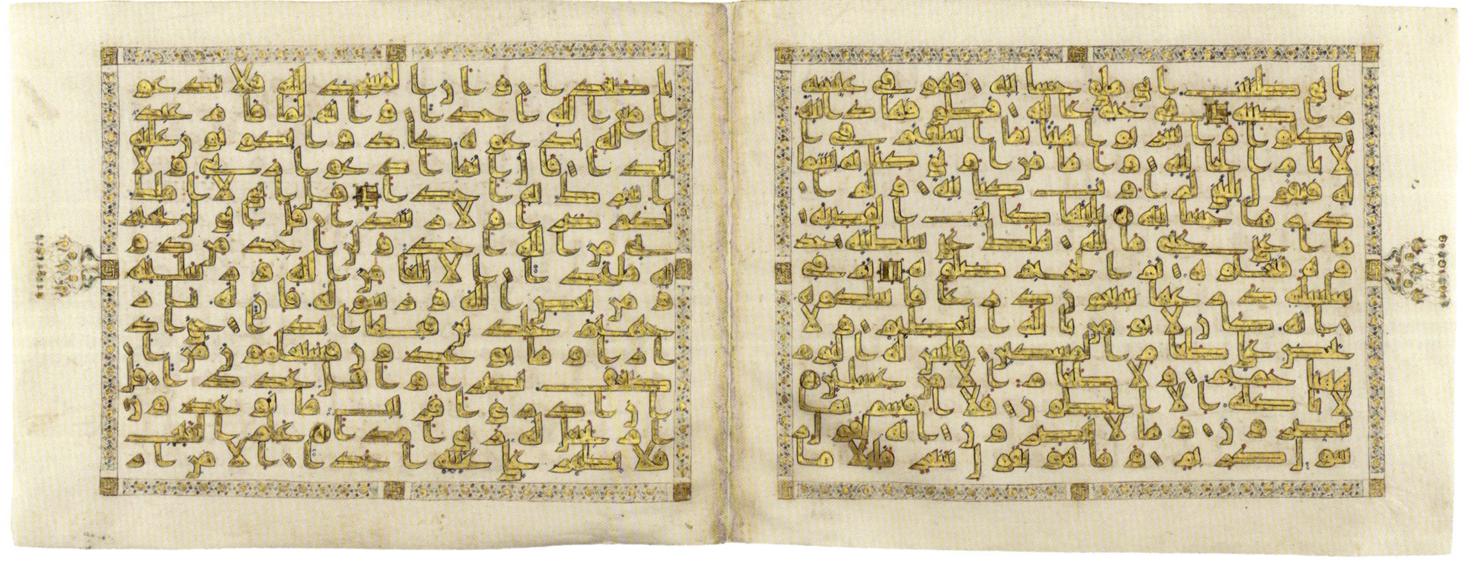

Folio 2, side A

Folio 1, side B

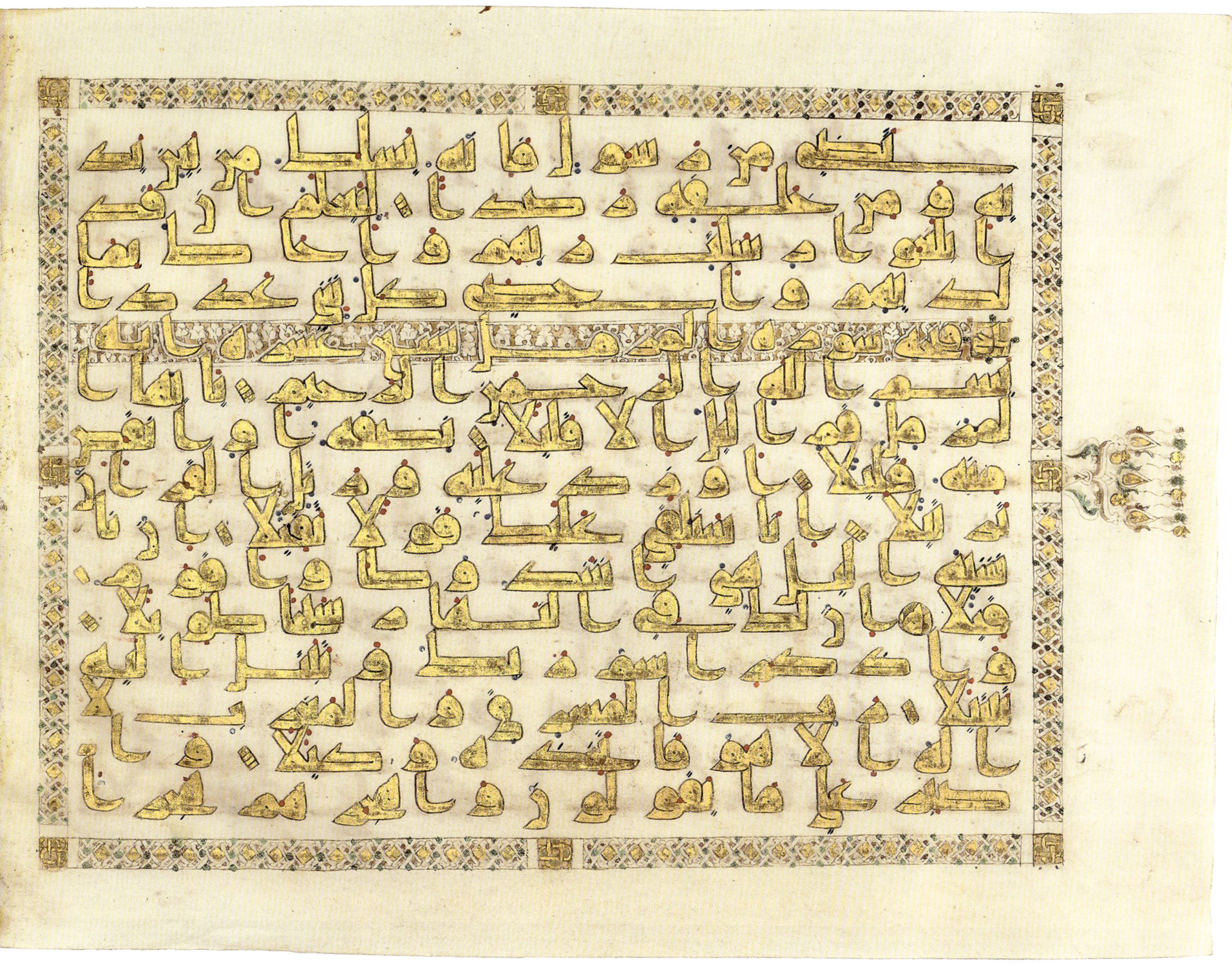

Folio 2, side B

6

Bifolio from a Qur'an Manuscript

North Africa or Central Islamic Lands, 9th century
Ink, opaque watercolor, and gold on parchment
Open: 10 13/16 × 29 3/16 inches (27.5 × 74.1 cm); 15 lines
Closed: 10 13/16 × 14 9/16 inches (27.5 × 37 cm)
Folio 1, side A: sura 69, *al-Haqqa* (The Concrete Reality), verses 7–19
Folio 1, side B: sura 69, *al-Haqqa* (The Concrete Reality), verses 20–41
Folio 2, side A: sura 72, *al-Jinn* (The Jinns), verses 17–27
Folio 2, side B: sura 72, *al-Jinn* (The Jinns), verses 27–28–sura 73, *al-Muzzammil* (The Enwrapped), verses 1–10
Text in gold Kufic script outlined in brown ink; vocalization in red and blue dots; letter-pointing in single and double diagonal brown lines; verse markers composed of diagonal gold line; verse counters of five are registered by the letter *ha'* (in gold Kufic script) set in a circle, and counters of ten as square boxes containing an Arabic letter corresponding to their numerical value in the *abjad* system; text panels are framed by borders composed of rotated squares—which mirror each other across openings—set amid an interlacing band studded with dots in red and green with knotted motifs at the centers and corners all done in gold outlined in brown; the outer margin features a finial resembling a fluttering tassel done in the same materials as the framing border; the chapter title is enclosed within a floriate border over a brown ground.
TR:290-2015

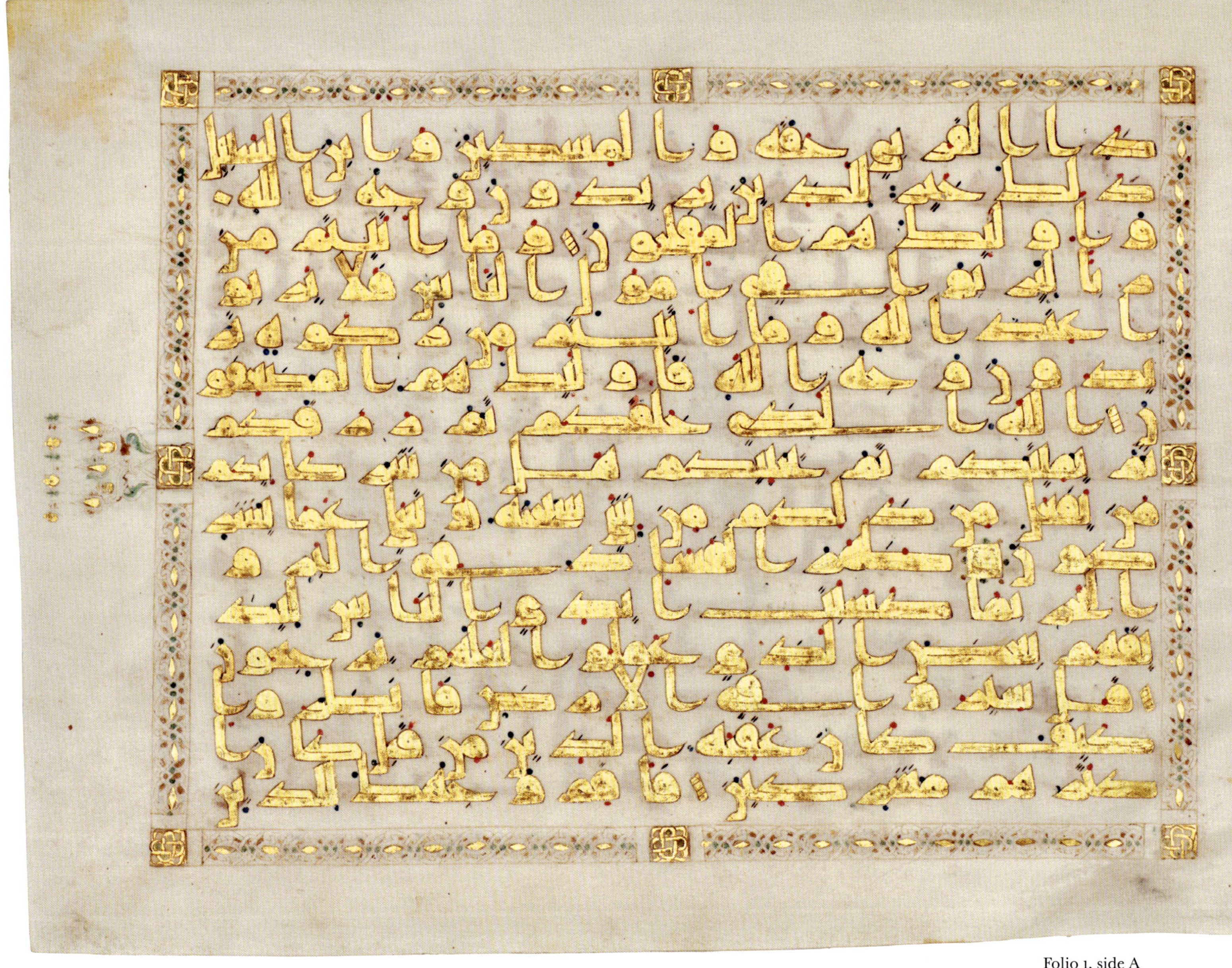

Folio 1, side A

7

Bifolio from a Qur'an Manuscript

North Africa or Central Islamic Lands, 9th century
Ink, opaque watercolor, and gold on parchment
Overall (each folio): 10 3/4 × 14 1/4 inches (27.3 × 36.2 cm); 15 lines
Open: 10 3/4 × 28 1/2 inches (27.3 × 72.4 cm)
Folio 1, side A: sura 30, *al-Rum* (The Romans), verses 38–43
Folio 1, side B: sura 30, *al-Rum* (The Romans), verses 43–48
Folio 2, side A: sura 30, *al-Rum* (The Romans), verses 48–55
Folio 2, side B: sura 30, *al-Rum* (The Romans), verses 56–60–sura 31, *Luqman* (Luqman), verses 1–4
Text in gold Kufic script outlined in brown ink; vocalization in red and blue dots; letter-pointing in single and double diagonal brown lines; verse markers composed of diagonal gold line; verse counters of five are registered by the letter *ha'* (in gold Kufic script) set in a circle, and counters of ten as square boxes containing an Arabic letter corresponding to their numerical value in the *abjad* system; text panels are framed by borders composed of gold lozenges—which mirror each other across openings—set amid an interlacing band studded with dots in red and green with knotted motifs at the centers and corners all done in gold outlined in brown; the outer margin features a finial resembling a fluttering tassel done in the same materials as the framing border; the chapter title is enclosed within a floriate border over a green-brown ground.
The Museum of Fine Arts, Houston, gift of Hossein Afshar, 2017.430

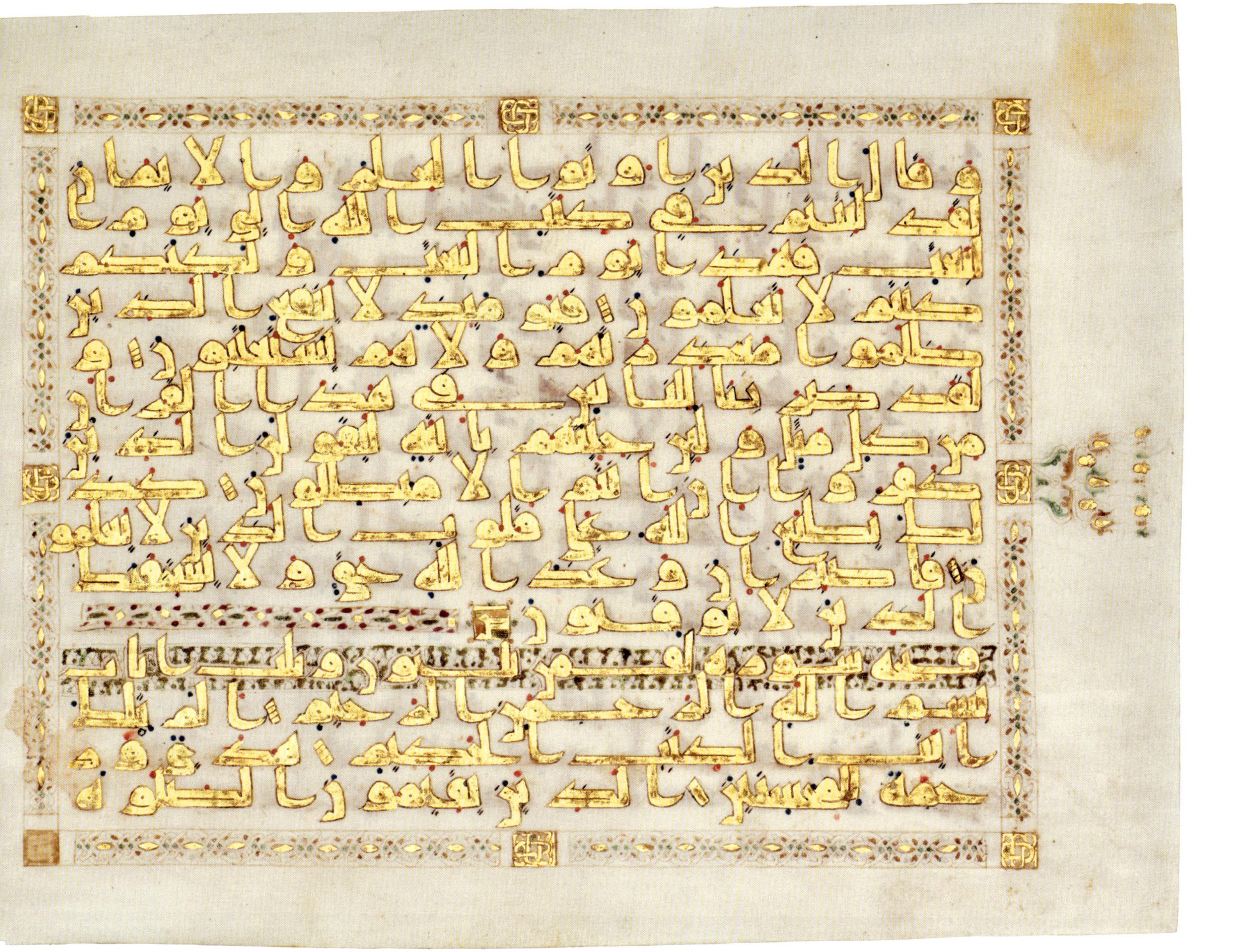

Folio 2, side B

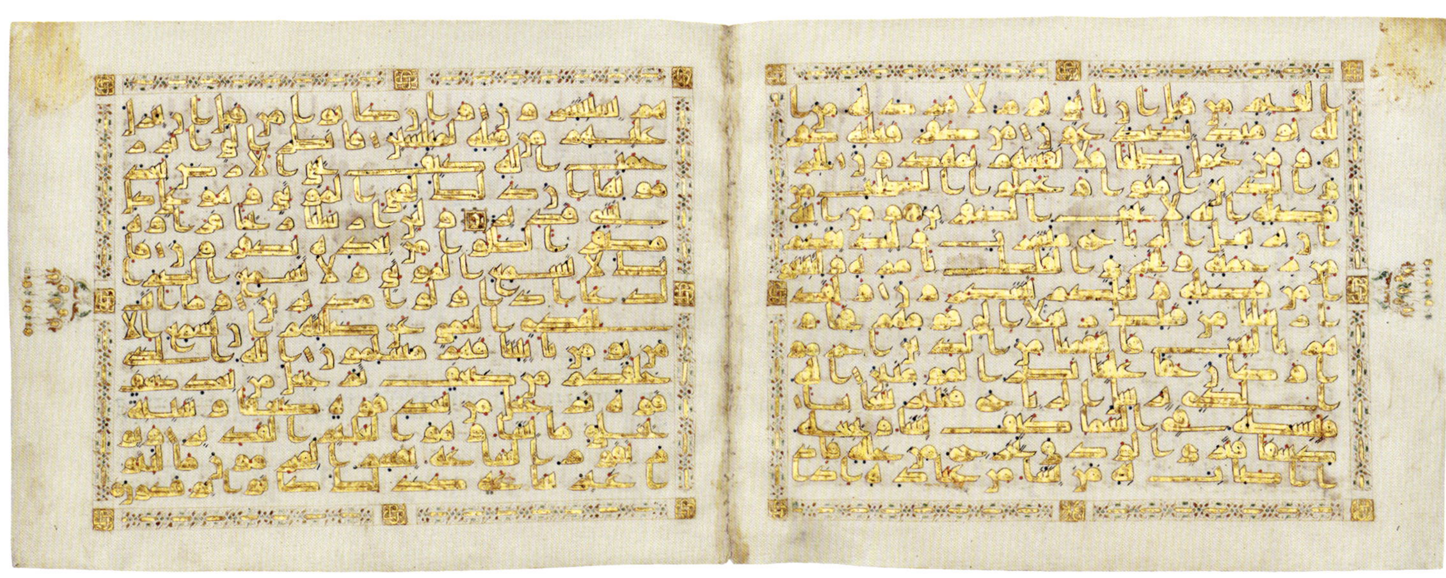

Folio 2, side A

Folio 1, side B

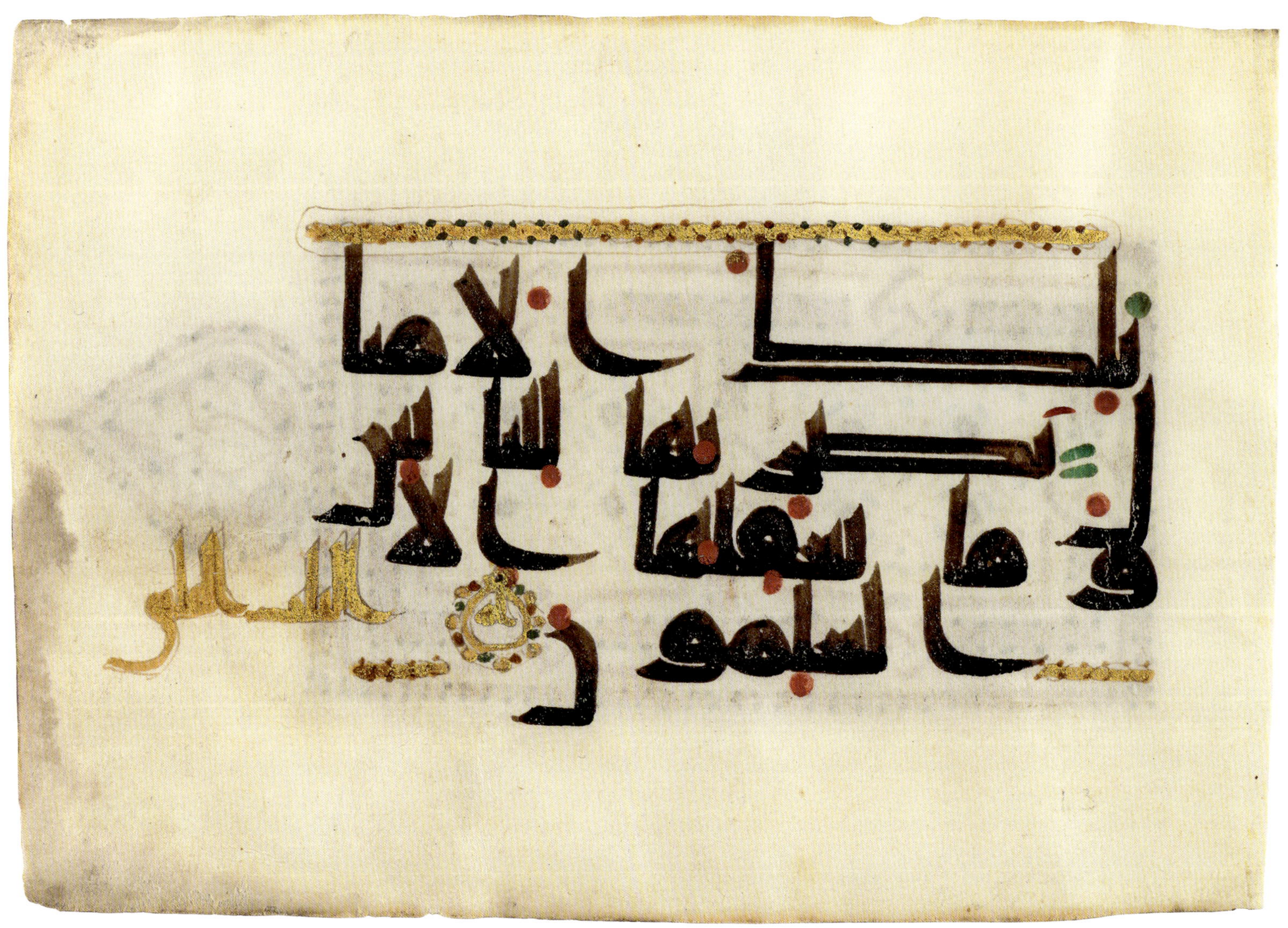

Side A

Following spread: Detail from side B

8

Folio from the Twentieth Part (*Juz'*) of a Qur'an Manuscript

North Africa or Central Islamic Lands, 9th century
Ink, opaque watercolor, gold, and silver on parchment
4 5/8 × 6 11/16 inches (11.7 × 17 cm); 4 lines
Side A: sura 29, *al-'Ankabut* (The Spider), verse 43
Side B: illuminated finispiece
Text copied in Kufic script in black ink; vocalization in red and blue dots; on side A, rope border in gold outlined in brown and accented by blue and red dots across top and bottom, with verse marker composed as a gold rosette with red and green dots; finispiece on side B composed as a panel of two squares (each divided into four parts with rotated squares at their centers) interconnected by a knotted border and a tear-shaped finial extending into the margin (all executed in gold with red and blue dots).
TR:288-2015

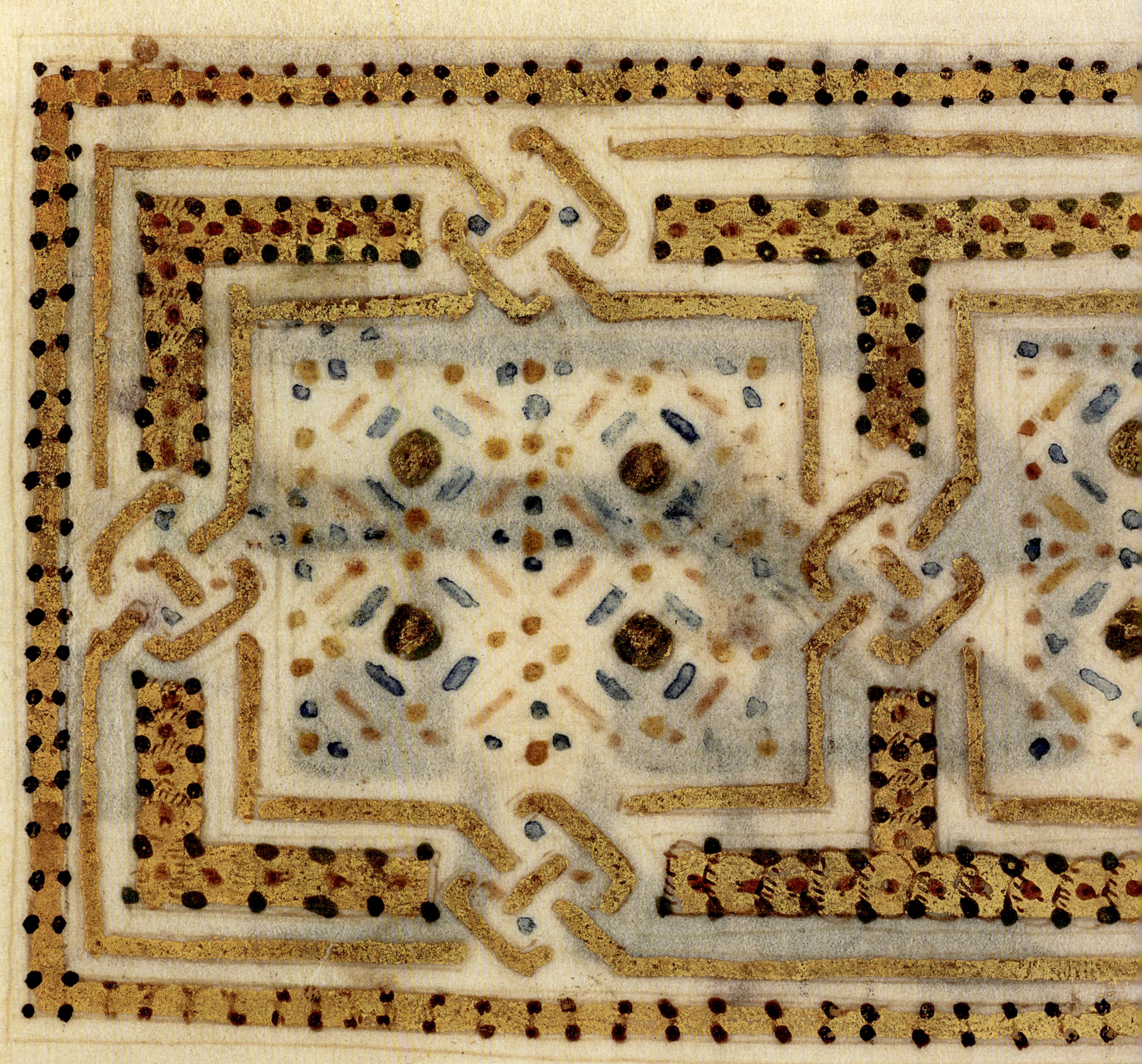

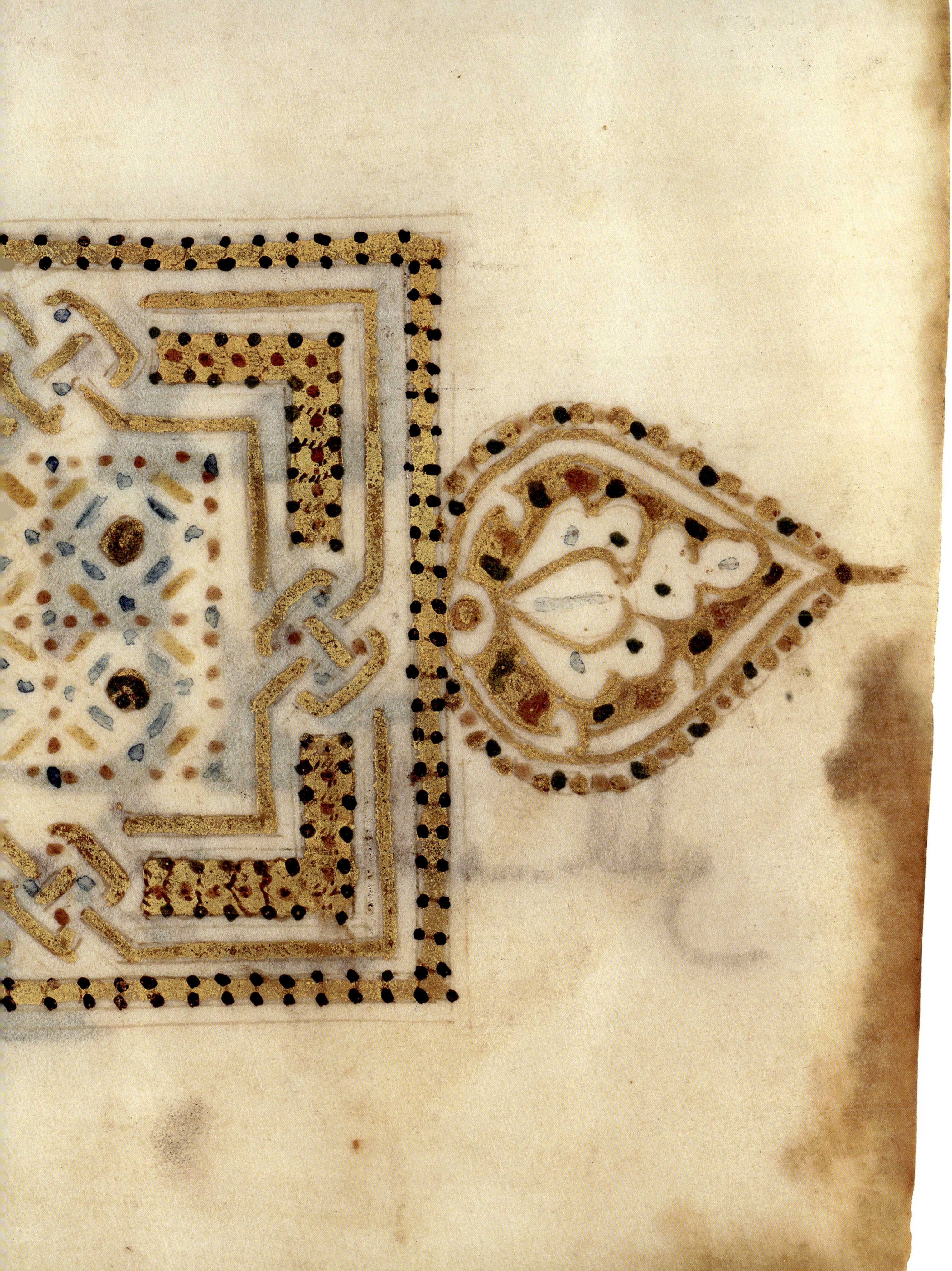

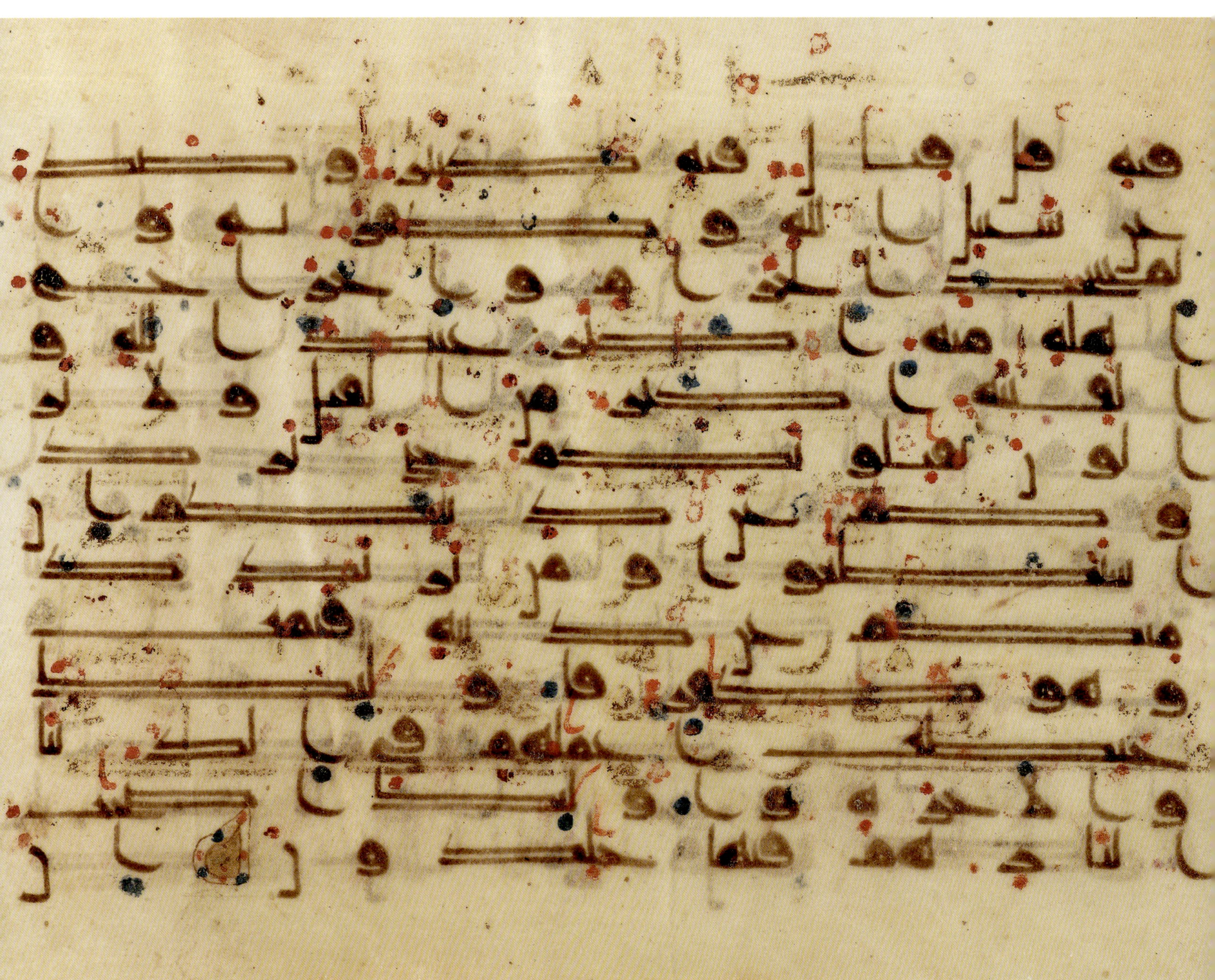

Folio 1, side A

9

Bifolio from a Qur'an Manuscript

North Africa or Central Islamic Lands, 9th–10th century
Ink and opaque watercolor on parchment
Overall: 5 15/16 × 14 1/4 inches (15.1 × 36.2 cm); 13 lines
Folio 1, side A: sura 2, *al-Baqara* (The Cow), verses 217–18
Folio 1, side B: sura 2, *al-Baqara* (The Cow), verses 218–20
Folio 2, side A: sura 2, *al-Baqara* (The Cow), verses 245–46
Folio 2, side B: sura 2, *al-Baqara* (The Cow), verses 246–47
Text copied in Kufic script in brown-black ink; vocalization in red and blue dots; verse markers indicated by gold disks enclosed by red and blue dots.
TR:1663-2015

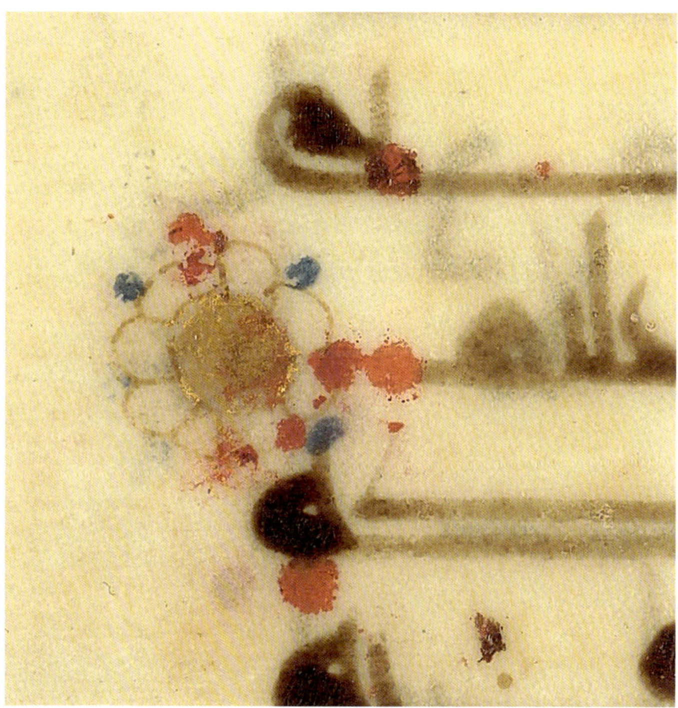

Detail of verse marker, folio 2, side B

10

Folio from a Qurʾan Manuscript

North Africa, 9th–10th century
Ink, opaque watercolor, and gold on parchment (folio cropped and mounted in paper border)
Overall: 12 13/16 × 15 1/2 inches (32.5 × 39.3 cm); 16 lines
Side A: sura 76, *al-Insan* (Man), verse 31–sura 77, *al-Mursalat* (The Emissaries), verses 1–26
Side B: sura 77, *al-Mursalat* (The Emissaries), verses 26–49
Text copied in Kufic script in brown-black ink; vocalization in red dots and doubled consonants in green (*shadda*); letter-pointing in single and double black dots; verse counters of five (in shape of letter *haʾ*) and ten (disk enclosed by border composed of smaller circles) in gold and black; sura 77 indicated by line of interconnected ovals in gold outlined in black; sura title in gold Kufic outlined in black, and floriate pendant in margin (also in gold and black).
TR:376-2015

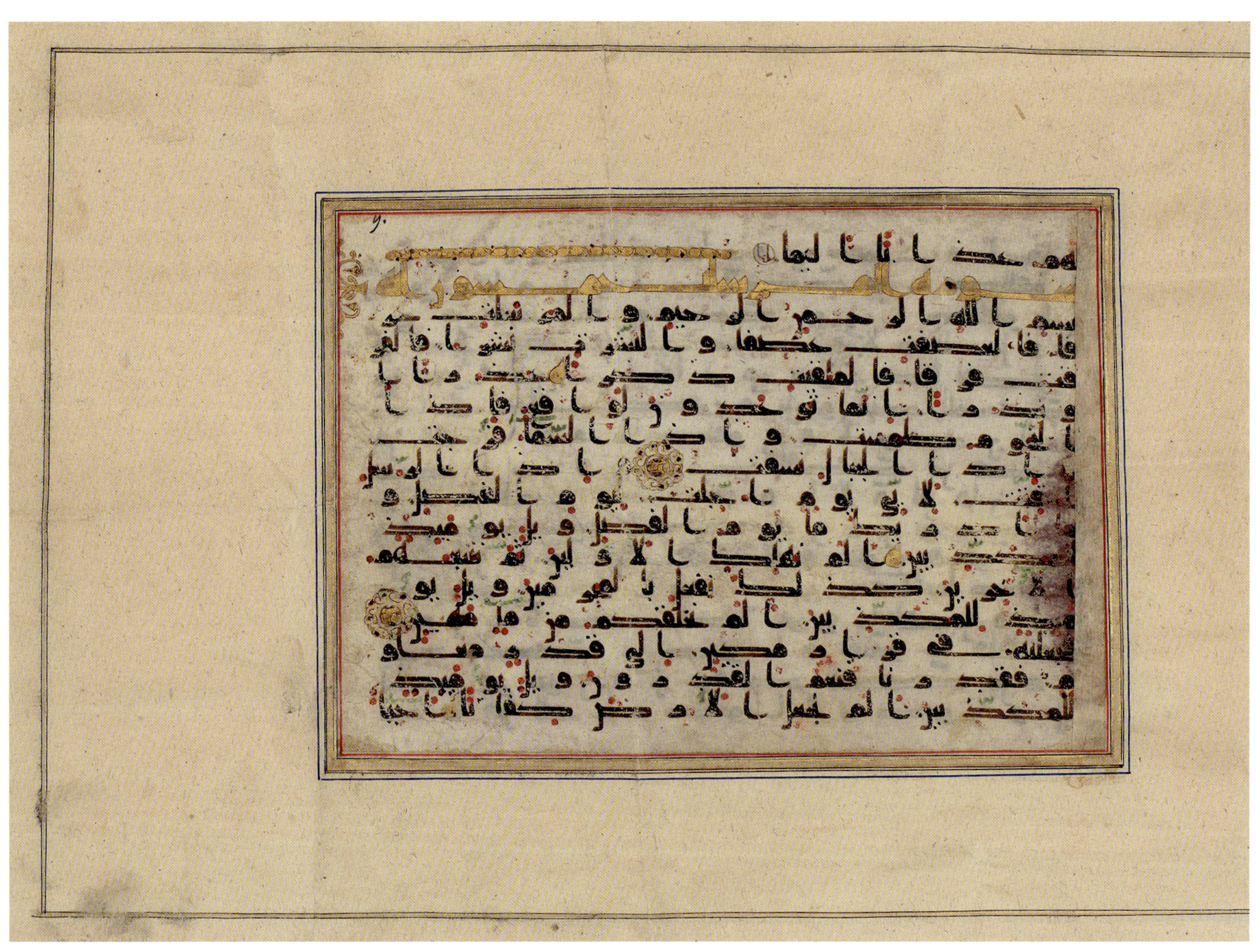

Side A

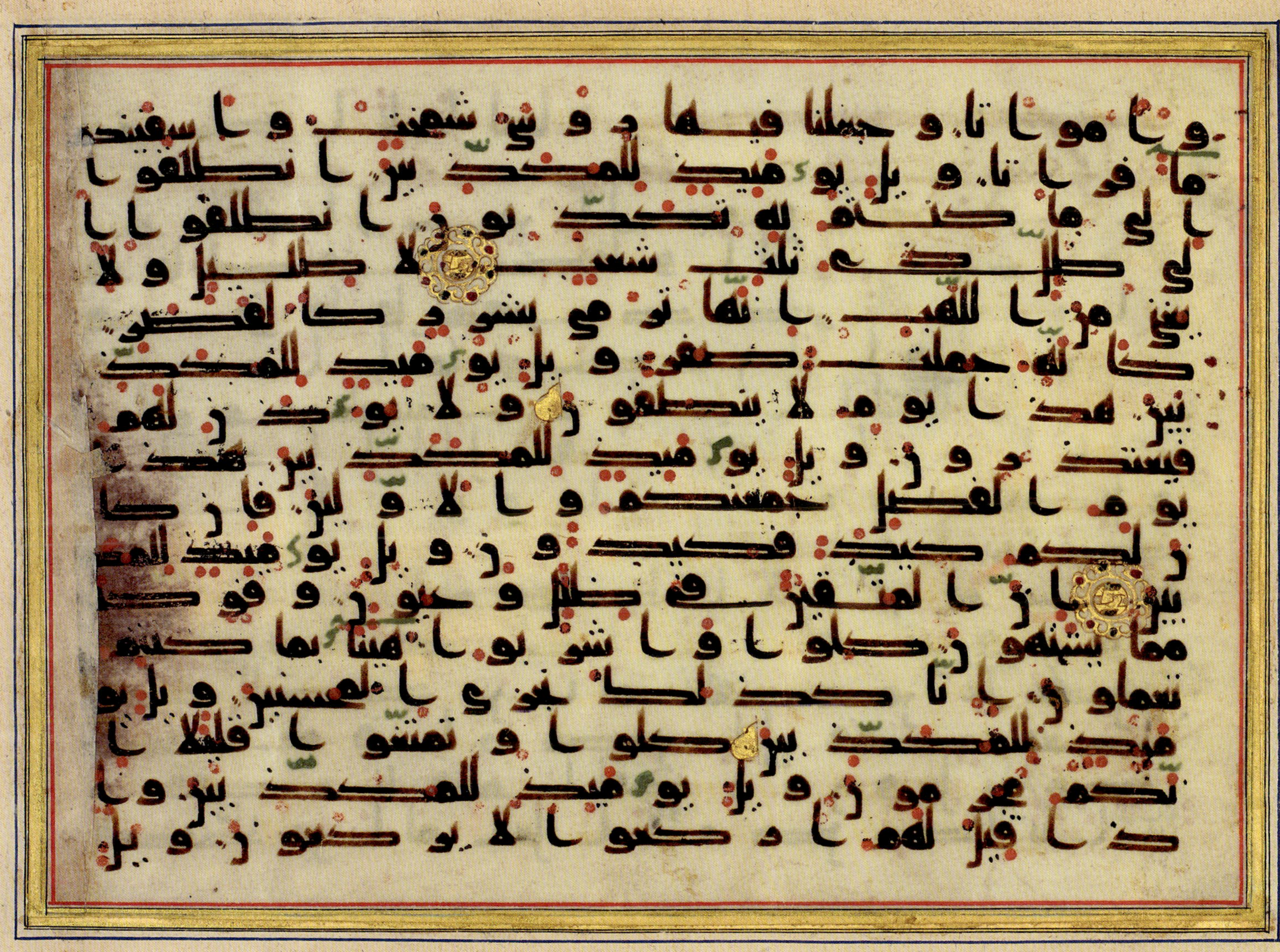

Side B

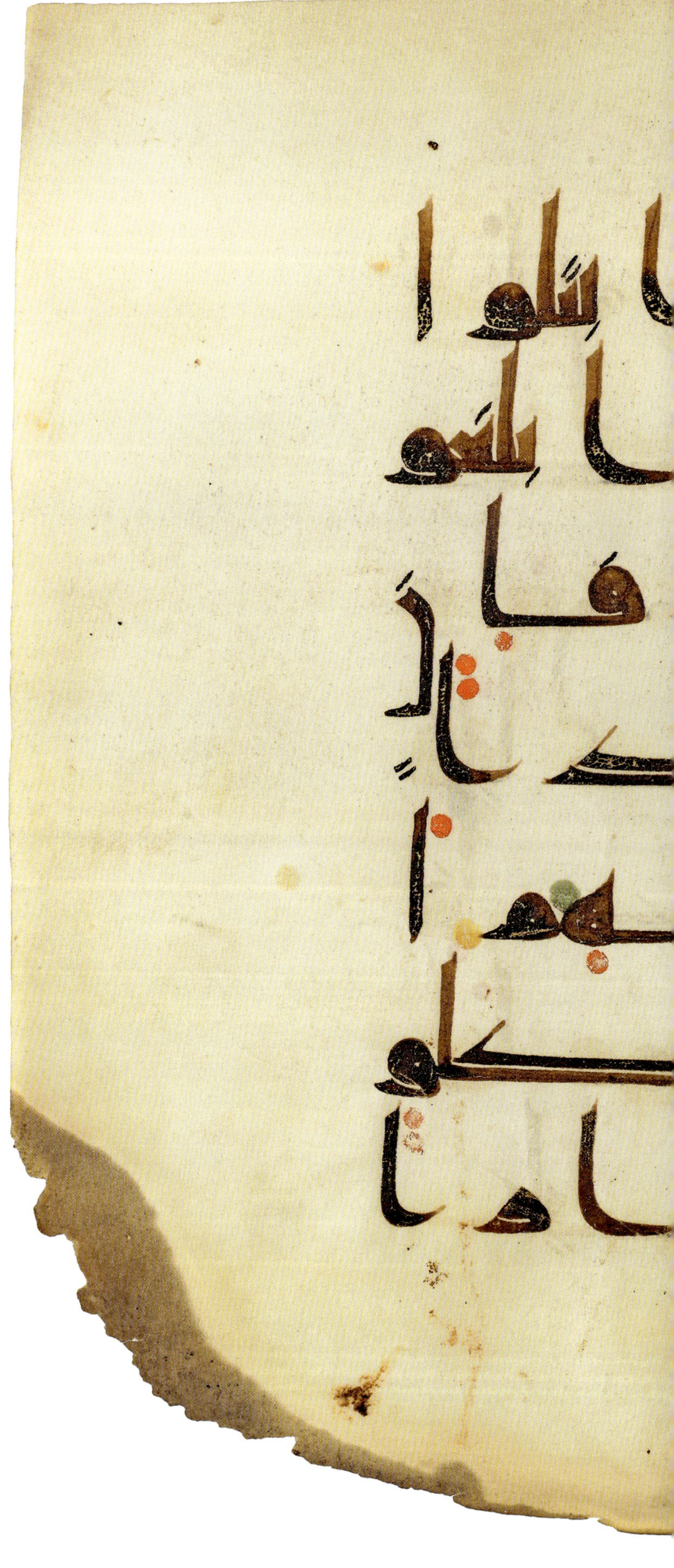

11

Folio from a Qur'an Manuscript

North Africa or Central Islamic Lands, 9th–10th century
Ink, opaque watercolor, and gold on parchment
Overall: 9 7/8 × 13 1/8 inches (25.1 × 33.3 cm); 7 lines
Side A: sura 4, *al-Nisa'* (The Women), verses 5–6
Side B: sura 4, *al-Nisa'* (The Women), verse 6
Text copied in Kufic script in brown-black ink; vocalization in red, green, and yellow dots; letter-pointing in single and double diagonal black lines; verse marker (disk in gold).
TR:1696-2015

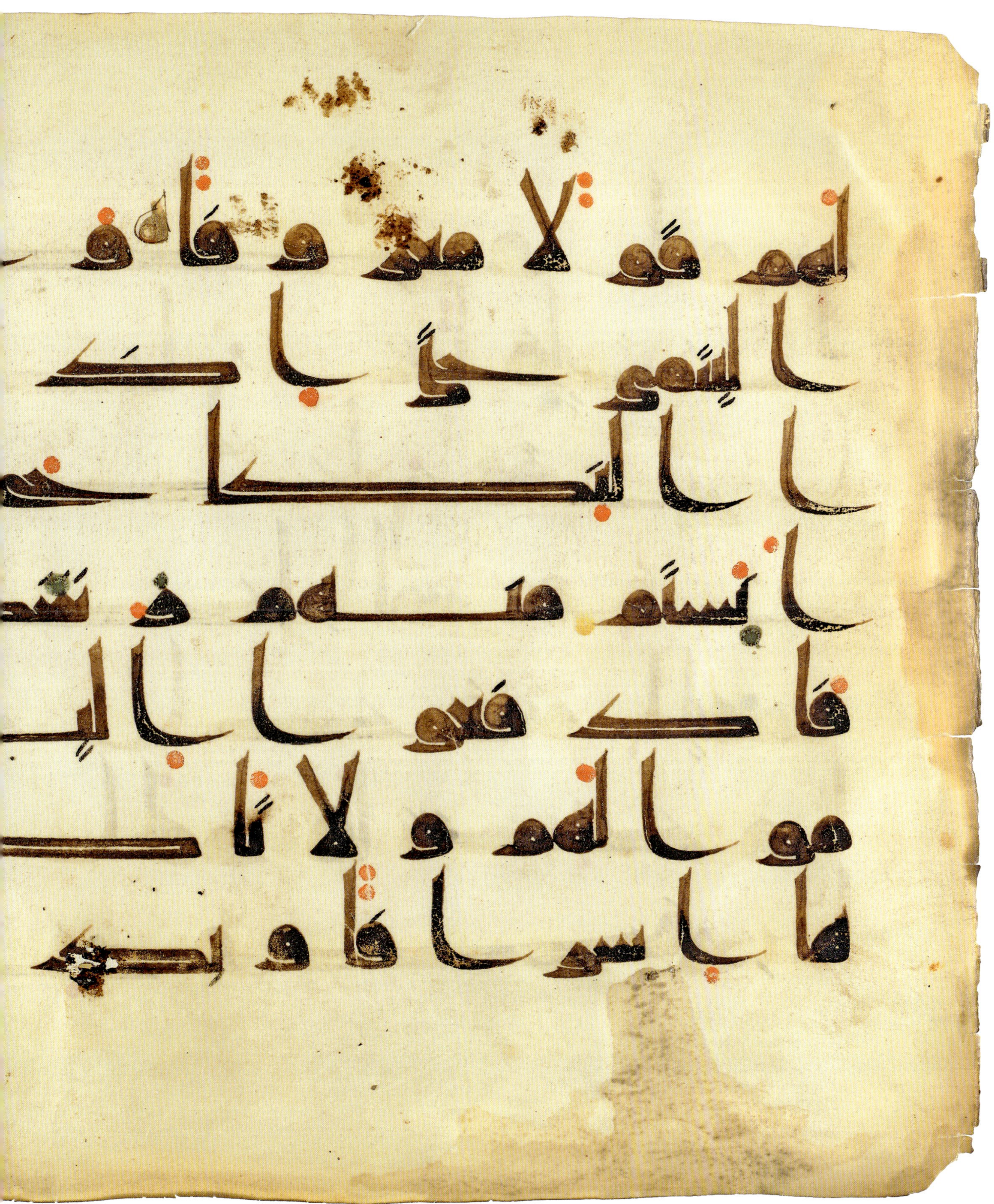

Side A

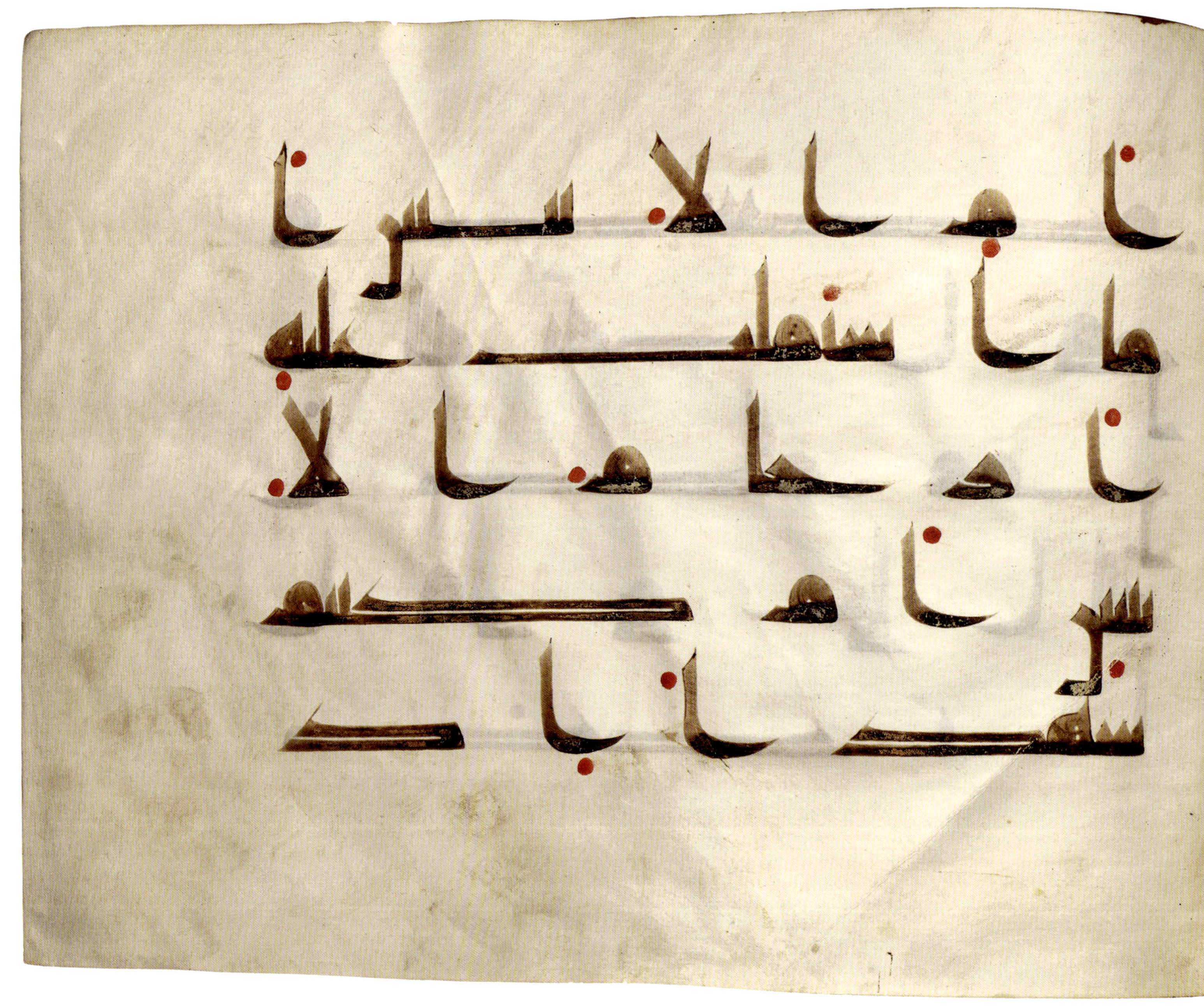

Folio 2, side A

12

Bifolio from a Qur'an Manuscript

North Africa or Central Islamic Lands, 9th–10th century
Ink and opaque watercolor on parchment
Overall (each folio): 11 7/16 × 15 3/4 inches (29 × 40 cm); 5 lines
Folio 1, side A: sura 6, *al-An'am* (The Cattle), verse 141
Folio 1, side B: sura 6, *al-An'am* (The Cattle), verses 141–42
Folio 2, side A: sura 6, *al-An'am* (The Cattle), verse 144
Folio 2, side B: sura 6, *al-An'am* (The Cattle), verse 144
Text copied in Kufic script in brown-black ink; vocalization in red dots.
TR:296-2015

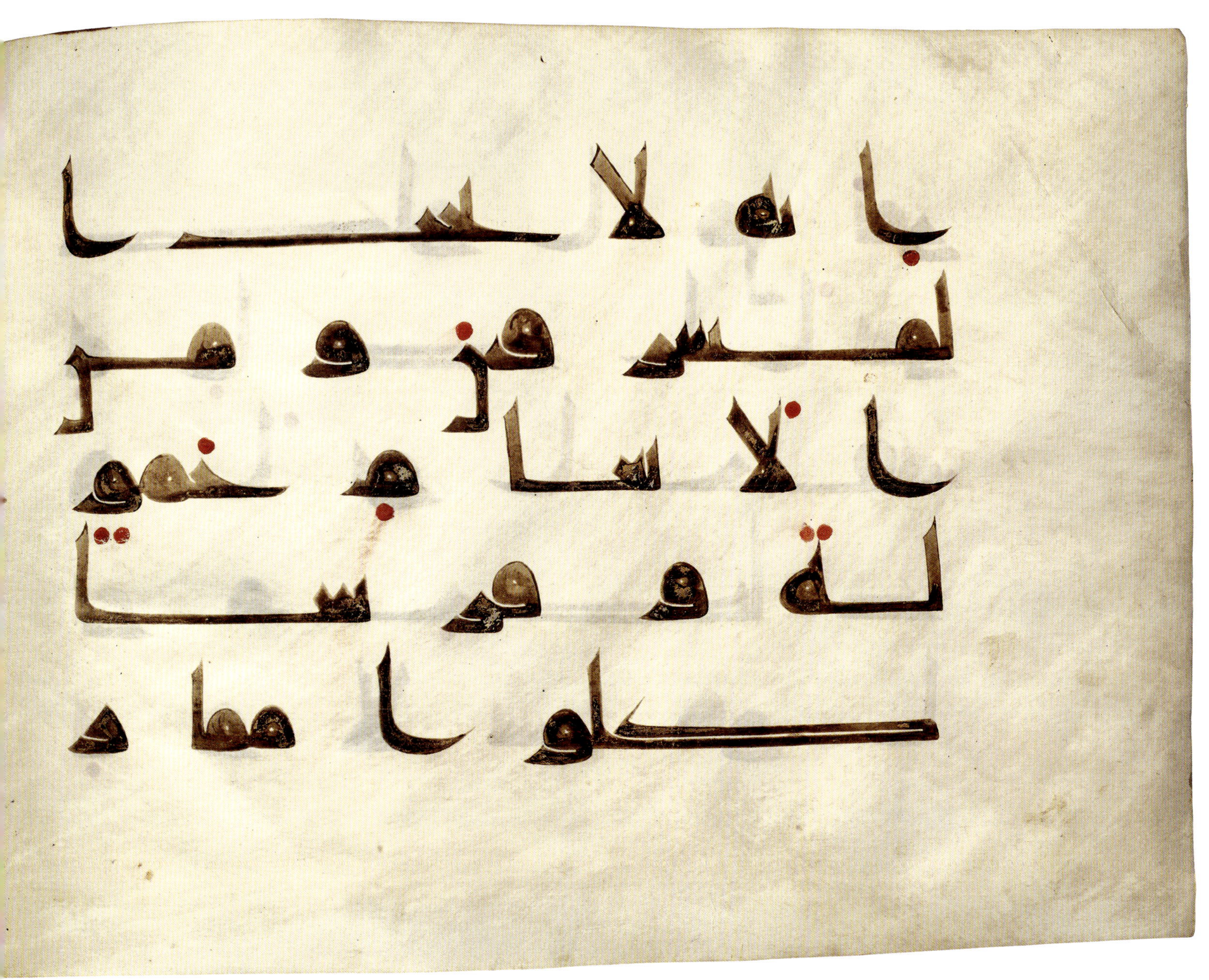

Folio 1, side B

13

Folio from a Qur'an Manuscript

North Africa or Central Islamic Lands, 9th–10th century
Ink, opaque watercolor, and gold on parchment
Overall: 9 13/16 × 13 inches (25 × 33 cm); 7 lines
Side A: sura 3, *Al 'Imran* (The Family of Imran), verses 117–118
Side B: sura 3, *Al 'Imran* (The Family of Imran), verse 118
Text copied in Kufic in brown-black ink; vocalization in red dots; letter-pointing in single and double diagonal black lines; verse marker composed as a gold rosette.
TR:502-2017

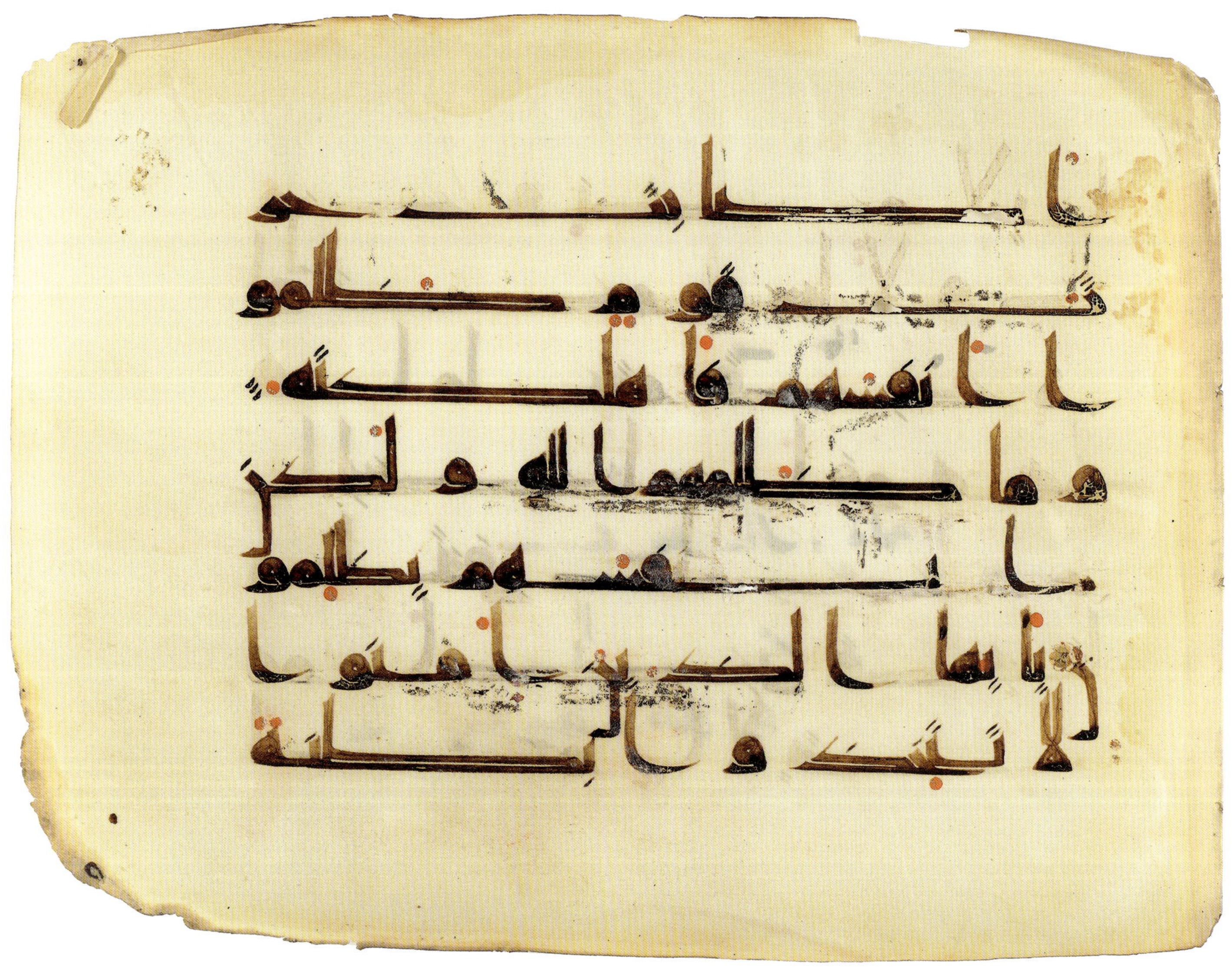

Side A

14

Folio from a Qur'an Manuscript

North Africa or Central Islamic Lands, 9th–10th century
Ink, opaque watercolor, and gold on parchment
Overall: 9 7/8 × 13 1/16 inches (25.1 × 33.2 cm); 7 lines
Side A: sura 3, *Al 'Imran* (The Family of Imran), verses 148–49
Side B: sura 3, *Al 'Imran* (The Family of Imran), verses 149–51
Text copied in Kufic script in brown-black ink; vocalization in red and green dots; letter-pointing in single and double diagonal black lines; verse counter composed as a gold disk with red spots (at end of verse 150).
TR:503-2017

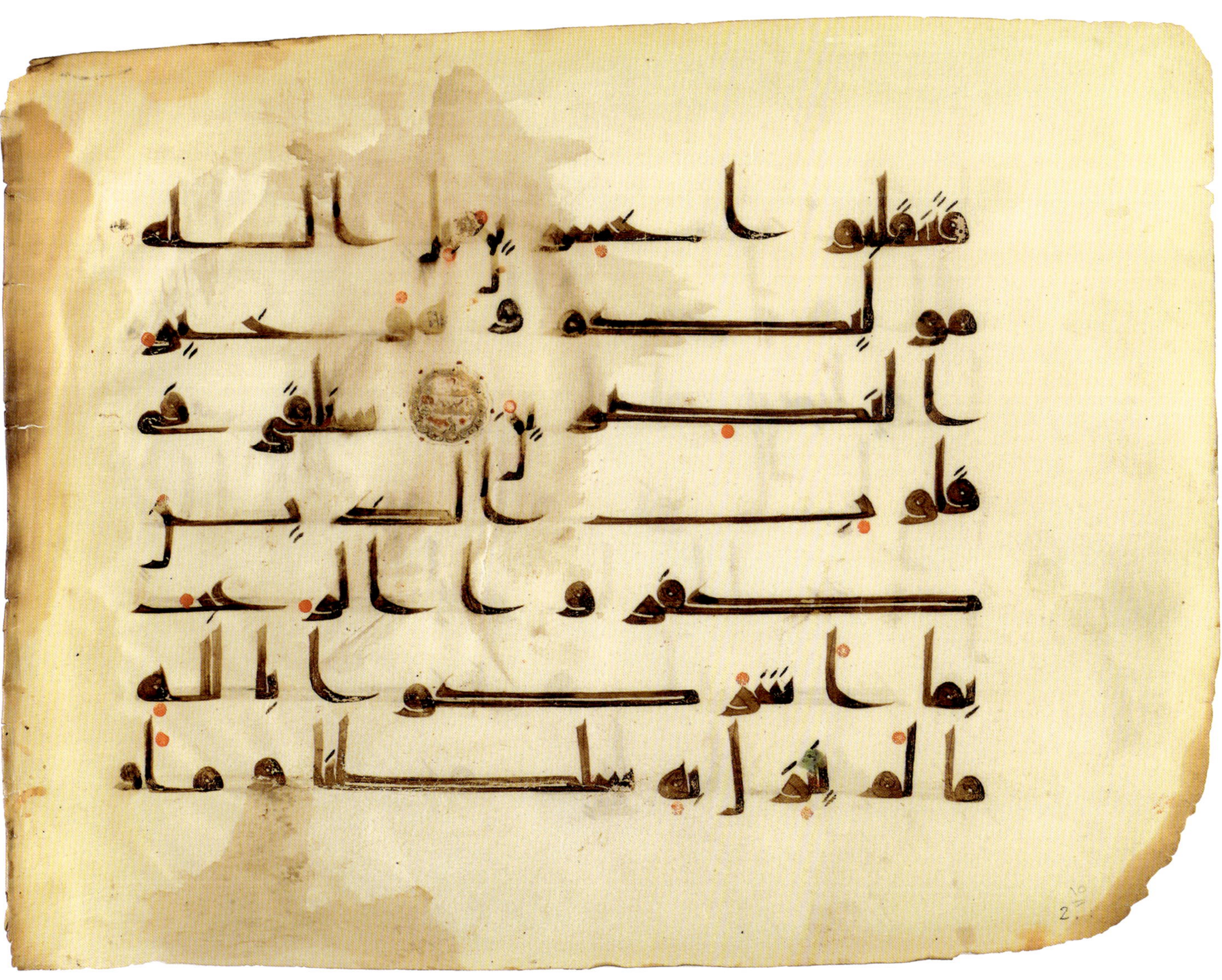

Side B

15

Folio from a Qur'an Manuscript

North Africa or Central Islamic Lands, 9th–10th century
Ink, opaque watercolor, and gold on parchment
Overall: 9 13/16 × 13 3/8 inches (25 × 34 cm); 7 lines
Side A: sura 4, *al-Nisa'* (The Women), verses 1–2
Side B: sura 4, *al-Nisa'* (The Women), verses 2–3
Text copied in Kufic script in black-brown ink; vocalization in red dots; letter-pointing in single and double diagonal black lines; verse marker between verses 2 and 3 composed as gold rosette with green center.
TR:499-2017

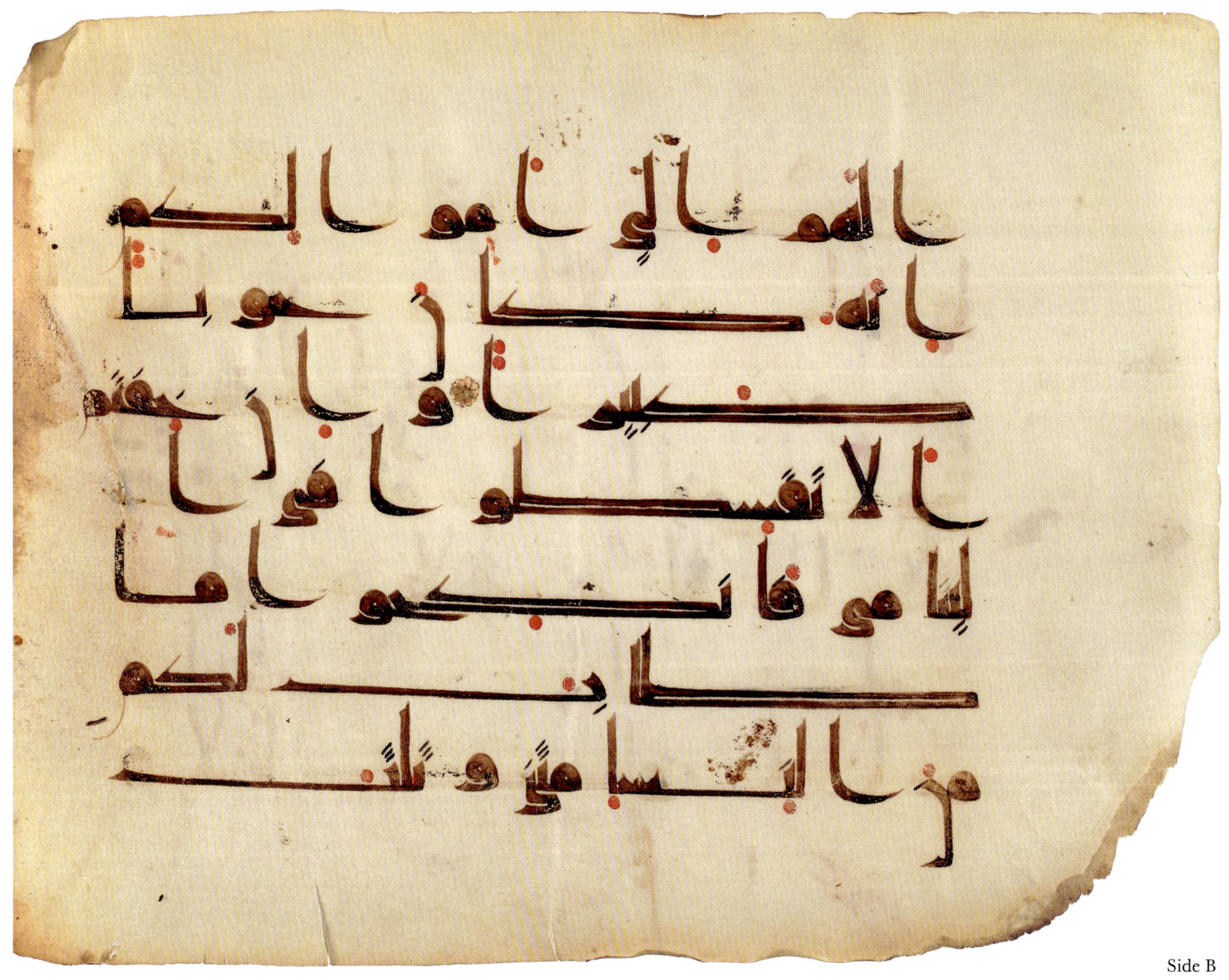

Side B

16

Folio from a Qur'an Manuscript

North Africa or Central Islamic Lands, 9th–10th century
Ink, opaque watercolor, and gold on parchment
Overall: 9 7/8 × 12 7/8 inches (25.1 × 32.7 cm); 7 lines
Side A: sura 4, *al-Nisa'* (The Women), verses 22–23
Side B: sura 4, *al-Nisa'* (The Women), verse 23
Text copied in Kufic script in brown-black ink; vocalization in red dots; letter-pointing in single and double diagonal black lines; verse marker between verses 22 and 23 composed as gold rosette outlined in purple-brown ink.
TR:1650-2015

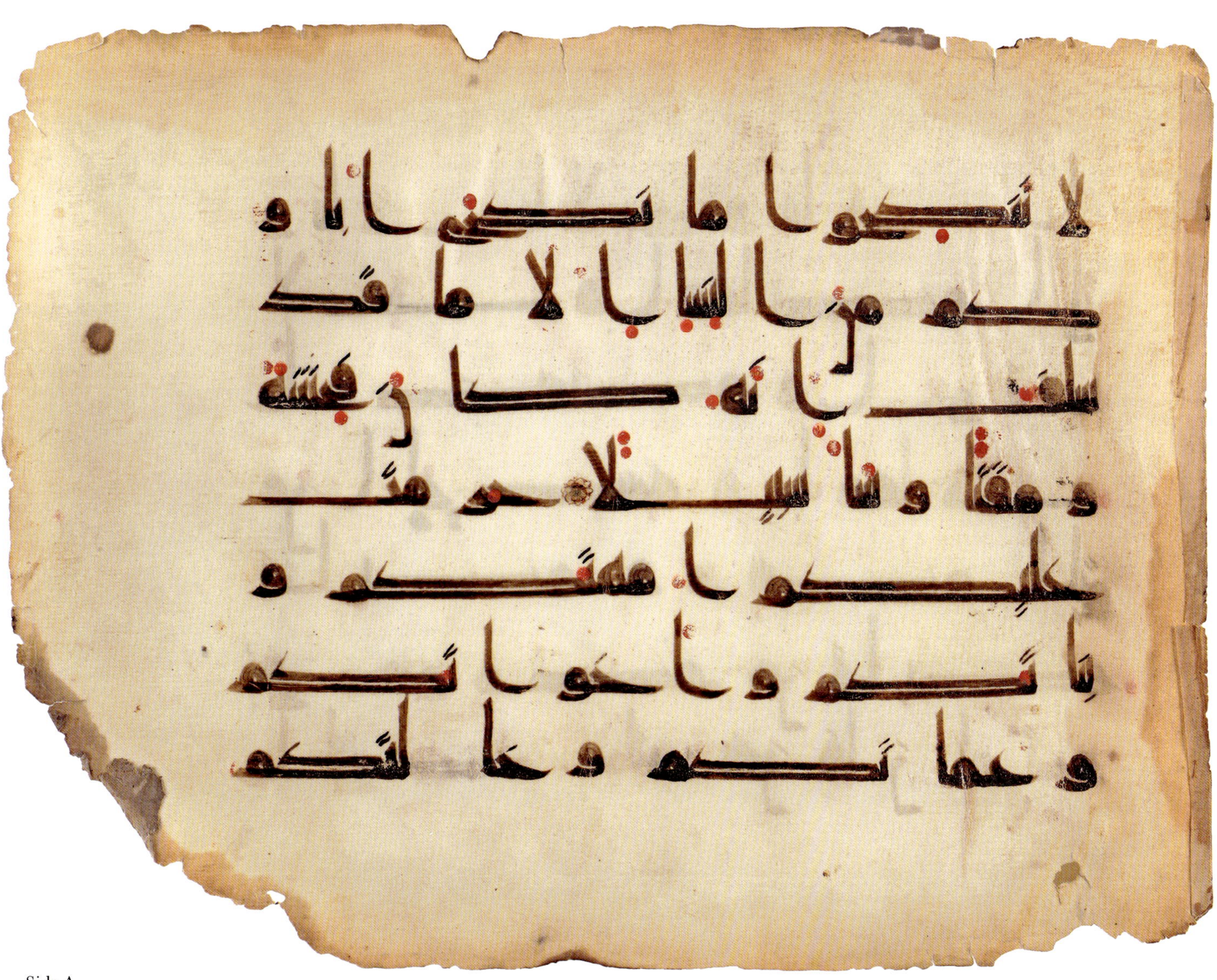

Side A

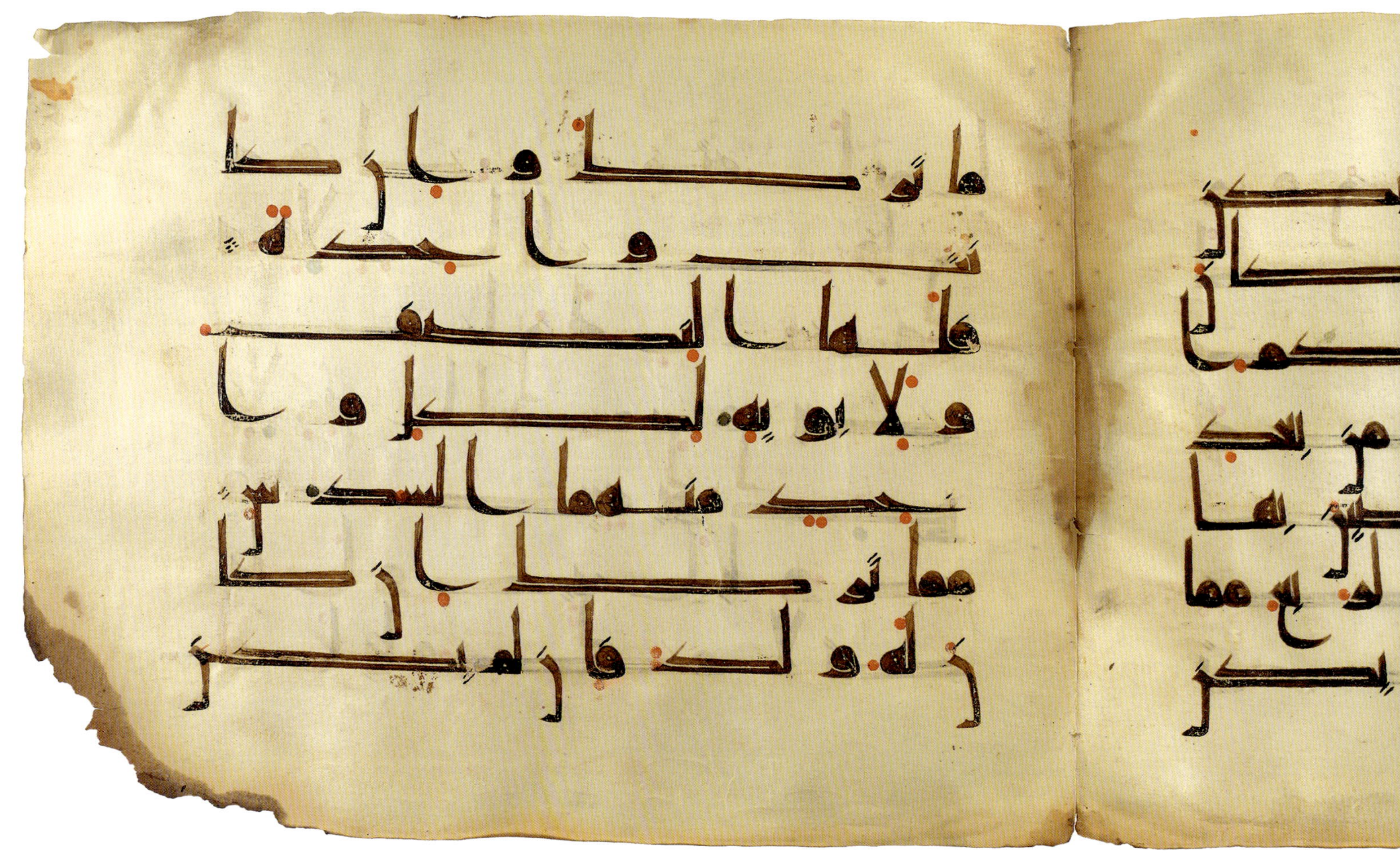

Cat. 17: Folio 1, side A

17

Bifolio from a Qur'an Manuscript

North Africa or Central Islamic Lands, 9th–10th century
Ink, opaque watercolor, and gold on parchment
Overall: 9 7/8 × 26 inches (25.1 × 66 cm); 7 lines
Folio 1, side A: sura 4, *al-Nisa'* (The Women), verse 11
Folio 1, side B: sura 4, *al-Nisa'* (The Women), verse 11
Folio 2, side A: sura 4, *al-Nisa'* (The Women), verses 11–12
Folio 2, side B: sura 4, *al-Nisa'* (The Women), verse 12
Text copied in Kufic script in brown-black ink; vocalization in red and blue dots; verse marker between verses 11 and 12 composed as gold rosette outlined in purple-brown ink.
TR:498-2017

18

Folio from a Qur'an Manuscript

Tunisia, 9th–10th century
Ink, opaque watercolor, and gold on parchment
Overall: 7 7/8 × 11 5/16 inches (20 × 28.7 cm); 6 lines
Side A: sura 4, *al-Nisa'* (The Women), verses 80–81
Side B: sura 4, *al-Nisa'* (The Women), verses 81–82
Text copied in Kufic script in black ink; vocalization in red and bluish green dots; letter-pointing in single and double diagonal black lines; verse markers on both sides composed as disks formed by border of looping circles studded with red and green dots.
TR:504-2017

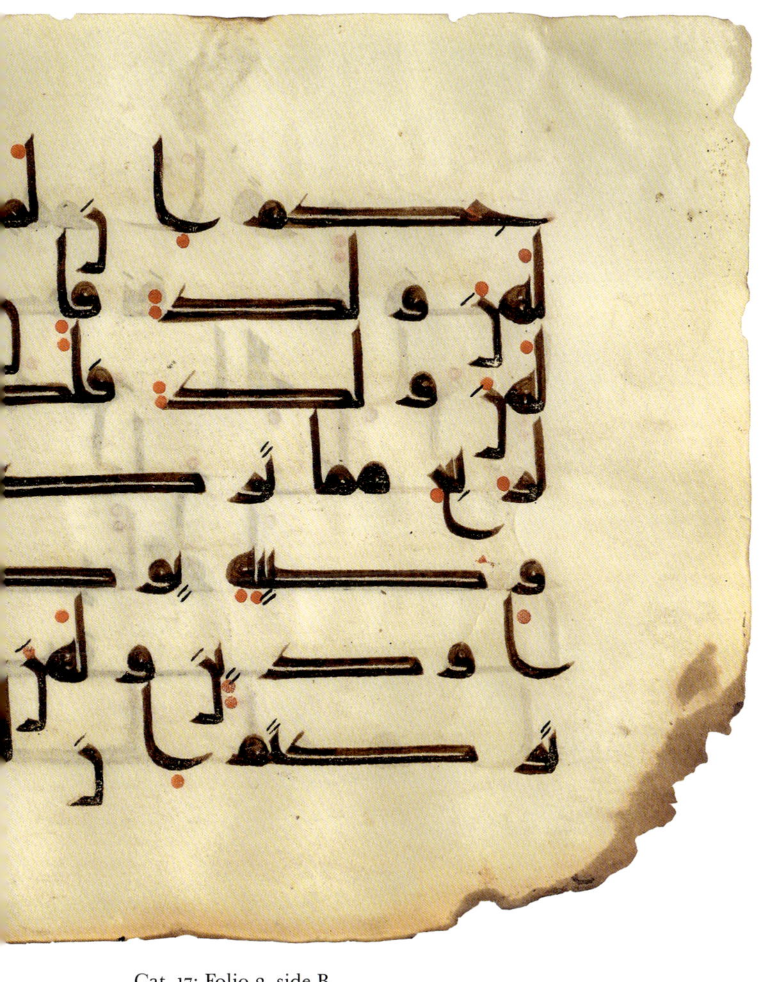
Cat. 17: Folio 2, side B

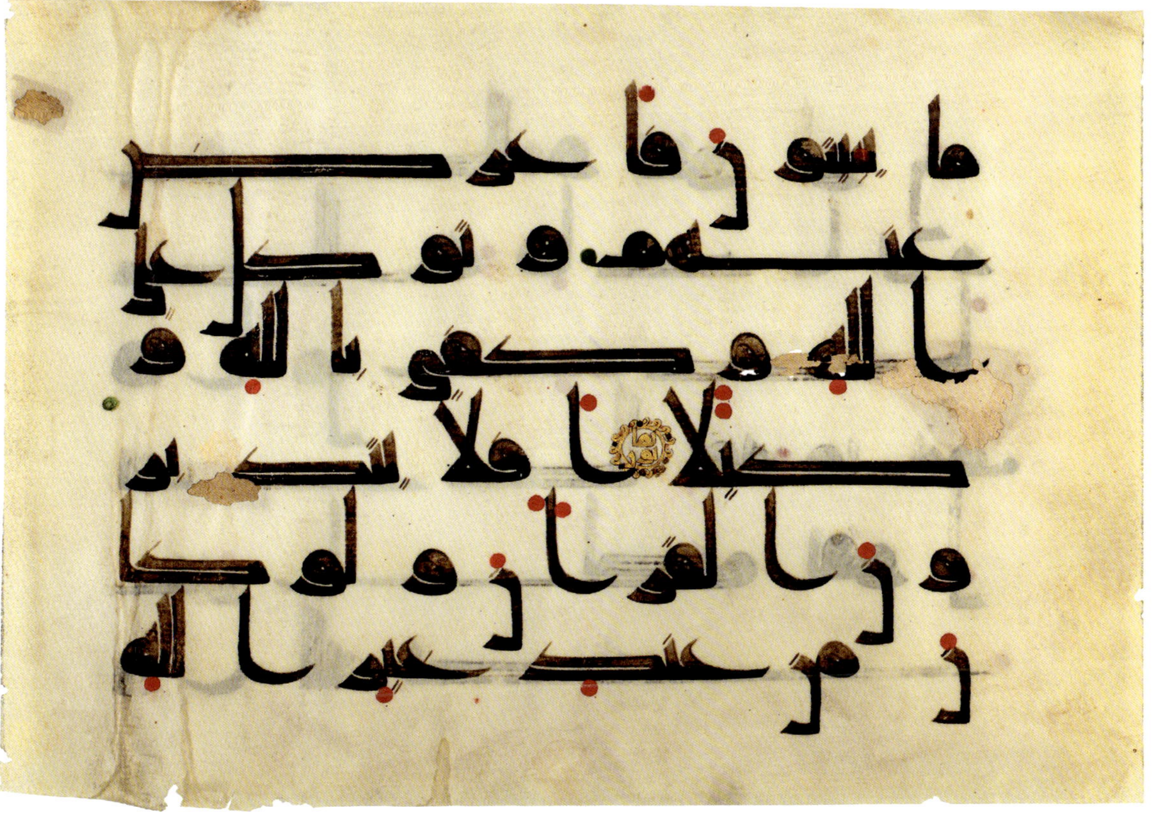
Cat. 18: Side B
Detail of side B on the following pages

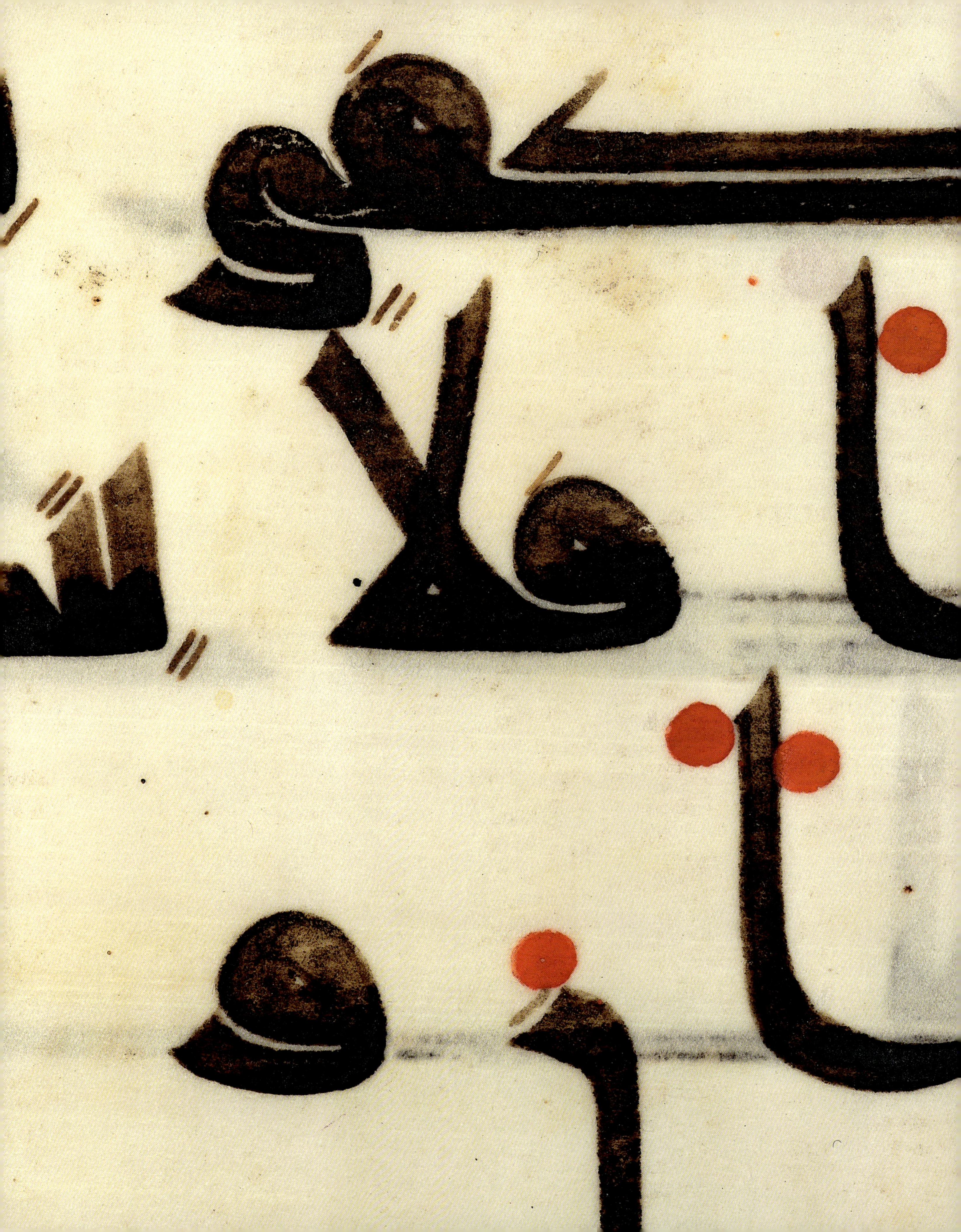

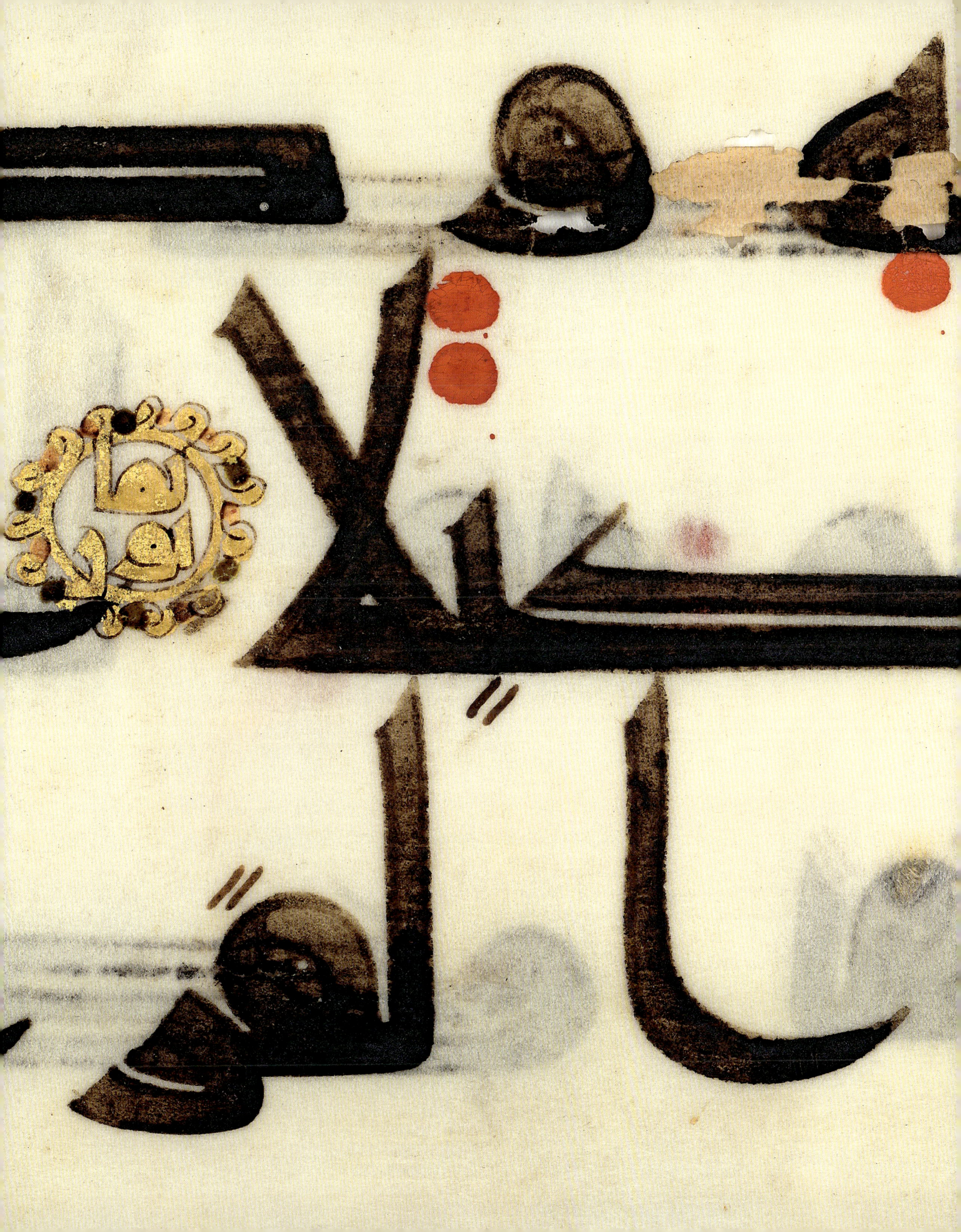

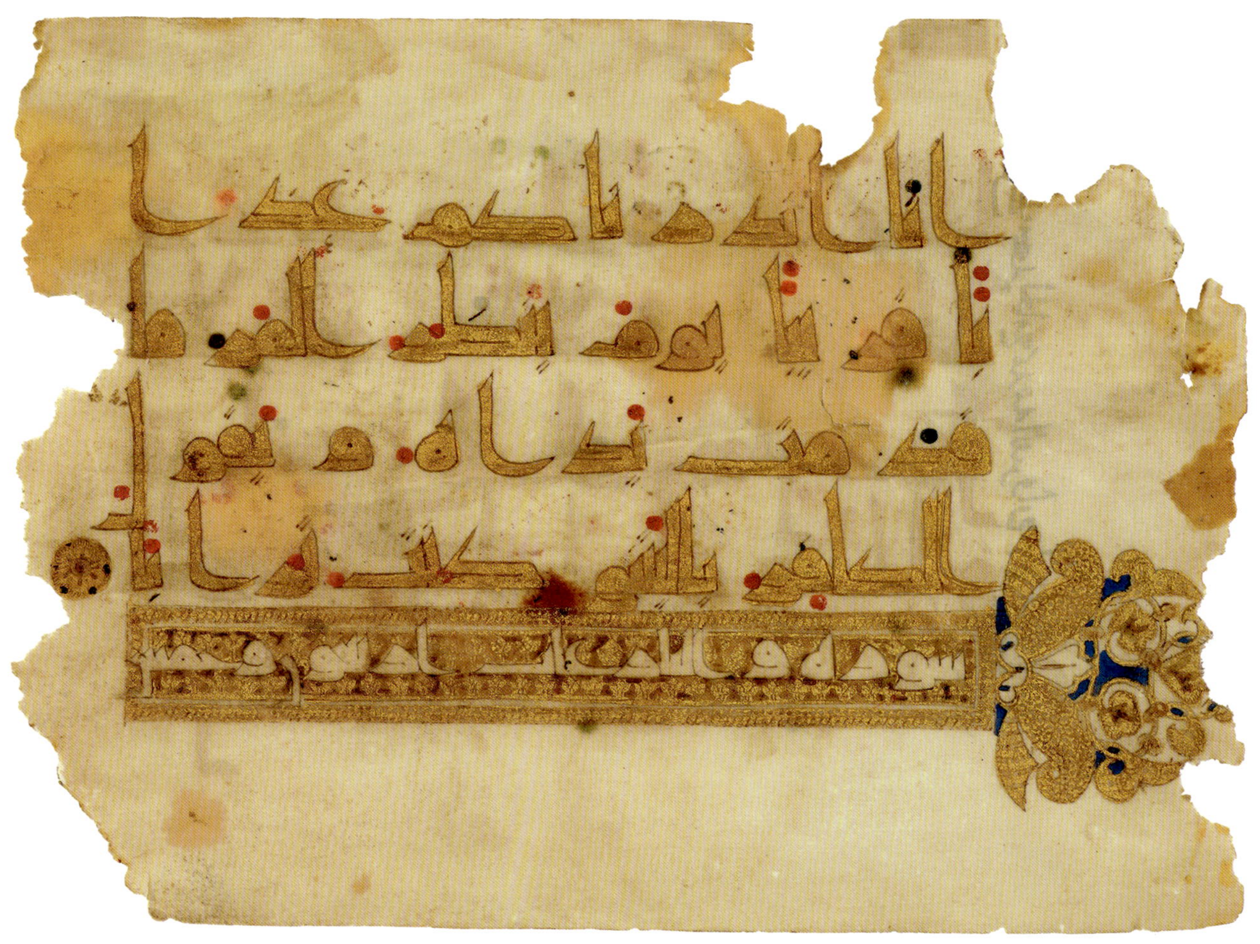

Side B

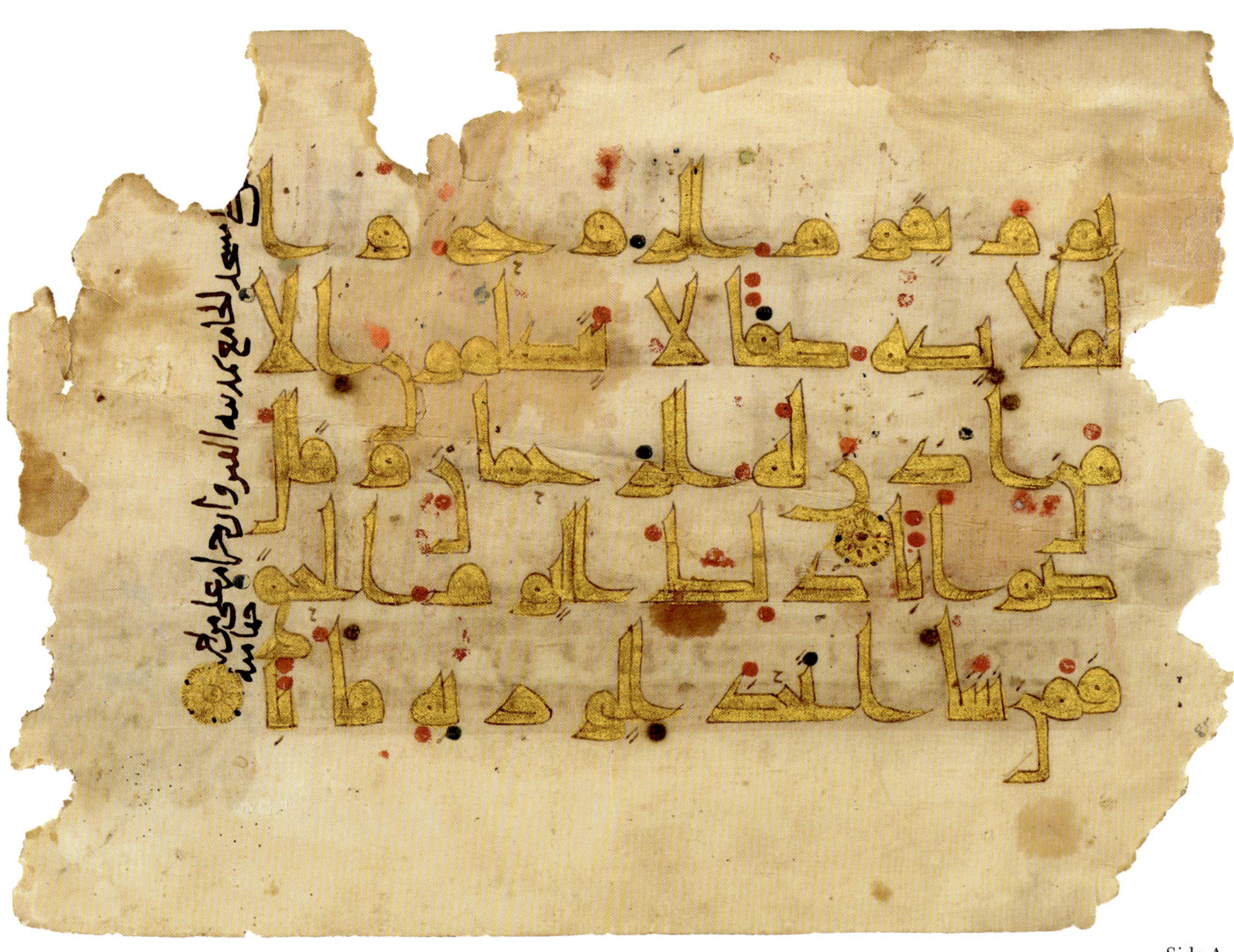

Side A

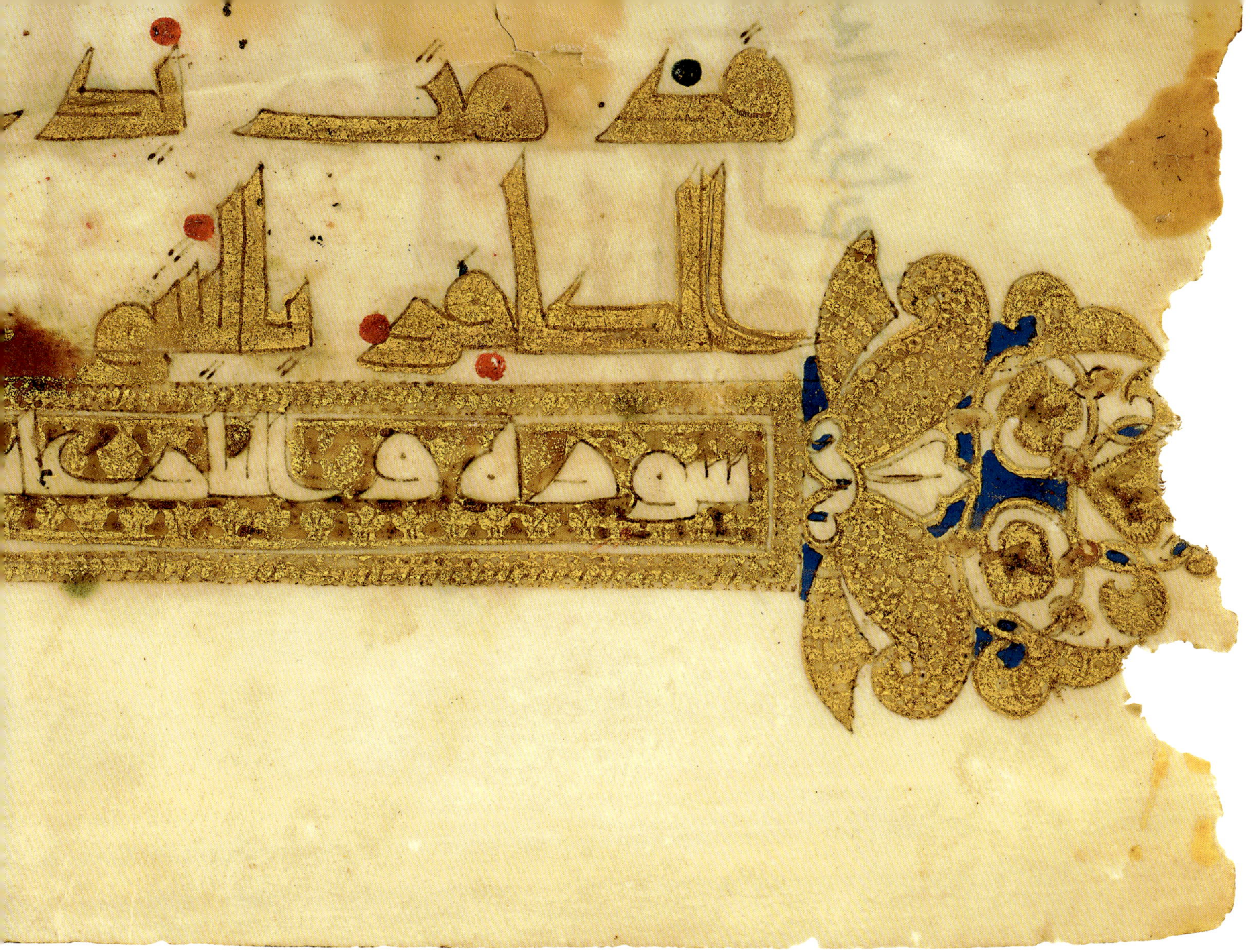

Side B (*detail*)

19

Folio from a Qur'an Manuscript

North Africa, possibly Kairouan, Tunisia, 9th–10th century
Ink, opaque watercolor, gold, and silver on parchment
5 5/8 × 7 7/8 inches (14.3 × 20 cm); 5 lines
Side A: sura 78, *al-Naba'* (The Announcement), verses 38–39
Side B: sura 78, *al-Naba'* (The Announcement), verse 40–heading for sura 79, *al-Nazi'at* (Those Who Pull and Withdraw)
Text in gold Kufic script; vocalization in red and blue dots; letter-pointing in single and double diagonal brown lines; verse markers gold rosettes with blue and brown dots; chapter heading for sura 79 on side B composed as a thin panel—with the title of the chapter reserved in the color of the parchment—of foliate motifs in gold against a brown ground enclosed by a rope border in the same materials; a large floriate finial, extending from the chapter title, is composed of multiple elements, including split palmettes, with patterned surfaces of stripes and disks executed in gold with brown outlines and some of the voids filled with blue; a notation on side A records the endowment of the Qur'an to the Friday Mosque (Masjid al-Jami') in the "town of Kairouan."
TR:1662-2015

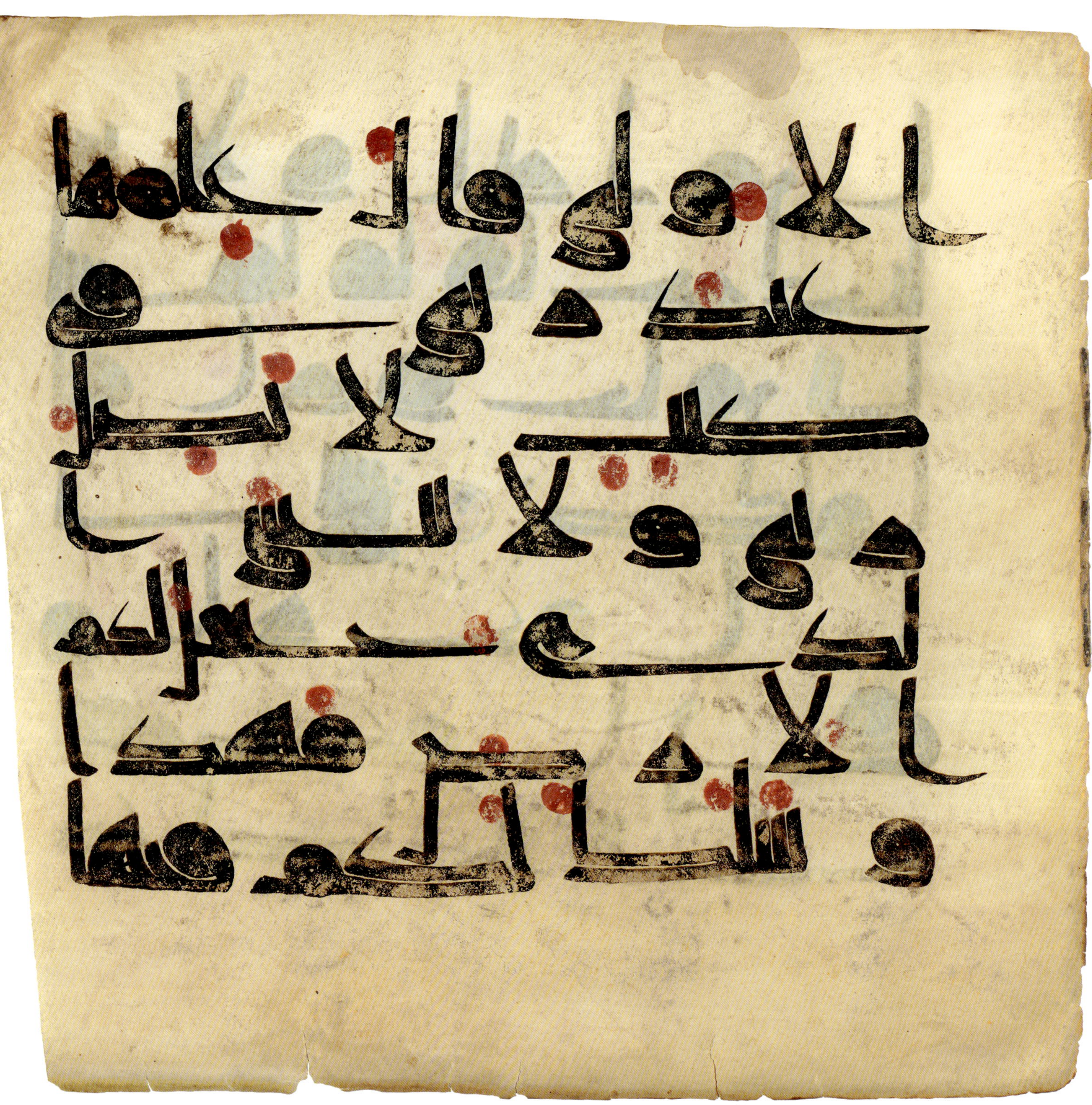

Side A

20

Folio from a Qurʾan Manuscript

Iran or North Africa, 9th–10th century
Ink and opaque watercolor on parchment
10 7/8 × 11 7/16 inches (27.6 × 29 cm); 7 lines
Side A: sura 20, *Ta' Ha'* (Ta Ha), verses 51–53
Side B: sura 20, *Ta' Ha'* (Ta Ha), verses 53–54
Text copied in Kufic script in black ink; vocalization in red dots; verse marker comprising gold disk studded with blue and red lines and dots, enclosed within rosette of faint black lines with red and blue dots on petals.
TR:501-2017

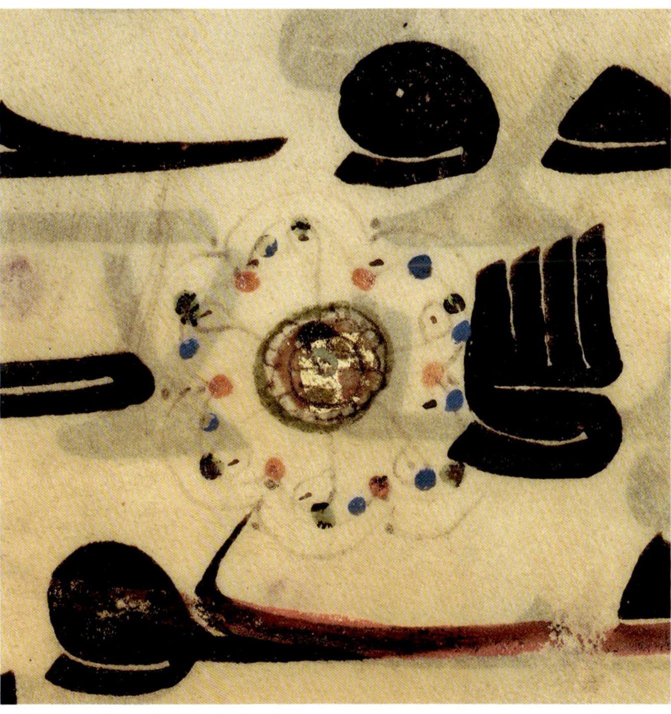

Side B (*detail*)

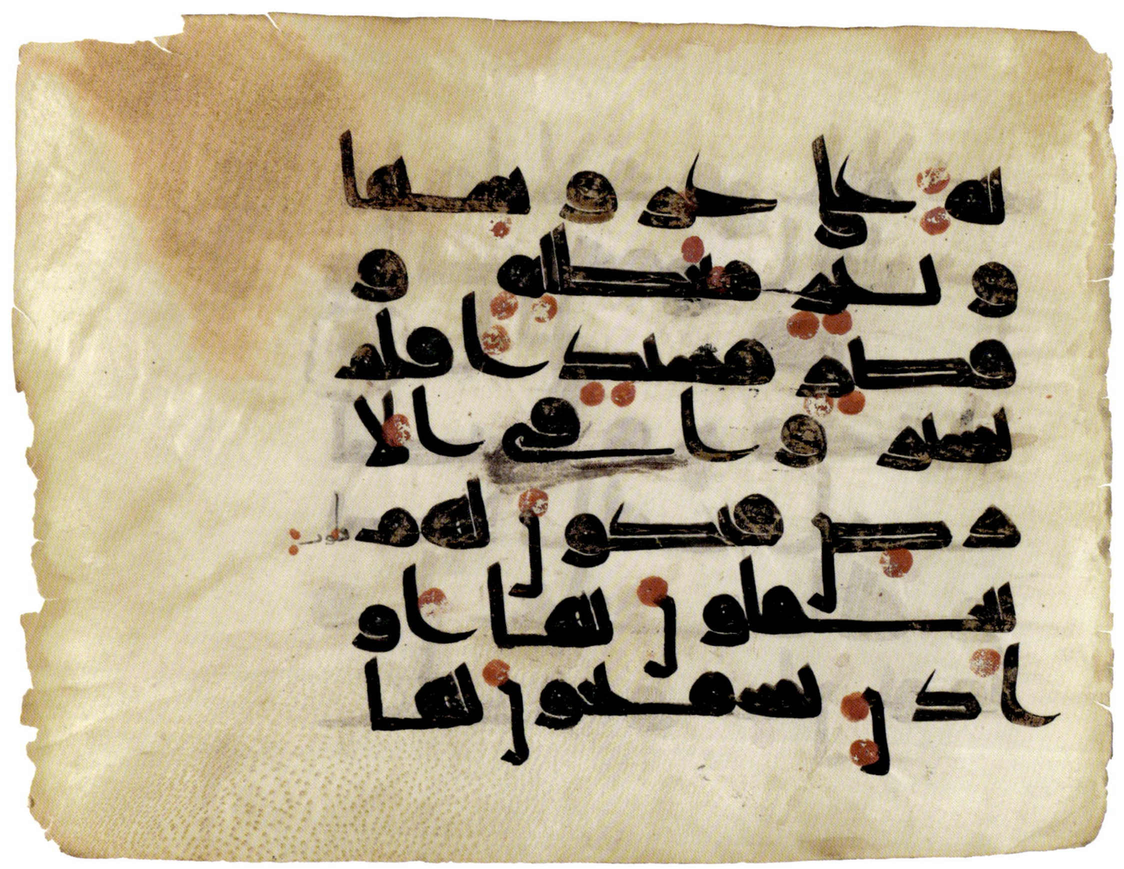

Side A *(above; detail on opposite page)*

21

Folio from a Qur'an Manuscript

Iran or North Africa, 9th–10th century
Ink and opaque watercolor on parchment
11 × 14 3/4 inches (28 × 37.5 cm); 7 lines
Side A: sura 22, *al-Hajj* (The Pilgrimage), verses 45–46
Side B: sura 22, *al-Hajj* (The Pilgrimage), verses 46–47
Text copied in Kufic script in black ink; vocalization in red dots; verse marker (on side B) composed as a rosette with a gold and black disk at center enclosed by a circle whose outline is modulated with spots of bluish green, red, and yellow.
TR:1680-2015

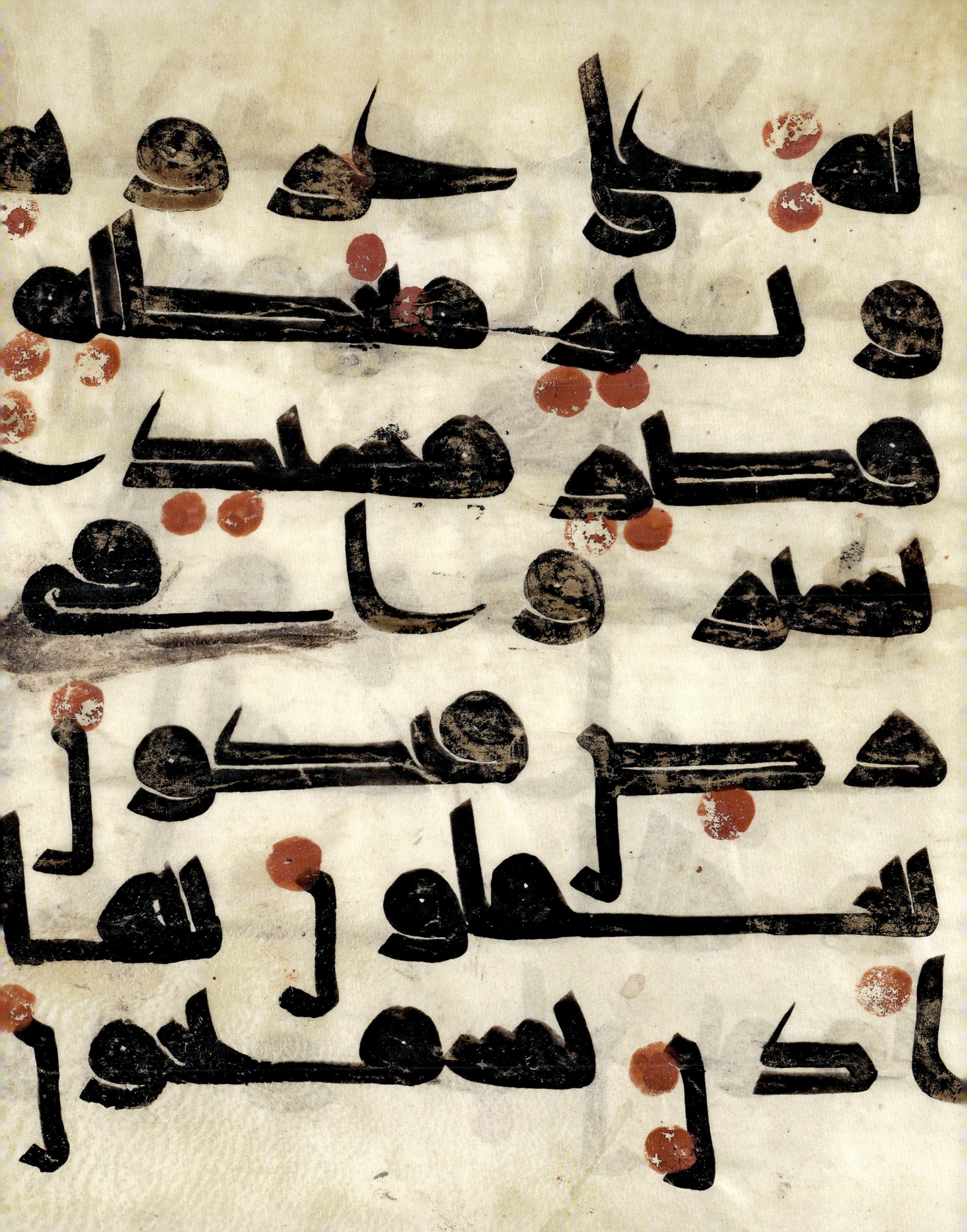

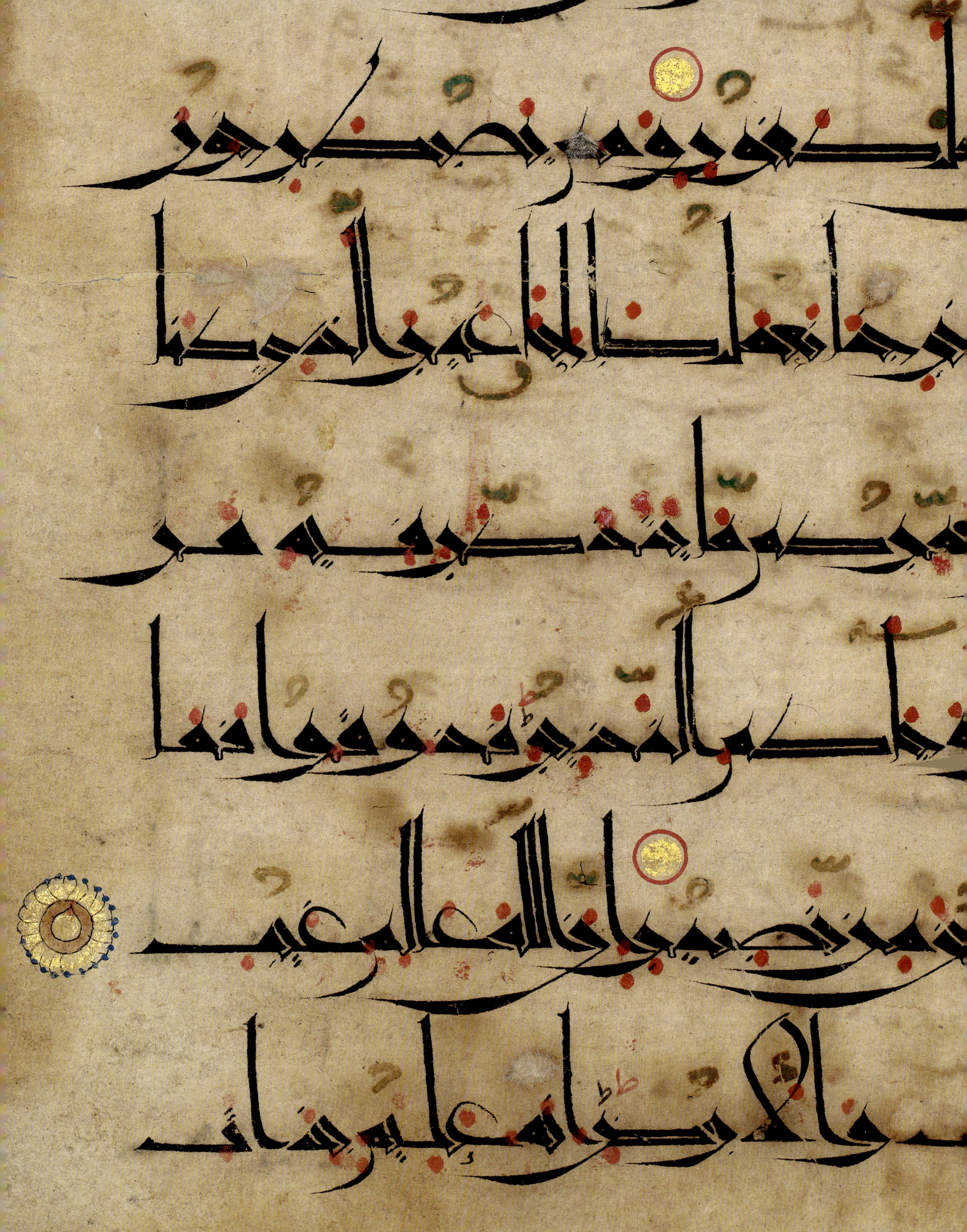

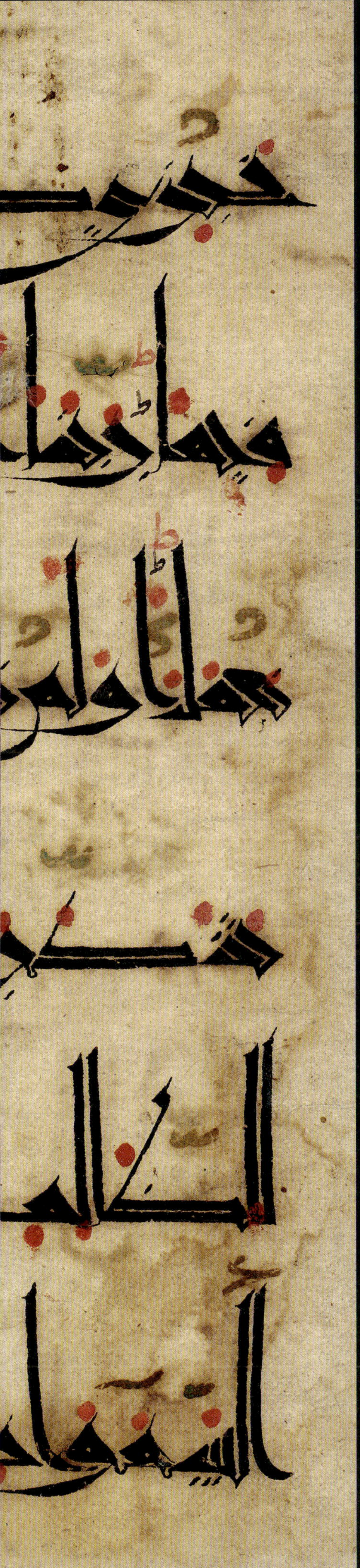

TRANSFORMATION

10TH–12TH CENTURY

TRANSFORMATIONS, 10TH–12TH CENTURY

Innovation of various kinds steadily transformed copies of the Qur'an from the tenth through twelfth centuries. One of the most important was the growing availability of paper, made from recycled rags, linen, and cordage, which supplanted papyrus—whose use was largely confined to Egypt—and parchment made from animal skins. The chronology and rate with which paper was adopted as the medium of choice for Qur'ans differed across the Islamic lands.[9] While the availability of paper effectively eliminated the use of other mediums as a writing support in most regions by the eleventh century, parchment continued to be used for Qur'ans in western Africa and the Iberian Peninsula into the thirteenth and fourteenth centuries (while paper was used for other kinds of texts). Another change coincident with the rise, and eventual dominance, of paper was a change in the orientation of the folio, a rectangular format now vertical in its orientation as the earliest Qur'ans copied in Hijazi script of the seventh–eighth centuries had been.

Script may be added to the changes affected by paper and format. One of the most celebrated developments of the tenth century, attributed to Ibn Muqla (886–940 CE), was the formation of a new canon of the "six scripts/pens" (*al-aqlam al-sitta*) and the "proportioned script" (*al-khatt al-mansub*; the adjective *mansub* also carries the sense of regulated or being brought into relation). According to written sources, Ibn Muqla selected six scripts (*naskh*, *thuluth*, *muhaqqaq*, *rayhani*, *riqa*ʿ, and *tawqi*ʿ), which were common in scribal use, and elevated them by subjecting the alphabet of each script to geometrical principles and fixed proportional interrelations according to the measure of the *alif*.[10] Conjoined to canon formation and proportional systematization was a system of vocalization and letter-pointing applied uniformly to the transcription of the Qur'an (a creation attributed to al-Khalil b. Ahmad al-Farahidi [d. 786 CE]). Orthographic consistency rendered the text fully legible and readable even to those people who had not memorized the Qur'an. While Ibn Muqla's reforms took place in the context of the Abbasid chancellery and formed a canon of scribal scripts used for secular purposes, the "six scripts/pens" were steadily accepted for the purpose of Qur'anic calligraphy.

The adoption of the reformed cursive scripts, created in Baghdad, took place at differing rates throughout the Islamic lands. Another script, Eastern Kufic (also dubbed "the New Style"), was used widely from the early tenth century until the early thirteenth century.[11] As a more cursive and rounded relative of Kufic, and with greater attenuation and thinness in its pen strokes, Eastern Kufic steadily supplanted Kufic. Eastern Kufic was itself gradually superseded by the cursive "six scripts" across the Islamic lands—from North Africa to Central Asia—by the thirteenth century. Yet another common form of script named Maghribi, confined to the Iberian Peninsula and western Africa, appears to have developed in the late eleventh century as another cursive variant of Kufic. The usage of several new types of script, formats, and systems of vocalization and letter-pointing took place in different combinations and in differing time frames that also varied by region. This diversity makes the period one of the most dynamic in the history of Islamic calligraphy.

22

Folio from a Qur'an Manuscript

North Africa, 10th century
Ink, opaque watercolor, and gold on parchment
7 3/8 × 11 7/8 inches (18.7 × 30.2 cm); 3 lines
Side A: sura 65, *al-Talaq* (Divorce), verse 12
Side B: sura 65, *al-Talaq* (Divorce), verse 12–heading for sura 66, *al-Tahrim* (Prohibition), verse 1
Text copied in Kufic script in brown-black ink; vocalization in red and green dots; letter-pointing in single and double diagonal black lines; verse marker composed of a stacked pyramid of gold dots outlined in black; illuminated chapter heading on side B comprises a rectangular panel—with the title of the verse in Kufic outlined in gold and reserved in the color of the parchment—whose ground is formed from gold floriate motifs outlined in reddish brown, the panel enclosed by a knotted border, and a floriate finial in the margin.
TR:505-2017

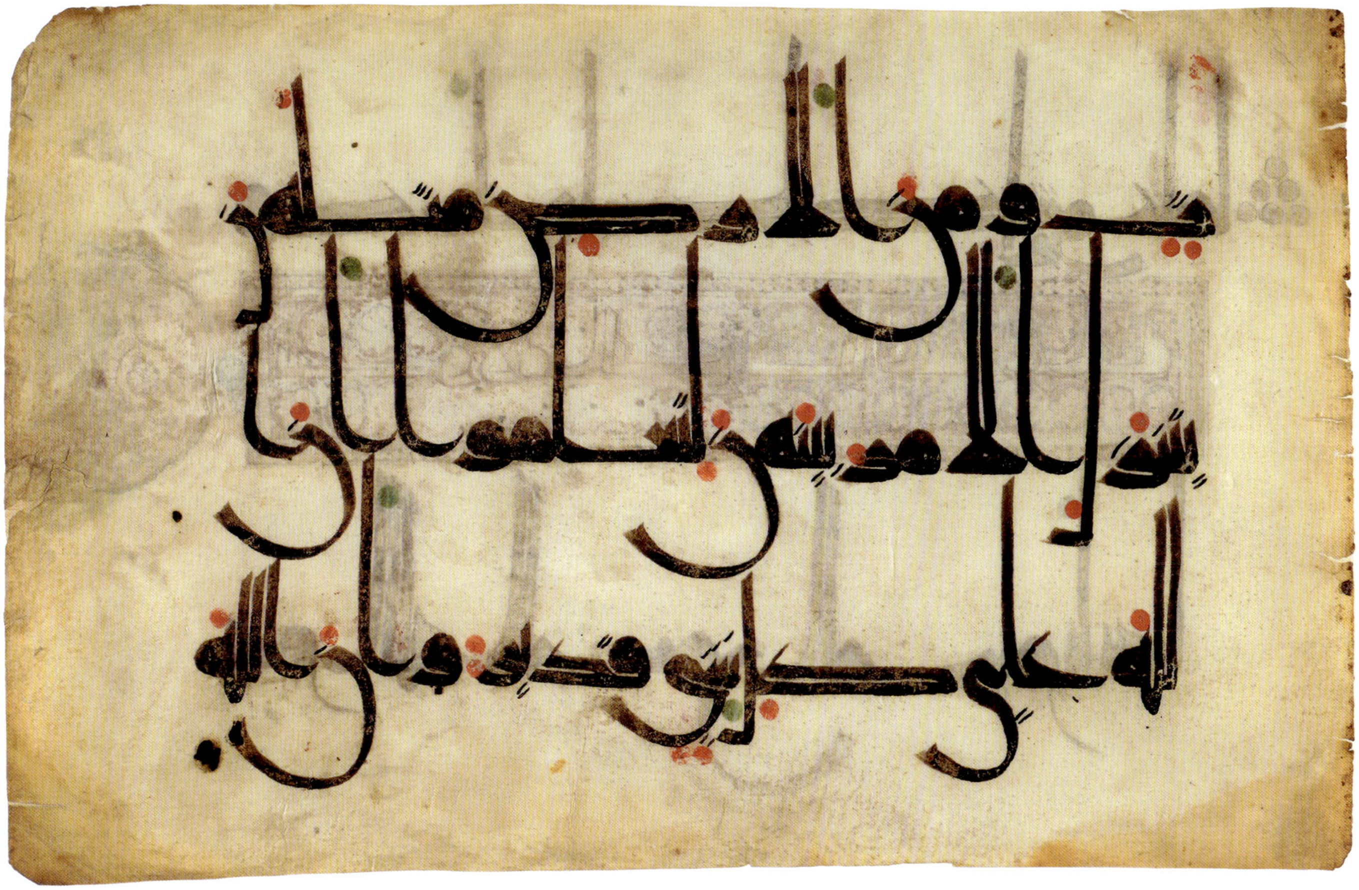

Side A

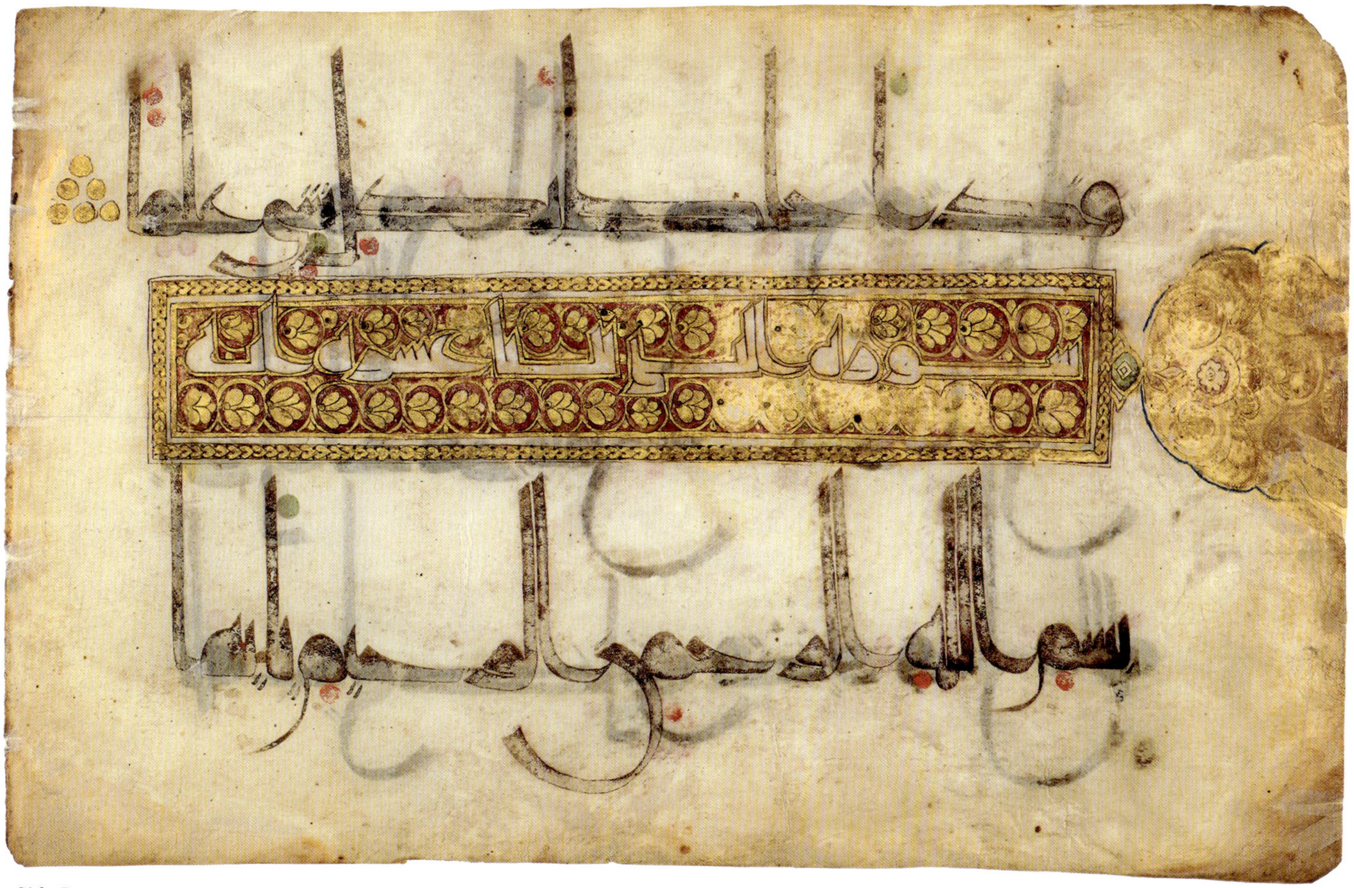

Side B

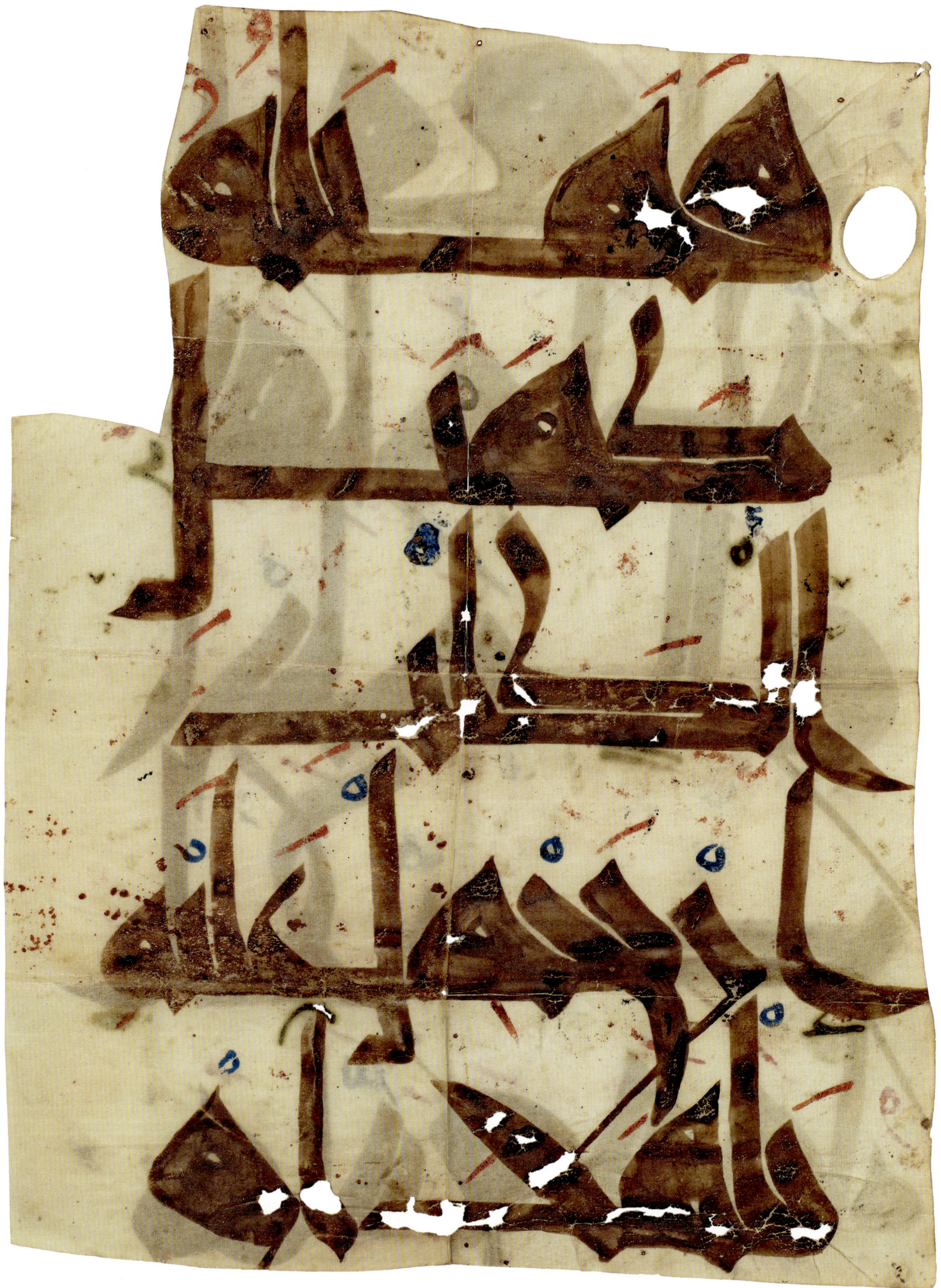

Side A

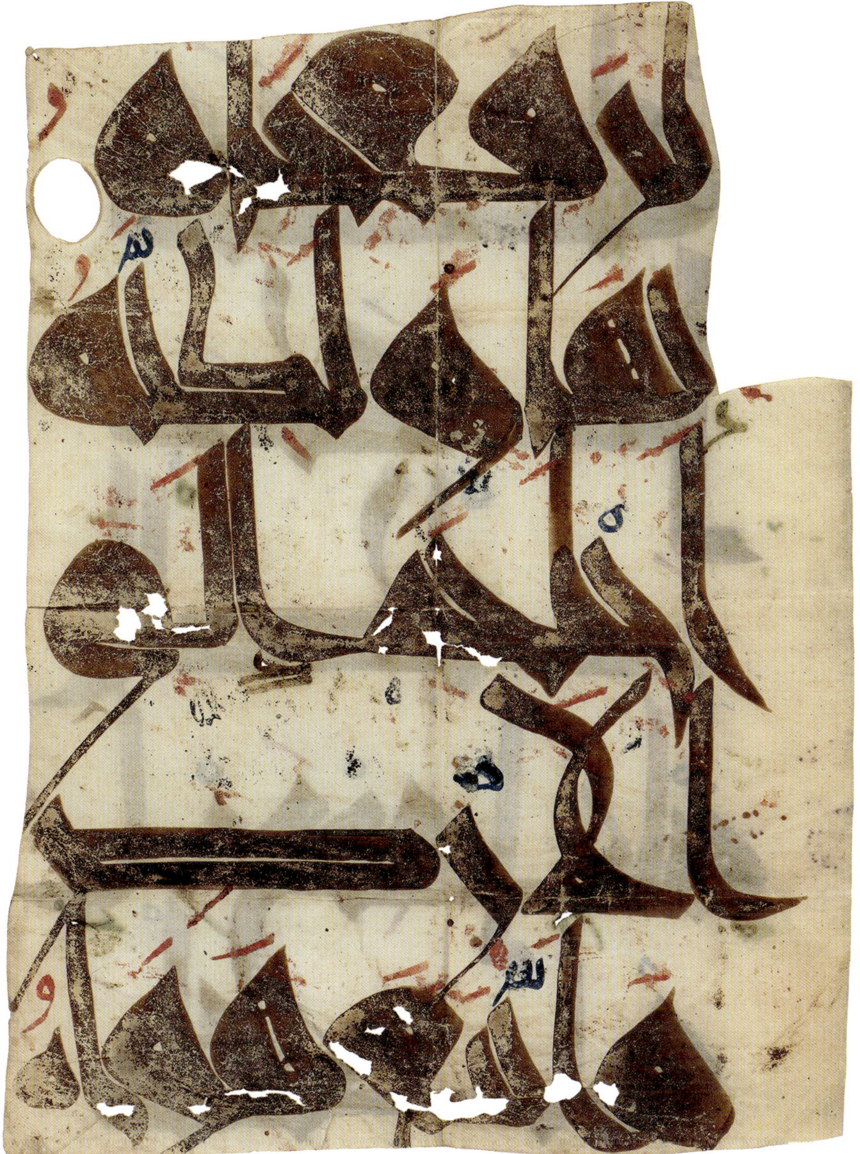

Side B

23

Folio from the Nurse's Qur'an (*Mushaf al-Hadina*)

Tunisia, Kairouan, AH 410/1019–1020 CE
Ink and opaque watercolor on parchment
Overall: 9 1/8 × 12 1/16 inches (23.1 × 30.6 cm); 5 lines
Side A: sura 7, *al-Aʿraf* (Wall between Heaven and Hell), verse 176
Side B: sura 7, *al-Aʿraf* (Wall between Heaven and Hell), verse 176
Text copied in Eastern Kufic script in brown ink; vocalization in red, blue, and green (for short vowels [*fatha*, *damma*, *kasra*], doubled consonants [*shadda*], silences [*sukun*], *hamza*, and glottal stop [*madda*]).
The "Nurse's Qur'an" is named after its patron who was a nursemaid (*hadina*) of the ruler al-Muʿizz b. Badis (r. 1016–1062 CE). Ibn Badis was a ruler of the Zirid dynasty that governed the territory of central North Africa based in Kairouan.
TR:298-2015

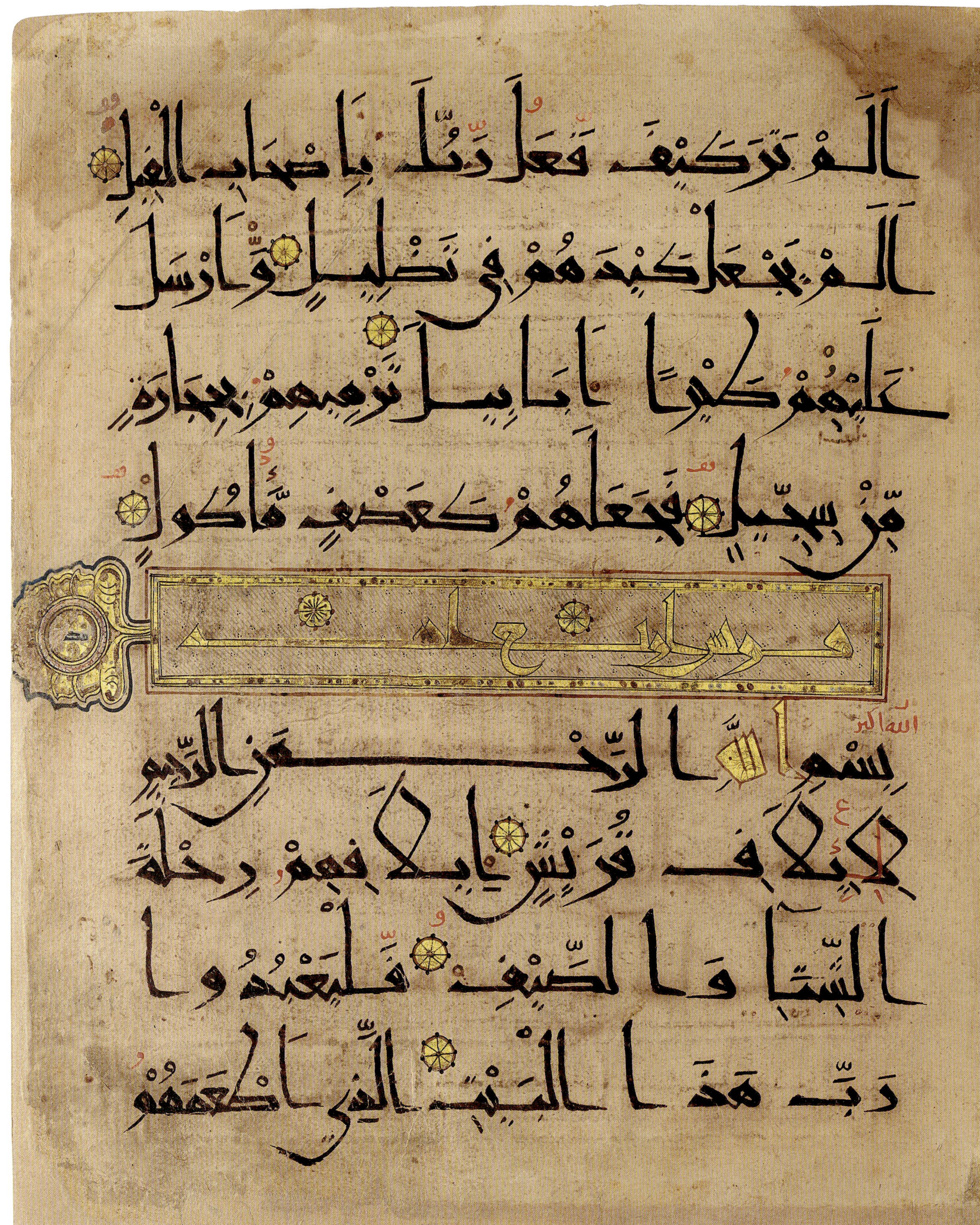
ألم تر كيف فعل ربك بأصحاب الفيل
ألم يجعل كيدهم في تضليل وأرسل
عليهم طيرا أبابيل ترميهم بحجارة
من سجيل فجعلهم كعصف مأكول
بسم الله الرحمن الرحيم
لإيلاف قريش إيلافهم رحلة
الشتاء والصيف فليعبدوا
رب هذا البيت الذي أطعمهم

Folio 2, side A

24

Bifolio from a Qur'an Manuscript

Iran, 11th–12th century
Ink, opaque watercolor, and gold on paper
Open: 15 5/8 × 26 1/2 inches (39.8 cm × 67.3 cm)
Closed: 15 5/8 × 13 1/4 inches (39.8 × 33.6 cm); 9 lines
Folio 1, side A: sura 102, *al-Takathur* (Plenitude), verses 3–8–illuminated chapter heading for sura 104, *al-Humaza* (The Slanderer)
Folio 1, side B: sura 104, *al-Humaza* (The Slanderer), verses 1–9–illuminated chapter heading for sura 105, *al-Fil* (The Elephant) and *basmala*
Folio 2, side A: sura 105, *al-Fil* (The Elephant), verses 1–5–illuminated chapter heading for sura 106, *Quraysh* (Quraysh), verses 1–4
Folio 2, side B: sura 106, *Quraysh* (Quraysh), end of verse 4–illuminated chapter heading for sura 107, *al-Ma'un* (Things of Common Use), verses 1–7–illuminated chapter heading for sura 108, *al-Kawthar* (Preeminence)
Text copied in Eastern Kufic script in black ink (the name of God written in gold outlined in black); vocalization and letter-pointing in black ink; verse markers are gold disks encircled by brown and blue dots; chapter headings are composed as thin rectangular panels with floriate finials in the margin; the headings record the chapter title in gold Kufic outlined in black against a ground formed from hatched brown lines punctuated by gold rosettes with articulated petals.
TR:381-2015

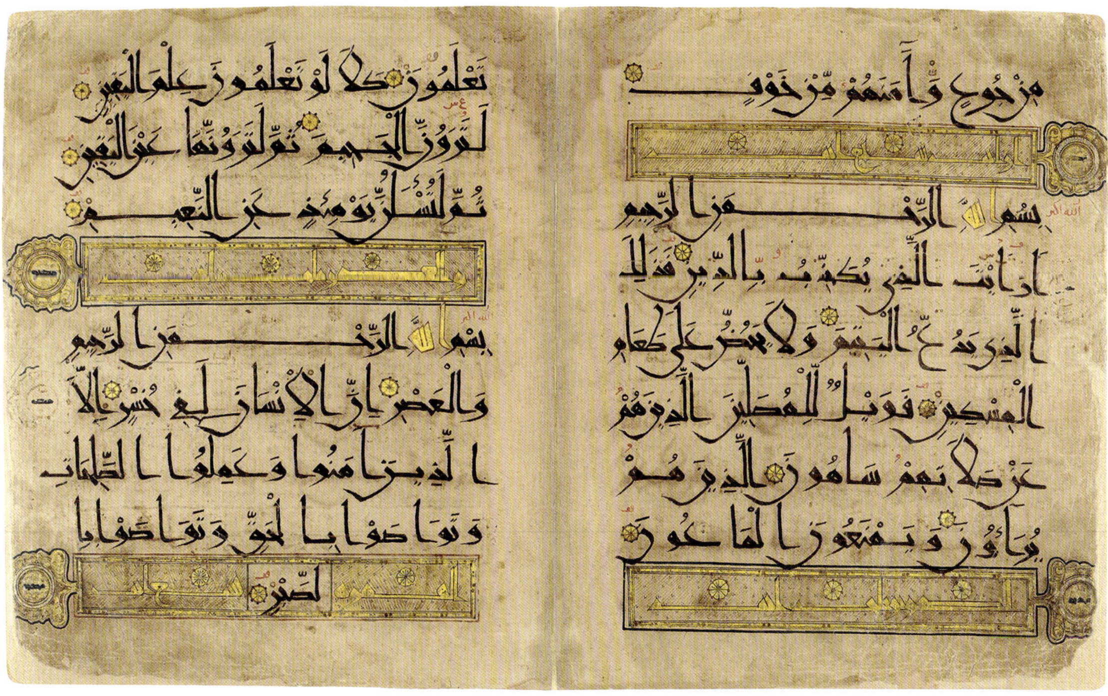

Folio 1, side A — Folio 2, side B

25

Folio from a Qur'an Manuscript

Eastern Islamic Lands, 12th century
Ink, opaque watercolor, and gold on paper
Overall: 22 1/16 × 16 1/8 inches (56 × 41 cm); 10 lines
Side A: sura 35, *al-Fatir* (The Originator), verses 14–19
Side B: sura 35, *al-Fatir* (The Originator), verses 20–27
Text copied in Eastern Kufic in black ink; vocalization in red dots; black lines for the vowels *fatha* and *kasra*; green shapes for the vowel *damma*, double consonant (*shadda*), and silence (*sukun*); variety of verse markers and counters composed as gold disks outlined with red and as rosettes of gold with brown with blue dots or red outlines.
TR:807-2015

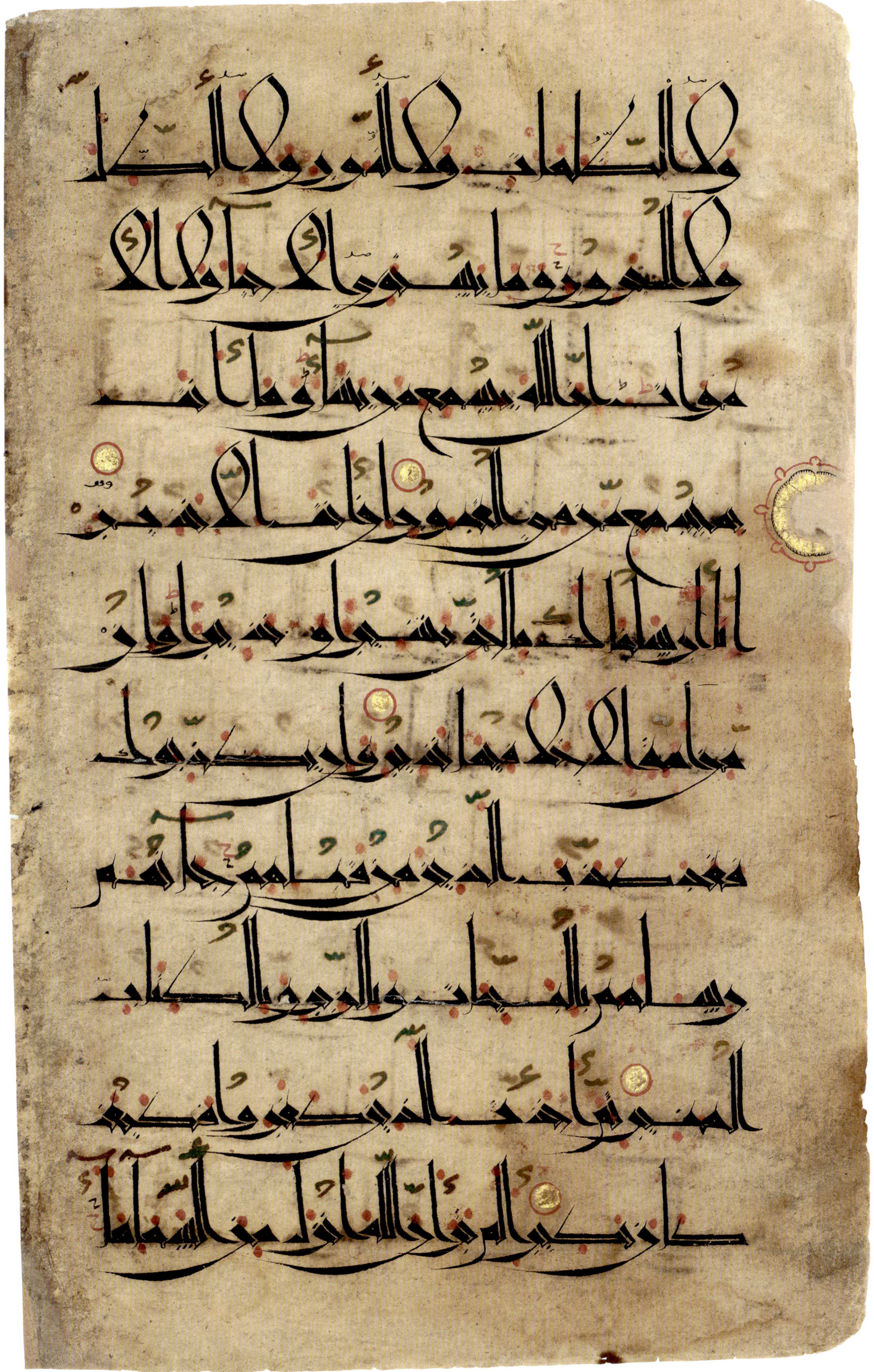

Side B

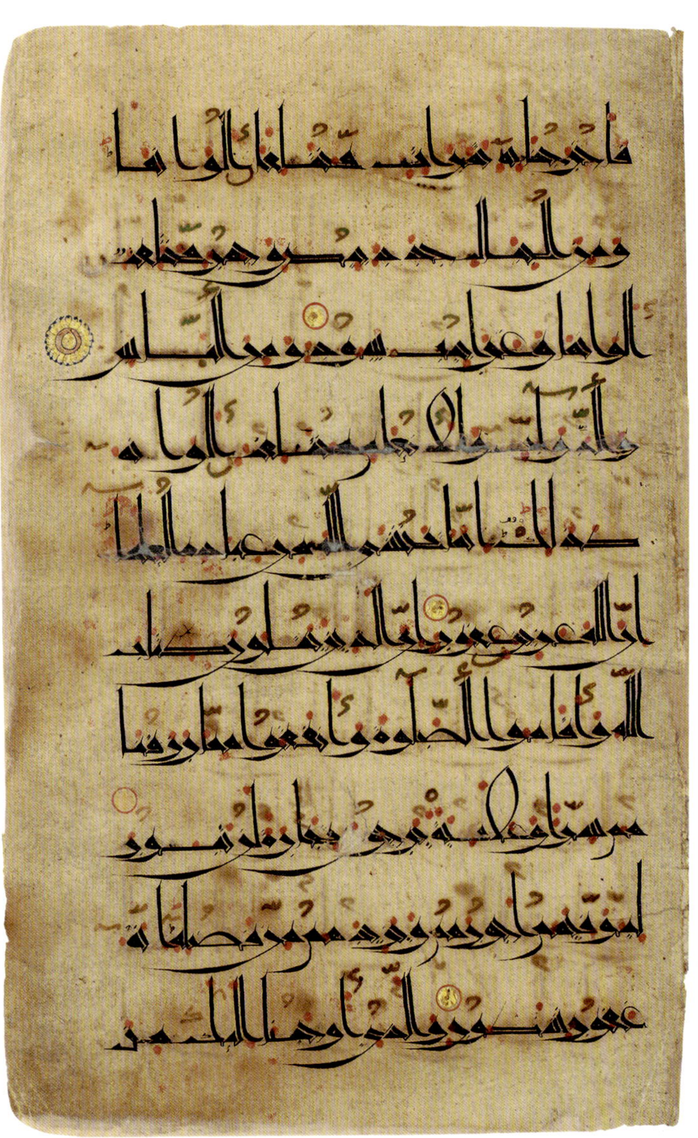

Cat. 26: Side A

26

Folio from a Qur᾿an Manuscript

Eastern Islamic Lands, 12th century
Ink, opaque watercolor, and gold on paper
Overall: 22 1/16 × 16 1/8 inches (56 × 41 cm); 10 lines
Side A: sura 35, *al-Fatir* (The Originator), verses 27–31
Side B: sura 35, *al-Fatir* (The Originator), verses 31–35
Text copied in Eastern Kufic in black ink; vocalization in red dots, black lines for vowels *fatha* and *kasra*; green shapes for the vowel *damma*, double consonant (*shadda*), and silence (*sukun*); variety of verse markers and counters composed as gold disks outlined with red and as rosettes of gold with brown with blue dots or red outlines.
TR:810-2015

27

Folio from a Qur᾿an Manuscript

Eastern Islamic Lands, 12th century
Ink, opaque watercolor, and gold on paper
Overall: 12 5/16 × 7 7/8 inches (31.3 × 20 cm); 10 lines
Side A: sura 35, *al-Fatir* (The Originator), verses 35–38
Side B: sura 35, *al-Fatir* (The Originator), verses 38–41
Text copied in Eastern Kufic in black ink; vocalization in red dots; black lines for vowels *fatha* and *kasra*; green shapes for the vowel *damma*, double consonant (*shadda*), and silence (*sukun*); variety of verse markers and counters composed as gold disks outlined with red and as rosettes of gold with brown with blue dots or red outlines.
TR:809-2015

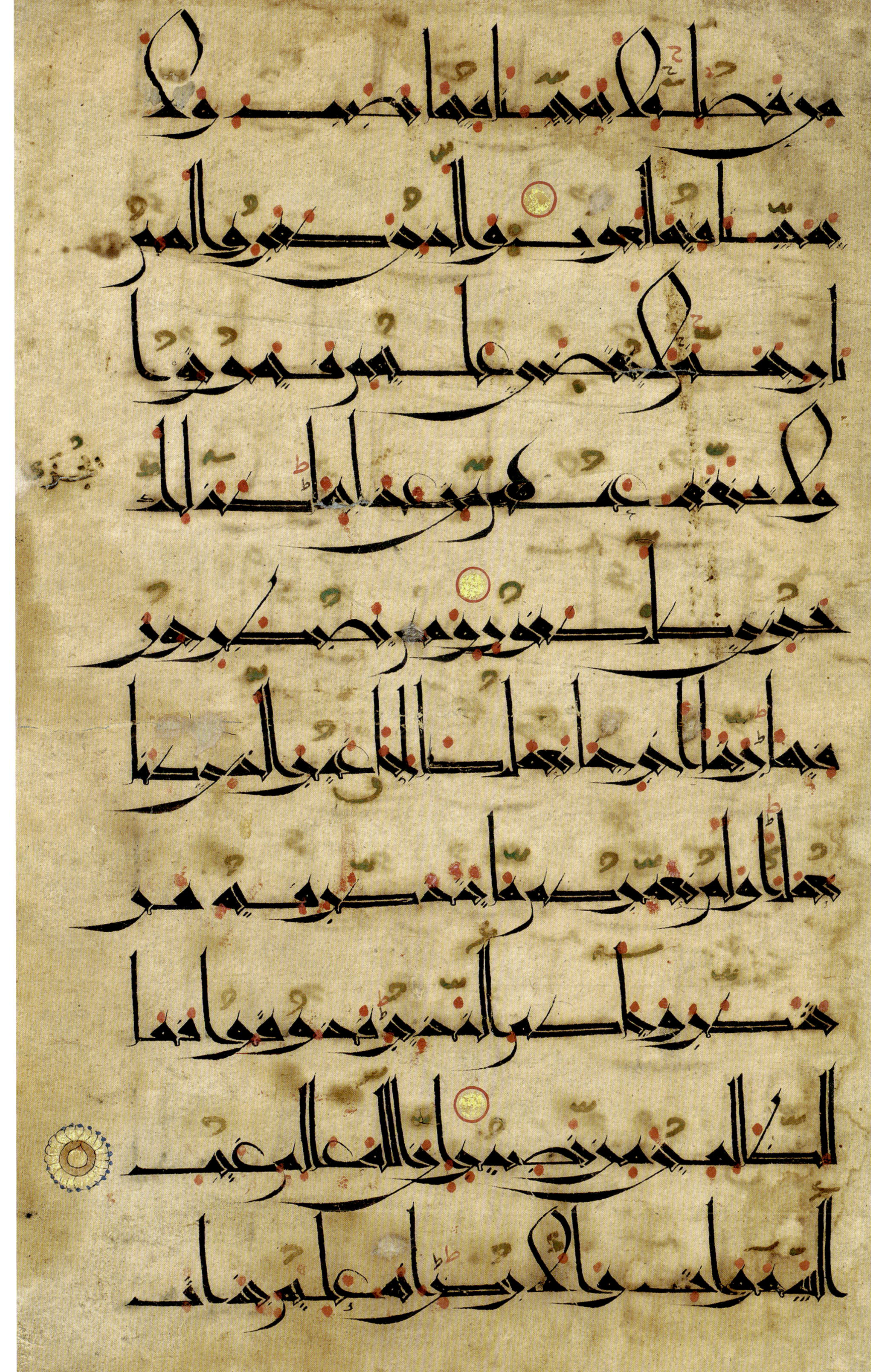

Cat. 27: Side A

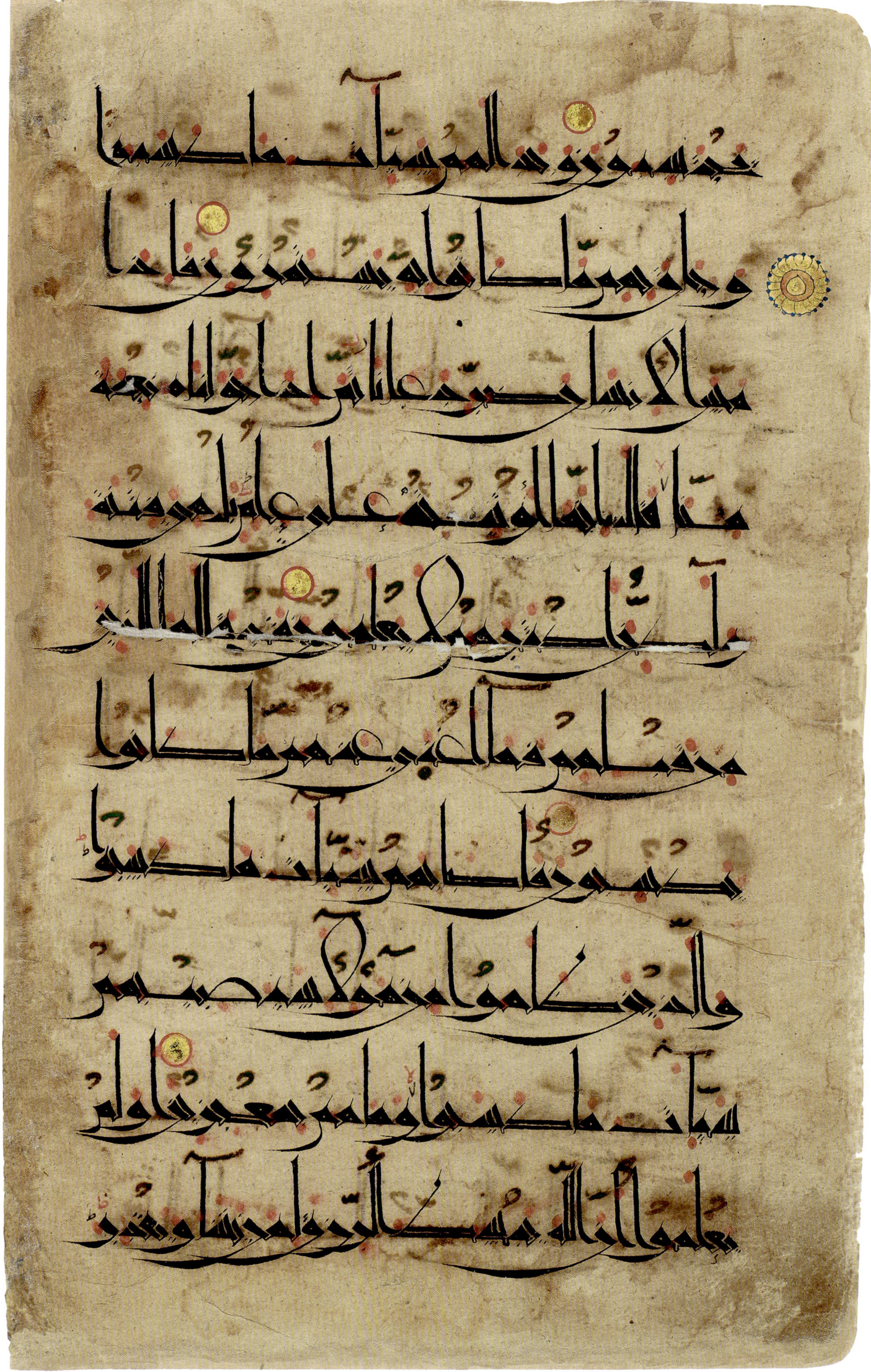

Cat. 28: Side B

28

Folio from a Qur'an Manuscript

Eastern Islamic Lands, 12th century
Ink, opaque watercolor, and gold on paper
12 5/16 × 7 7/8 inches (31.3 × 20 cm); 10 lines
Side A: sura 39, *al-Zumar* (The Small Groups), verses 43–47
Side B: sura 39, *al-Zumar* (The Small Groups), verses 47–52
Text copied in Eastern Kufic in black ink; vocalization in red dots; black lines for vowels *fatha* and *kasra*, green shapes for the vowel *damma*, double consonant (*shadda*), and silence (*sukun*); variety of verse markers and counters composed as gold disks outlined with red and as rosettes of gold with brown with blue dots or red outlines.
TR:812-2015

29

Folio from a Qur'an Manuscript

Eastern Islamic Lands, 12th century
Ink, opaque watercolor, and gold on paper
Overall: 22 1/16 × 16 1/8 inches (56 × 41 cm); 10 lines
Side A: sura 39, *al-Zumar* (The Small Groups), verses 19–22
Side B: sura 39, *al-Zumar* (The Small Groups), verses 22–25
Text copied in Eastern Kufic in black ink; vocalization in red dots; black lines for vowels *fatha* and *kasra*, green shapes for the vowel *damma*, double consonant (*shadda*), and silence (*sukun*); variety of verse markers and counters composed as gold disks outlined with red and as rosettes of gold with brown with blue dots or red outlines.
TR:811-2015

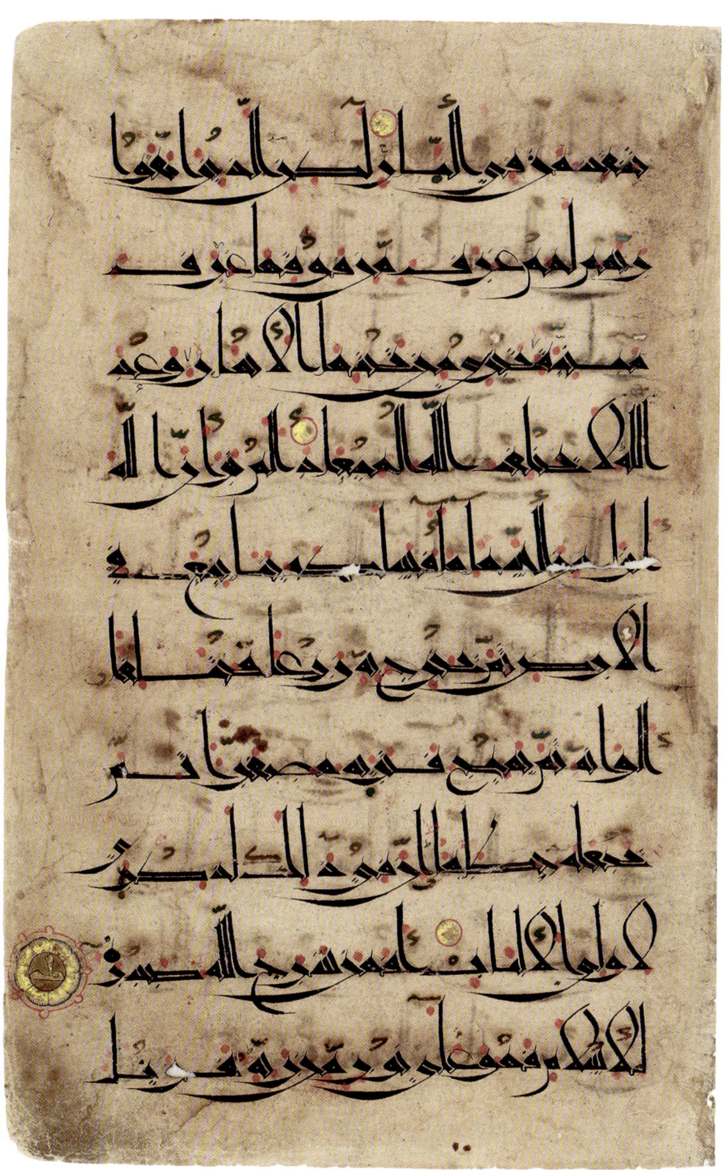

Cat. 29: Side A
Detail of side B on the following pages

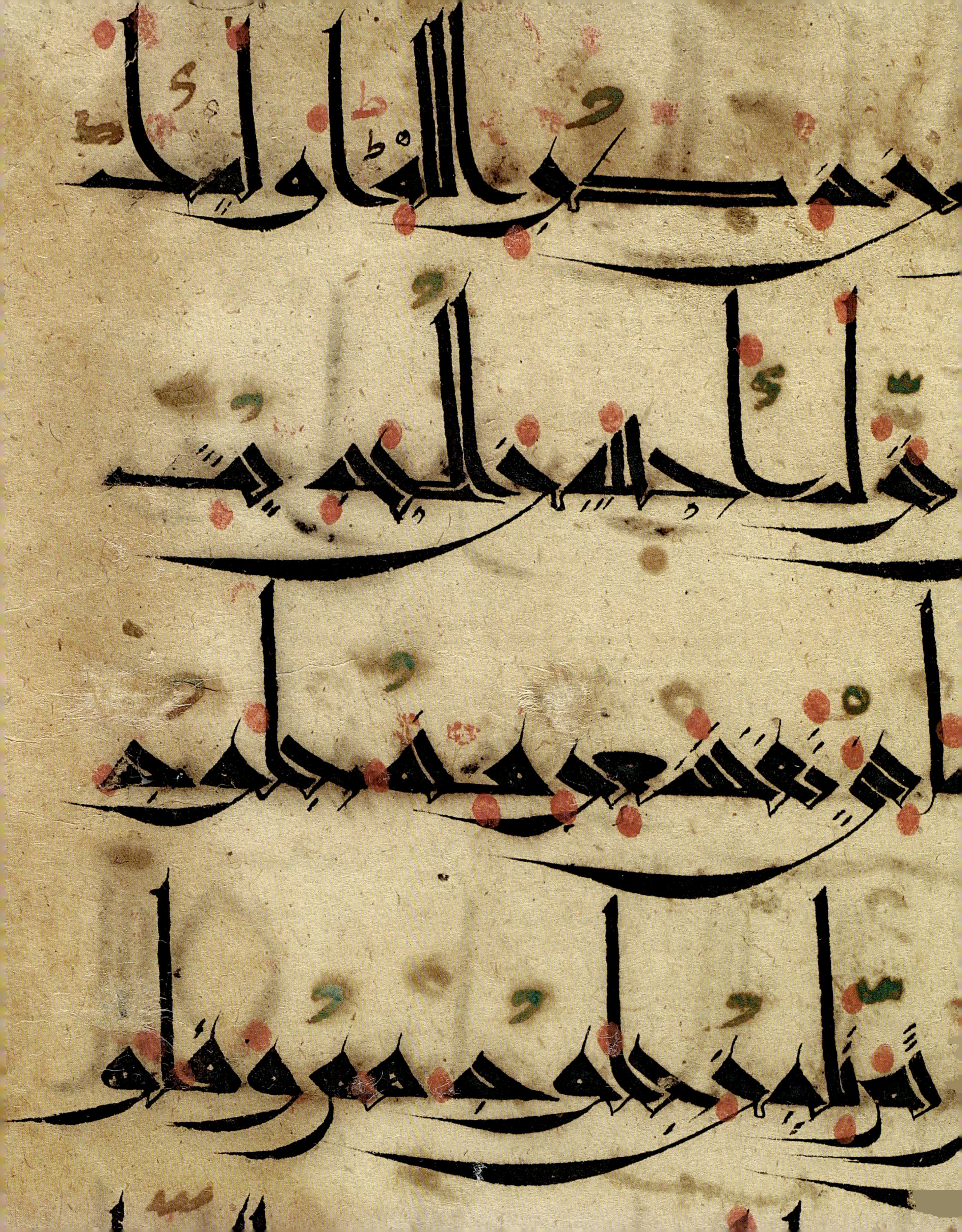

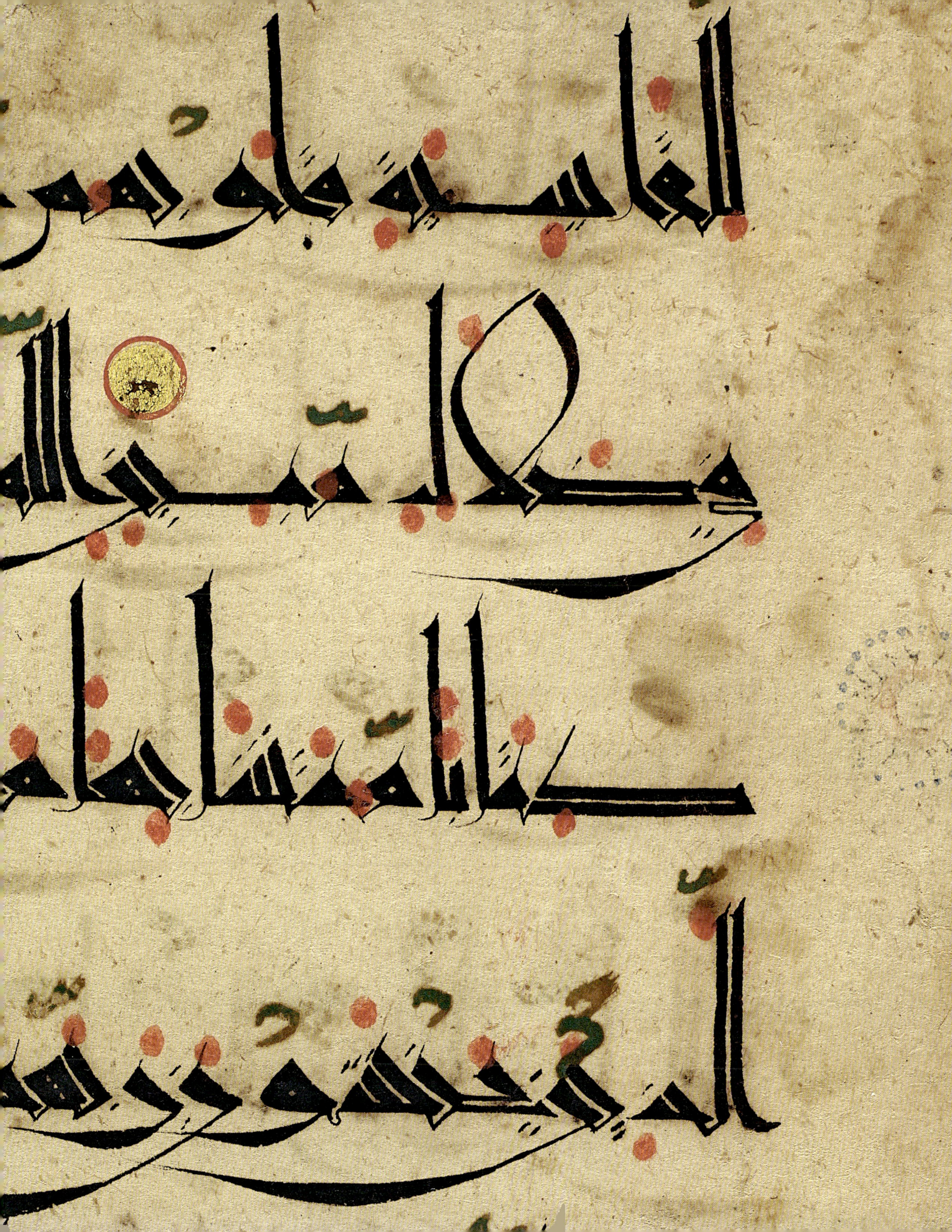

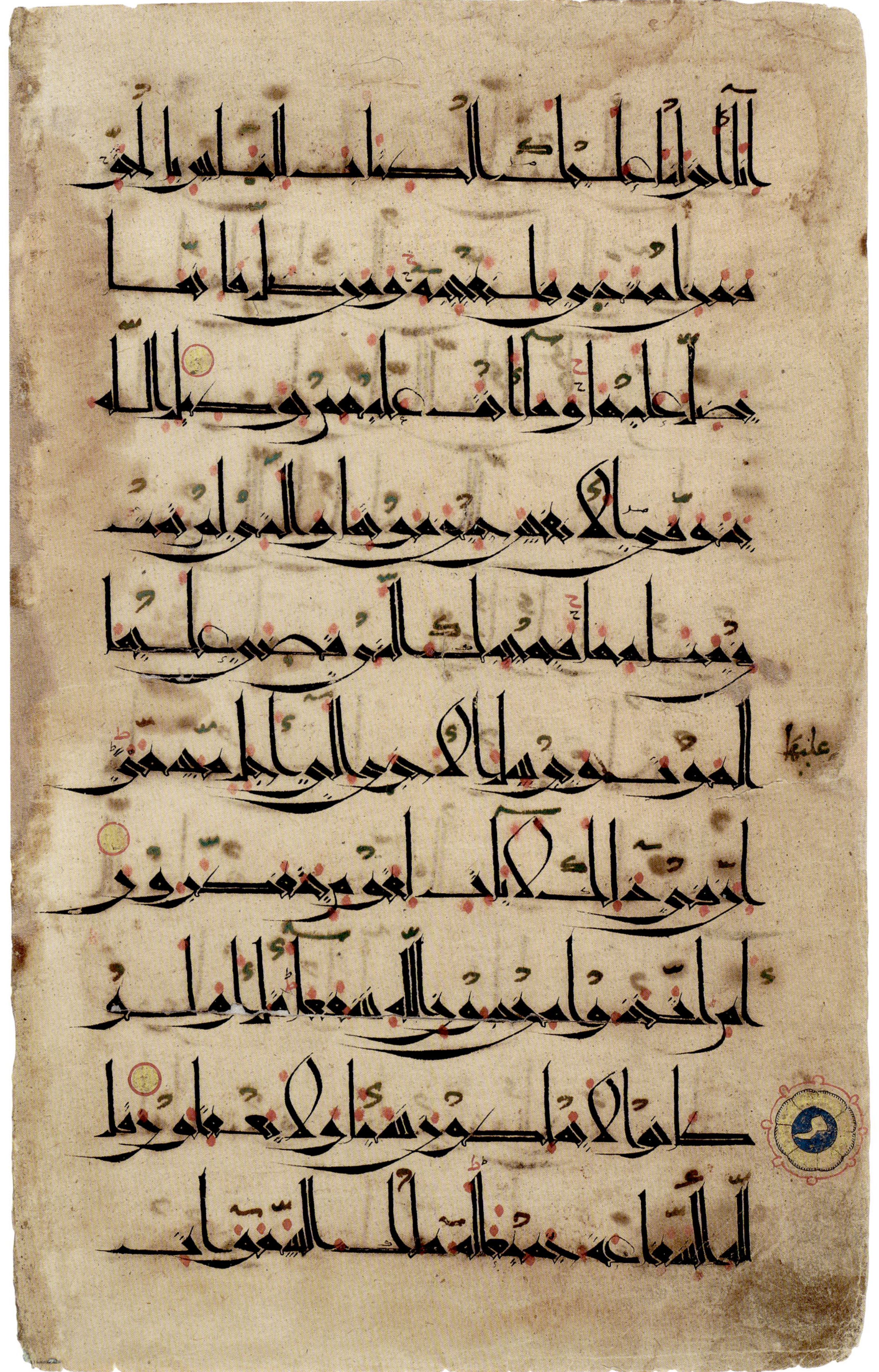

Cat. 30: Side B

30

Folio from a Qur'an Manuscript

Eastern Islamic Lands, 12th century
Ink, opaque watercolor, and gold on paper
Overall: 22 1/16 × 16 1/8 inches (56 × 41 cm); 10 lines
Side A: sura 39, *al-Zumar* (The Small Groups), verses 37–40
Side B: sura 39, *al-Zumar* (The Small Groups), verses 41–44
Text copied in Eastern Kufic in black ink; vocalization in red dots; black lines for vowels *fatha* and *kasra*, green shapes for the vowel *damma*, double consonant (*shadda*), and silence (*sukun*); variety of verse markers and counters composed as gold disks outlined with red and as rosettes of gold with brown with blue dots or red outlines.
TR:808-2015

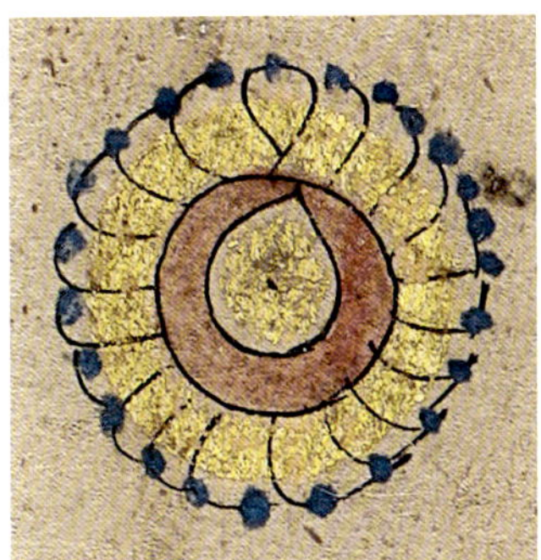

Detail of verse marker

31 (*see following pages*)

Two Folios from a Qur'an Manuscript

Eastern Islamic Lands, 12th century
Ink, opaque watercolor, and gold on paper
Each folio 11 × 7 1/4 inches (27.9 × 18.4 cm); 10 lines
Folio 1, side A: sura 36, *Ya' Sin* (Ya Sin), verses 18–27
Folio 1, side B: sura 36, *Ya' Sin* (Ya Sin), verses 27–34
Folio 2, side A: sura 38, *Sad* (Sad), verses 22–26
Folio 2, side B: sura 38, *Sad* (Sad), verses 26–29
Text copied in Eastern Kufic in black ink; vocalization in red dots; black lines for vowels *fatha* and *kasra*, green shapes for the vowel *damma*, double consonant (*shadda*), and silence (*sukun*); variety of verse markers and counters composed as gold disks outlined with red and as rosettes of gold with brown with blue dots or red outlines; folios set in paper borders.
TR:1651-2015

Following pages: Cat. 31: Folio 1, side A and folio 2, side B

أليم قالوا طائركم معكم أئن ذكرتم

بل أنتم قوم مسرفون وجاء من أقصا المدينة

رجل يسعى قال يا قوم اتبعوا المرسلين

اتبعوا من لا يسألكم أجرا وهم مهتدون

وما لي لا أعبد الذي فطرني وإليه

ترجعون أأتخذ من دونه آلهة إن يردن الرحمن

بضر لا تغن عني شفاعتهم شيئا ولا ينقذون

إني إذا لفي ضلال مبين إني آمنت

بربكم فاسمعون قيل ادخل الجنة قال يا

ليت قومي يعلمون بما غفر لي ربي وجعلني

فاحكم بين الناس بالحق ولا تتبع الهوى

فيضلك عن سبيل الله ان الذين يضلون

عن سبيل الله لهم عذاب شديد بما نسوا

يوم الحساب وما خلقنا السماء والارض

وما بينهما باطلا ذلك ظن الذين

كفروا فويل للذين كفروا من النار

ام نجعل الذين امنوا وعملوا الصالحات

كالمفسدين في الارض ام نجعل

المتقين كالفجار كتاب انزلنه اليك

مبارك ليدبروا ءايته وليتذكر

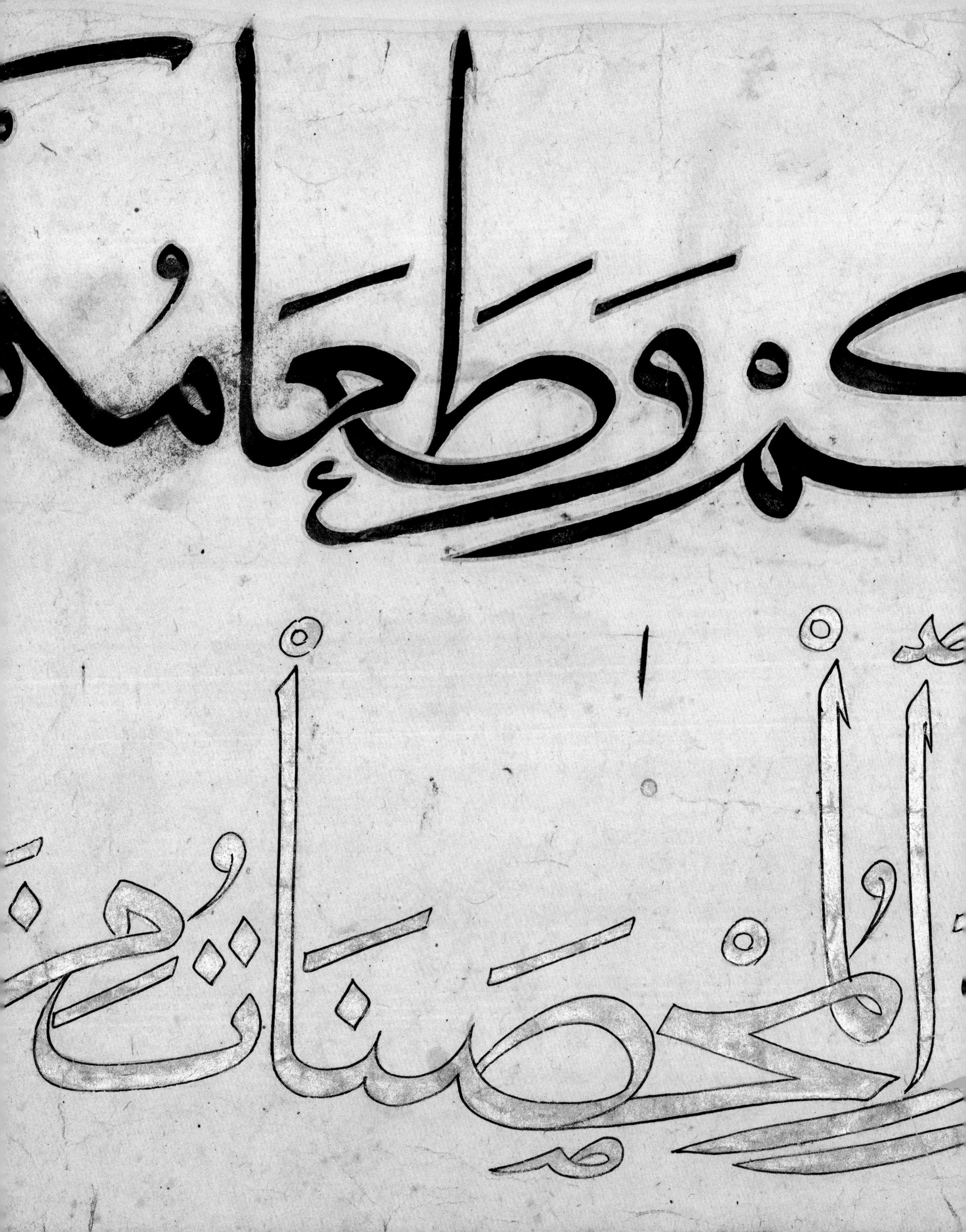

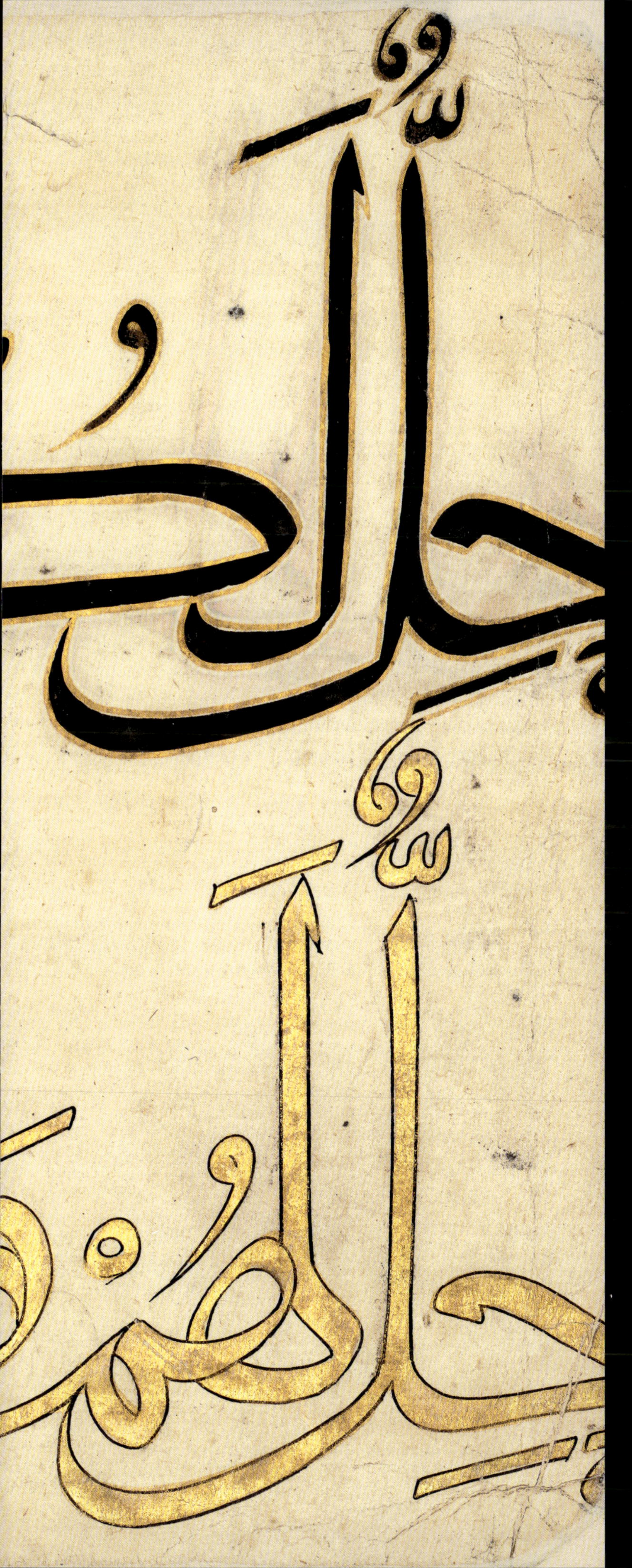

CODIFICATION

13TH–16TH CENTURY

CODIFICATION, 13TH–16TH CENTURY

With the steady ascent of the "six scripts/pens," and their supplanting what had come before, emerged another uniformity in the scribal practices of copying the Qur'an. The steady refinement of the canonical six scripts, attributed to Ibn Muqla (d. 940 CE), beautified by Ibn al-Bawwab (d. 1022 CE), and further perfected by Yaqut al-Musta'simi (d. c. 1298 CE)—a sequence of master calligraphers reiterated by numerous contemporary writers on the history of Islamic calligraphy in Arabic, Persian, and Turkish—resulted in their codification and specific applications.[12] Qur'ans were most commonly copied in *naskh* or *muhaqqaq* with *thuluth* reserved for titles. Kufic continued to be used as a script of the most venerable heritage but was confined to illuminated chapter headings, a highly circumscribed use compared against the extensive application of the repertoire of cursive scripts. The presence of Kufic instantiated a trace of the Qur'an's historical production within its matrix—another mode of self-referentiality—and was perhaps connected to a history remembered between the thirteenth through sixteenth centuries and most palpably expressed in references to extant specimens of "Kufi" calligraphed by the likes of 'Ali b. Abi Talib (d. 661 CE) and his descendants.[13]

The enhanced legibility of the six scripts, particularly due to their consistent habits of orthography, and their capacity for denser coverage on a single folio without compromising clarity, made the possibility of producing a Qur'an as a single volume easily attainable. This had important implications: it was now increasingly possible for a much broader clientele, though certainly still buyers of means, to acquire personal copies of the sacred book. That noted, it is also the case that multipart Qur'ans continued to be made in large-sized formats of paper with extensive programs of complex, elaborate illumination, particularly as endowed gifts to religious institutions—especially mosques and madrasas—constituting a form of inalienable property.[14] Some of the most astonishing examples of the Qur'an were made between the thirteenth and sixteenth centuries under imperial sponsorship by rulers and elite courtly patrons of the Mamluk, Ilkhanid, Jalayirid, Timurid, Ottoman, and Safavid dynasties and produced in workshops in Baghdad, Cairo, Herat, Istanbul, Tabriz, Samarkand, and Shiraz, with the most eminent calligraphers and illuminators of the age hired to do the work.[15] In addition to a mode of production supported by royal patrons, there was also a bookmaking industry, speculative in nature, that provided manuscripts of the Qur'an as a commodity to non-royal classes of individuals.

An increasing emphasis on calligraphic authorship—especially calligraphers connected by pedagogical lineages to venerated masters—was accompanied by growing specialization in the skills required to make fine copies of the Qur'an, ranging from illuminators to rulers to binders, and by an emphasis on the high quality of raw and prepared materials sourced from diverse regions of the Islamic world. The material ecology of the art of the Qur'an—and the arts of the book generally—acquired a distinctive prominence in the period between the thirteenth and sixteenth centuries, for example, the high-quality papers produced in Baghdad and Samarqand. Ever narrowing specialization was joined by an elaboration of materials, their application, and their resulting effects.

The text of the Qur'an might be transcribed or produced in alternating sizes of script or in different colors of ink and gold or other metals over plain or colored papers. Papers could also be adorned with gold sprinkling and the unit of the bifolio, now not merely a single sheet of paper folded along its middle but assembled from texts carrying writing set inside margins. Such new forms of embellishment, reflecting the skills and imagination of their makers, responded to aesthetic priorities and predilections and established a new benchmark of refinement that was simply different from the values of earlier historical periods but inherently no better than them.

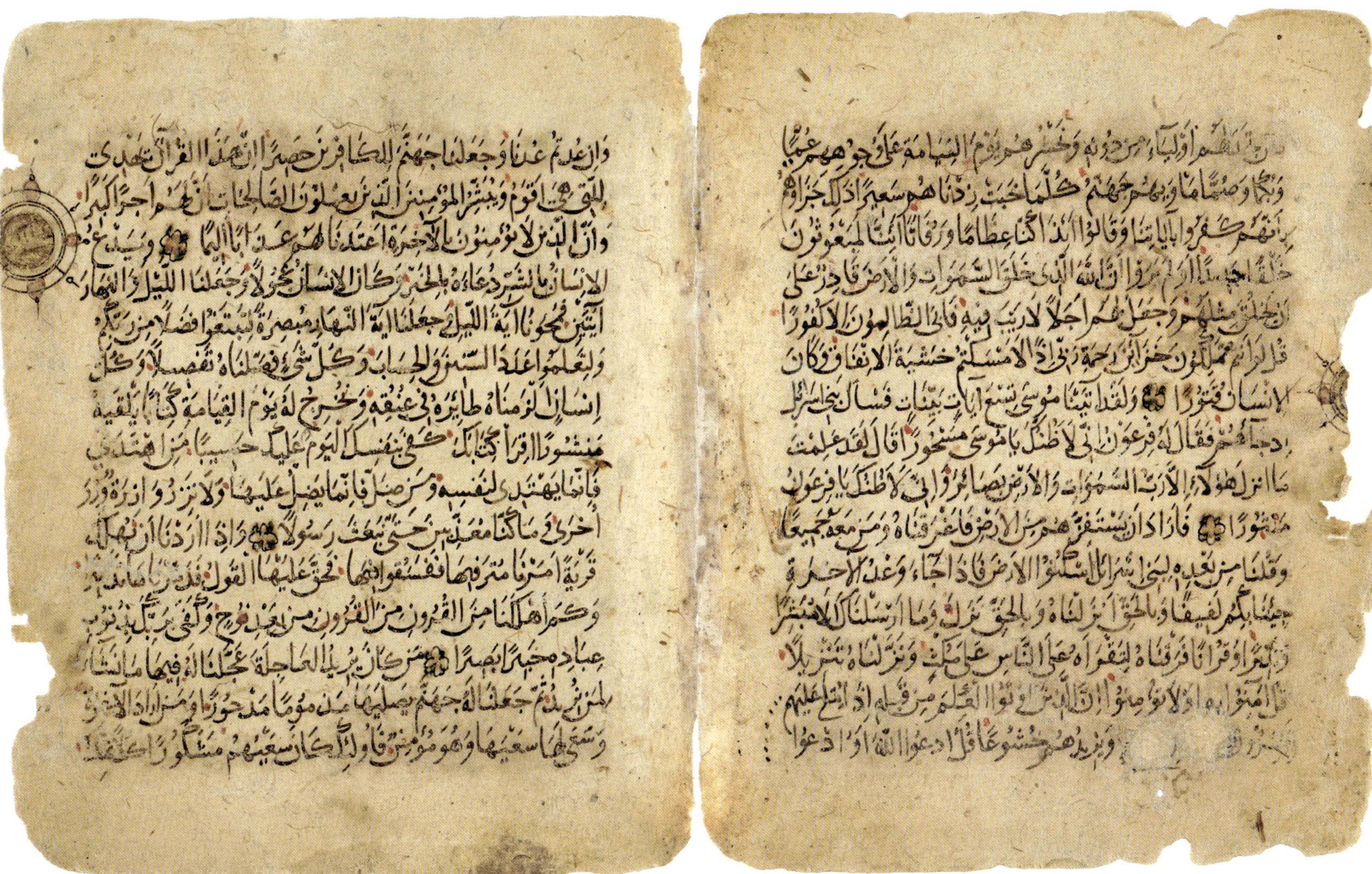

Folio 1, side A

Folio 2, side B

32

Bifolio from a Qur'an Manuscript

Iran or Iraq, 12th–13th century
Ink and opaque watercolor on paper
Overall: 11 × 7 7/8 inches (28 × 20 cm); 15 lines
Folio 1, side A: sura 17, *al-Isra'* (The Night Journey), verses 8–19
Folio 1, side B: sura 17, *al-Isra'* (The Night Journey), verses 20–33
Folio 2, side A: sura 17, *al-Isra'* (The Night Journey), verses 83–97
Folio 2, side B: sura 17, *al-Isra'* (The Night Journey), verses 97–110
Text copied in *naskh* script in brown-black ink; vocalization and letter-pointing in black; verse markers (gold quatrefoil with blue dots) and counters (gold disk set in concentric circles drawn in black with rays, some augmented with gold ovals).
TR:814-2015

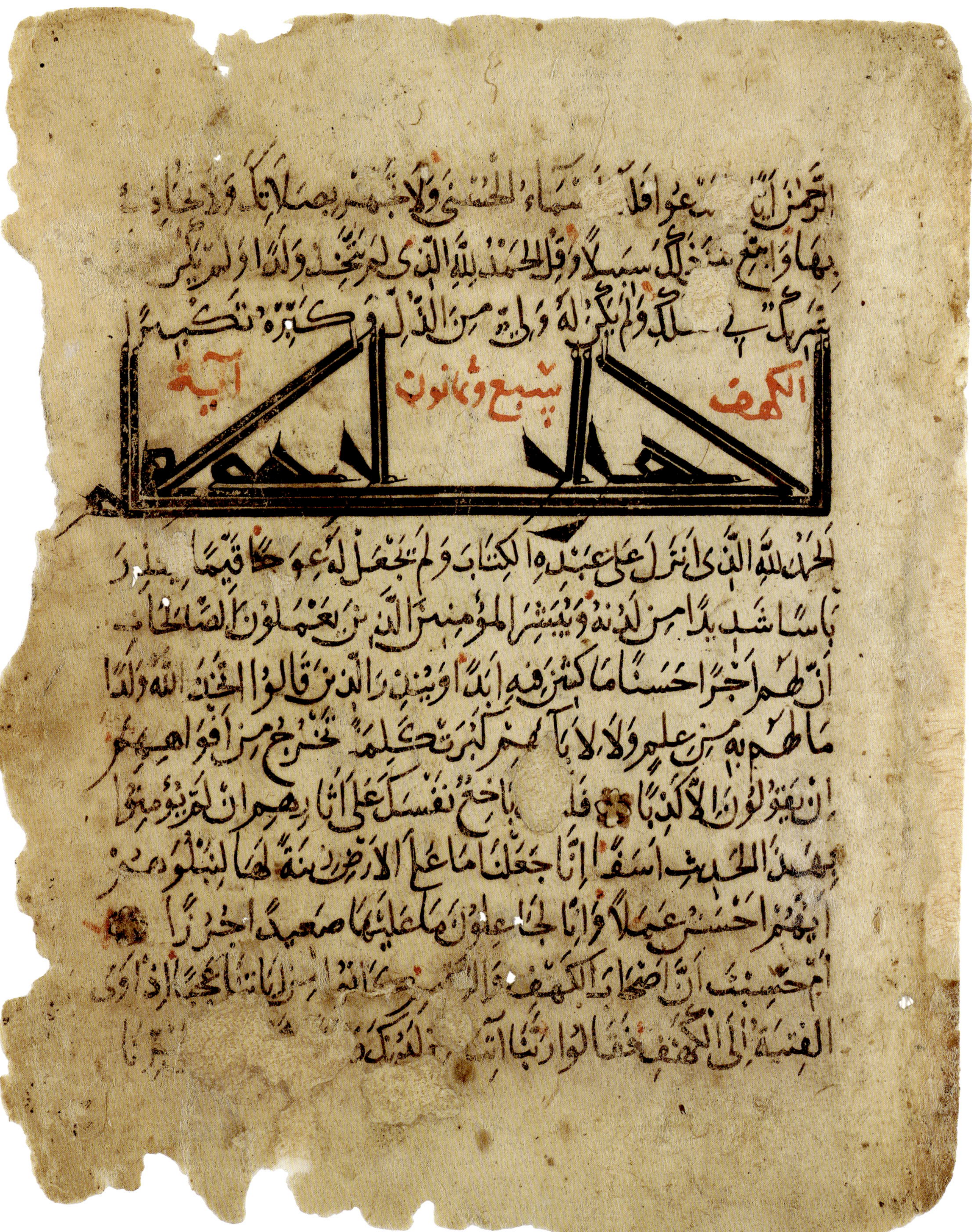

Cat. 33: Side A

33

Folio from a Qur'an Manuscript

Iran or Iraq, 12th–13th century
Ink and opaque watercolor on paper
Overall: 11 × 7 7/8 inches (28 × 20 cm); 15 lines
Side A: sura 17, *al-Isra'* (The Night Journey), verses 110–11–sura 18, *al-Kahf* (The Cave), verses 1–10
Side B: sura 18, *al-Kahf* (The Cave), verses 11–19
Text copied in *naskh* script; verse markers; side A has a chapter heading composed of the sura's name and number of verses (87) written in red ink with the *basmala* for the chapter in black Kufic script.
TR:816-2015

34

Two Folios from a Qur'an Manuscript

Iran or Iraq, 12th–13th century
Ink and opaque watercolor on paper
Overall: 11 × 7 7/8 inches (28 × 20 cm); 15 lines
Folio 1, side A: sura 17, *al-Isra'* (The Night Journey), verses 33–47
Folio 1, side B: sura 17, *al-Isra'* (The Night Journey), verses 47–58
Folio 2, side A: sura 17, *al-Isra'* (The Night Journey), verses 59–69
Folio 2, side B: sura 17, *al-Isra'* (The Night Journey), verses 69–92
Text copied in *naskh* script in brown-black ink; vocalization and letter-pointing in black; verse markers (gold quatrefoil with blue dots) and counters (gold disk set in concentric circles drawn in black with rays, some augmented with gold ovals).
TR:815-2015

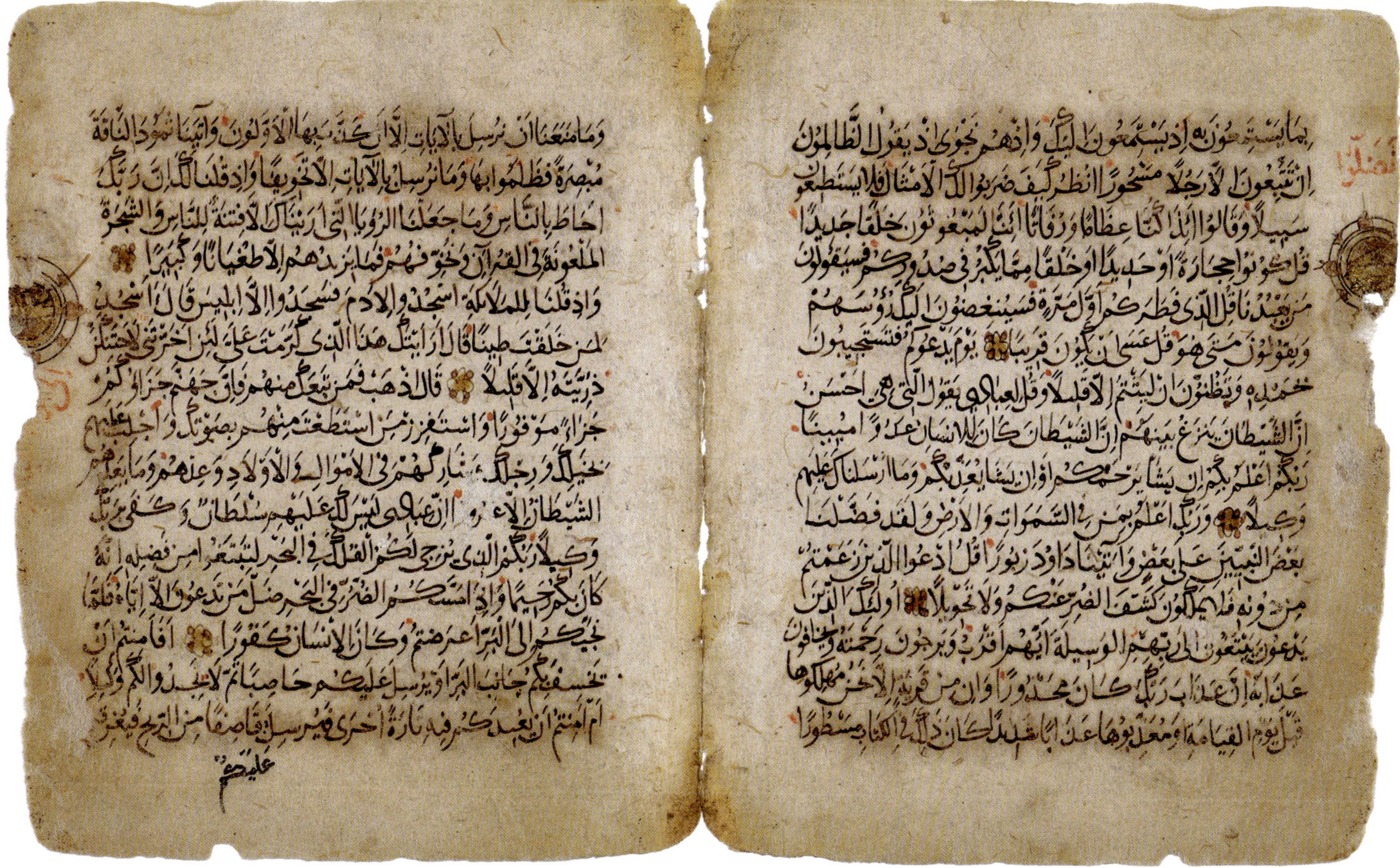

Cat. 34: Folio 2, side A

Cat. 34: Folio 1, side B

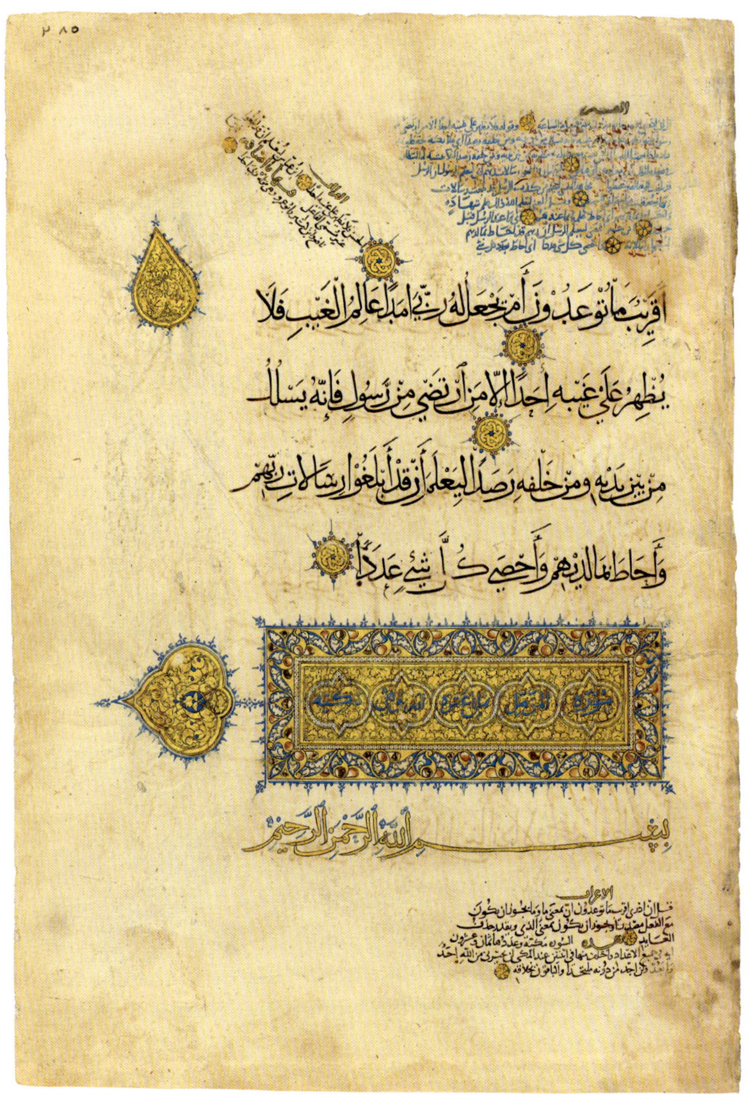

Side A

35

Folio from a Qur'an Manuscript

Egypt, probably Cairo, late 13th–early 14th century
Ink, opaque watercolor, and gold on paper
Overall: 13 3/8 × 19 3/16 inches (34 × 48.8 cm); 7 lines
Side A: sura 72, *al-Jinn* (The Jinns), verses 25–28–illuminated chapter heading for sura 73, *al-Muzzammil* (The Enwrapped), *basmala*
Side B: sura 73, *al-Muzzammil* (The Enwrapped), verses 1–13
Text copied in *muhaqqaq* script in black ink; illuminated verse markers (gold disks with knotted motifs encircled by blue and brown dots) and counters (tear drops and disks in gold with motifs and geometric figures drawn in black); chapter heading for sura 73 composed of rectangular box with cusped medallion finial; ground of box provides sura name—divided into five sections each in a cartouche—in blue *muhaqqaq* over gold ground enclosed by floriate border in gold, lapis lazuli, and brown, with lapis lazuli rays around outer edge; marginal notations in *naskh* script, contemporary to the Qur'an's production, on both sides A and B—in red, black, and blue inks—provide commentaries on aspects of interpretation (*tafsir*), including grammar, meaning, and reading.
TR:306-2015.A, .B

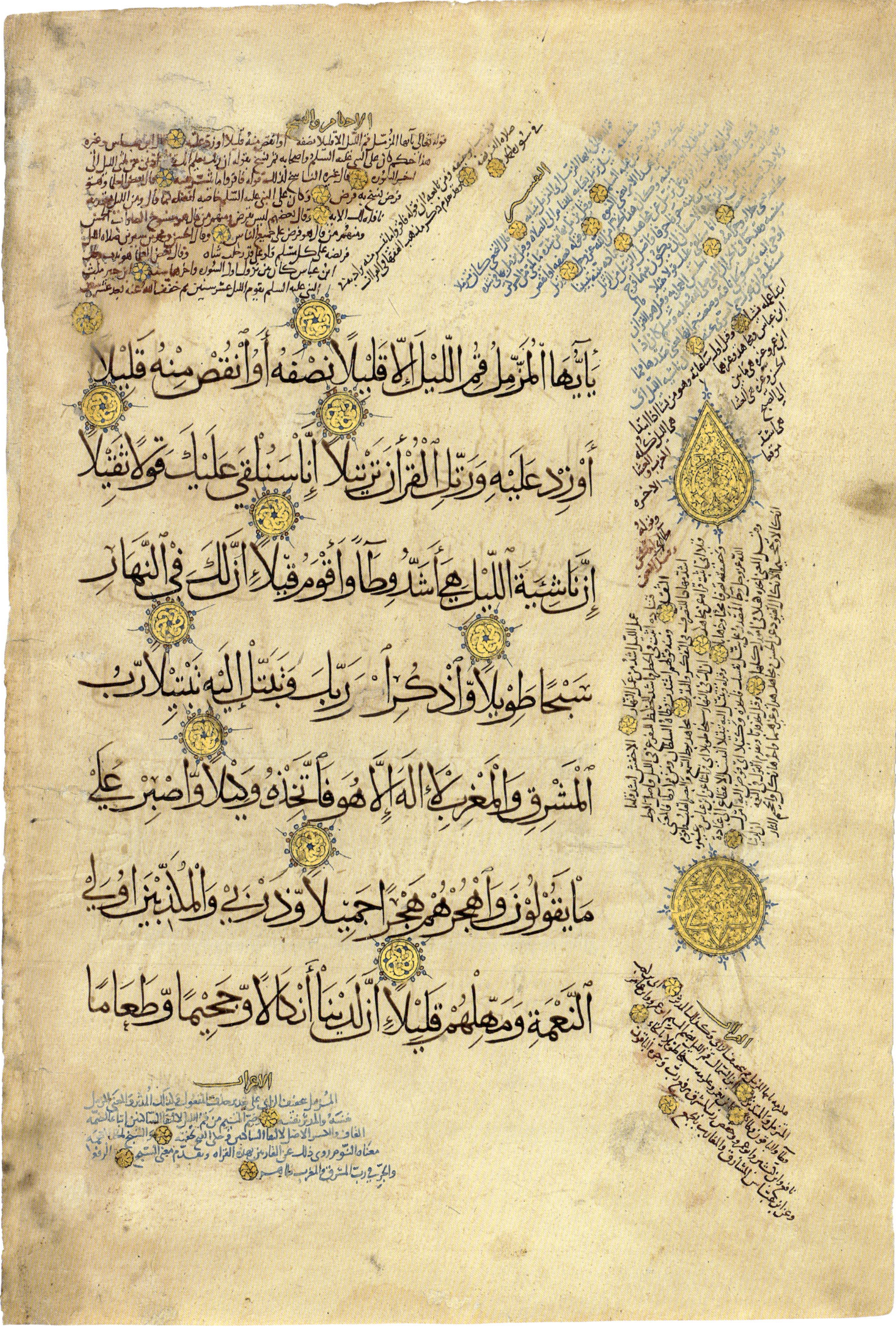

يا أيها المزمل قم الليل إلا قليلا نصفه أو انقص منه قليلا
أو زد عليه ورتل القرآن ترتيلا إنا سنلقي عليك قولا ثقيلا
إن ناشئة الليل هي أشد وطأ وأقوم قيلا إن لك في النهار
سبحا طويلا واذكر اسم ربك وتبتل إليه تبتيلا رب
المشرق والمغرب لا إله إلا هو فاتخذه وكيلا واصبر على
ما يقولون واهجرهم هجرا جميلا وذرني والمكذبين أولي
النعمة ومهلهم قليلا إن لدينا أنكالا وجحيما وطعاما

Side B

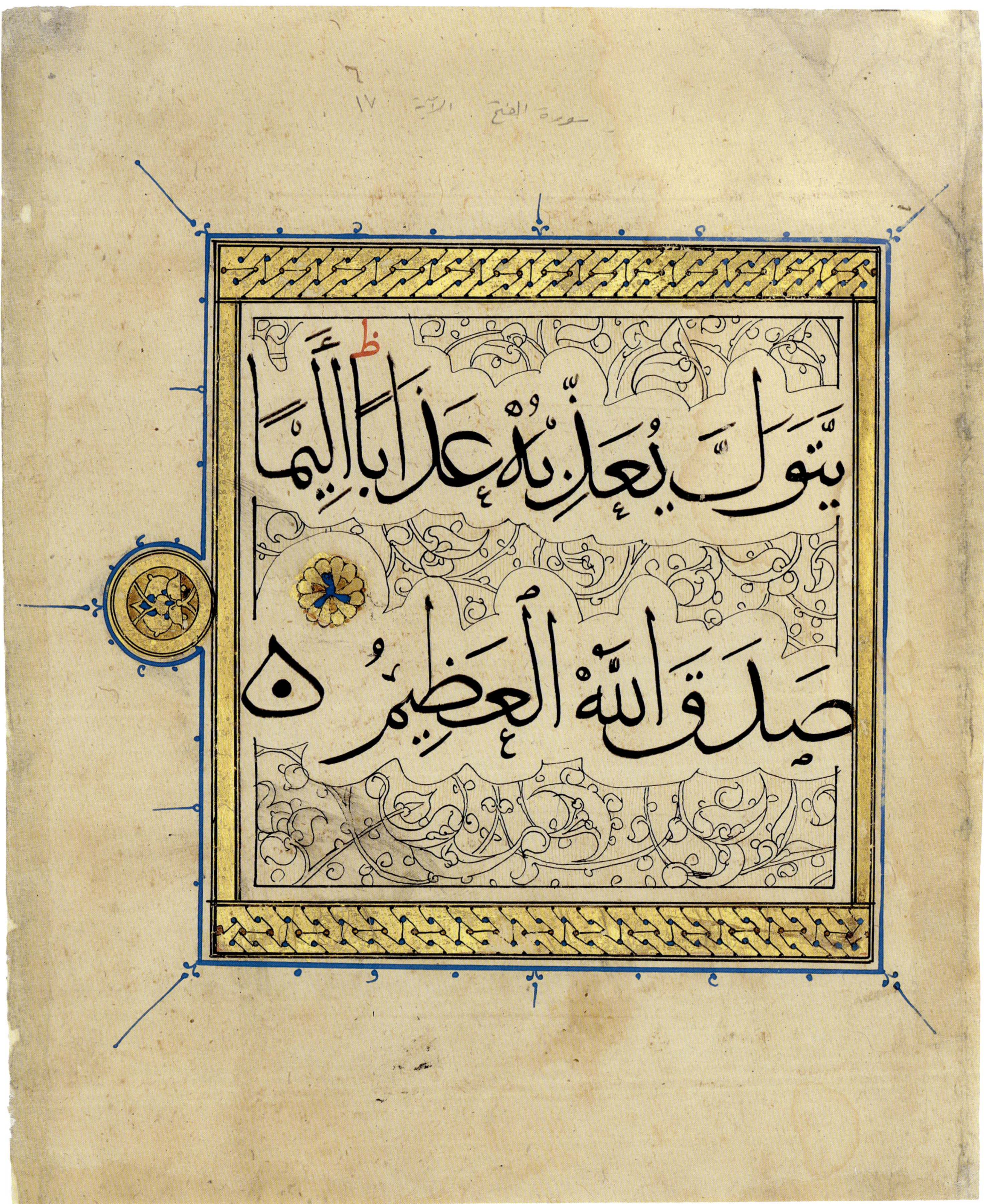

Cat. 36: Side A

36

Folio from the Twenty-Sixth Part (*Juz'*) of a Qur'an Manuscript

Egypt, 14th century
Ink, opaque watercolor, and gold on paper
Overall: 9 1/8 × 7 1/2 inches (23.2 × 19 cm); 2 lines
Side A: sura 48, *al-Fath* (The Victory), end of verse 17 followed by "the Almighty God speaks the truth" (*sadaqa Allah al-'azim*), a formula typically used to mark the end of a Qur'anic quotation
Side B: blank
Text copied in *thuluth* script in black ink amid cloudbands of reserved paper; the ground an arabesque of palmettes and split palmettes in black ink set over hatching in brown; vocalization and letter-pointing in black ink; verse marker (gold rosette with blue and red center); enclosed in a golden frame with an attached medallion, all in gold with blue and red, and an outer line and rays in lapis lazuli; the folio is the last of the first half (*hizb*) of the twenty-sixth part (*juz'*) of the Qur'an.
TR:384-2015

37 (*see following pages*)

Folio from a Thirty-Part Qur'an Manuscript

Anatolia, Iran, or Central Asia, early to mid-14th century
Ink, opaque watercolor, and gold on paper
Overall: 11 5/16 × 7 3/8 inches (28.8 × 18.8 cm); 3 lines
Side A: sura 5, *al-Ma'ida* (The Feast), part of verse 52, with interlinear Persian translation
Side B: sura 5, *al-Ma'ida* (The Feast), part of verse 52, with interlinear Persian translation
Text copied in *muhaqqaq* script with interlinear text in *naskh* script (both in black ink); vocalization and letter-pointing in black ink; illuminated verse markers (gold rosettes); decorative borders framing the text, on both sides A and B, along upper, lower, and outer sides are later additions and comprise knotted motifs and texts (of traditions of the Prophet Muhammad [*hadith*] and exegesis [*tafsir*]) in red and blue Kufic script over golden floral scrolls.
TR:940-2015.A,.B

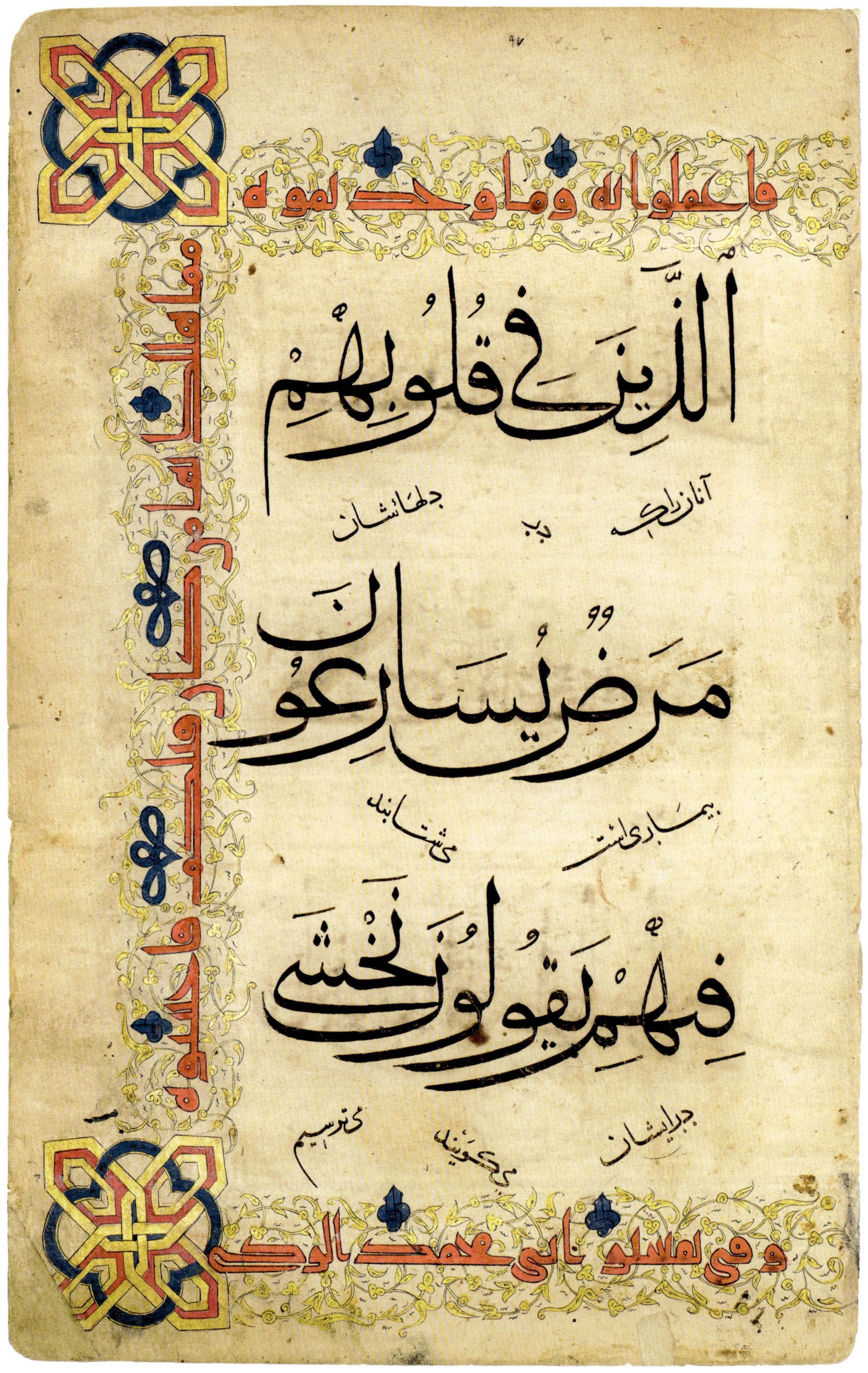

Cat. 37: Side A

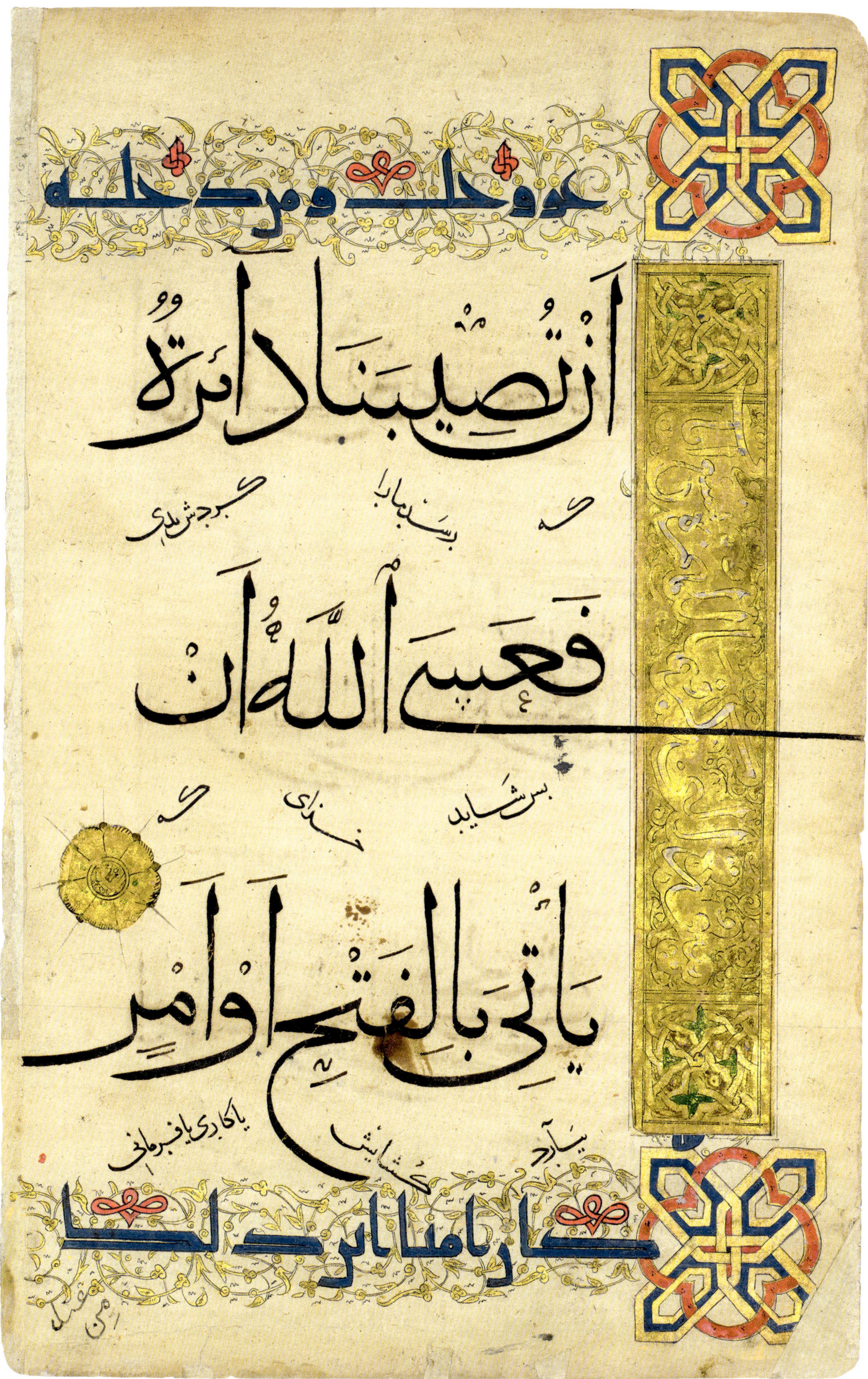

Cat. 37: Side B

38

Lines from a Qur'an Manuscript

Calligraphy attributed to Ahmad b. al-Shaykh al-Suhrawardi al-Bakri (d. 1320/21 CE)
Iraq, Baghdad, probably AH 707/1307–1308 CE
Ink and gold on paper
Calligraphy 1: 7 1/2 × 11 1/8 inches (19.1 × 28.3 cm)
Calligraphy 2: 7 5/8 × 11 3/8 inches (19.4 × 28.9 cm)
Overall: 22 × 16 inches (55.9 × 40.6 cm)
Calligraphy 1: sura 5, *al-Ma'ida* (The Feast), part of verse 4
Calligraphy 2: sura 5, *al-Ma'ida* (The Feast), part of verse 5
Text is copied in *muhaqqaq* script in alternating lines of black outlined with gold and gold outlined with black with matching vocalization and letter-pointing.
TR:506-2017

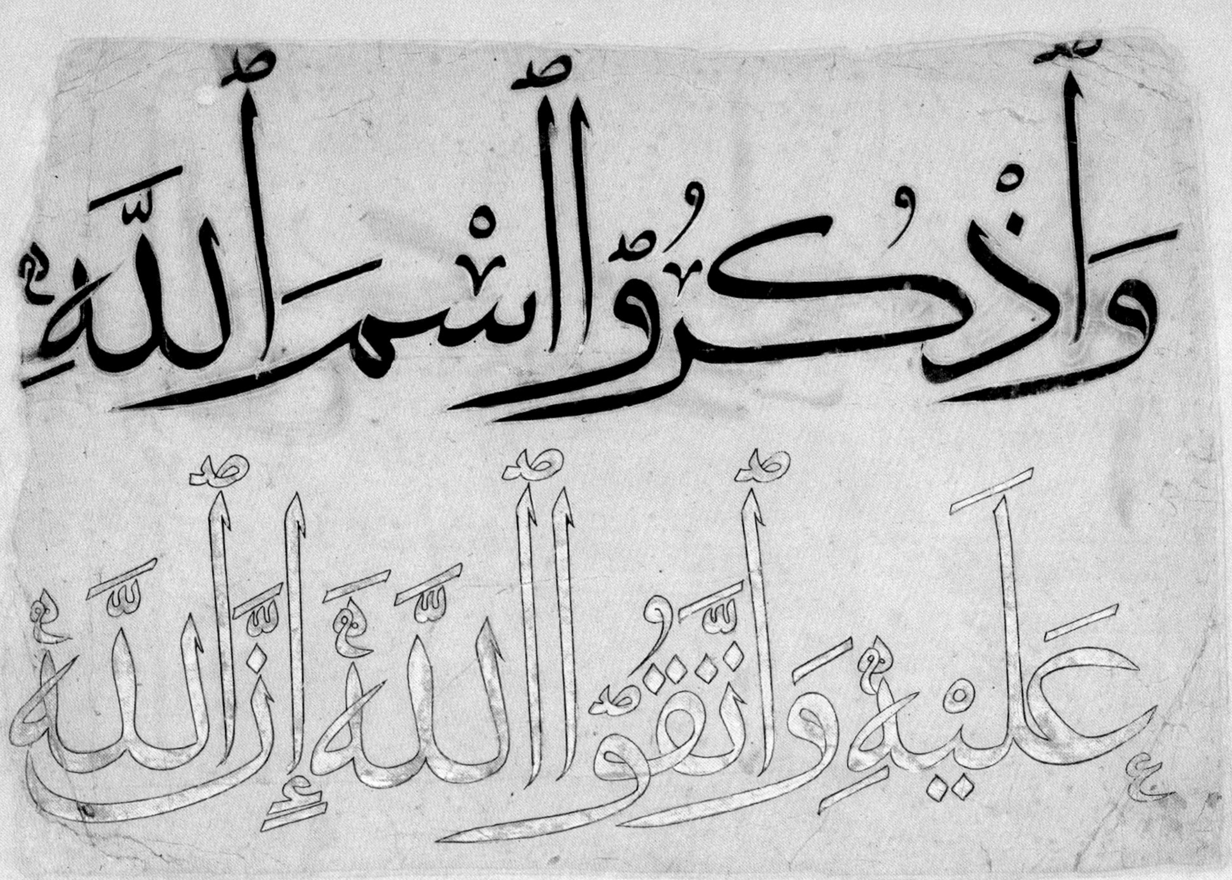
واذكروا اسم الله
عليه واتقوا الله إن الله

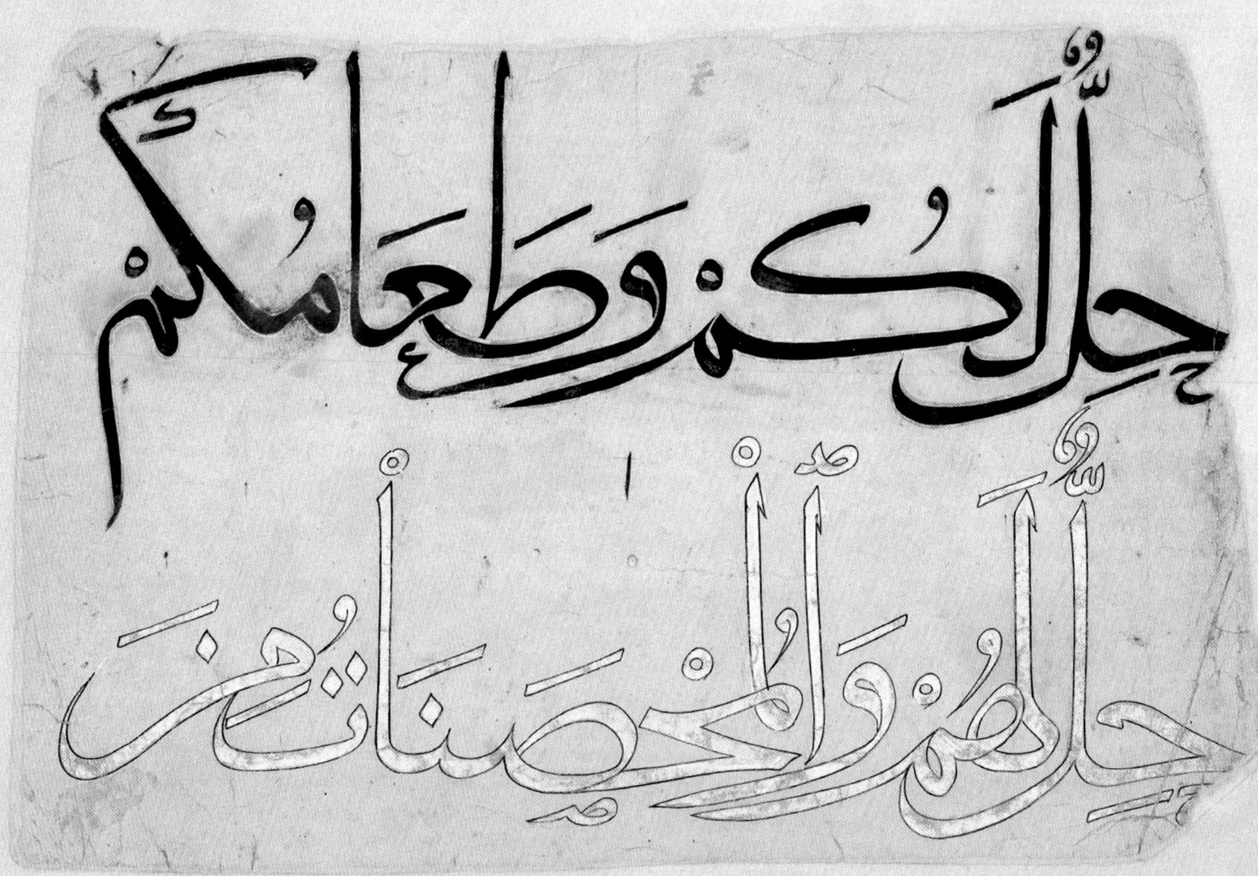
حل لكم وطعامكم
حل لهم والمحصنات

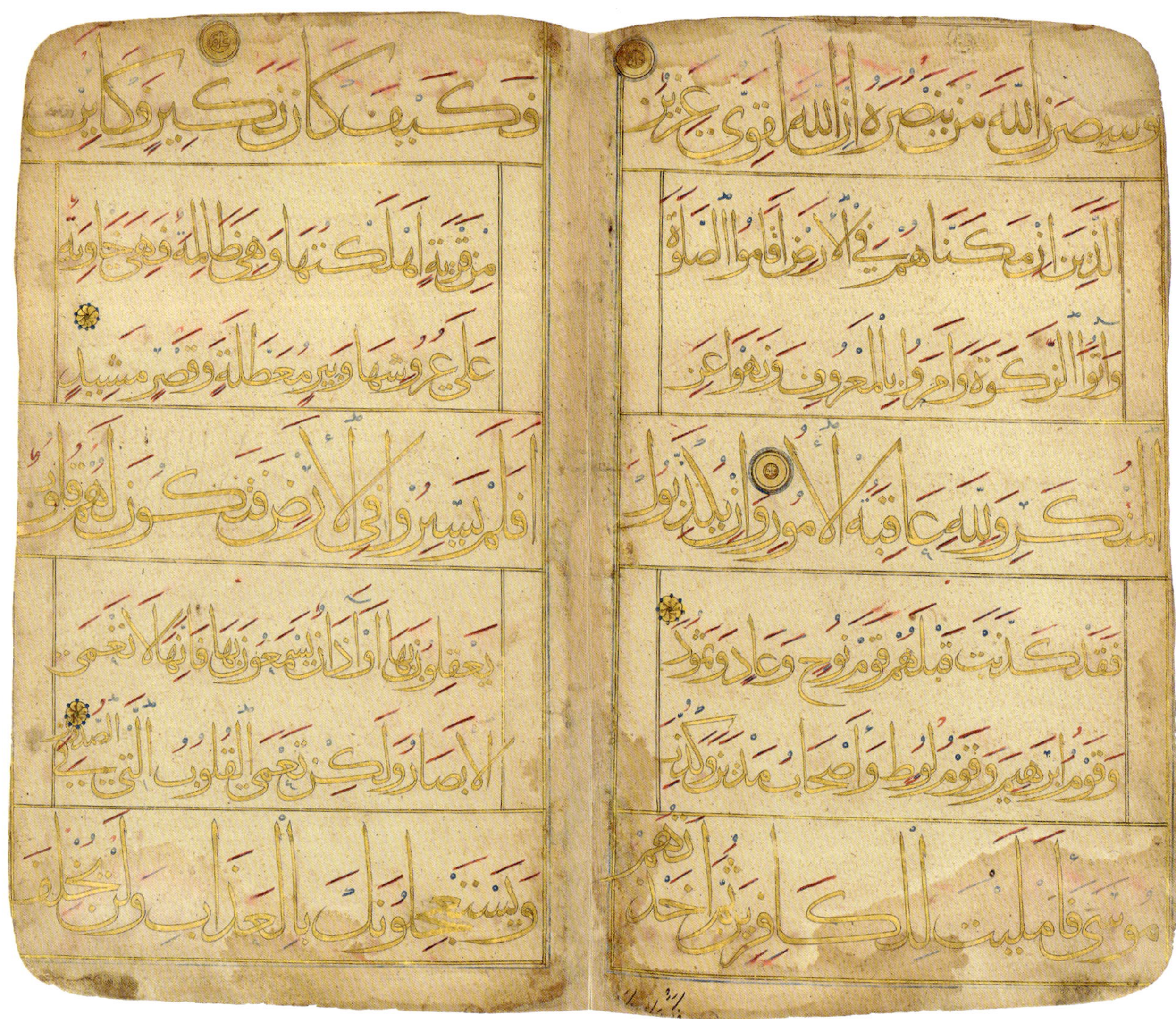

Folio 2, side A

Folio 1, side B

39

Bifolio from a Qur'an Manuscript

Iran, probably Shiraz, mid-14th century
Ink, opaque watercolor, and gold on paper
Open: 17 9/16 × 20 7/8 inches (44.6 × 53.1 cm)
Closed: 17 9/16 × 10 7/16 inches (44.6 × 26.5 cm); 7 lines
Folio 1, side A: sura 22, *al-Hajj* (The Pilgrimage), verses 37–40
Folio 1, side B: sura 22, *al-Hajj* (The Pilgrimage), verses 40–44
Folio 2, side A: sura 22, *al-Hajj* (The Pilgrimage), verses 44–47
Folio 2, side B: sura 22, *al-Hajj* (The Pilgrimage), verses 47–52
Text is copied in *muhaqqaq* script in gold outlined in black ink; vocalization in red and blue inks and letter-pointing in gold outlined in black; illuminated verse markers (rosettes with reddish brown and blue) and counters (gold disks with blue and reddish brown).
TR:387-2015

Opposite: Folio 2, detail of side B

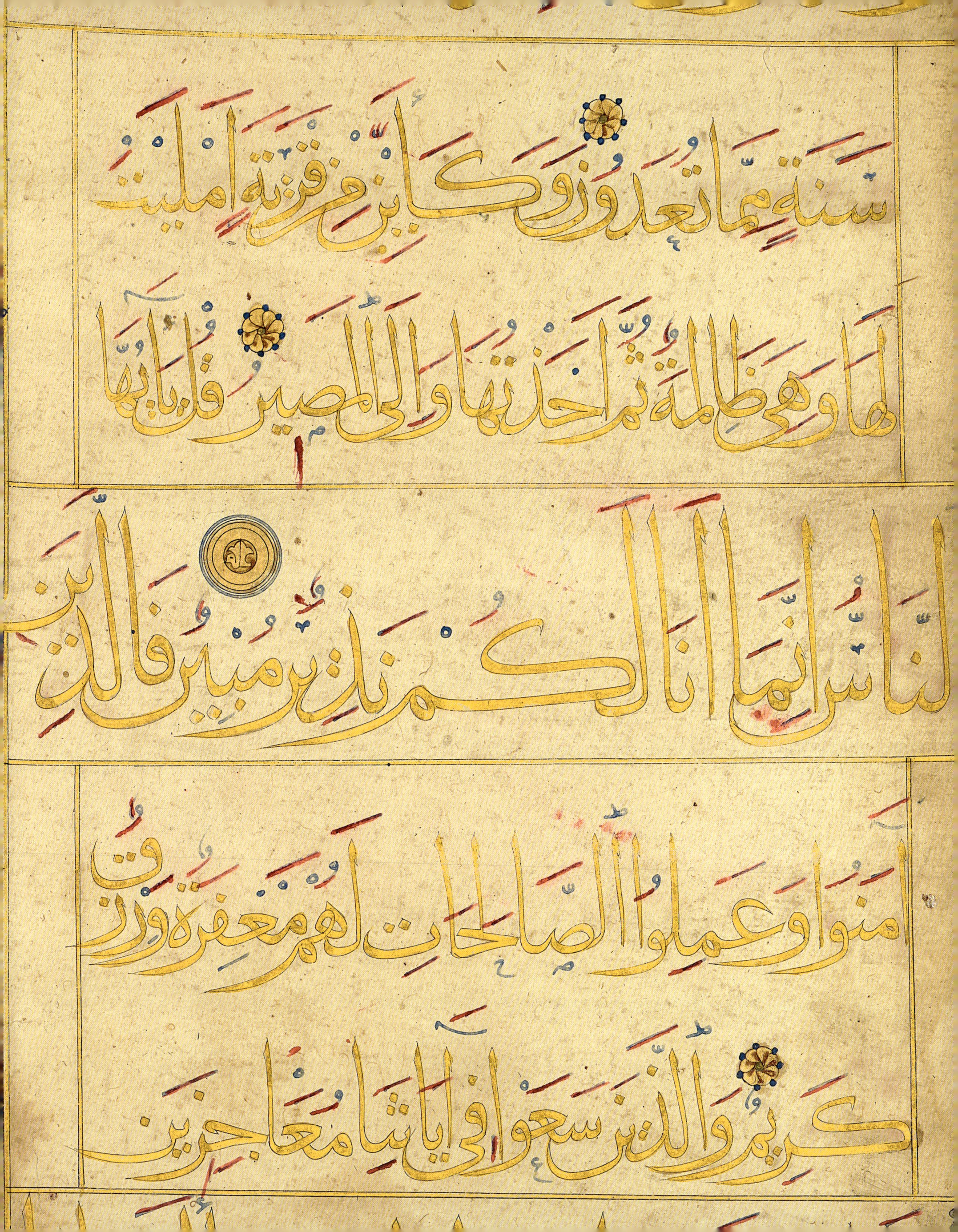
سنة مما تعدون وكأين من قرية أمليت
لها وهي ظالمة ثم أخذتها وإلى المصير قل يا أيها
الناس إنما أنا لكم نذير مبين فالذين
آمنوا وعملوا الصالحات لهم مغفرة ورزق
كريم والذين سعوا في آياتنا معاجزين

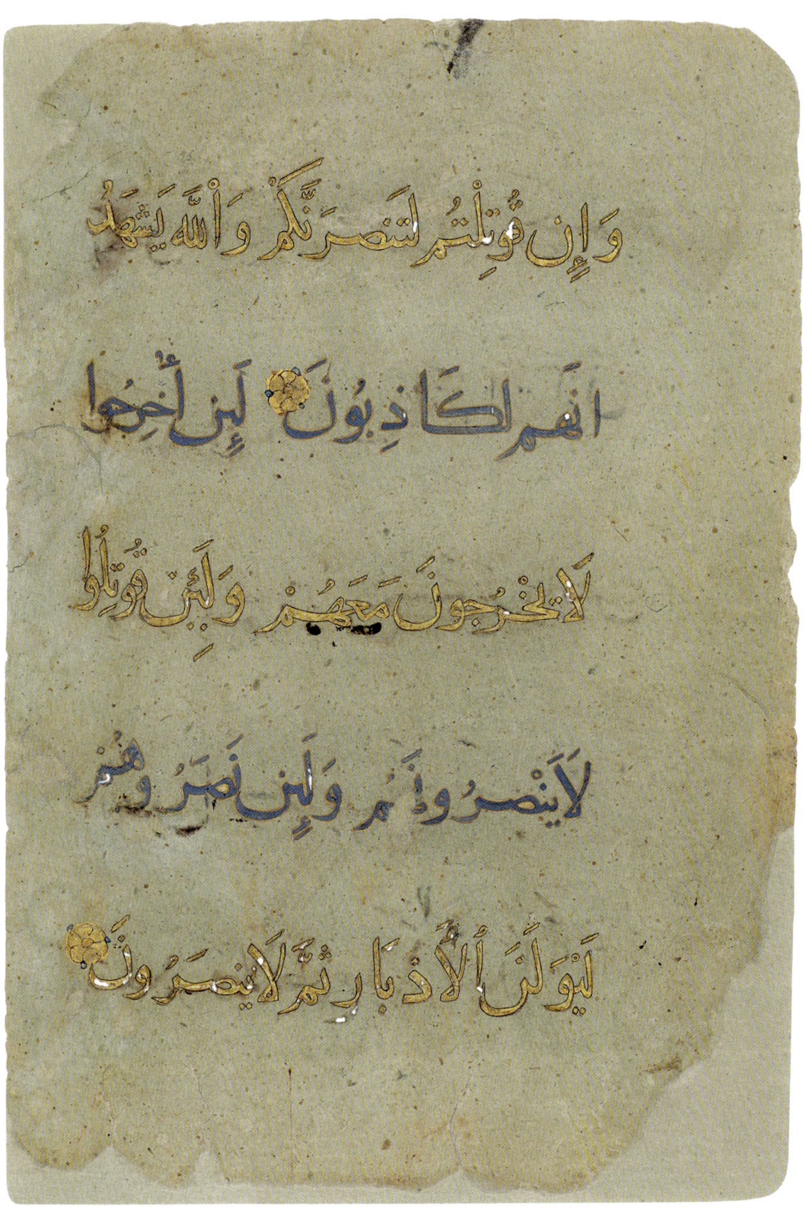

Cat. 40: Side B

40

Folio from a Qur'an Manuscript

Central Islamic Lands, 14th century
Ink, opaque watercolor, and gold on paper
Overall: 10 1/16 × 7 inches (25.5 × 17.7 cm); 5 lines
Side A: sura 59, *al-Hashr* (Confrontation), verses 10–11
Side B: sura 59, *al-Hashr* (Confrontation), verses 11–12
Text is copied in *naskh* script in alternating lines of gold outlined in black and blue outlined in gold with corresponding vocalization and letter-pointing; verse markers gold rosettes spotted with dots of blue and red.
TR:806-2015

41

Folio from a Qur'an Manuscript

Central Islamic Lands, 14th century
Ink, opaque watercolor, and gold on paper
9 13/16 × 7 1/16 inches (25 × 17.9 cm); 5 lines
Side A: sura 62, *al-Jumu'a* (The Congregation), verses 8–10
Side B: sura 62, *al-Jumu'a* (The Congregation), verses 10–11
Text is copied in *naskh* script in alternating lines of gold outlined in black and blue outlined in gold with corresponding vocalization and letter-pointing; verse markers gold rosettes spotted with dots of blue and red.
TR:401-2015

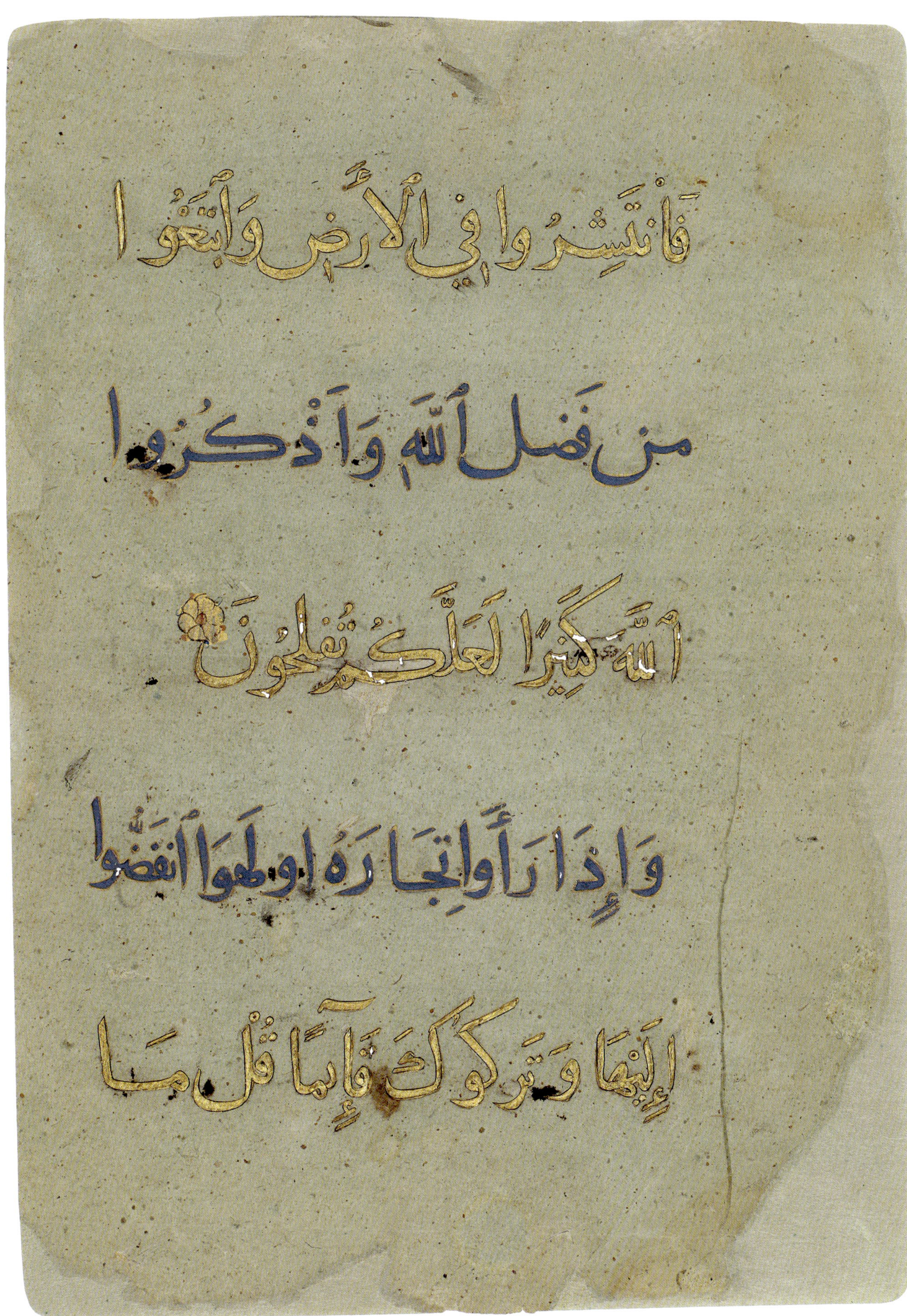

Cat. 41: Side B

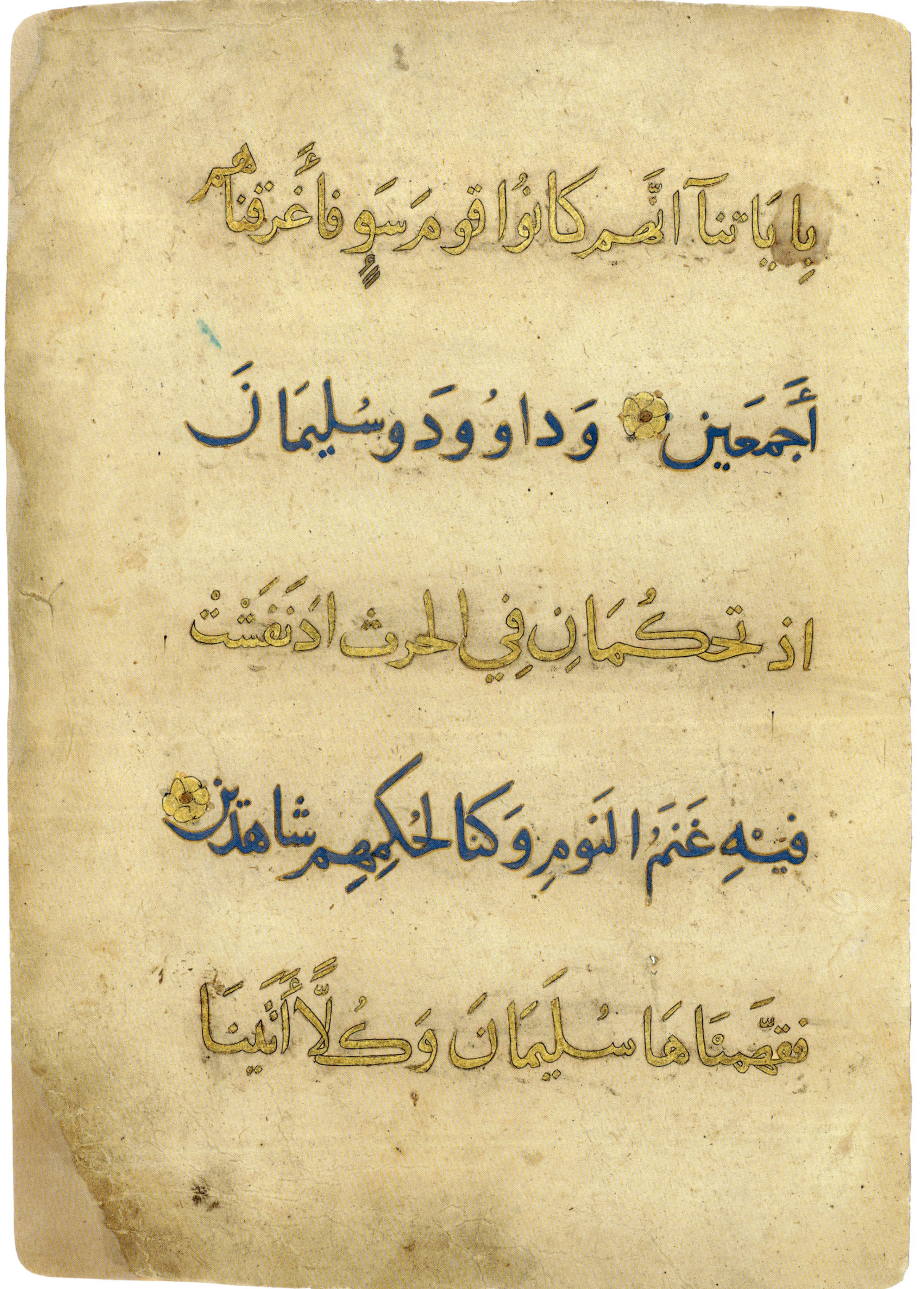
بآياتنا انهم كانوا قوم سوء فأغرقناهم
أجمعين ۝ وداود وسليمان
اذ يحكمان في الحرث اذ نفشت
فيه غنم القوم وكنا لحكمهم شاهدين ۝
ففهمناها سليمان وكلا آتينا

Cat. 42: Side A

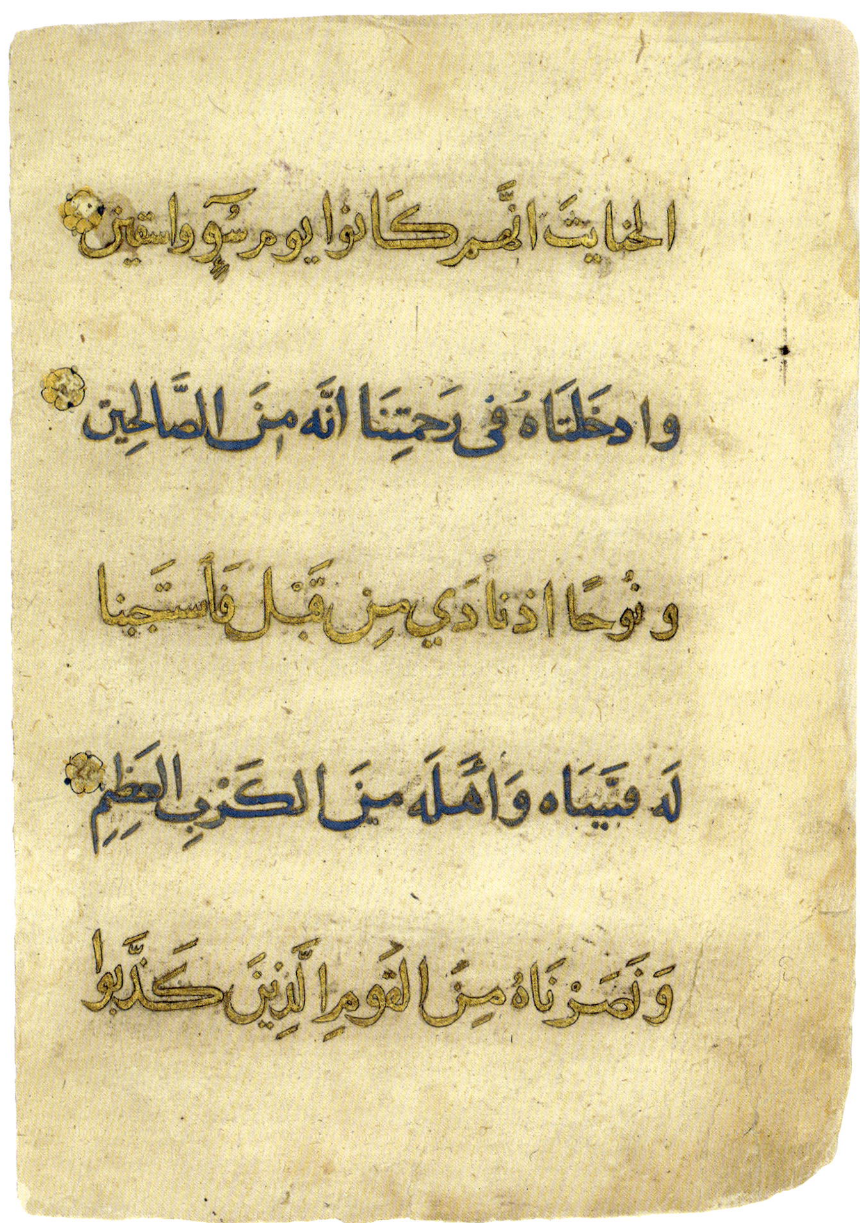

Cat. 43: Side B

42

Folio from a Qurʾan Manuscript

Central Islamic Lands, 14th century
Ink, opaque watercolor, and gold on paper
9 13/16 × 7 1/16 inches (25 × 18 cm); 5 lines
Side A: sura 21, *al-Anbiyaʾ* (The Prophets), verses 77–79
Side B: sura 21, *al-Anbiyaʾ* (The Prophets), verses 79–81
Text is copied in *naskh* script in alternating lines of gold outlined in black and blue outlined in gold with corresponding vocalization and letter-pointing; verse markers gold rosettes spotted with dots of blue and red.
TR:804-2015.A,.B

43

Folio from a Qurʾan Manuscript

Central Islamic Lands, 14th century
Ink, opaque watercolor, and gold on paper
9 13/16 × 7 1/16 in. (25 × 18 cm); 5 lines
Side A: sura 21, *al-Anbiyaʾ* (The Prophets), verses 73–74
Side B: sura 21, *al-Anbiyaʾ* (The Prophets), verses 74–77
Text is copied in *naskh* script in alternating lines of gold outlined in black and blue outlined in gold with corresponding vocalization and letter-pointing; verse markers gold rosettes spotted with dots of blue and red.
TR:803-2015.A,.B

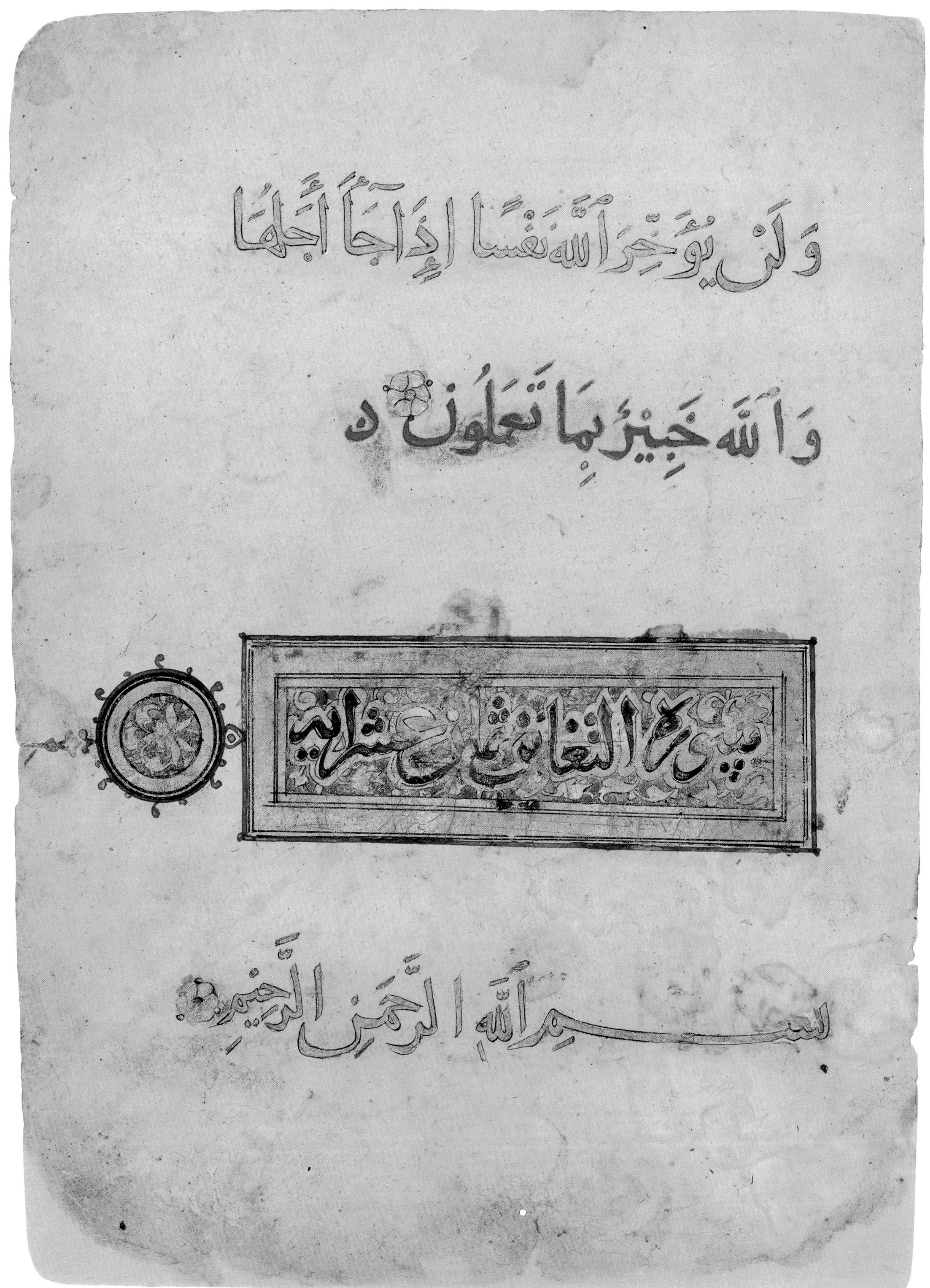
وَلَن يُؤَخِّرَ ٱللَّهُ نَفْسًا إِذَا جَآءَ أَجَلُهَا

وَٱللَّهُ خَبِيرٌۢ بِمَا تَعْمَلُونَ

سورة التغابن ثماني عشرة آية

بِسْمِ ٱللَّهِ ٱلرَّحْمَٰنِ ٱلرَّحِيمِ

Side A

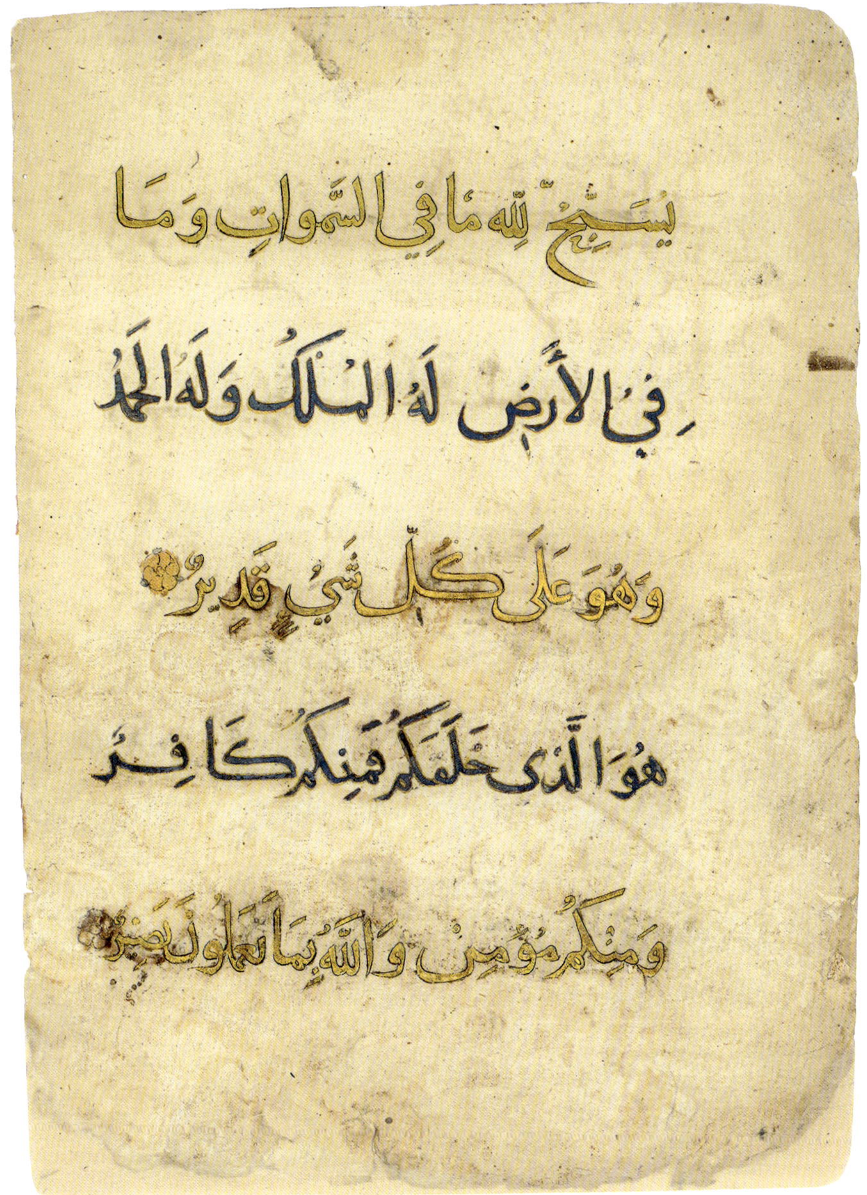
يسبح لله ما في السموات وما
في الأرض له الملك وله الحمد
وهو على كل شيء قدير
هو الذي خلقكم فمنكم كافر
ومنكم مؤمن والله بما تعملون بصير

Side B

44

Folio from a Qur'an Manuscript

Egypt or Iraq, 14th century
Ink, opaque watercolor, and gold on paper
10 1/8 × 7 3/8 inches (25.7 × 18.7 cm); 5 lines
Side A: sura 63, *al-Munafiqun* (The Hypocrites), verse 11–illuminated chapter heading for sura 64, *al-Taghabun* (Exposition) and *basmala*
Side B: sura 64, *al-Taghabun* (Exposition), verses 1–2
Text is copied in *naskh* script in alternating lines of gold outlined in black and blue outlined in gold with corresponding vocalization and letter-pointing; verse markers gold rosettes spotted with dots of blue and red; chapter heading for sura 64 (in *thuluth* script) composed of a rectangular panel with medallion in margin in palette of gold, lapis lazuli, and reddish brown.
TR:938-2015

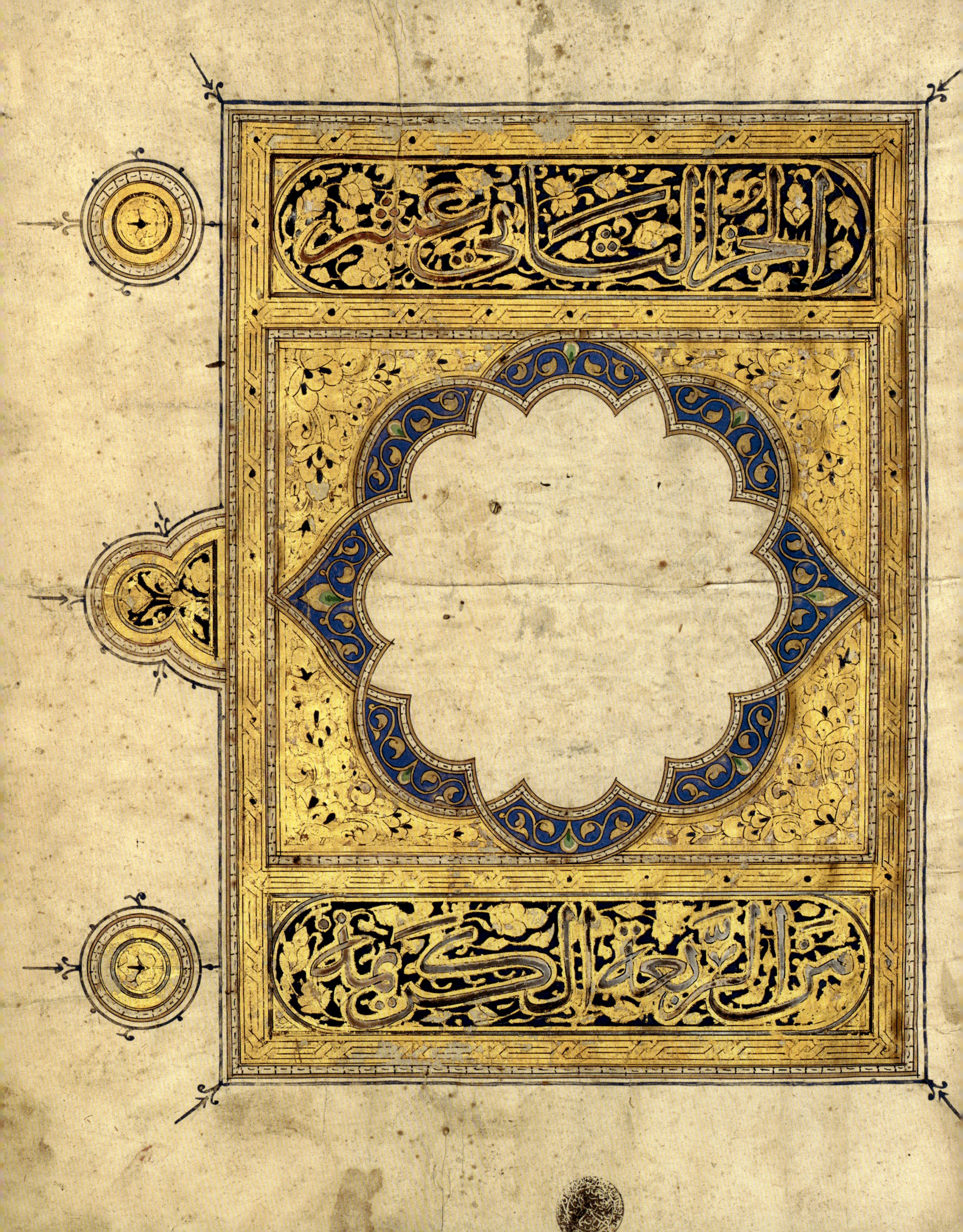
الجزء الثاني عشر
من الربعة الكريمة

45

Twelfth Part (*Juz'*) of a Qur'an Manuscript

Signed by Ahmad al-Isfahani
Cairo, dated 10 Dhu al-Hijja AH 789/December 22, 1387
Ink, opaque watercolor, and gold on paper; leather binding, stamped and tooled (modern replacement)
Open: 17 1/8 × 24 5/8 inches (43.5 × 62.6 cm)
Overall (each folio): 1/2 × 17 1/8 × 12 5/8 inches (1.3 × 43.5 × 32 cm); 4–10 lines
Folios 3, side A–19, side B, sura 11, *Hud* (Hud), verses 1–123, and sura 12, *Yusuf* (Joseph), verses 1–52
Text is copied in *muhaqqaq* script in black script alternating large and small sizes with some lines in gold outlined in black; vocalization and letter-pointing in black; illuminated frontispiece in a palette of gold, lapis lazuli, white, and green (folio 3, side A) composed of two rectangular panels (with the title of the *juz'* in *thuluth* script over a floral scroll) above and below an eight-pointed medallion with three marginal finials; double-page text frontispiece (folios 3, side B–4, side A), script set in cloudbands of reserved paper over a ground formed by an arabesque in gold with blue and green flowers and pale brown hatching; chapter headings (folios 3, side A, and 14, side A) repeat palette and motifs of frontispiece; verse markers (small gold rosettes) and counters (gold disks); the colophon (folio 19b) records that the manuscript was copied in the madrasa endowed by the Mamluk Sultan al-Malik al-Zahir Abu Sa'id (r. 1382–99).
TR:400-2015

Opposite: Illuminated frontispiece, folio 3, side A

Following pages: Cat. 45: Folio 4, side A, and folio 3, side B

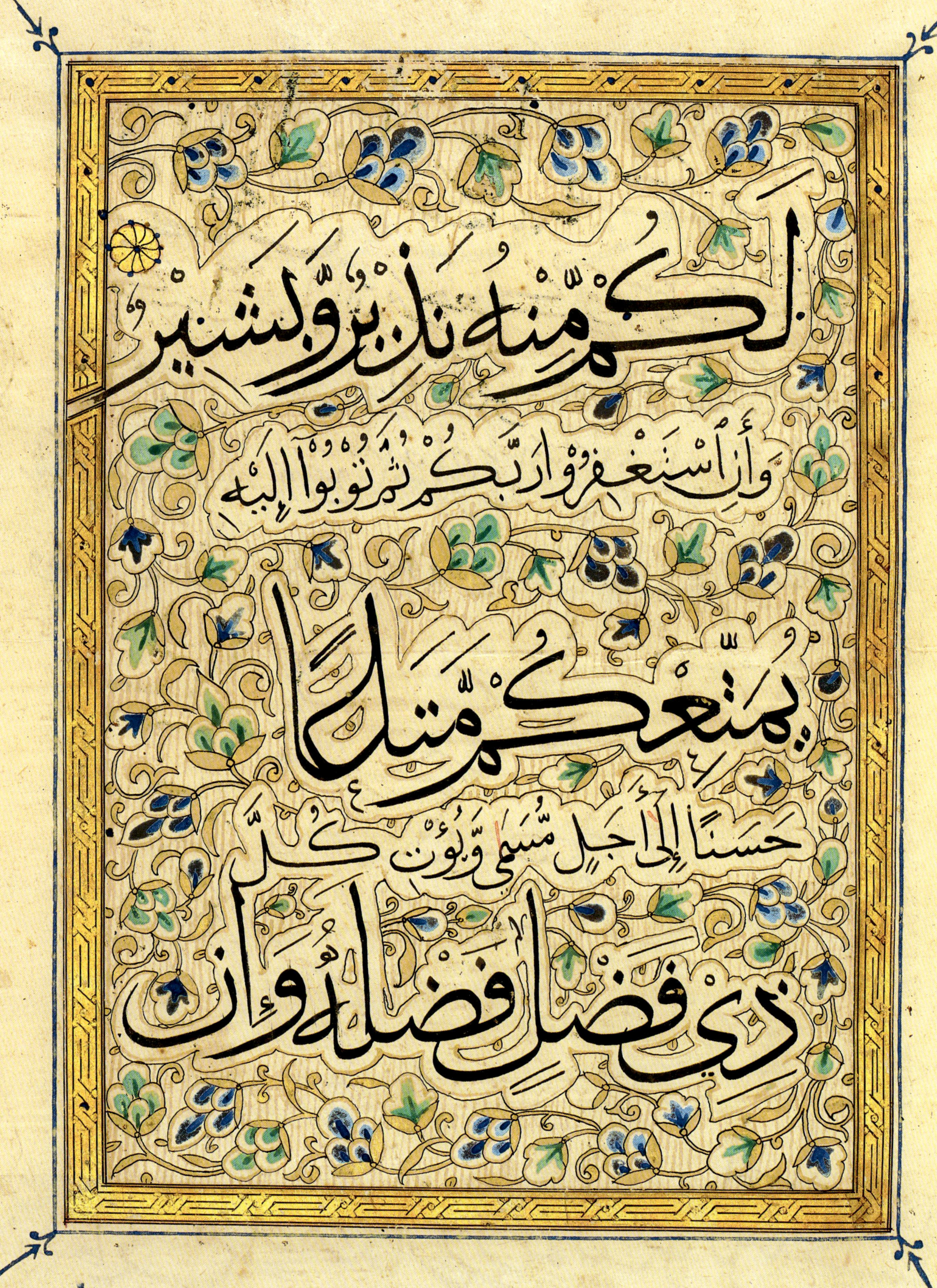
لكم منه نذير وبشير
وأن استغفروا ربكم ثم توبوا إليه
يمتعكم متاعا
حسنا إلى أجل مسمى ويؤت كل
ذي فضل فضله وإن

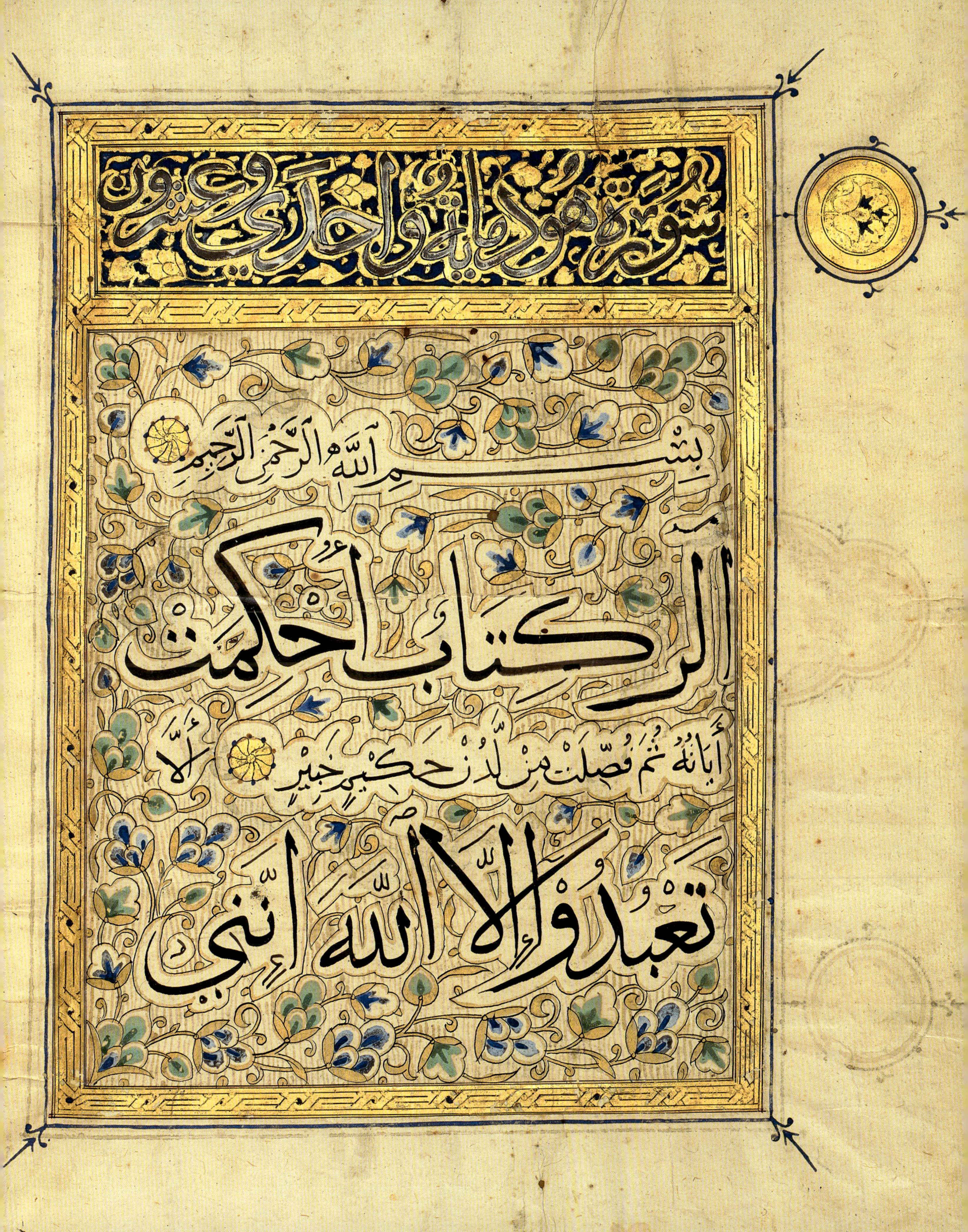

سورة هود مائة واحدى وعشرون
بسم الله الرحمن الرحيم
الر كتاب أحكمت
آياته ثم فصلت من لدن حكيم خبير ألا
تعبدوا إلا الله إنني

على ربهم ألا لعنة الله على الظالمين
الذين يصدون عن سبيل الله ويبغونها عوجا وهم بالآخرة
هم كافرون أولئك لم يكونوا معجزين في الأرض
وما كان لهم من دون الله من أولياء يضاعف لهم العذاب
ما كانوا يستطيعون السمع وما كانوا يبصرون
أولئك الذين خسروا أنفسهم وضل
عنهم ما كانوا يفترون لا جرم أنهم في الآخرة هم
الأخسرون إن الذين آمنوا وعملوا الصالحات وأخبتوا
إلى ربهم أولئك أصحاب الجنة هم فيها خالدون مثل
الفريقين كالأعمى والأصم والبصير والسميع هل يستويان مثلا
أفلا تذكرون ولقد أرسلنا نوحا

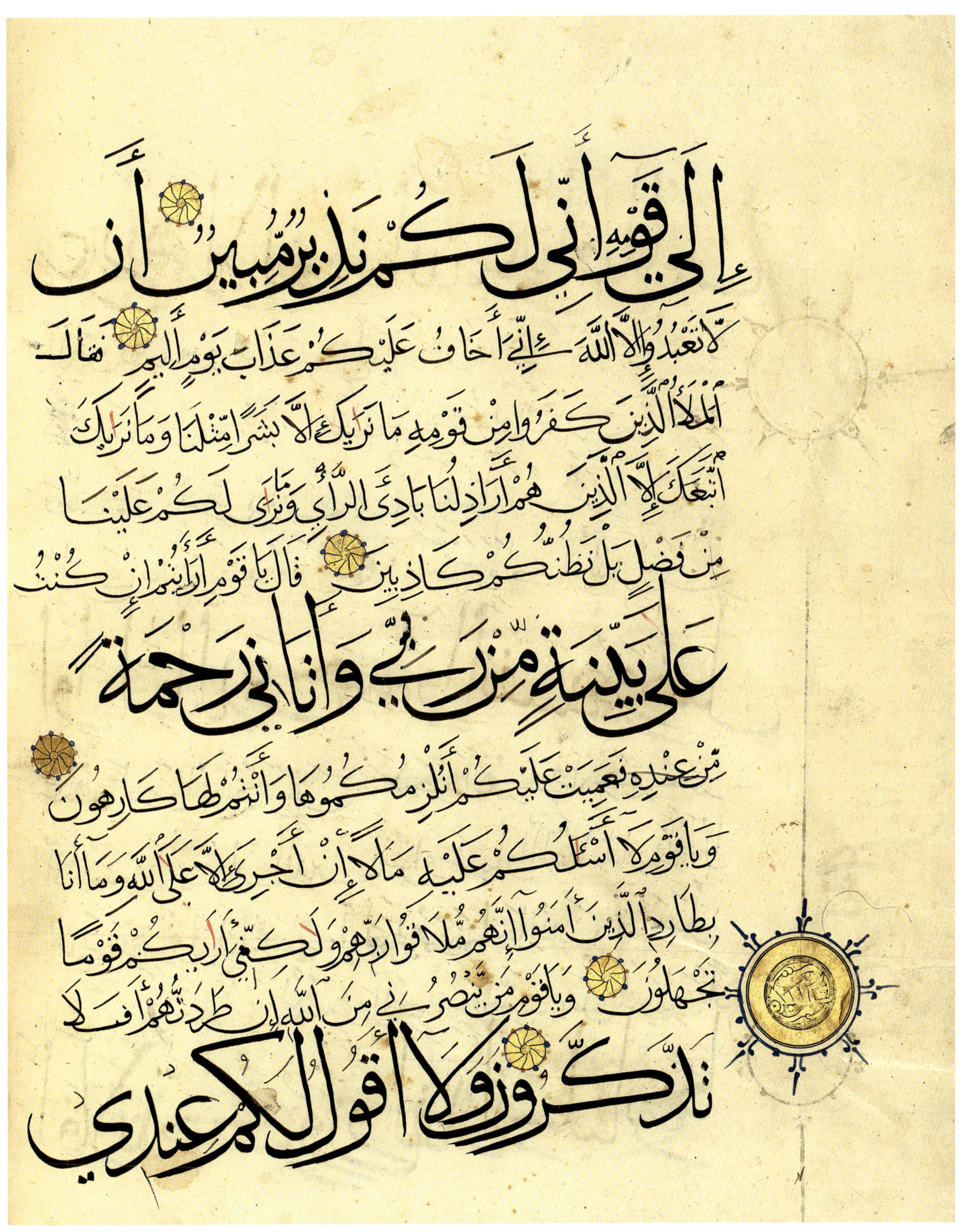

Above: Cat. 45: Folio 6, side B

Opposite: Cat. 45: Folio 6, side A

كلما ألقي فيها فوج سألهم خزنتها ألم يأتكم نذير ۞ قالوا بلى قد جاءنا نذير فكذبنا وقلنا ما نزل الله
من شيء إن أنتم إلا في ضلال كبير ۞ وقالوا لو كنا نسمع أو نعقل ما كنا في أصحاب السعير

رحمته من يشاء لو تزيلوا لعذبنا الذين كفروا
منهم عذابا اليما ۞ اذ جعل الذين كفروا في قلوبهم
الحمية حمية الجاهلية فانزل الله سكينته على رسوله وعلى
المؤمنين والزمهم كلمة التقوى وكانوا احق بها
واهلها وكان الله بكل شيء عليما ۞ لقد صدق الله
رسوله الرؤيا بالحق لتدخلن المسجد الحرام ان شاء الله
امنين محلقين رءوسكم ومقصرين لا تخافون فعلم ما لم
تعلموا فجعل من دون ذلك فتحا قريبا ۞ هو الذي
ارسل رسوله بالهدى ودين الحق ليظهره على الدين كله

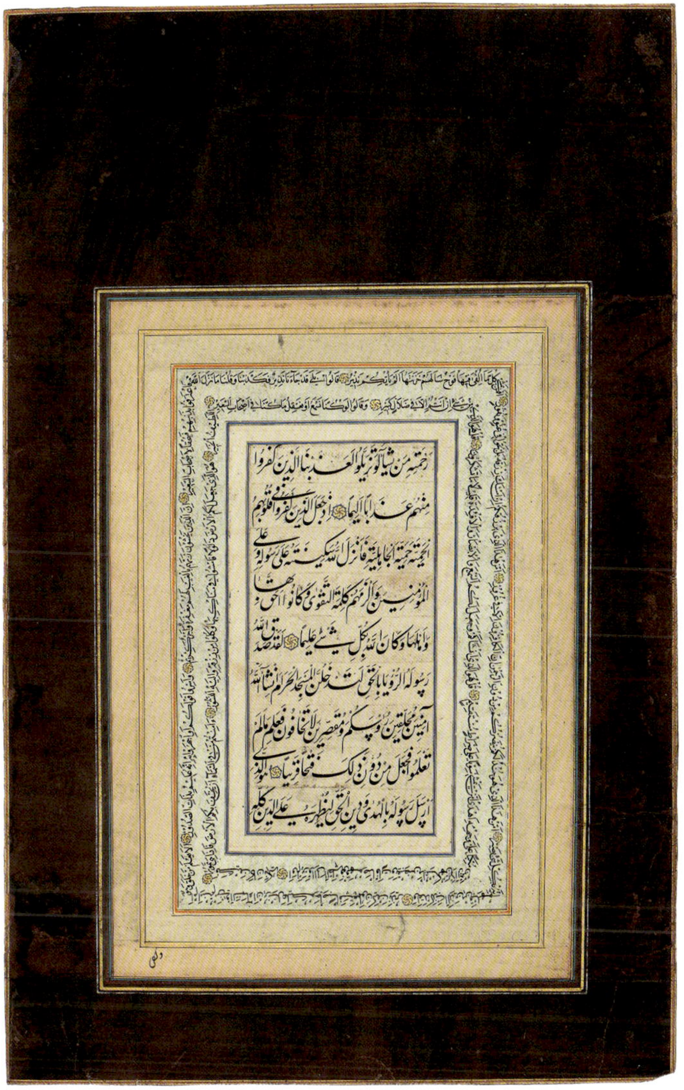

46

Calligraphic Specimen Composed of Selections from the Qurʾan

Calligraphy attributed to Shah Mahmud Nishapuri (active 16th century)
Iran, 16th century
Ink, opaque watercolor, and gold on paper
Overall: 18 3/8 × 11 3/4 inches (46.7 × 29.9 cm)
Calligraphy: 9 3/16 × 5 3/4 inches (23.4 × 14.6 cm)
Central text: sura 48, *al-Fath* (Victory), verses 25–28
Border text: sura 67, *al-Mulk* (Dominion), verses 8–24
Central panel copied in *nastaʿliq* script in black ink with vocalization and letter-pointing in black; verse markers knotted gold rosettes (the original specimen has been reformatted by reducing the spaces between the lines of script). Border text copied in a form of *naskh* script in black ink with vocalization and letter-pointing in black; verse markers small gold rosettes. Central and border texts are further distinguished by the color of paper on which they are written and separated by rulings in lapis lazuli and gold; the specimen has been mounted to an album folio.
TR:388-2015

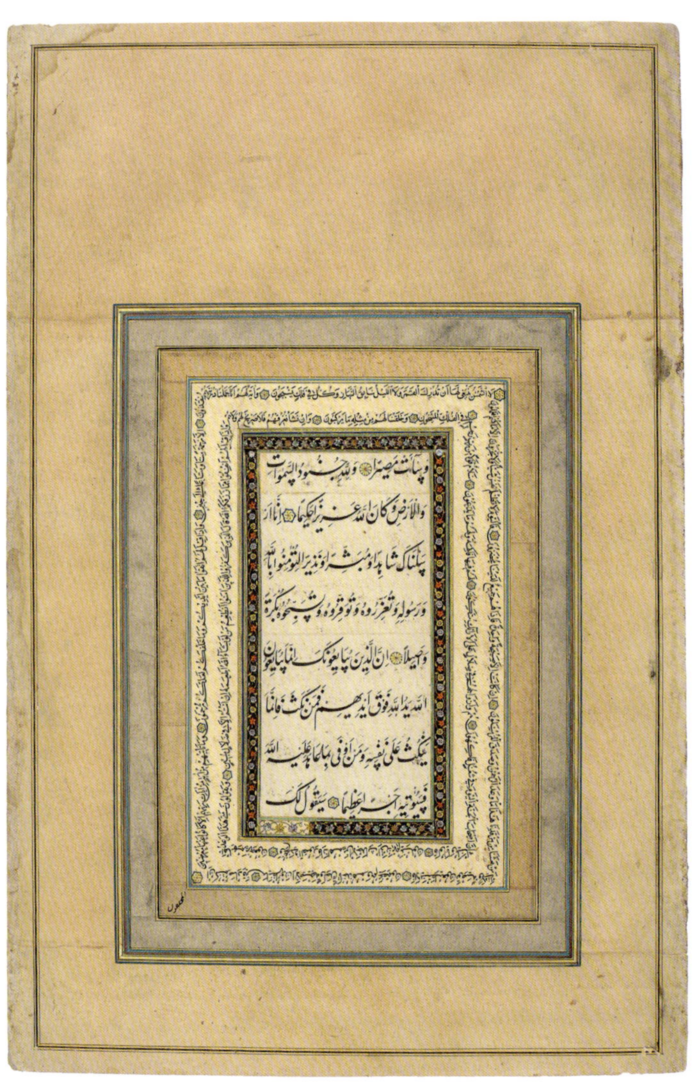

47

Calligraphic Specimen Composed of Selections from the Qur'an

Calligraphy attributed to Shah Mahmud Nishapuri (active 16th century)
Iran, 16th century
Ink, opaque watercolor, and gold on paper
Overall: 19 3/16 × 12 13/16 inches (48.7 × 32.5 cm)
Calligraphy: 9 1/8 × 5 7/8 inches (23.2 × 14.9 cm)
Central text: sura 48, *al-Fath* (Victory), verses 6–11
Border text around margin starting in upper-right corner: sura 36, *Ya' Sin* (Ya Sin), verses 40–58
Central panel copied in *nasta'liq* script in black ink with vocalization and letter-pointing in black; verse markers gold rosettes (the original specimen has been partially reformatted by reducing the spaces between the lines of script). Border text copied in a form of *naskh* script in black ink with vocalization and letter-pointing in black; verse markers gold rosettes. The central and border texts are further distinguished by the color of paper on which they are written—which is also gold-sprinkled—and separated by a sequence of rulings in green and gold and an illuminated floral border; the specimen has been mounted to an album folio.
TR:923-2015

لا الشمس ينبغي لها ان تدرك القمر ولا الليل سابق النهار وكل في فلك يسبحون وآية لهم انا حملنا ذريتهم
في الفلك المشحون وخلقنا لهم من مثله ما يركبون وان نشأ نغرقهم فلا صريخ لهم ولا

وساءت مصیرا ولله جنود السموات
والارض وکان الله عزیزا حکیما انا ار
سلناک شاهدا ومبشرا ونذیرا لتؤمنوا بالله
ورسوله وتعزروه وتوقروه وتسبحوه بکرة
واصیلا ان الذین یبایعونک انما یبایعون
الله ید الله فوق ایدیهم فمن نکث فانما
ینکث علی نفسه ومن اوفی بما عاهد علیه الله
فسیؤتیه اجرا عظیما سیقول لک

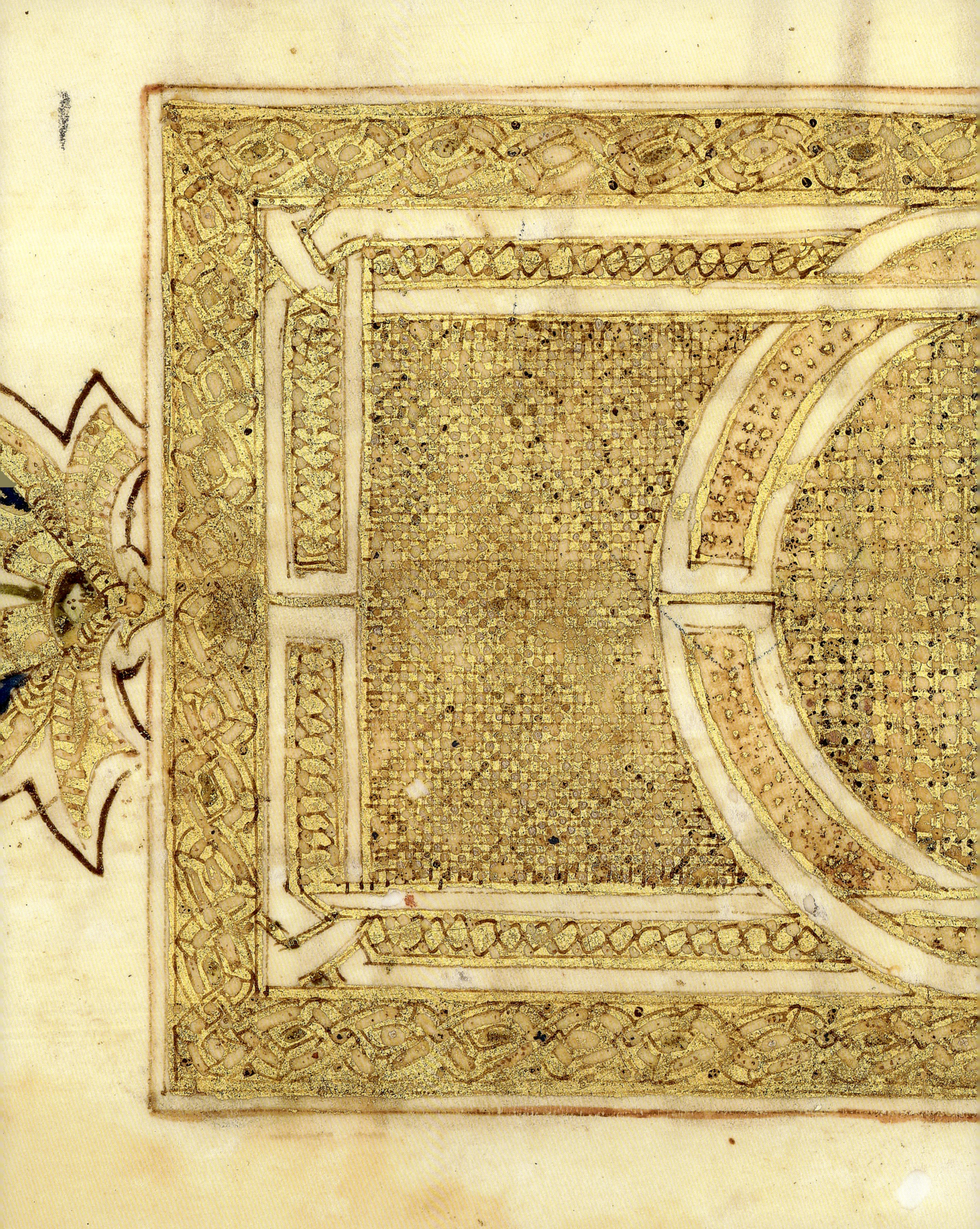

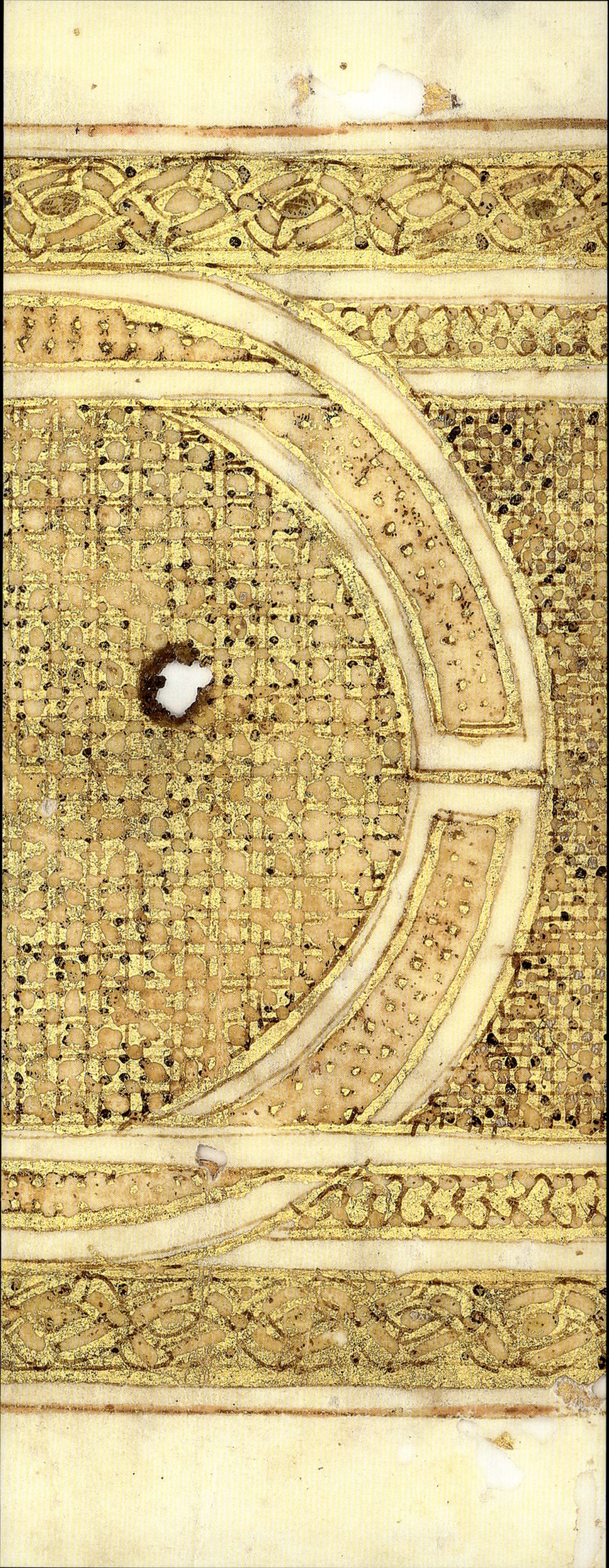

ILLUMINATIONS

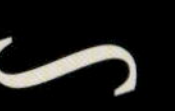

ILLUMINATIONS

Illuminations in manuscripts of the Qur'an were simultaneously functional and aesthetic. This was true regardless of the scope of the illuminated program, which varied widely from manuscript to manuscript, reflective of the relative level of resources allocated to the project (whether a multipart—e.g., of seven or thirty—or single volume Qur'an) and of the attitudes about the embellishment of the *mushaf*. In functional terms, illumination provided the text of the Qur'an with a visible structure, a form of internal wayfinding useful to the reader, by punctuating its major divisions (chapters), separating the verses by marking their endings, providing verse counters of five and ten, and signaling the beginning and ending of parts (*juz'*) through frontispieces and finispieces. While early copies of the Qur'an employed illuminated motifs to mark chapter divisions, and often also individual verses, as well as verse counters, and in larger compositions to form the frontispieces and finispieces of individual *juz'*, programs of illumination became steadily more complex and extensive from the tenth century onward. Additional elements that became commonplace—again reflecting available resources—included an expansion and elaboration through single- and double-page frontispieces (arranged as "carpet pages" or medallions [*shamsas*]), single- and double-page text frontispieces with illuminated borders framing the text, commissioning certificates, colophons, and marking the middle of the Qur'an—at sura 18, *al-Kahf* (The Cave)—through elaborated borders.[16] Illumination could also extend beyond these elements to surround the text, providing a patterned, embellished ground. In broad terms, illumination always carried a symbolic function as a physical analogue to the spiritual illumination provided by the Qur'an and the messages it contained. Adhered metals on the surfaces of parchment and paper caught the light as the folios were turned, while their inherent reflective properties could be enhanced by pricking and punching the surface of the metals—applied either as leaf or as a colored ink—to texture their surfaces and thereby catch light from different angles even when the folio was static. Such effects of surface manipulation began to become more common in the fourteenth century and after.

The materials used for illumination included opaque watercolor, black and colored inks, and metals (e.g., gold, silver, copper, tin), which were applied either as leaf or as powdered metal in a binder of glue or gum arabic.[17] Contrasting colors of gold were exploited—including those that were silver rich—while the use of ternary copper alloys simulated gold.[18] Various kinds of adhesives, prepared from animal sources (animal hides, fish, egg whites), were used to attach leaf to parchment and paper. Before the application of pigments and metals, the composition and elements of the design were formed through inscribed or scored lines made with a stylus, compass, and straight edge, or through an underdrawing formed with a pen or brush in a faint medium that could be concealed by the materials applied over it. Burnishing followed the application of these mediums to enhance their adherence and luster. While the design repertoire and aesthetics of illumination varied over time and region, common subjects included geometry and biomorphic forms (various kinds of plants and flowers) that were often combined.

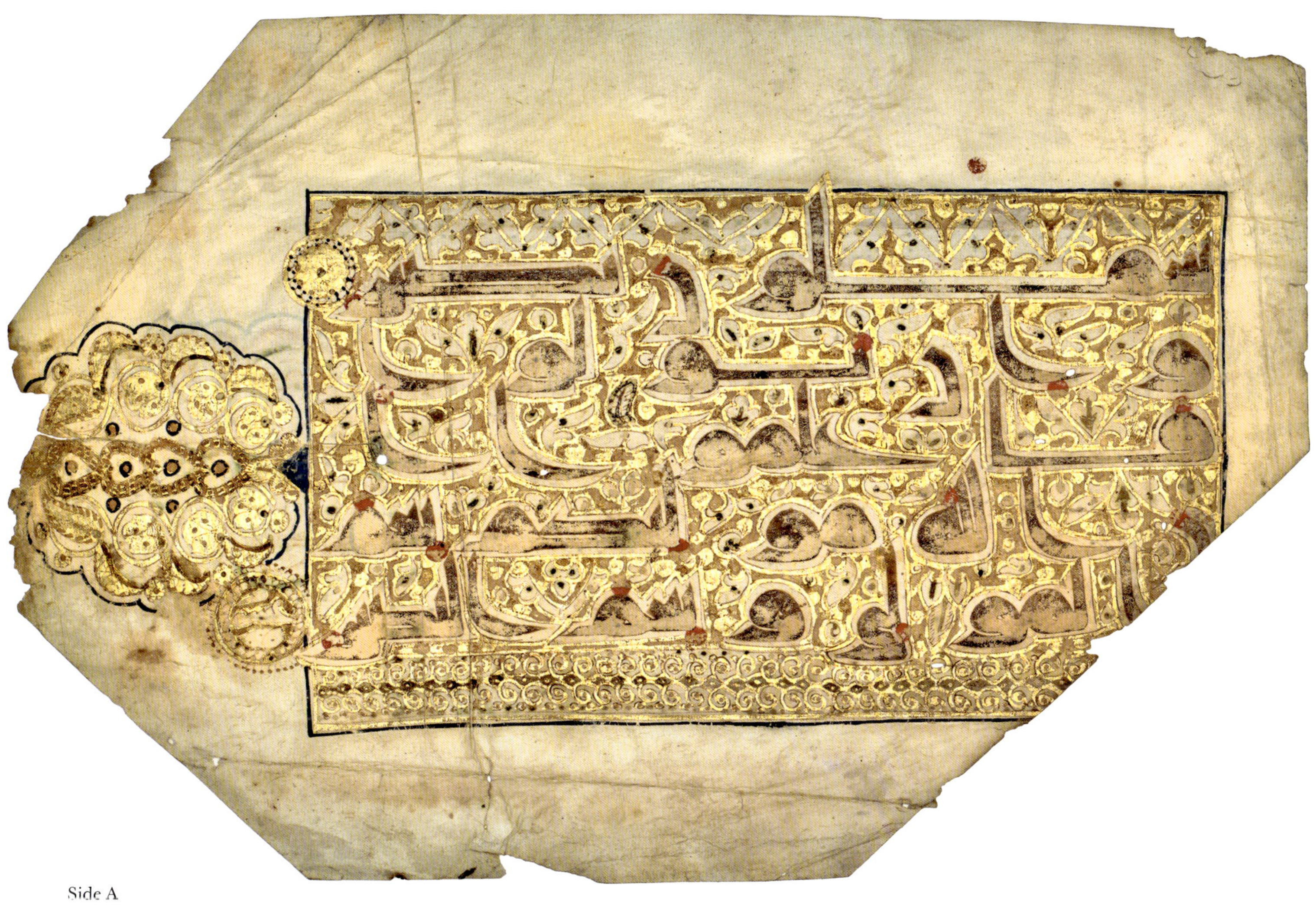

Side A

48

Folio from the Ninth Part (*Juz'*) of a Qur'an Manuscript

North Africa or Central Islamic Lands, 9th–10th century
Ink, opaque watercolor, and gold on parchment
6 11/16 × 9 1/16 inches (17 × 23 cm); 5 lines
Side A: sura 8, *al-Anfal* (Spoils of War), verses 39–40
Side B: illuminated finispiece
Text copied in Kufic script in brown ink; vocalization in red dots; ground of floriate motifs reserved in parchment over gold and reddish brown with a scrolling vine along the bottom edge; large floriate finial in the margin composed of several types of scrolling and interlocking leaves and flowers; verse marker (gold rosette) and counter (gold disk). Finispiece comprises a rectangular panel with a central field composed of rotated squares set inside a border with a large floriate finial extending into the margin.
TR:1738-2015

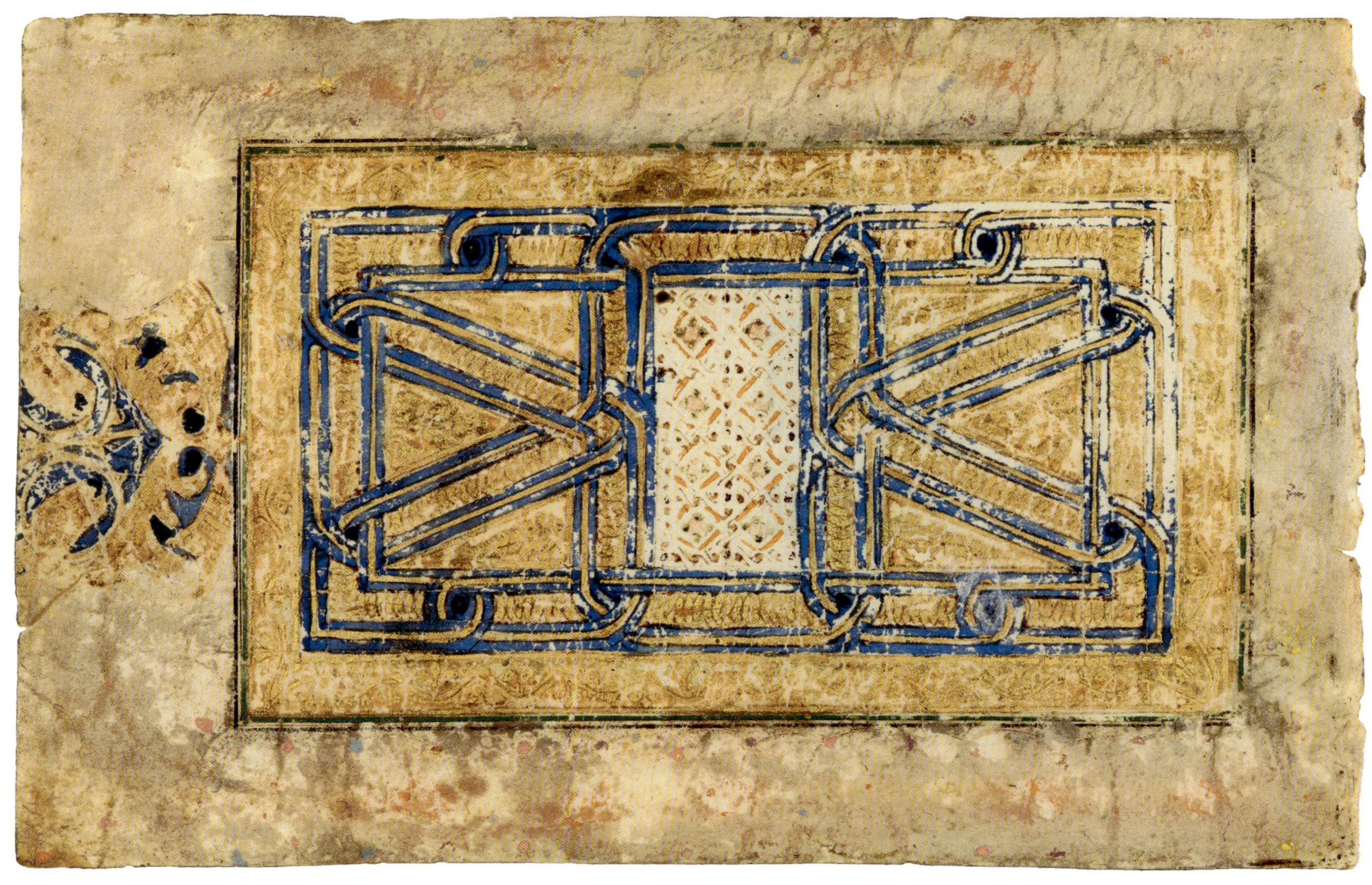

Side A

49

Illuminated Panel, Folio from a Qur'an Manuscript

North Africa or Central Islamic Lands, 9th–10th century
Ink, opaque watercolor, and gold on parchment
Overall: 4 1/16 × 6 9/16 inches (10.3 × 16.7 cm)
Illuminated panel comprising a rectangular panel with a floriated finial in a palette of gold, lapis lazuli, and brown; the panel features an intricately knotted design in blue over a gold ground of scrolling plants which frames a central rectangle whose ground, reserved in unpainted parchment, is decorated with a pattern of interconnected rotated squares.
TR:800-2015

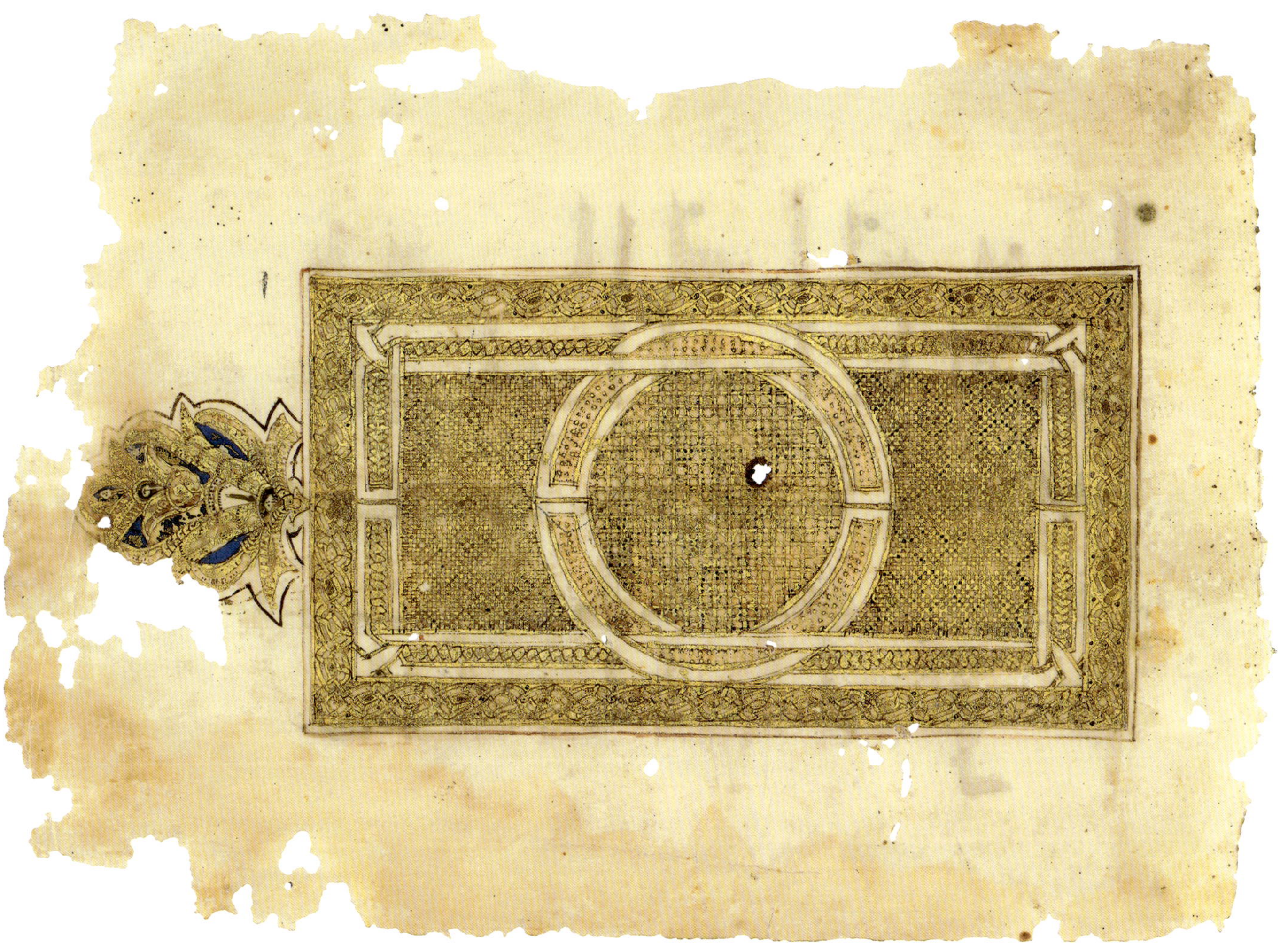

Side A
Following pages: cat. 50: Side B

50

Illuminated Panel, Folio from a Qurʾan Manuscript

North Africa or Central Islamic Lands, 9th–10th century
Ink, opaque watercolor, and gold on parchment
Overall: 5 13/16 × 8 1/8 inches (14.7 × 20.7 cm)
Illuminated panel comprising a rectangular panel with a floriated finial in a palette of gold, brown, and lapis lazuli; the panel features a circle on a central field and two borders, each interconnected by a knotted border; the fields of these separate forms are contrasted through different treatments, which include grids, lattices, and rope-like patterns; the contrasting biomorphic finial is composed of various kinds of leaves, its voids painted with lapis lazuli.
TR:293-2015

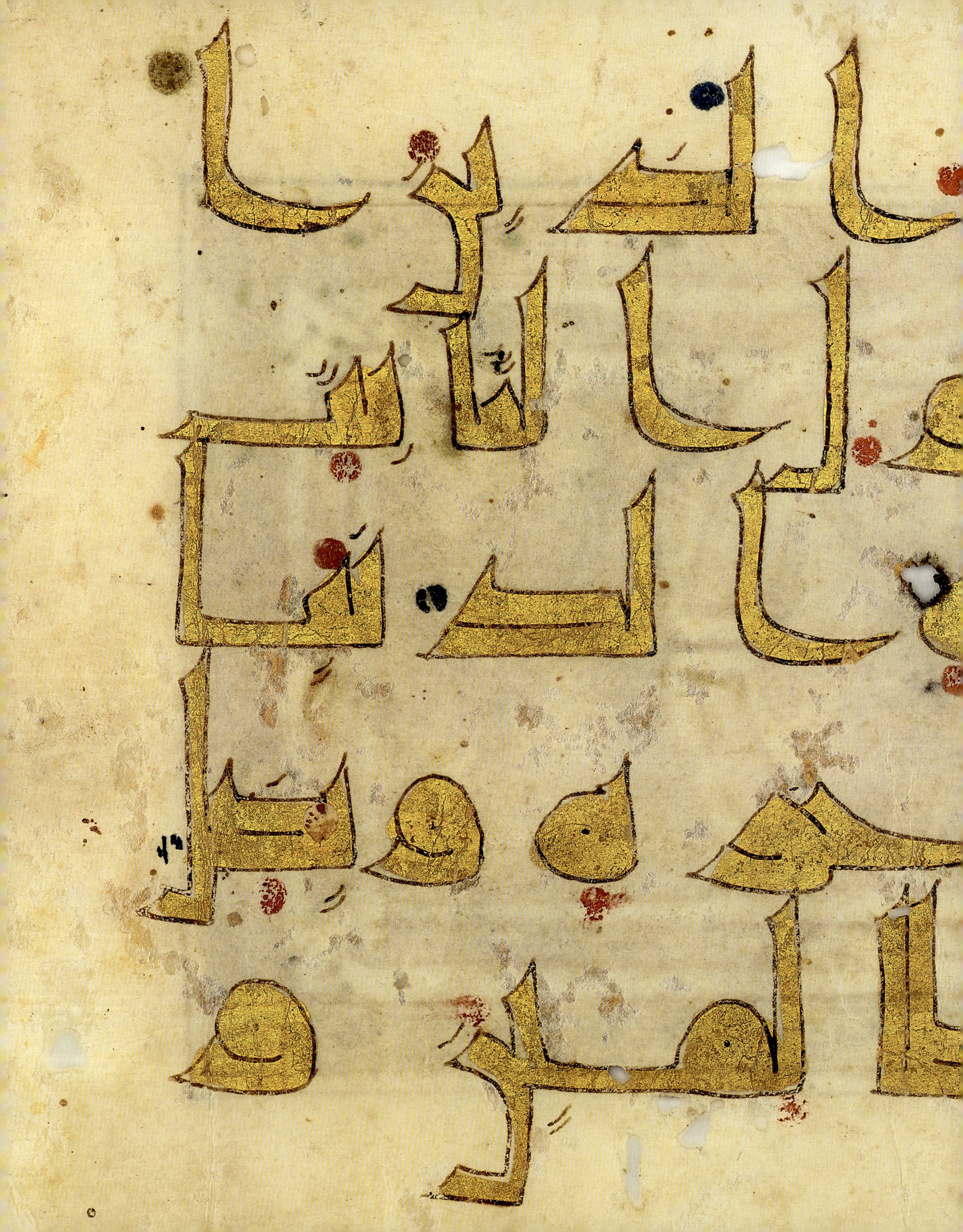

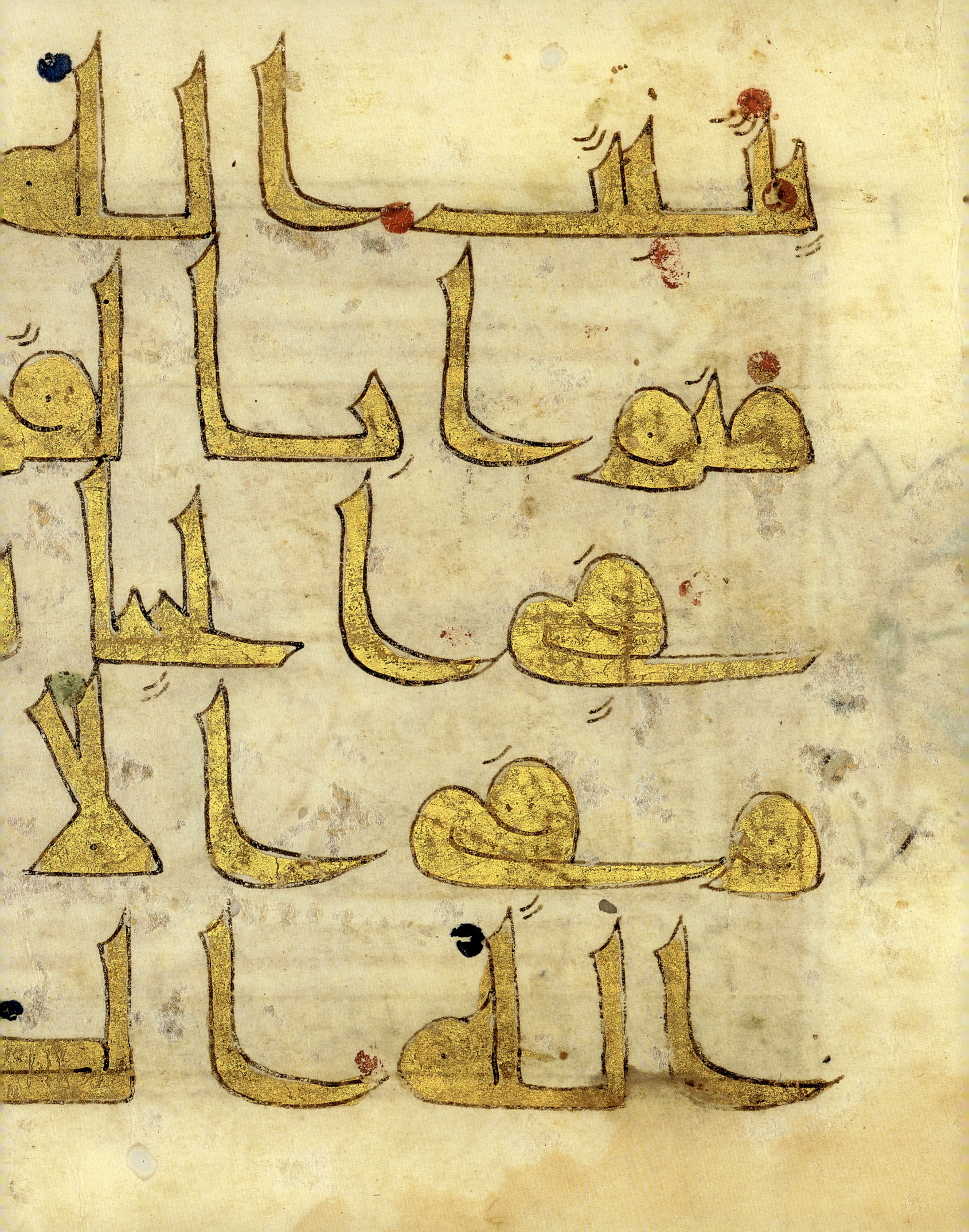

51

Folio from the Third Part (*Juz'*) of a Qur'an Manuscript

North Africa, Tunisia, or Western Islamic Lands, Sicily, late 10th–12th century
Ink, opaque watercolor, and gold on paper
4 1/4 × 6 inches (10.8 × 15.2 cm); 5 lines
Side A: illuminated frontispiece to the third *juz'* of the Qur'an
Side B: sura 2, *al-Baqara* (The Cow), verse 253
Text in gold Kufic script outlined with brown ink; vocalization in red, blue, and green dots (some discolored) and black line (for silences and double consonants); the side B features a medallion in gold, red, and lapis lazuli. The frontispiece on the side A comprises a rectangular panel with a floriate finial in the margin, all done in gold, lapis lazuli, and red; the central field of the panel features four interconnected quatrefoils with split palmettes between them set inside a border; the finial arranges its floriate forms in a tear-shaped medallion and also uses red and lapis lazuli as a background.
TR:1682-2015

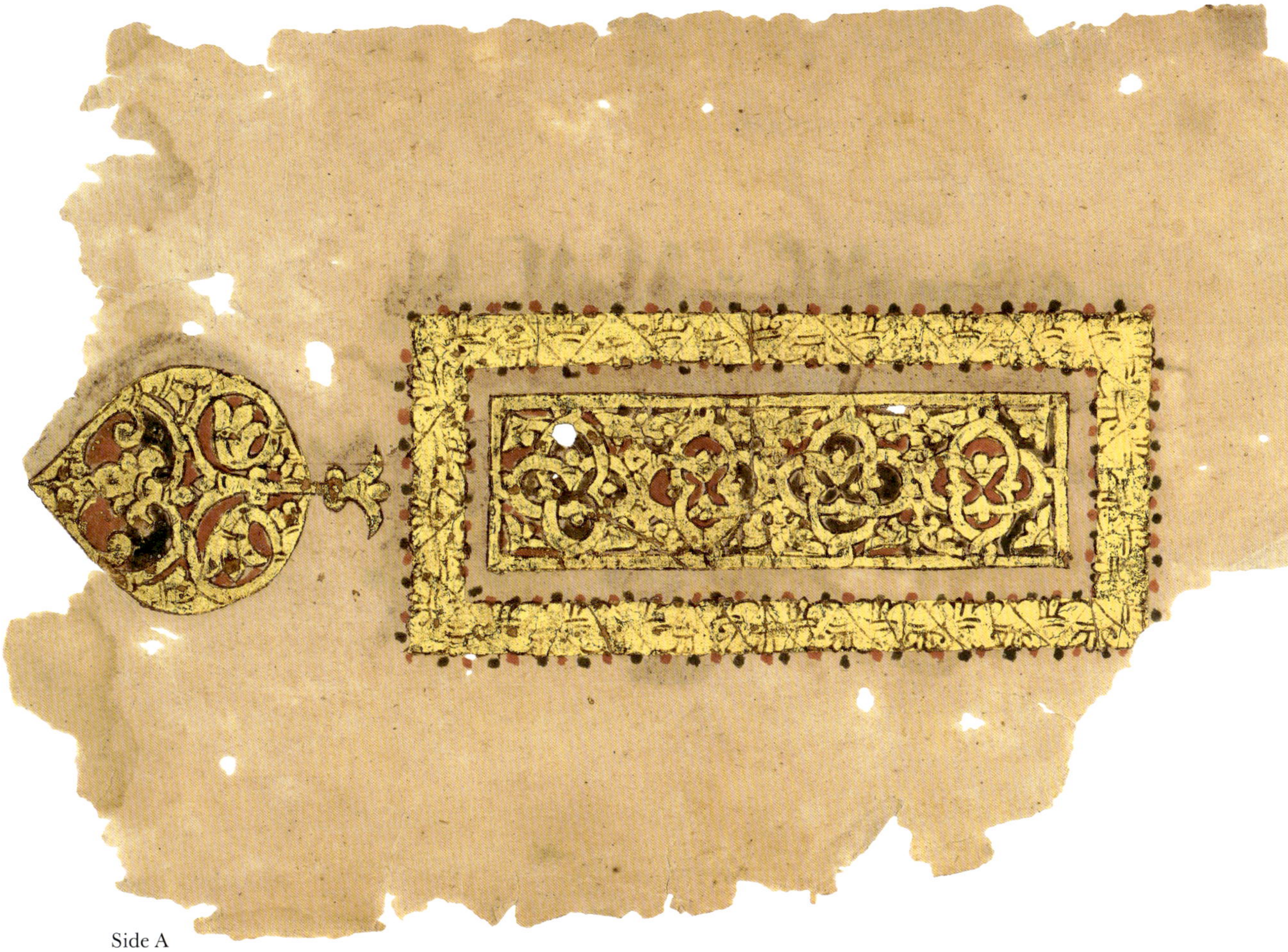

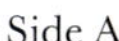

Side A

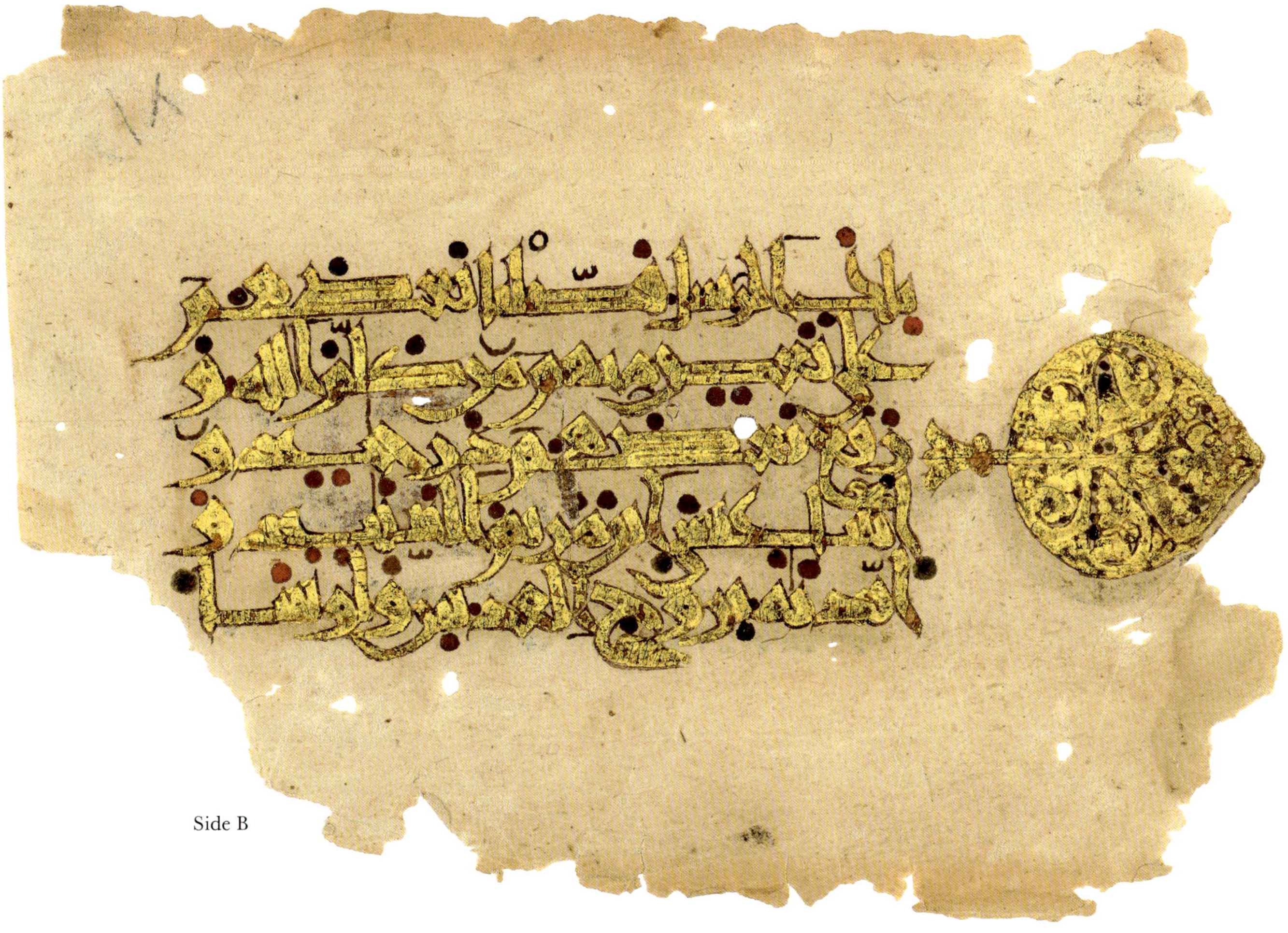

Side B

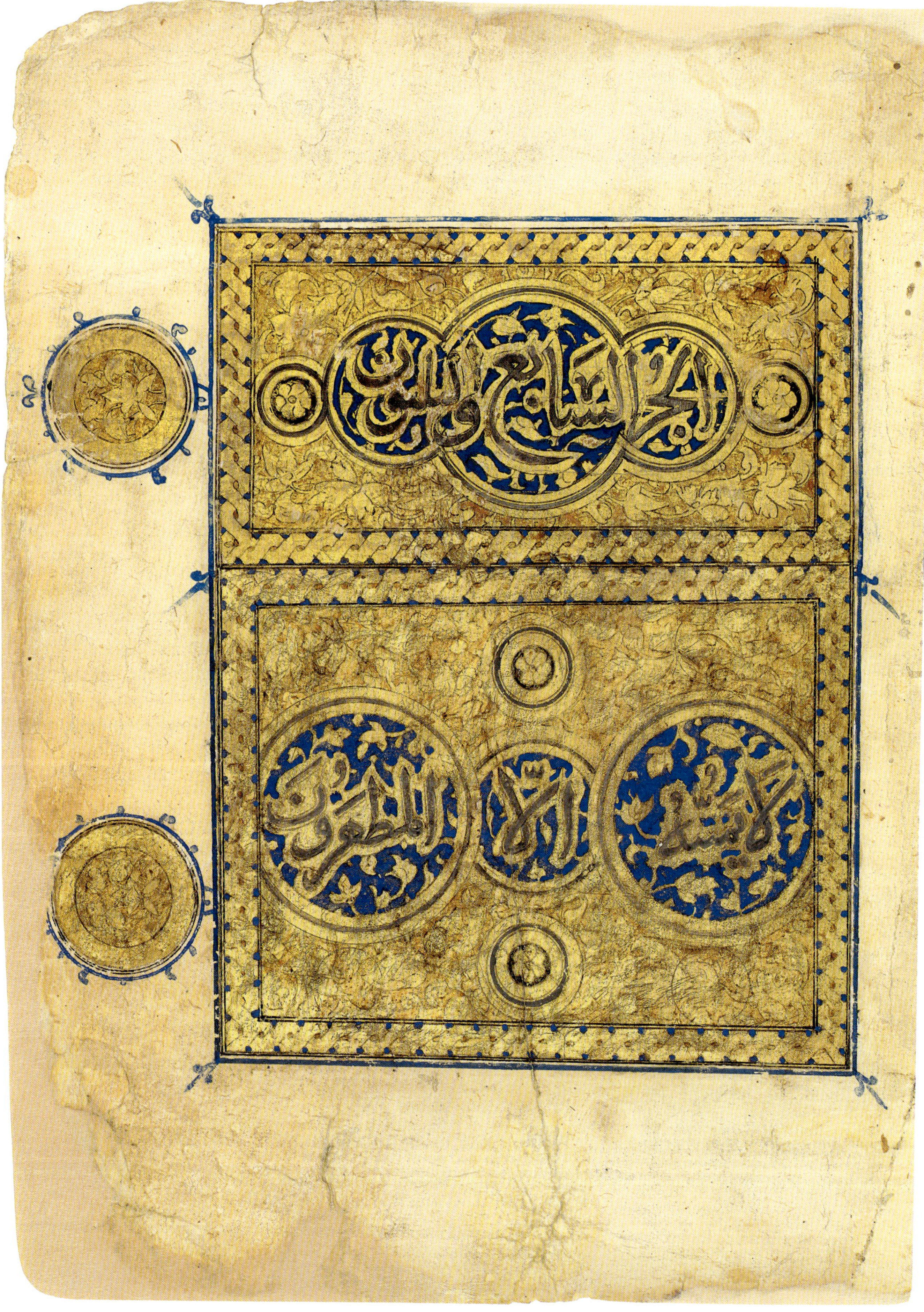

Side A

52

Folio from the Nineteenth Part (*Juz'*) of a Qur'an Manuscript

Egypt or Iraq, 14th century
Ink, opaque watercolor, and gold on paper
9 7/8 × 7 3/16 inches (25.1 × 18.3 cm); 5 lines
Side A: illuminated frontispiece with inscriptions in *thuluth* script in two lines: top, "the thirty-seventh *hizb*"; bottom, "only they can reach it who are clean [of mind]" (sura 56, *al-Waqi'a* [the Inevitable], verse 79)
Side B: sura 25, *al-Furqan* (The Criterion), verses 21–22
Text copied in *naskh* script in alternating lines of gold outlined in black and lapis lazuli outlined in gold with corresponding vocalization and letter-pointing; verse markers gold rosettes; first verse of sura 25 set inside a framed box with knotted border (gold disk finial in margin), its text set in cloudbands over a scroll of split palmettes and pale brown tinted ground. The frontispiece is composed as a rectangle divided in two parts of unequal height, each with a disk extending into the margin, in a palette of gold, lapis lazuli, and brown; knotted borders frame each of the two rectangles which contain text in *thuluth* script (perhaps executed in silver, now oxidized) divided between three circles; the *thuluth* is set over golden florals and lapis lazuli ground; the spaces enclosing the circles are treated with a floral scroll in gold over a brown ground.
TR:939-2015

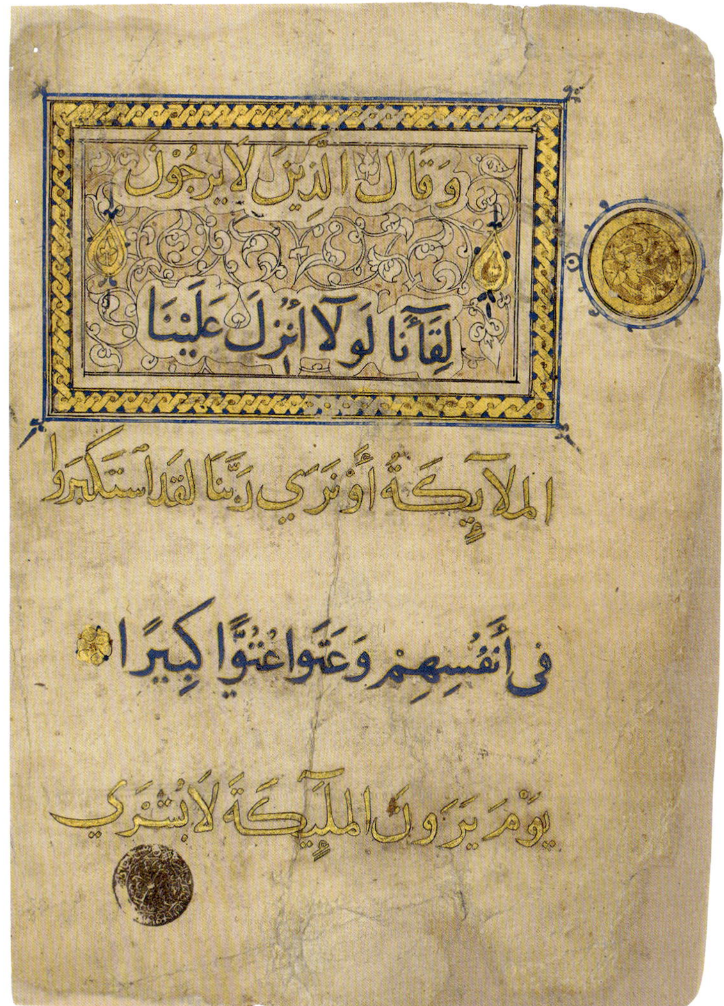
Side B

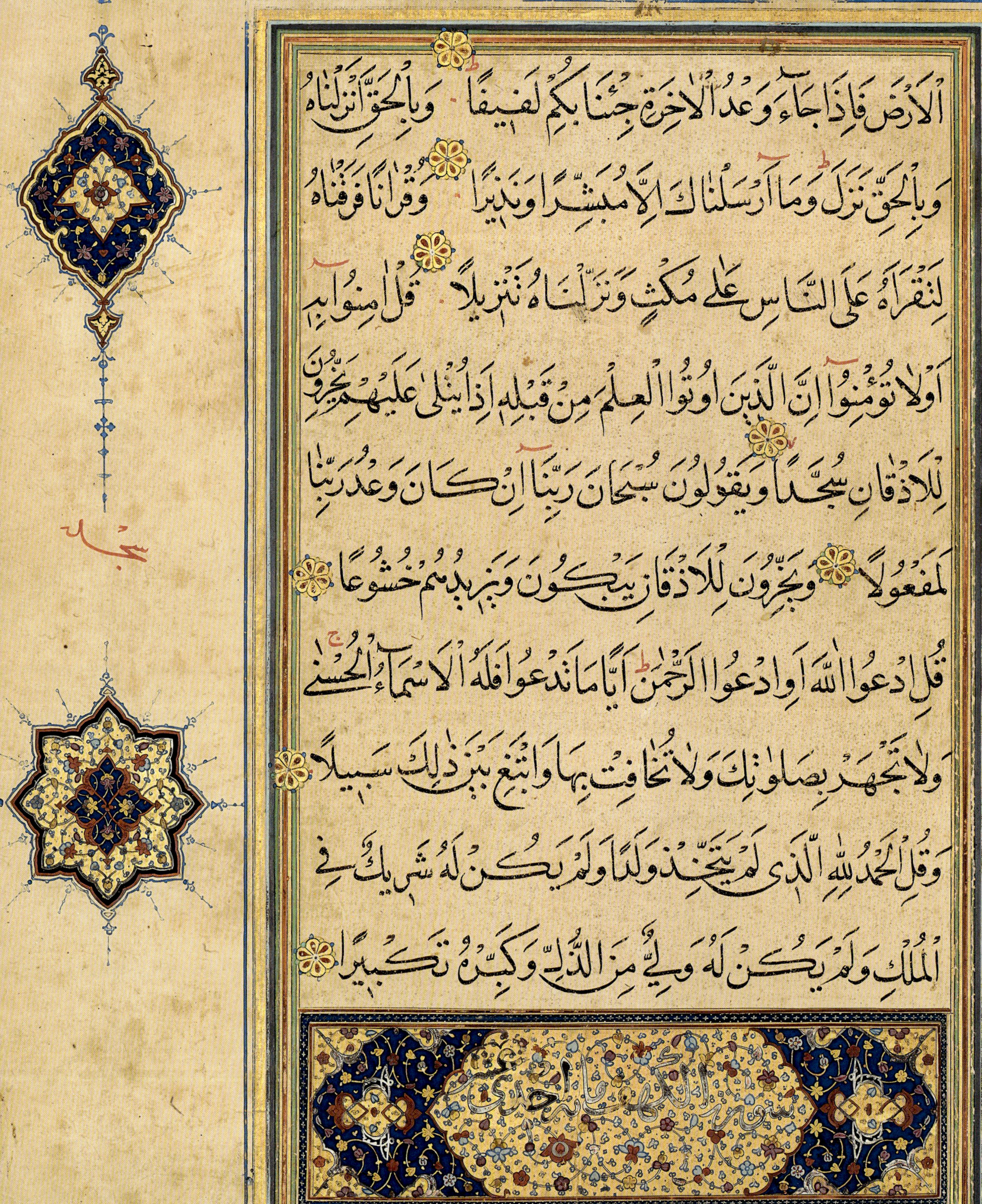
الأرض فإذا جاء وعد الآخرة جئنا بكم لفيفا وبالحق أنزلناه
وبالحق نزل وما أرسلناك إلا مبشرا ونذيرا وقرآنا فرقناه
لتقرأه على الناس على مكث ونزلناه تنزيلا قل آمنوا به
أو لا تؤمنوا إن الذين أوتوا العلم من قبله إذا يتلى عليهم يخرون
للأذقان سجدا ويقولون سبحان ربنا إن كان وعد ربنا
لمفعولا ويخرون للأذقان يبكون ويزيدهم خشوعا
قل ادعوا الله أو ادعوا الرحمن أيا ما تدعوا فله الأسماء الحسنى
ولا تجهر بصلاتك ولا تخافت بها وابتغ بين ذلك سبيلا
وقل الحمد لله الذي لم يتخذ ولدا ولم يكن له شريك في
الملك ولم يكن له ولي من الذل وكبره تكبيرا
سورة الكهف

53

Bifolio from a Qur'an Manuscript

Iran, late 16th century
Ink, opaque watercolor, and gold on paper
Open: 17 15/16 × 23 1/16 inches (45.5 × 58.6 cm); 12 lines
Closed: 17 15/16 × 11 9/16 inches (45.5 × 29.3 cm)
Folio 1, side A: sura 17, *al-Isra'* (The Night Journey), verses 104–111, illuminated chapter heading to sura 18, *al-Kahf* (The Cave)
Folio 1, side B: sura 18, *al-Kahf* (The Cave), verses 1–11; illuminated border enclosing text
Folio 2, side A: sura 18, *al-Kahf* (The Cave), verses 11–18; illuminated border enclosing text
Folio 2, side B: sura 18, *al-Kahf* (The Cave), verses 18–22
Text copied in *naskh* script in black ink within cloudbands of gold-sprinkled reserved paper on a golden ground with colored flowers; verse markers gold rosettes, verse counters rhomboid figures (for five) and eight-pointed stars (for ten); chapter heading on folio 1, side A, sets the title of sura and its number of verses (in white *thuluth* script) within a cusped cartouche of gold with a polychrome floral scroll enclosed by a lapis lazuli ground with floral scroll; illuminated borders of folio 1, side B–folio 2, side A use the same palette as the illuminated chapter heading and comprise a field of cusped medallions of various sizes against an arabesque of split palmettes and flowers.
TR:389-2015

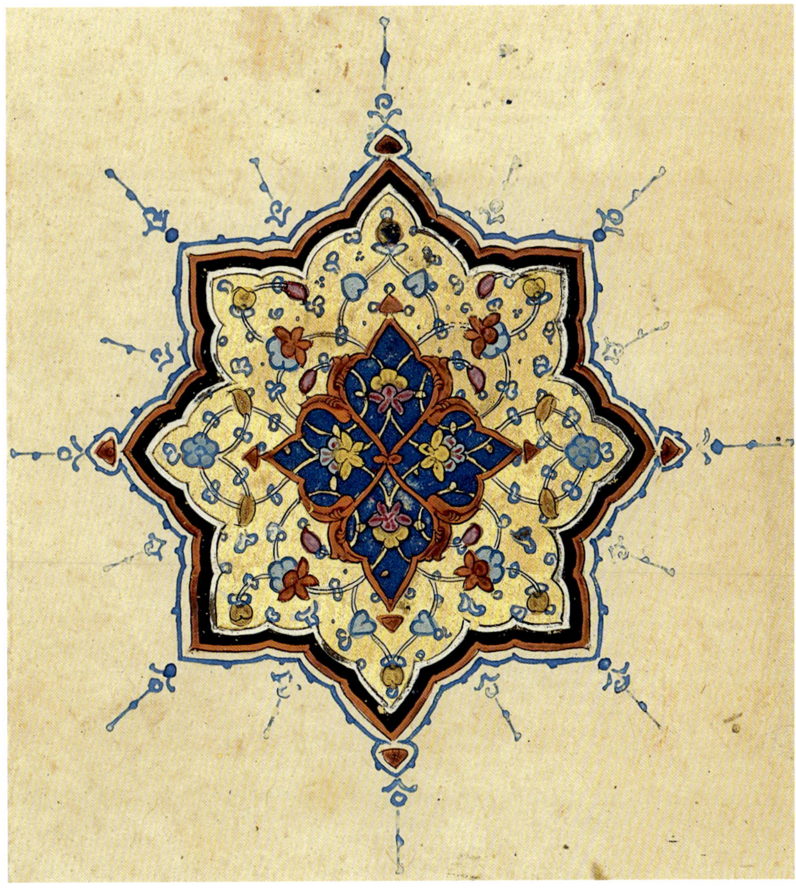

Folio 1, side A (*detail*)

Opposite: Folio 1, side A
Following pages: Folio 2, side A, and folio 1, side B

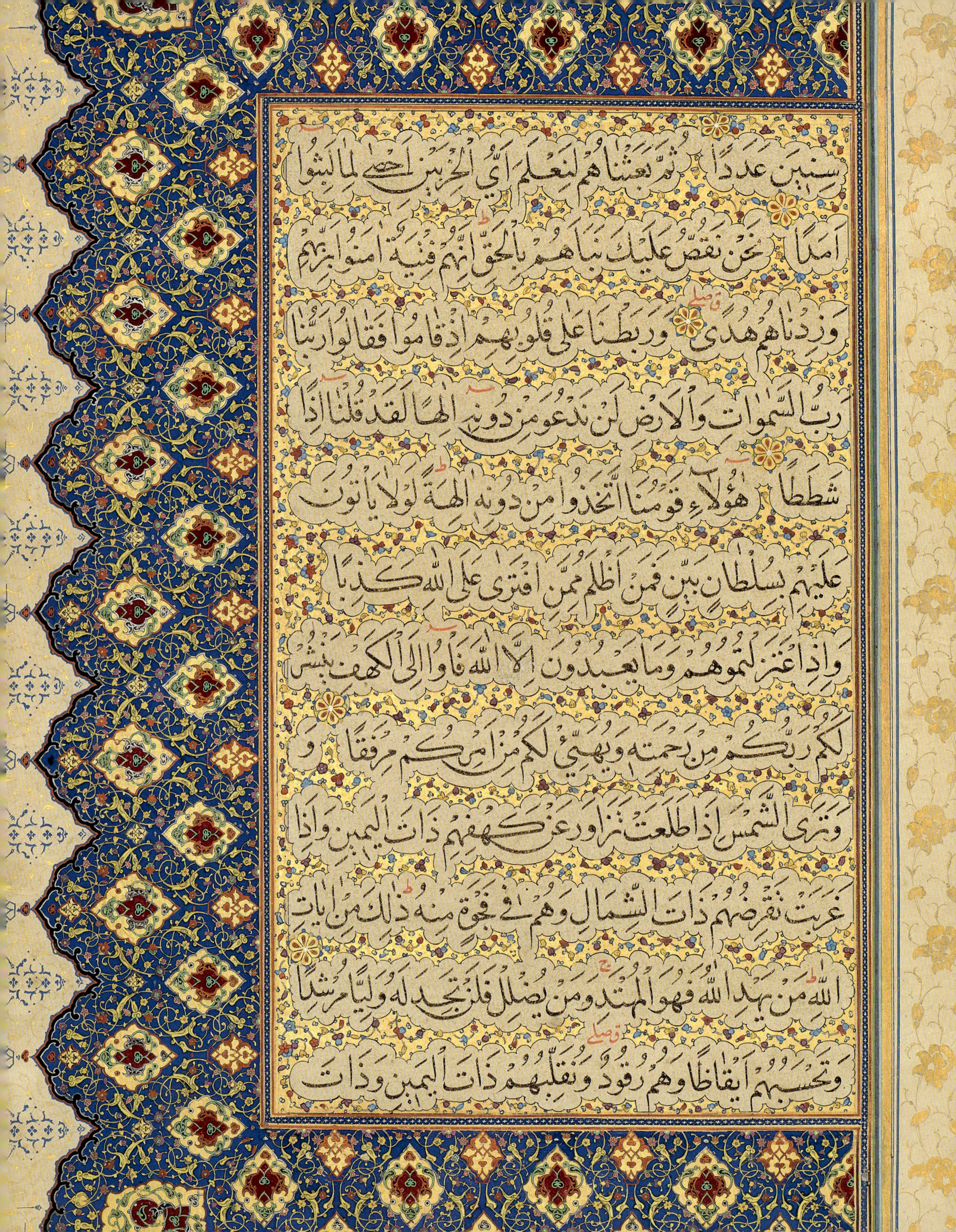

سنين عددا ثم بعثناهم لنعلم اي الحزبين احصى لما لبثوا
امدا نحن نقص عليك نباهم بالحق انهم فتية امنوا بربهم
وزدناهم هدى وربطنا على قلوبهم اذ قاموا فقالوا ربنا
رب السموات والارض لن ندعوا من دونه الها لقد قلنا اذا
شططا هؤلاء قومنا اتخذوا من دونه الهة لولا ياتون
عليهم بسلطان بين فمن اظلم ممن افترى على الله كذبا
واذ اعتزلتموهم وما يعبدون الا الله فاووا الى الكهف ينشر
لكم ربكم من رحمته ويهيئ لكم من امركم مرفقا و
وترى الشمس اذا طلعت تزاور عن كهفهم ذات اليمين واذا
غربت تقرضهم ذات الشمال وهم في فجوة منه ذلك من ايات
الله من يهد الله فهو المهتد ومن يضلل فلن تجد له وليا مرشدا
وتحسبهم ايقاظا وهم رقود ونقلبهم ذات اليمين وذات

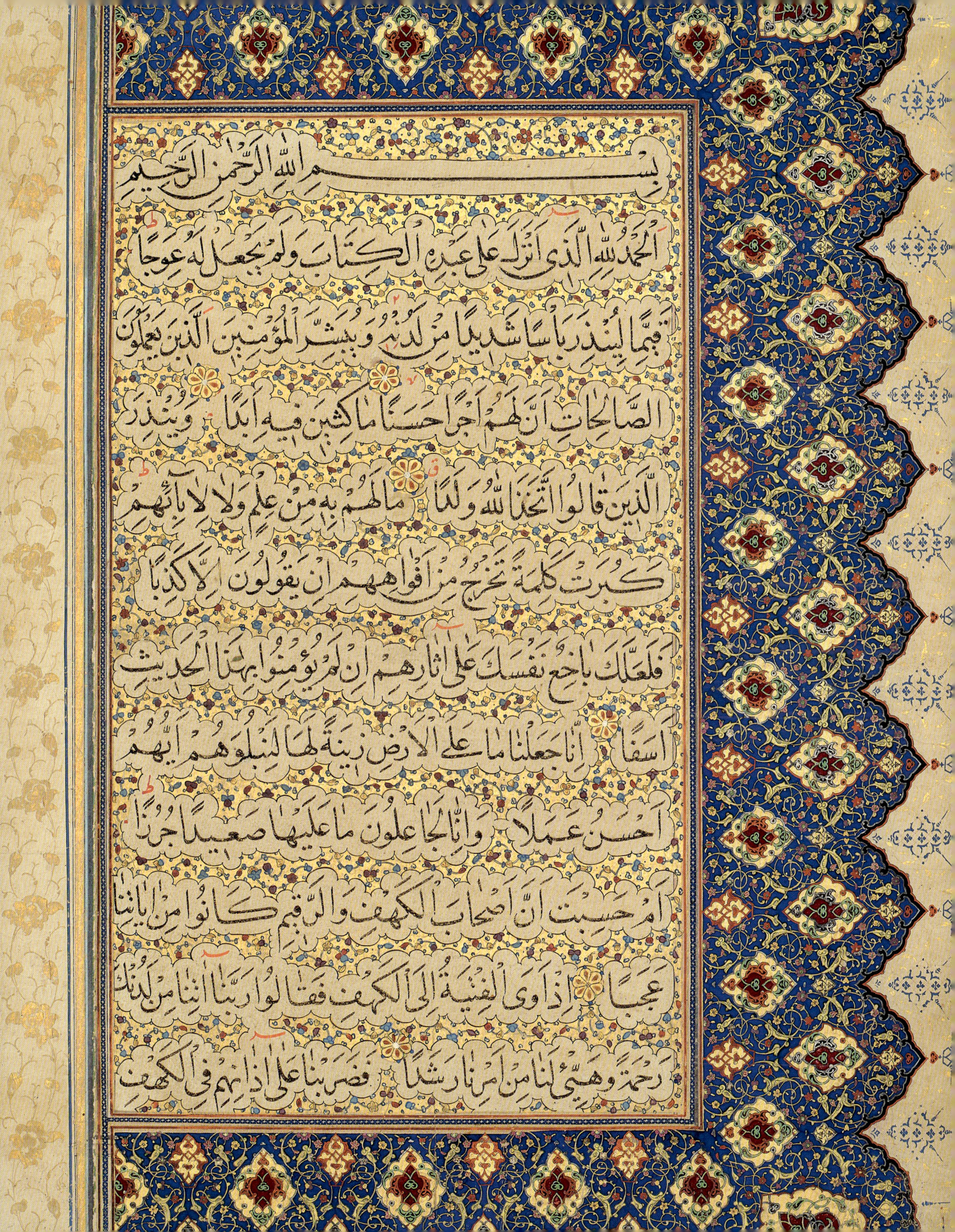
بسم الله الرحمن الرحيم

الحمد لله الذي انزل على عبده الكتاب ولم يجعل له عوجا
قيما لينذر باسا شديدا من لدنه ويبشر المؤمنين الذين يعملون
الصالحات ان لهم اجرا حسنا ماكثين فيه ابدا ويُنذر
الذين قالوا اتخذ الله ولدا ما لهم به من علم ولا لآبائهم
كبرت كلمة تخرج من افواههم ان يقولون الا كذبا
فلعلك باخع نفسك على آثارهم ان لم يؤمنوا بهذا الحديث
اسفا انا جعلنا ما على الارض زينة لها لنبلوهم ايهم
احسن عملا وانا لجاعلون ما عليها صعيدا جرزا
ام حسبت ان اصحاب الكهف والرقيم كانوا من آياتنا
عجبا اذ اوى الفتية الى الكهف فقالوا ربنا آتنا من لدنك
رحمة وهيئ لنا من امرنا رشدا فضربنا على آذانهم في الكهف

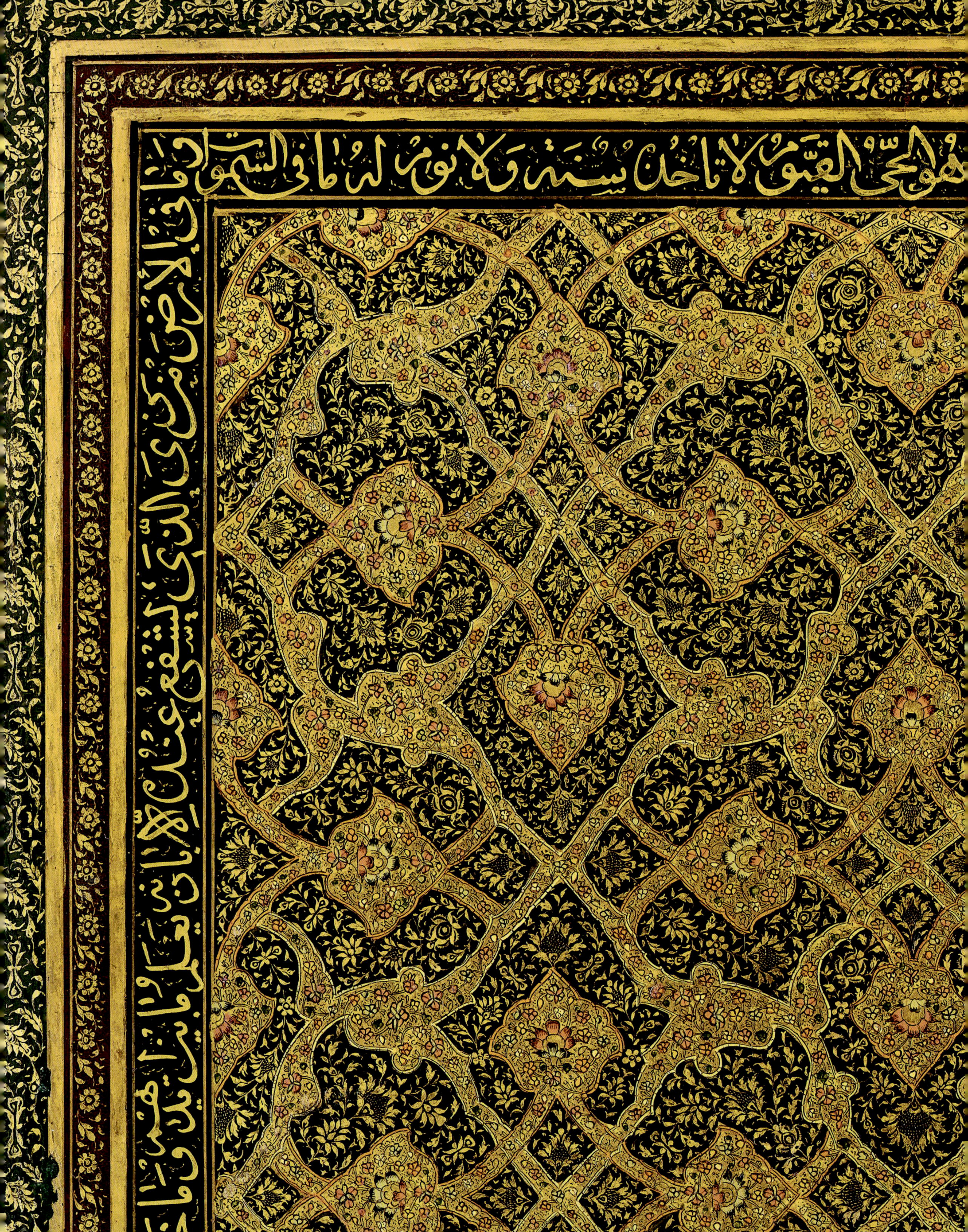
هو الحي القيوم لا تاخذه سنة ولا نوم له ما في السموات وما
في الارض من ذا الذي يشفع عنده الا باذنه يعلم ما بين ايديهم وما

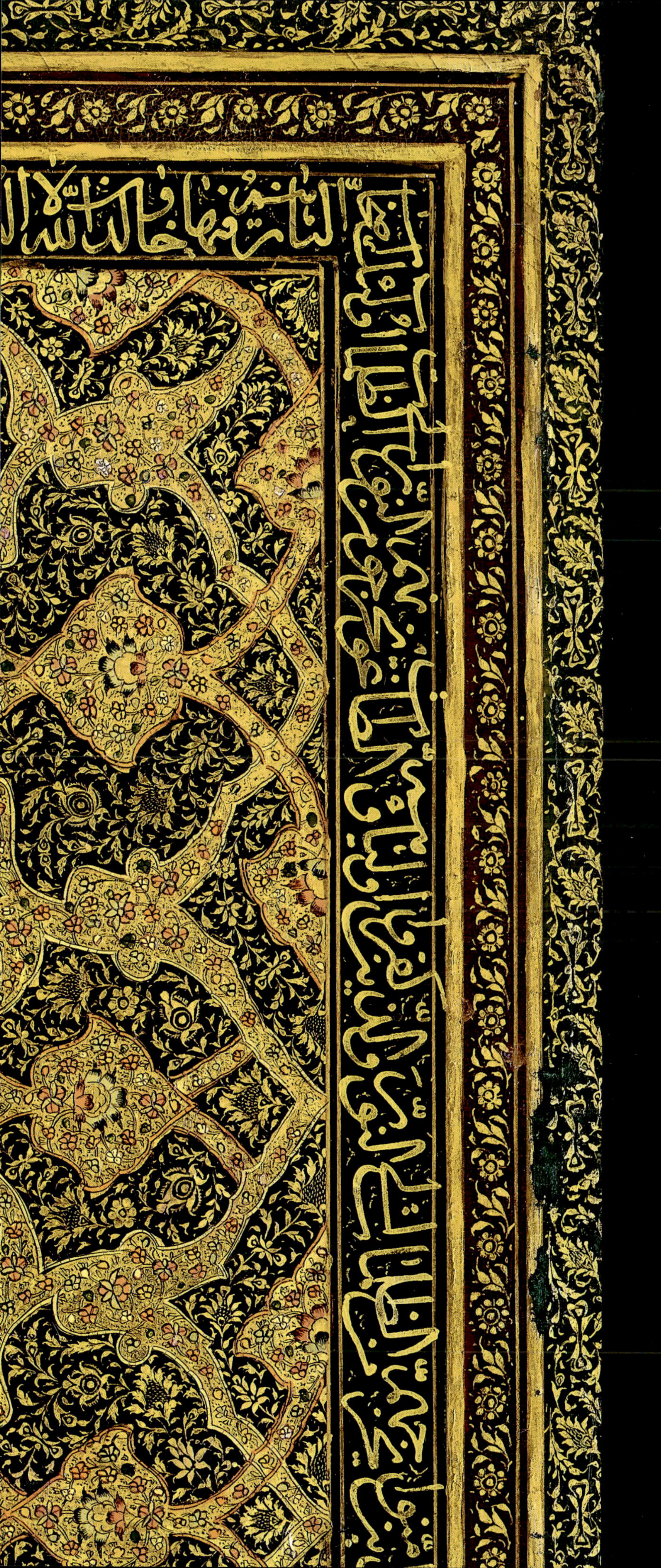

BOUND VOLUMES AND BOOK COVERS

BOUND VOLUMES AND BOOK COVERS

Throughout the Islamic lands a special prestige was attached to the skills and artistry required to make bookbindings. The importance of the craft is reflected in a specialist literature dedicated to the practice of making bindings, comprising treatises whose contents encompass descriptions of the necessary tools, of the preparation of materials and mediums, as well as the techniques entailed in production.[19] Praising the many specializations required of bookmaking generally, a letter of invitation/decree (*manshur*), composed by Sharaf al-Din Muhammad Yazdi and dated 1432 CE, invited the illuminator (*muzahhib*) Khwaja Nasir Muhammad to direct the workshop of Timurid prince Ibrahim Sultan (d. 1435 CE) in Shiraz, Iran. Stressing the properties of permanence, stability, and preservation—which would overcome the risk of dismemberment despite circulation and handling—Yazdi highlights the necessity of the "firm stitching of folios and gatherings one to the other in arranging a solid binding of pasteboard and skin."[20] The capacity of the book to endure, to withstand the vagaries of time, and to conserve knowledge and transmit it through writing from one generation to another was commonly praised in contrast to monumental architecture in medieval Islamic texts. For example, the polymath al-Jahiz (d. 868 or 869 CE) commented, "for there is no doubt that construction eventually perishes, and its traces disappear, while books handed from one generation to another, and from nation to nation, remain ever renewed."[21] For al-Jahiz, the power of the book represented the "victory" of memory over forgetfulness.

Although extant bindings from the first centuries of Qur'an production are rare, a defining feature of written copies of the revelation—the *mushaf*—was its enclosure "between two boards" (*bayna al-lawhayn*), the earliest forms of which were made of wood.[22] The bindings used for the codex form are much better represented by extant examples from the medieval period onward. The structure of bindings for Qur'ans was the same as that for other manuscripts. It comprised an upper and a lower cover connected by a spine (into which the textblock would be glued and hinged), commonly with an envelope flap attached to the outer edge of the lower cover: the fore-edge flap, adjoining the envelope flap to lower cover, was of approximately the same width as the spine. When the codex was closed, the textblock—including its outer edge—was housed in a protective, sturdy casing.[23] Bindings were made from wooden boards or pasteboards (composed of paper sheets glued together) with coverings adhered to their outer and inner surfaces. While these coverings were predominantly of tanned and dyed leather, surface treatments could include cloth and paper (mostly in combination with leather) from the fifteenth century onward. Lacquer over pasteboard bindings became increasingly common in the sixteenth century and later. Lacquer offered the possibility of more richly polychrome designs, which were, in effect, paintings protected under layers of varnish.

A wide repertoire of techniques was applied to embellish bindings. The supple leather on the outer covers and their inner surfaces (doublures) could be ruled, gilded, blind-tooled, and stamped with tools and pressed with engraved metal plates. Filigree (*munabbat-kari*), made of both paper and leather, formed intricate, lace-like patterns to adorn the less exposed doublures and enhanced by other means the property of relief across the binding's surfaces. The color palette of the binding could be augmented by filigree laid over a colored ground with fields of color changing to form complex geometric figures. While the decorative program of the outer and inner surfaces of bindings were often closely related, small changes were introduced to create subtle variations on themes. Principal design categories comprised geometry (e.g., complex geometric figures, interlocking motifs, medallions, pendants, cartouches, strapwork) and the natural world (e.g., flowers of various kinds, palmettes and split palmettes, cloud motifs). The natural motifs were constructed to form arabesques, scrolls, and sprays. The decoration of bindings could also be epigraphic, with textual programs composed of carefully chosen verses from the Qur'an, verses which often referenced the Qur'an itself. The self-referential aspect of such verses was also true of the artistic programs of bindings that manifest, on their surfaces, formal features, habits of composition, materials, and effects which found correspondences and echoes inside the Qur'ans' folios among its polychrome illuminations.

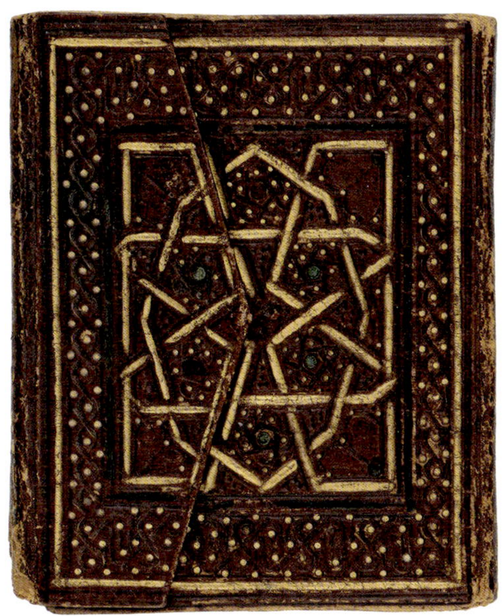

Upper cover

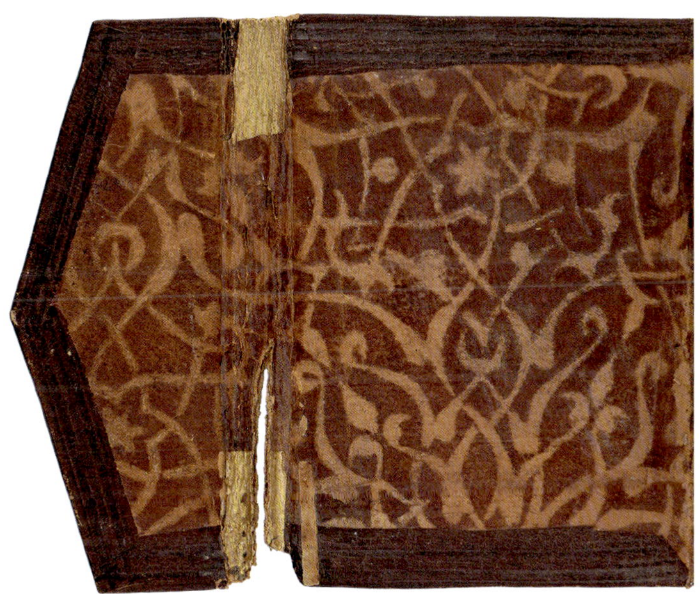
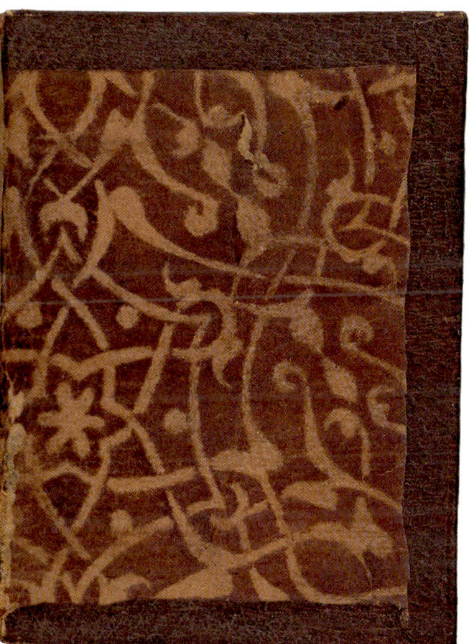

Inside cover

54

Fifth Part (*Juz'*) of a Qur'an Manuscript

Iran, late 13th–14th century
Ink, opaque watercolor, and gold on paper
Open: 2 1/4 × 4 13/16 inches (5.7 × 12.2 cm); 5 lines
Closed: 1/4 × 2 1/4 × 1 7/8 inches (0.6 × 5.7 × 4.7 cm)
Unpaginated manuscript, sura 4, *al-Nisa'* (The Women), verses 24–147
Binding (upper and lower covers and envelope flap): tooled, stamped, and gilded brown leather (central panel composed of interlocking geometric figures, outer border of intertwining lines studded with dots); doublures: brown leather patterned with an arabesque of split palmettes.
Text copied in *naskh* script; illuminated frontispiece, double-page text frontispiece (identifying manuscript as fifth *juz'* of thirty), and verse markers.
TR:403-2015

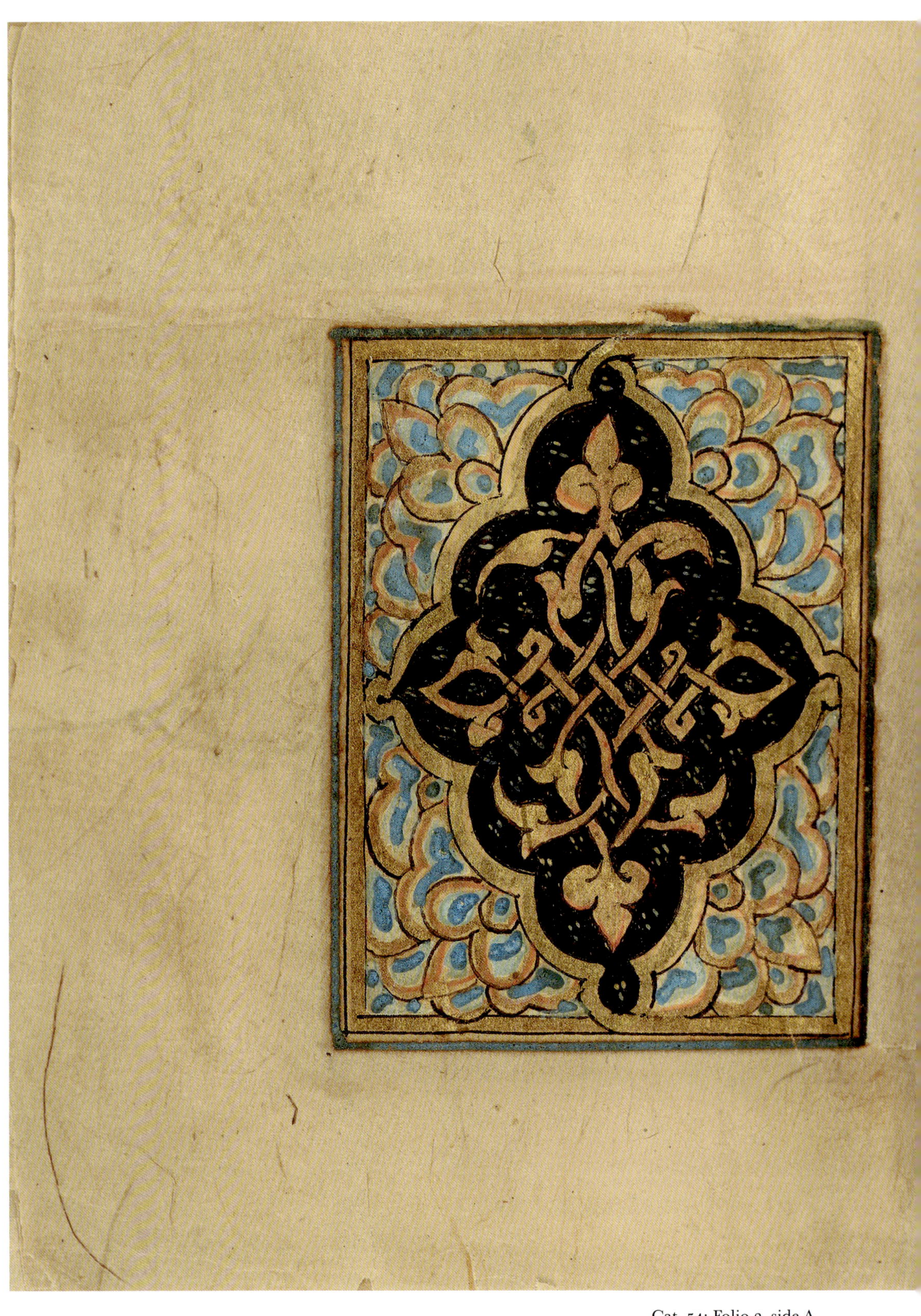

Cat. 54: Folio 2, side A

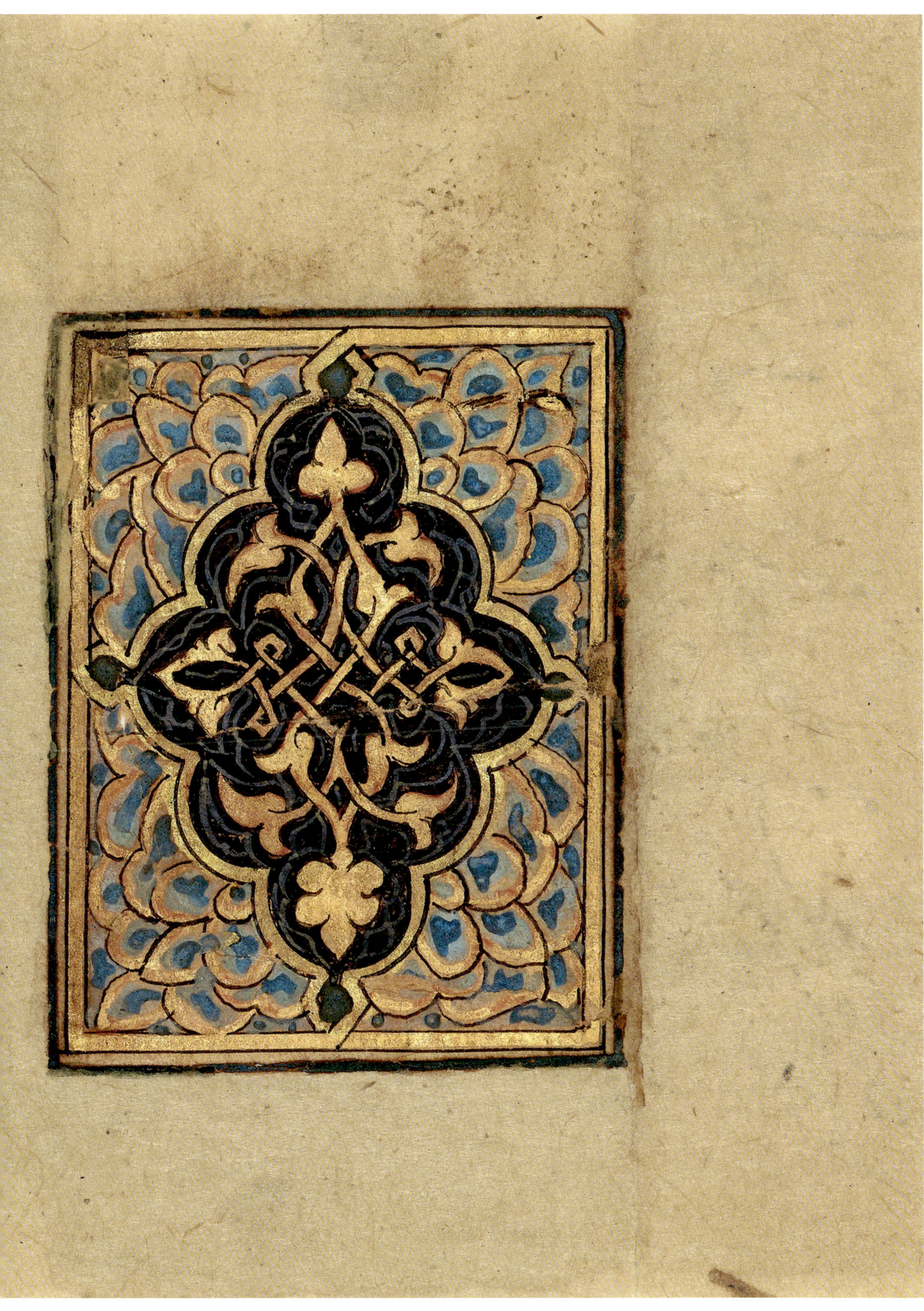

Cat. 54: Folio 1, side B

55

Fourteenth Part (*Juz'*) of a Qur'an Manuscript

Iran, mid-15th–mid-16th century
Ink, opaque watercolor, and gold on paper
Open: 2 3/4 × 3 5/16 inches (7 × 8.4 cm); 5 lines
Closed: 2 3/4 × 2 inches (7 × 5.1 cm)
Folios 2, side B–43 side A, sura 15, *al-Hijr* (al-Hijr), verses 2–99, to sura 16, *al-Nahl* (The Bees), verses 1–128
Binding (upper and lower covers and envelope flap): tooled, stamped, and gilded brown leather with lapis lazuli forming a field of split palmettes and flowers; doublures: arabesque in filigree red leather over a lapis lazuli ground; central four-lobed medallion flanked by two pendants over a gold ground. Text copied in *naskh* script; illuminated chapter headings and verse markers.
TR:366-2015

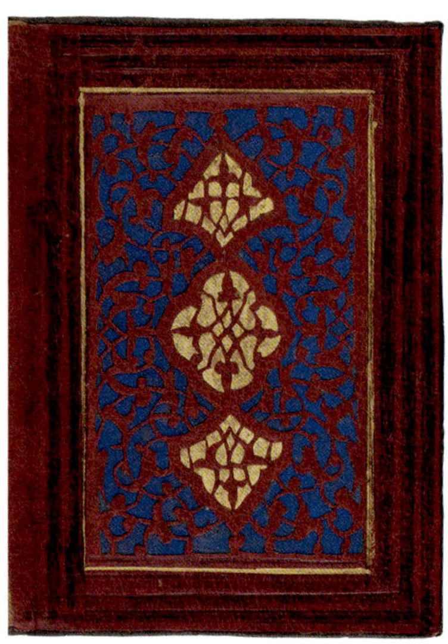

Doublure, upper cover

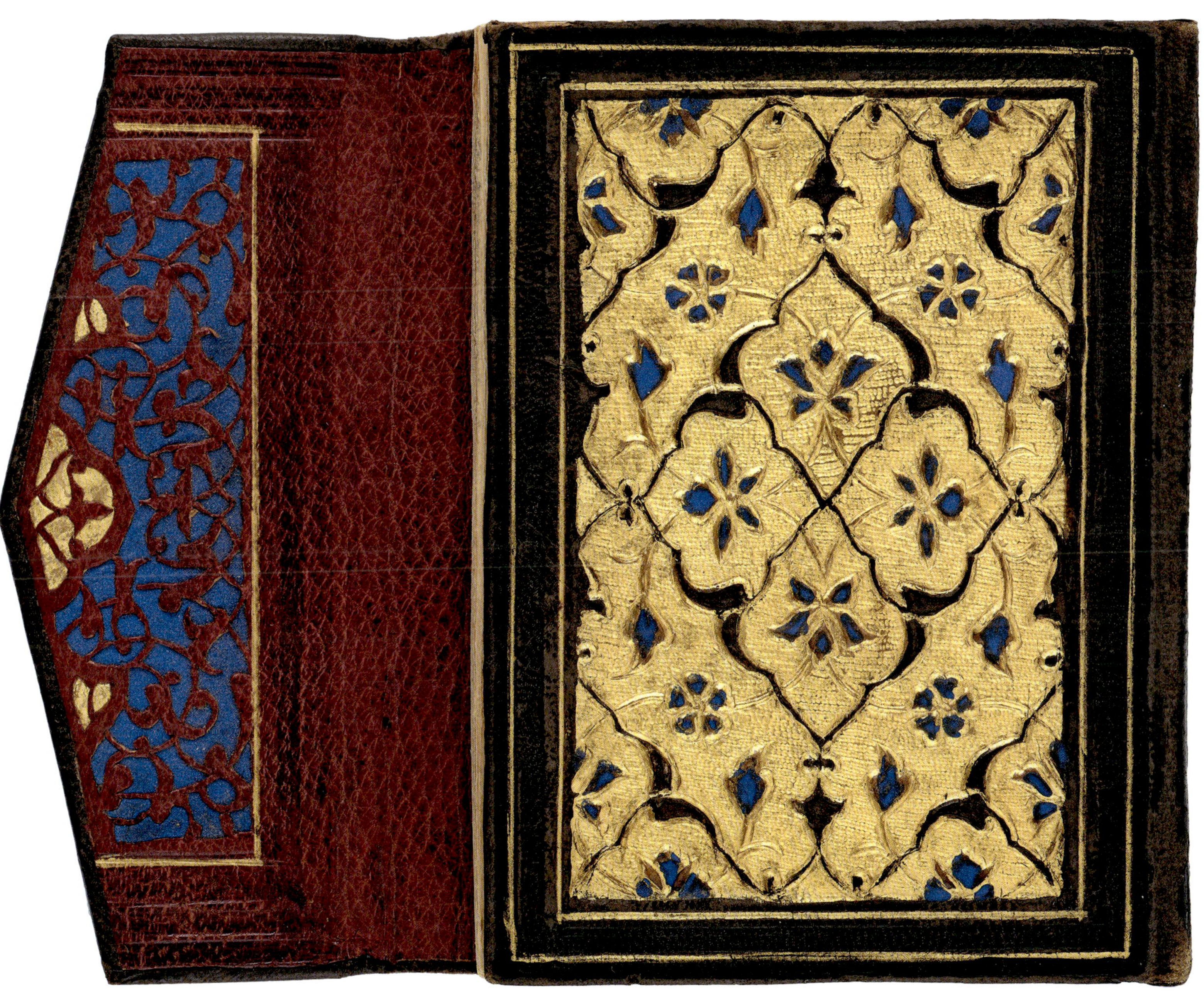

Upper cover and interior of envelope flap

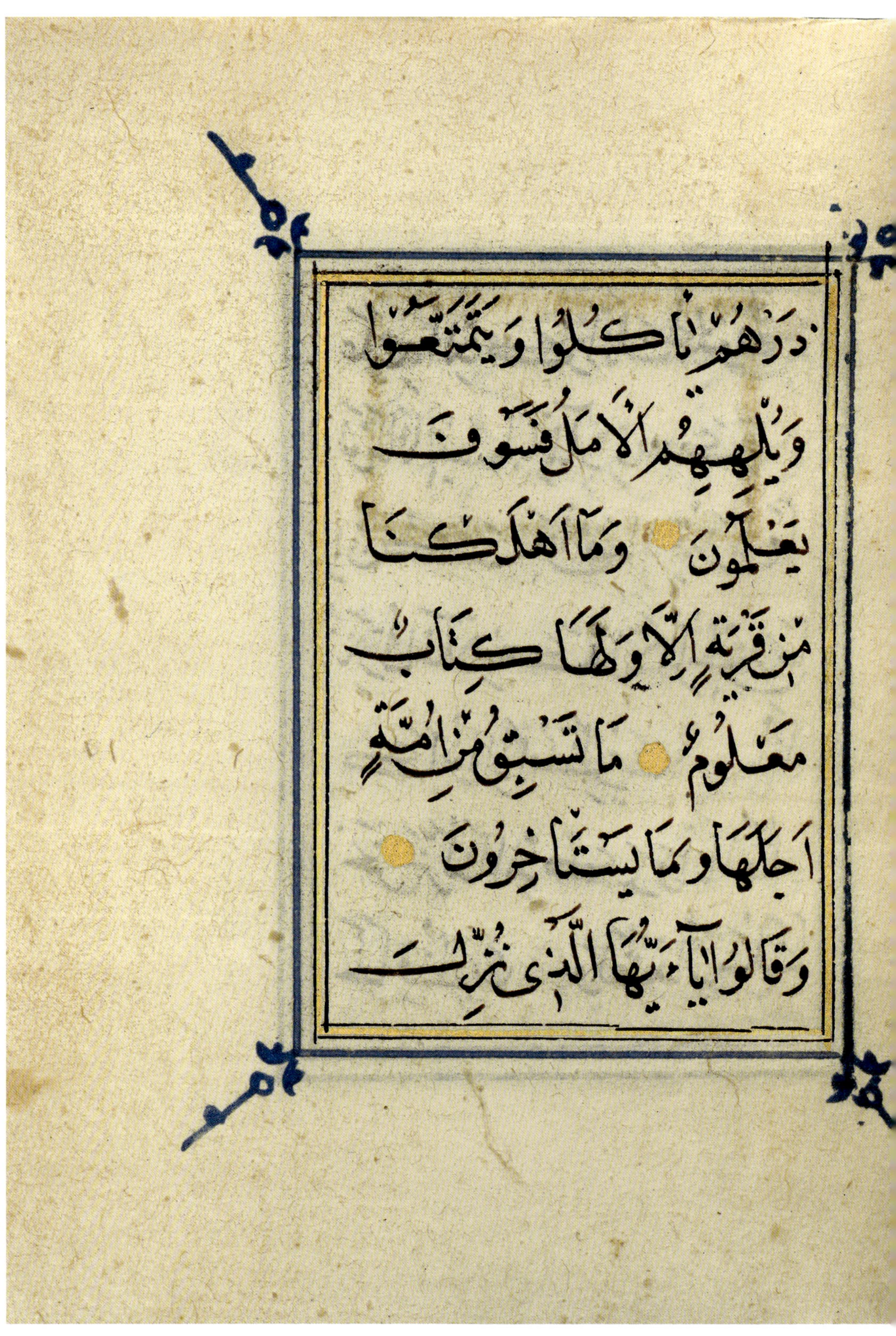

ذرهم يأكلوا ويتمتعوا
ويلههم الأمل فسوف
يعلمون • وما أهلكنا
من قرية إلا ولها كتاب
معلوم • ما تسبق من أمة
أجلها وما يستأخرون •
وقالوا يا أيها الذي نزل

Cat. 55: Folio 2, side A

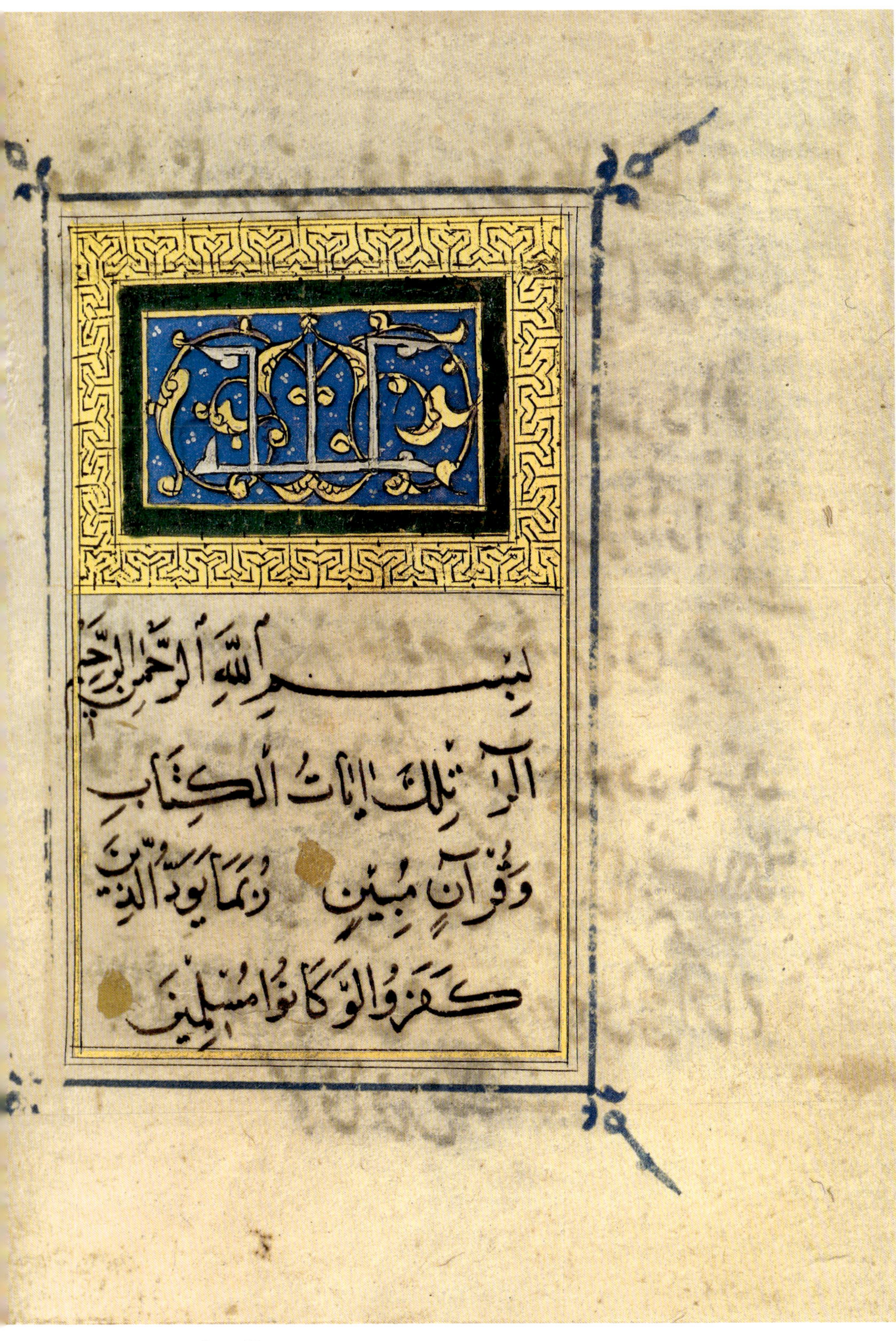
بسم الله الرحمن الرحيم
الر تلك آيات الكتاب
وقرآن مبين ربما يود الذين
كفروا لو كانوا مسلمين

Cat. 55: Folio 1, side B

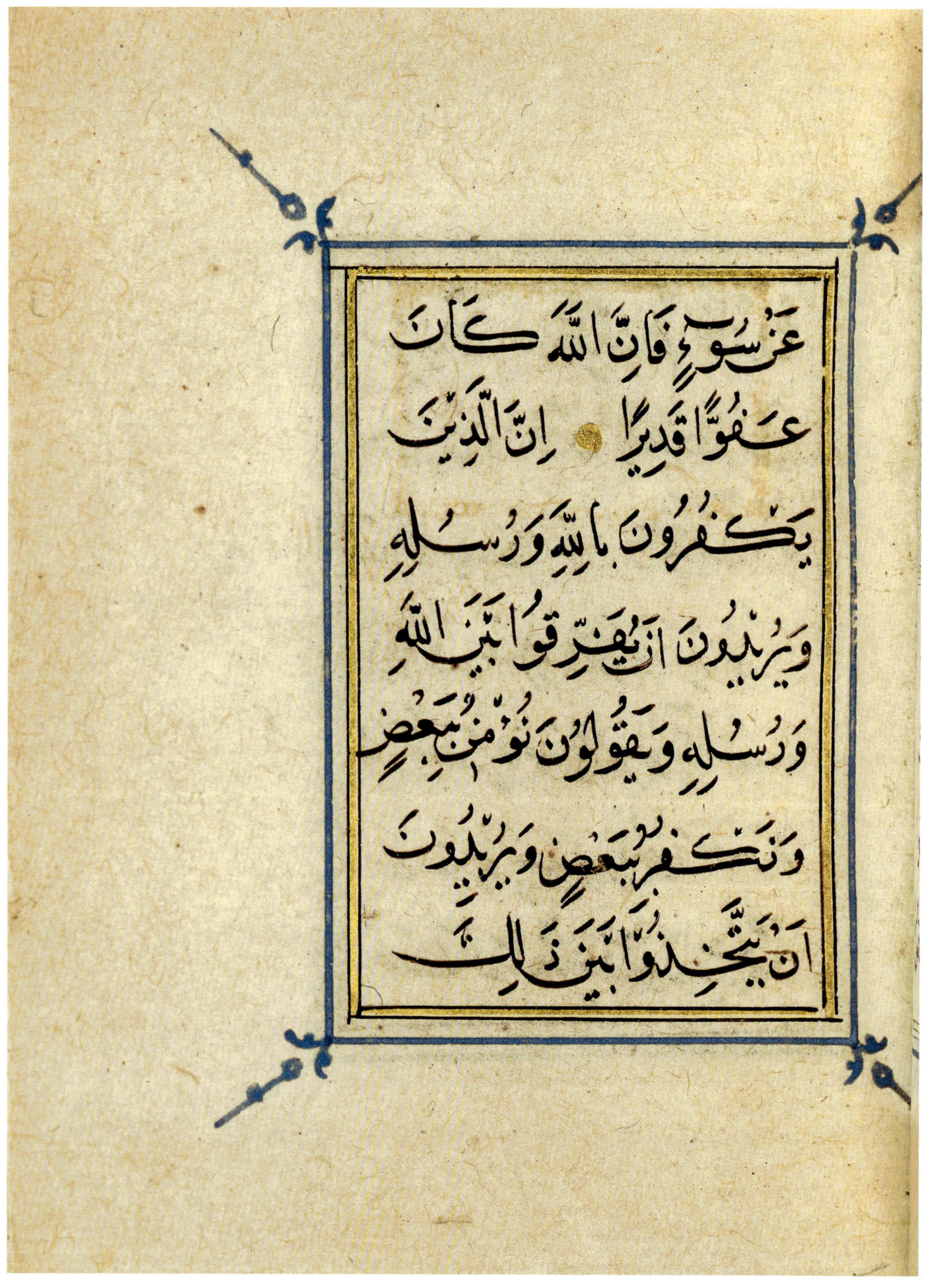
عن سوء فان الله كان
عفوا قديرا • ان الذين
يكفرون بالله ورسله
ويريدون ان يفرقوا بين الله
ورسله ويقولون نؤمن ببعض
ونكفر ببعض ويريدون
ان يتخذوا بين ذلك

Folio 2, side A

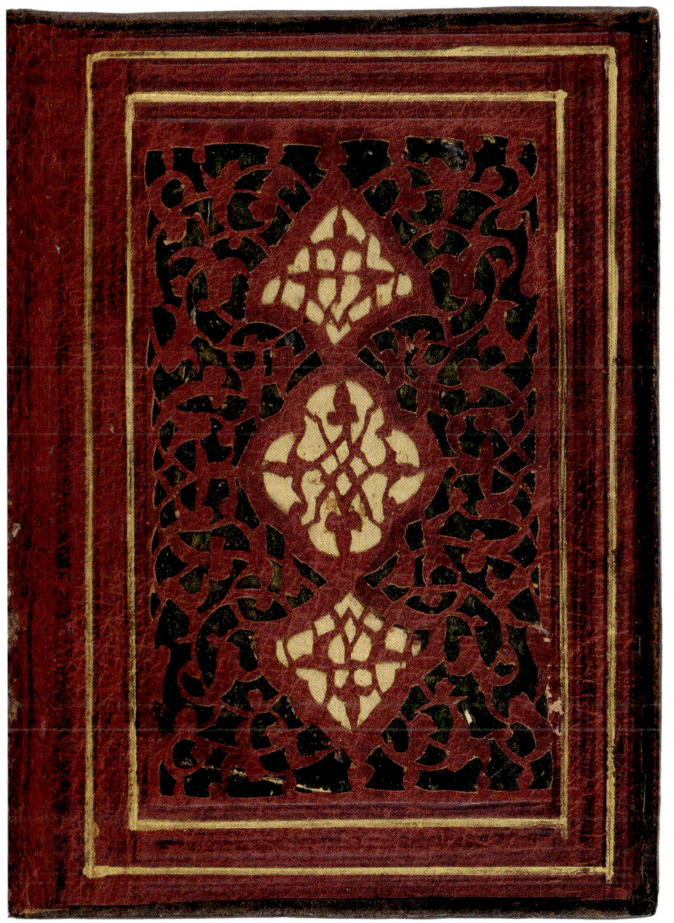

Doublure, upper cover

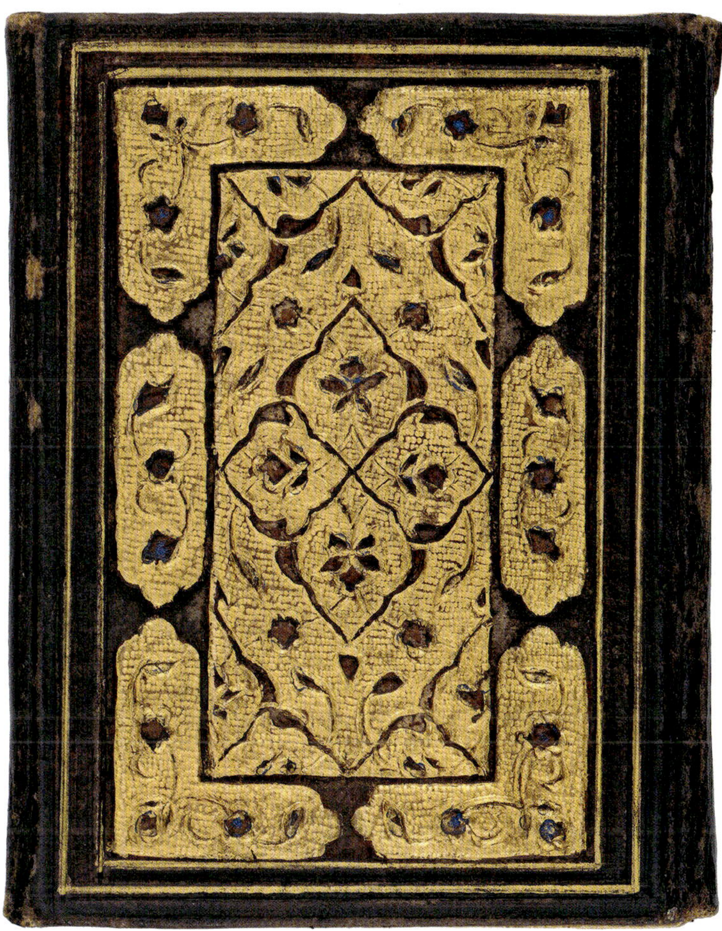

Upper cover

56

Sixth Part (*Juz'*) of a Qur'an Manuscript

Iran, mid-15th–mid-16th century
Ink, opaque watercolor, and gold on paper
Open: 2 3/4 × 5 5/16 inches (7 × 13.5 cm); 7 lines
Closed: 5/16 × 2 3/4 × 2 inches (0.9 × 7 × 5.1 cm)
Folios 2, side B–44, side B, sura 4, *al-Nisa'* (The Women), verses 148–76, to sura 5, *al-Ma'ida* (The Feast), verses 1–82
Binding (upper and lower covers and envelope flap): tooled, stamped, and gilded brown leather with lapis lazuli forming a field of split palmettes and flowers (central panel framed by border of cartouches); doublures: arabesque in filigree red leather over a brownish-green ground; central four-lobed medallion flanked by two pendants over a gold ground. Text copied in *naskh* script; chapter headings in *thuluth* script (in gold); illuminated chapter headings and verse markers.
TR:1628-2015

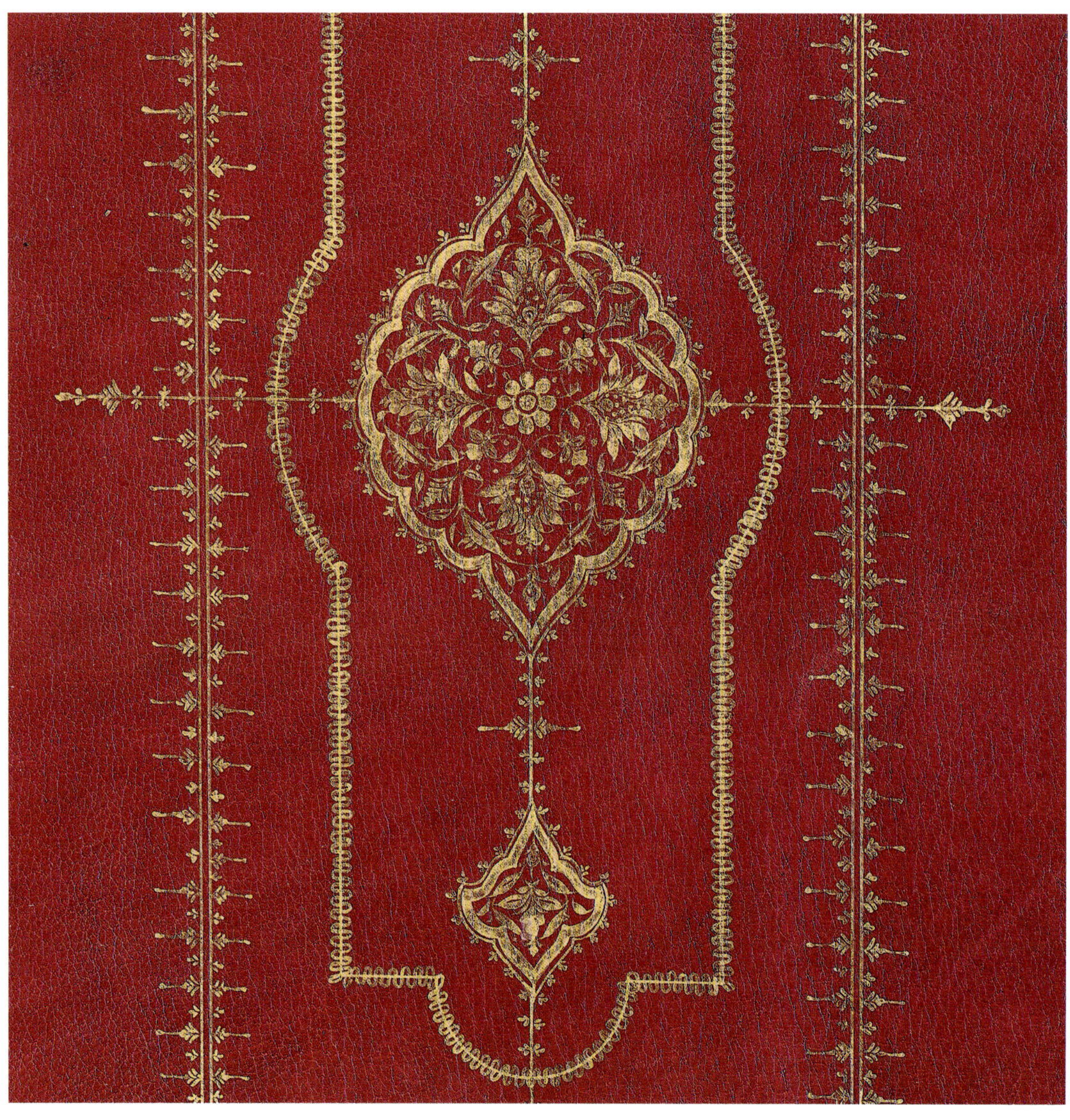

Doublure, lower cover (*detail*)

57

Qur'an Manuscript

Signed by Husayn al-Shirazi al-Fakhkhar (active 16th century)
Iran, possibly Shiraz, AH 961/1553–54 CE
Ink, opaque watercolor, and gold on paper
Open: 1 3/4 × 11 7/8 × 7 9/16 inches (4.4 × 30.2 × 19.2 cm); 14 lines
Closed: 11 7/8 × 12 15/16 inches (30.2 × 32.8 cm)
Binding: modern binding of black leather over pasteboard with gold stamping; doublures: red leather stamped and gilded. Text copied in *naskh* script (text field is gold-sprinkled, borders are plain); chapter headings in *thuluth* script; full program of illumination comprising text frontispiece (for sura 1, *al-Fatiha* [The Prologue]), chapter headings, verse markers and counters.
TR:879-2015

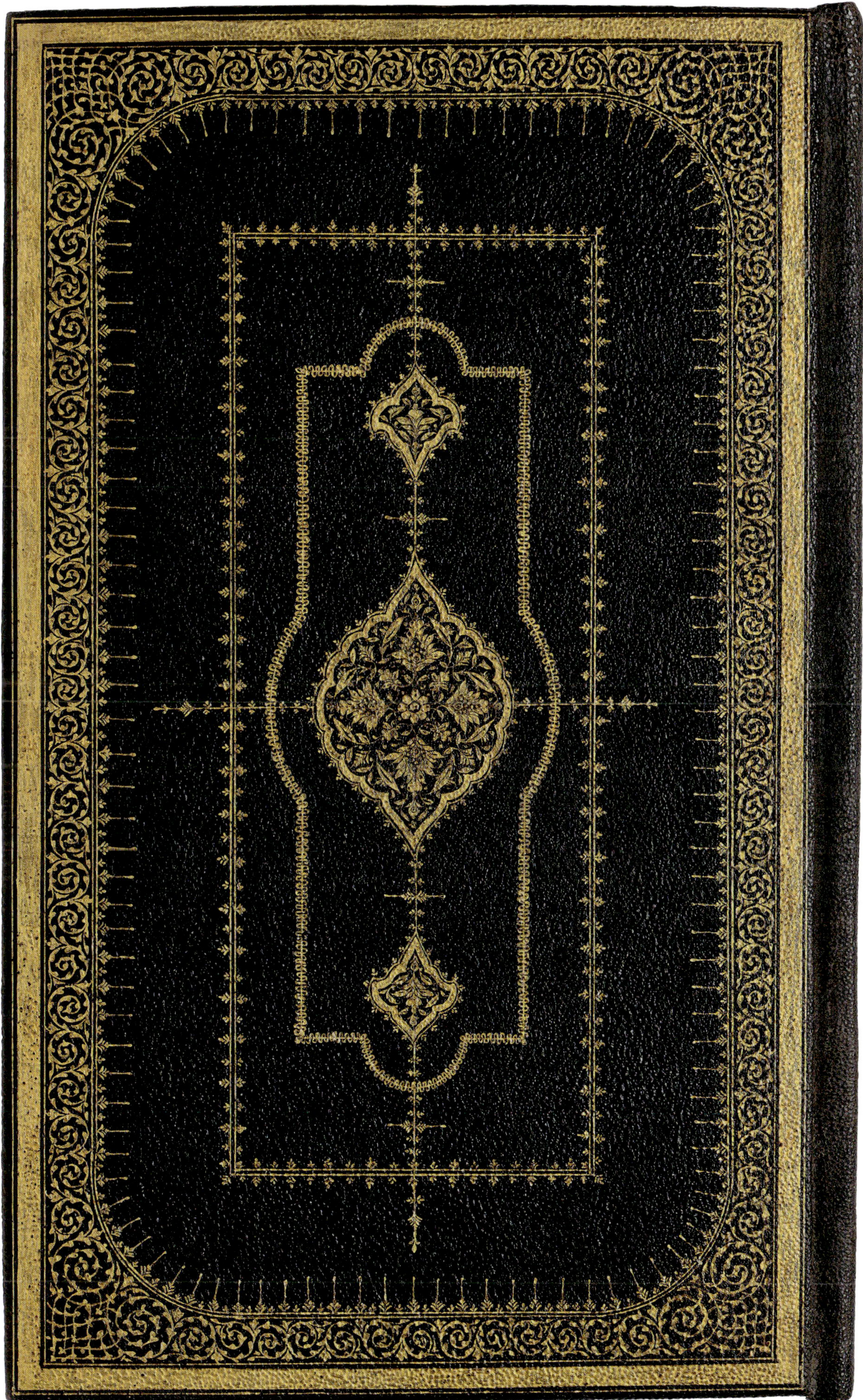

Upper cover

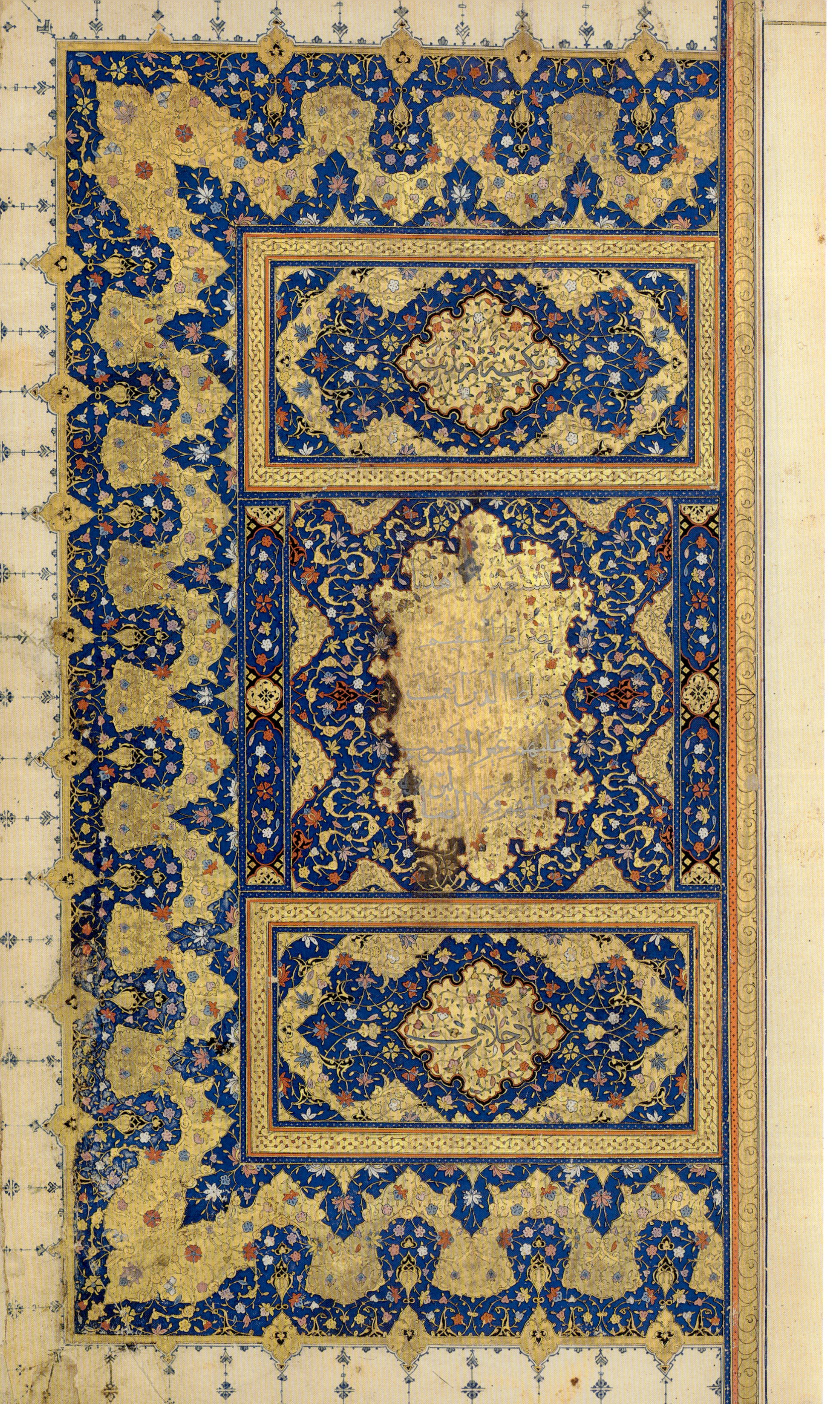

Cat. 57: Illuminated frontispiece, Folio 1, side A

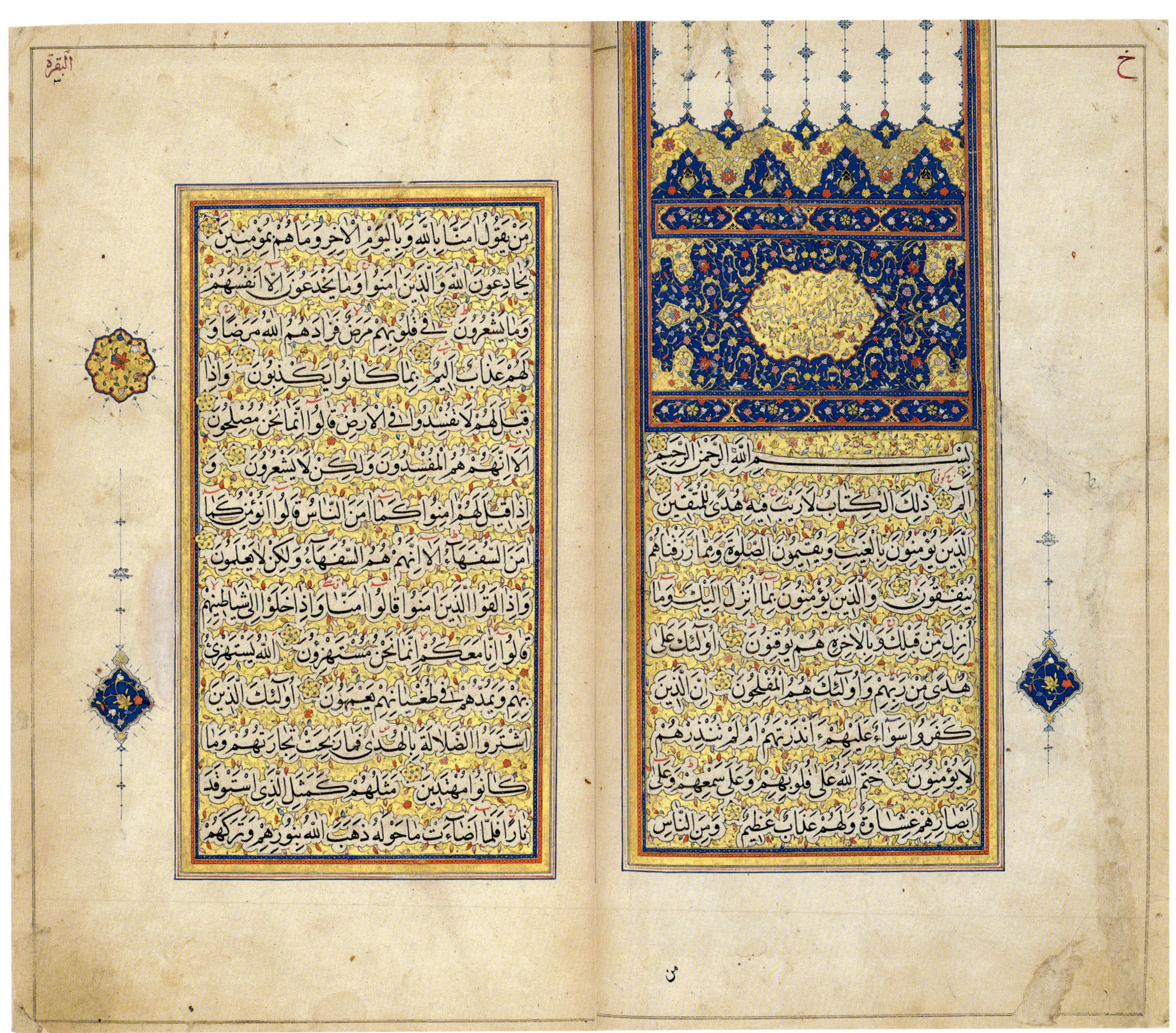

Cat. 57: Folio 2, side A, and folio 1, side B

Following pages: Cat. 57: Folio 321, side A, and folio 320, side B

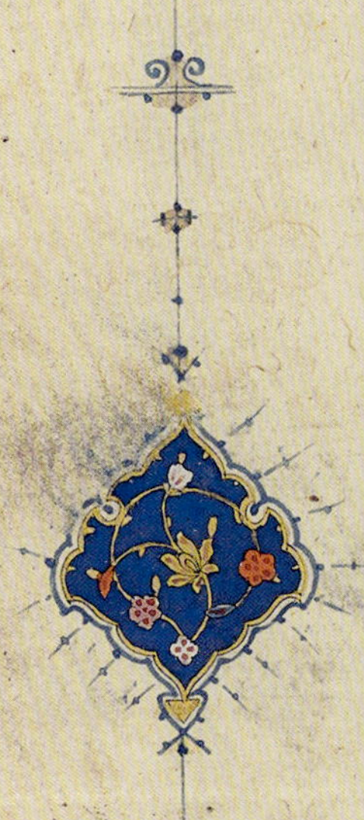

بسم الله الرحمن الرحيم

لم يكن الذين كفروا من اهل الكتاب والمشركين منفكين
حتى تاتيهم البينة ۝ رسول من الله يتلوا صحفا مطهرة
فيها كتب قيمة ۝ وما تفرق الذين اوتوا الكتاب
الا من بعد ما جاءتهم البينة ۝ وما امروا الا ليعبدوا
الله مخلصين له الدين حنفاء ويقيموا الصلوة ويؤتوا
الزكوة وذلك دين القيمة ۝ ان الذين كفروا من
اهل الكتاب والمشركين في نار جهنم خالدين فيها
اولئك هم شر البرية ۝ ان الذين امنوا وعملوا الصالحات
اولئك هم خير البرية ۝ جزاؤهم عند ربهم جنات
عدن تجري من تحتها الانهار خالدين فيها ابدا رضي الله
عنهم ورضوا عنه ذلك لمن خشي ربه ۝

سورة الزلزال ثمان آيات

راه استغنى ان الى ربك الرجعى ارايت الذى ينهى
عبدا اذا صلى ارايت ان كان على الهدى او
امر بالتقوى ارايت ان كذب وتولى الم يعلم
بان الله يرى كلا لئن لم ينته لنسفعا بالناصية
ناصية كاذبة خاطئة فليدع ناديه سندع
الزبانية كلا لا تطعه واسجد واقترب

سورة القدر مكية خمس آيات

بسم الله الرحمن الرحيم

انا انزلناه فى ليلة القدر وما ادريك ما ليلة القدر
ليلة القدر خير من الف شهر تنزل الملائكة و
الروح فيها باذن ربهم من كل امر سلام هى حتى مطلع الفجر

سورة البينة مدنية ثمان آيات

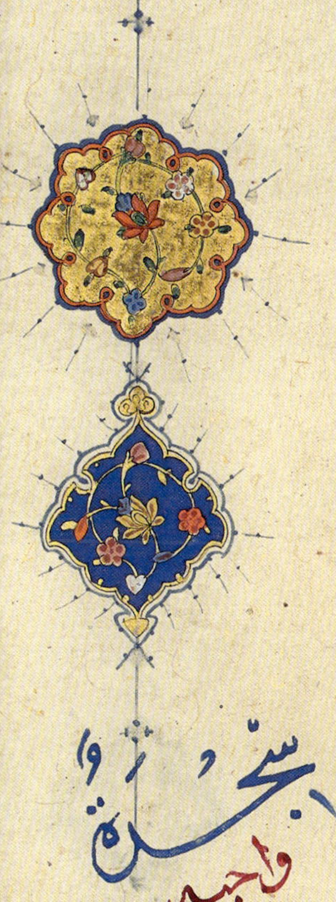

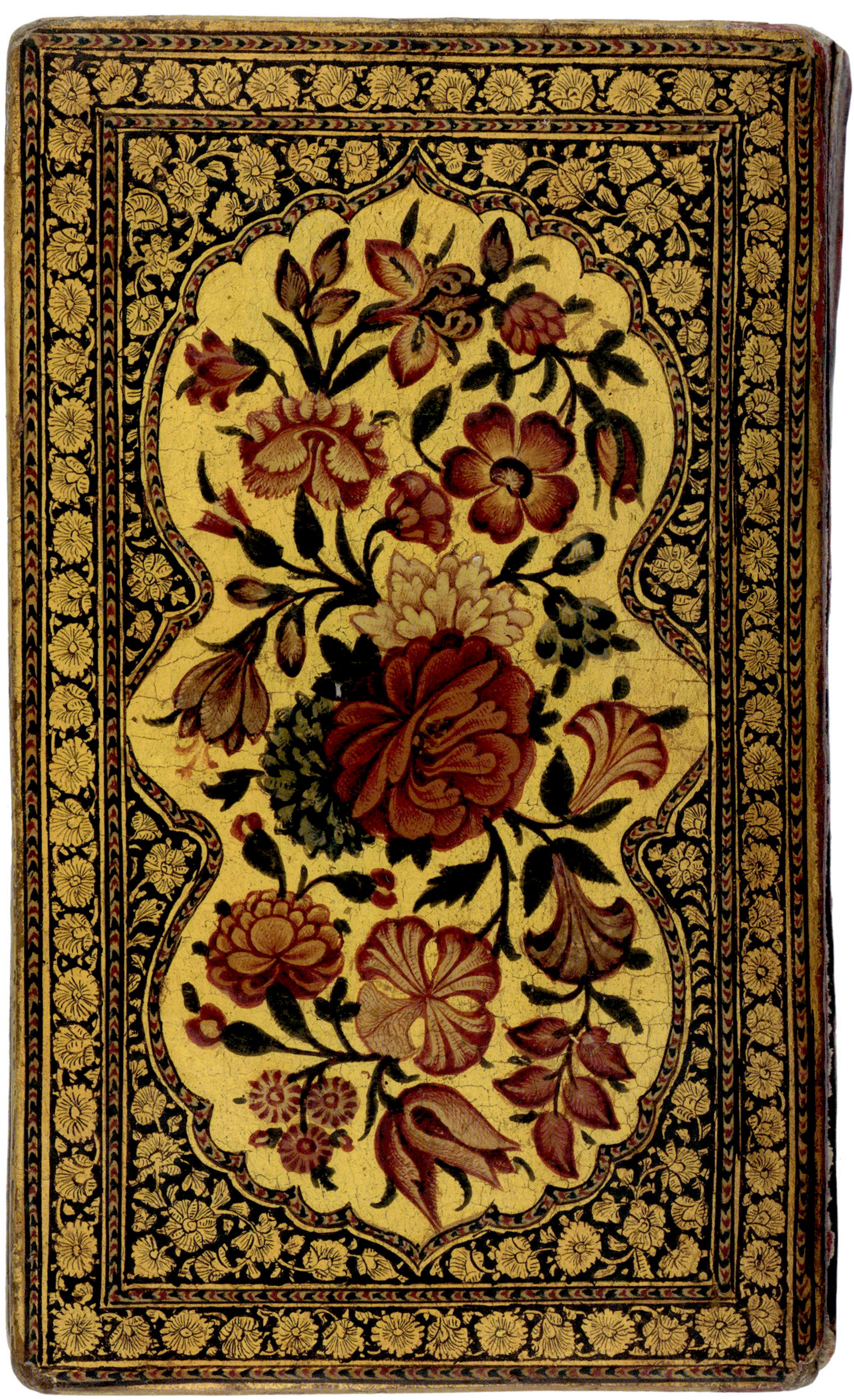

Front, upper cover

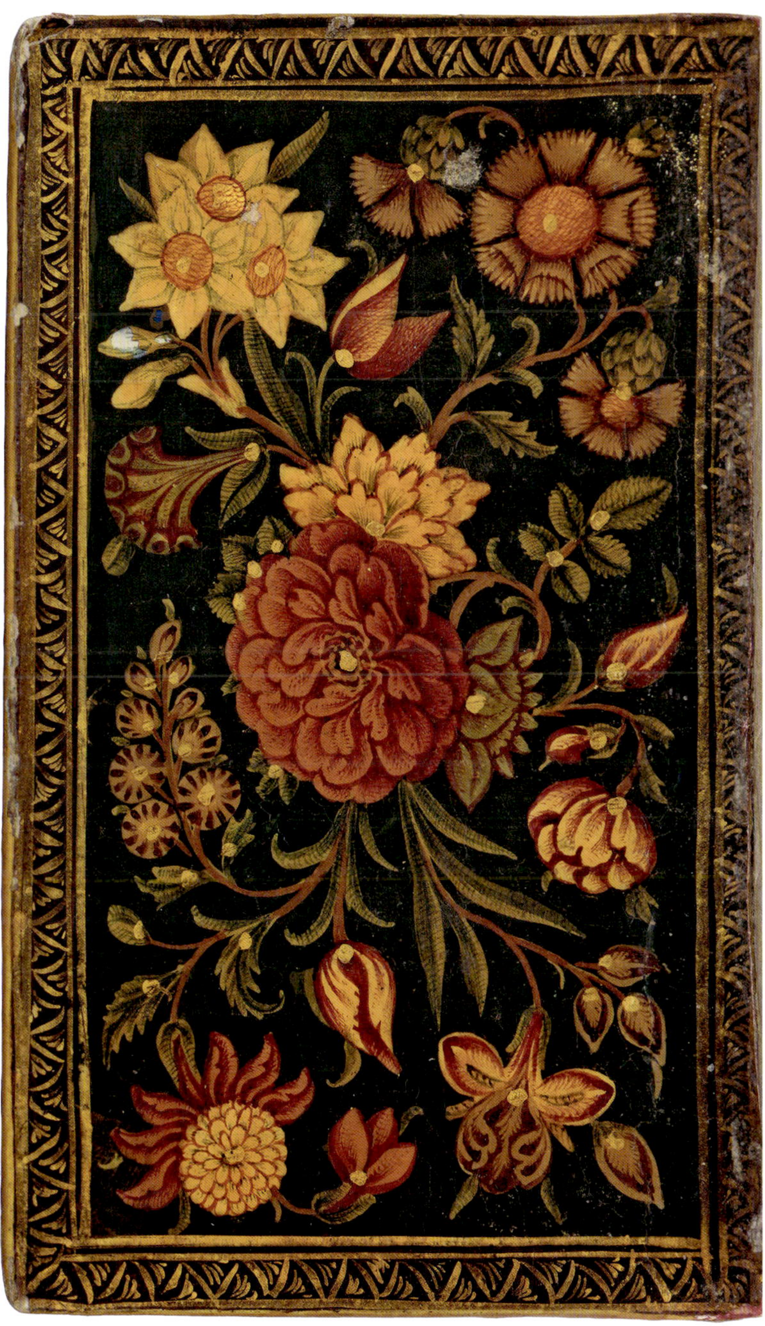

Doublure, lower cover

58

Qur'an Manuscript

India, AH 1123/1711–12 CE
Ink, opaque watercolor, and gold on paper
Open: 15/16 × 4 × 2 3/8 inches (2.4 × 10.1 × 6.1 cm); 17 lines
Closed: 4 × 4 1/2 inches (10.1 × 11.5 cm)
Binding: lacquer over pasteboard with opaque watercolor and gold; upper and lower covers composed as a spray of flowers over gold arranged in a cartouche, which is enclosed by golden flowers over a black ground; doublures composed as a spray of flowers over a black ground enclosed by a border of a zigzagging gold line over black.
Text copied in *naskh* script (text field enclosed by a floral scroll border); chapter headings in *thuluth* script (alternating blue script over gold ground, gold script over blue ground); full program of illumination comprising text frontispiece (for sura 1, *al-Fatiha* [The Prologue]), double-page text finispiece (for suras 113–14), chapter headings, and verse markers.
TR:881-2015

59

Qur'an Manuscript

Signed by Mir ʿAbd al-Karim Muhammad Sadiq al-Husayni al-Yazdi
Iran, dated AH 1260/1844–45 CE
Ink, opaque watercolor, and gold on paper
Open: 13 1/8 × 16 1/8 inches (33.4 × 41 cm); 14 lines
Closed: 2 5/8 × 13 1/8 × 8 5/8 inches (6.7 × 33.4 × 21.9 cm)
Binding: lacquer over pasteboard with opaque watercolor and gold; upper and lower covers each composed as a central field of interconnecting split palmettes and medallions (with colored flowers over gold) on a black ground with gold lotus flowers, a text border in gold *thuluth* script on black, and two outer borders in red and green (each with golden floral scrolls); doublures each composed as a spray of flowers with a rose and nightingale (a visual metaphor for the lover's unrequited love) over a gold ground, enclosed by black and red borders (enriched with gold motifs), and an outer text border in gold *thuluth* script on a green ground. Inscription on upper cover: sura 2, *al-Baqara* (The Cow), verses 255–57; inscription on lower cover: sura 24, *al-Nur* (The Light), verses 35–36, concluding with a prayer and the date AH 1260/1844–45 CE. Inscriptions on the doublures are each prayers mentioning the Prophet Muhammad and ʿAli b. Abi Talib. Text copied in *naskh* script (set in clouds of reserved paper enclosed by a gold ground with polychrome flowers); full program of illumination comprising double-page prayer of dedication, double-page table (*fihrist*) enumerating the names of the 114 suras, double-page text frontispiece (for suras 1–2), illuminated frame for sura 2, *al-Baqara* (The Cow), verses 4–22, chapter headings, and verse markers.
TR:404-2015

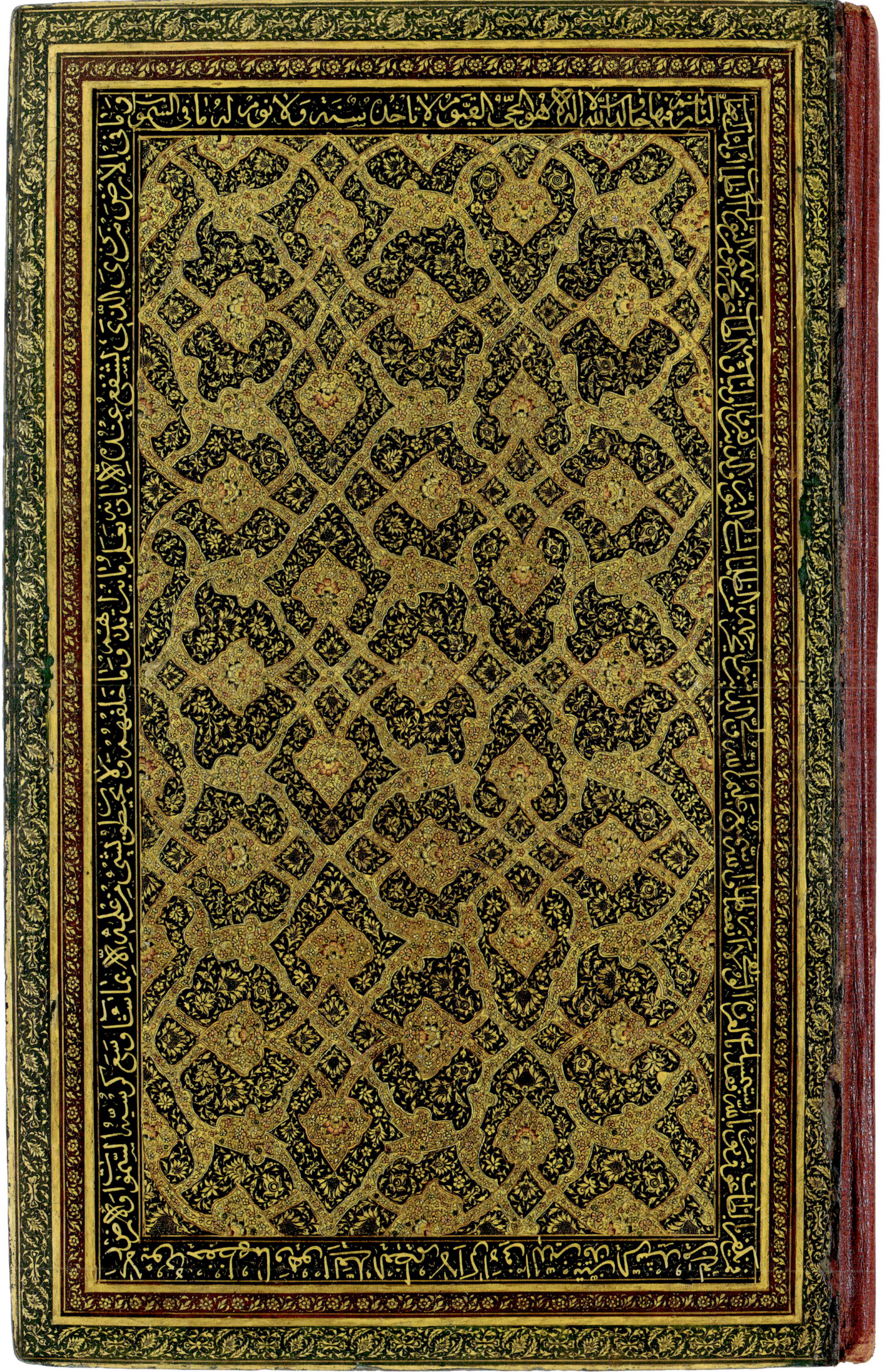

Upper cover

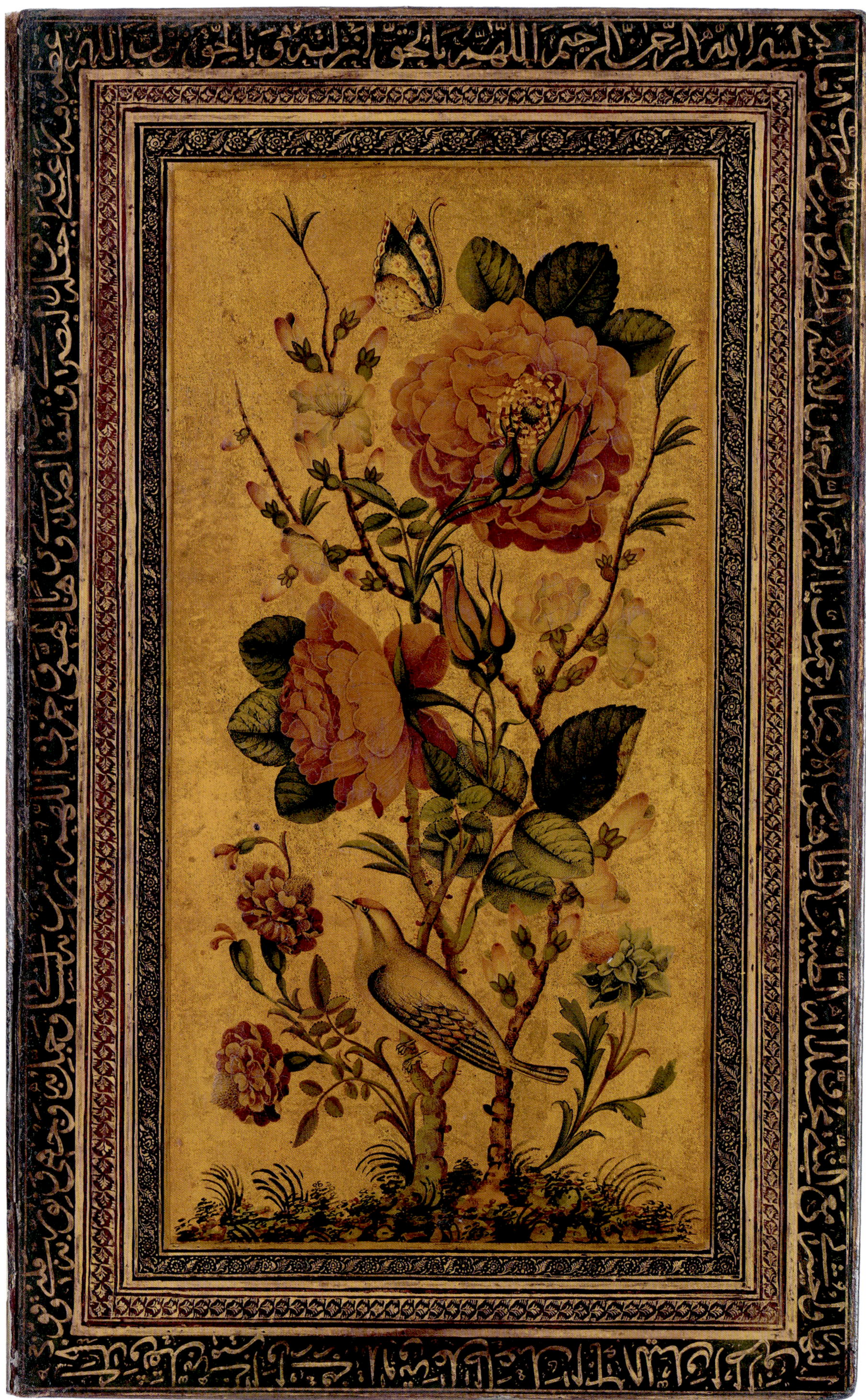

Cat. 59: Doublure, upper cover

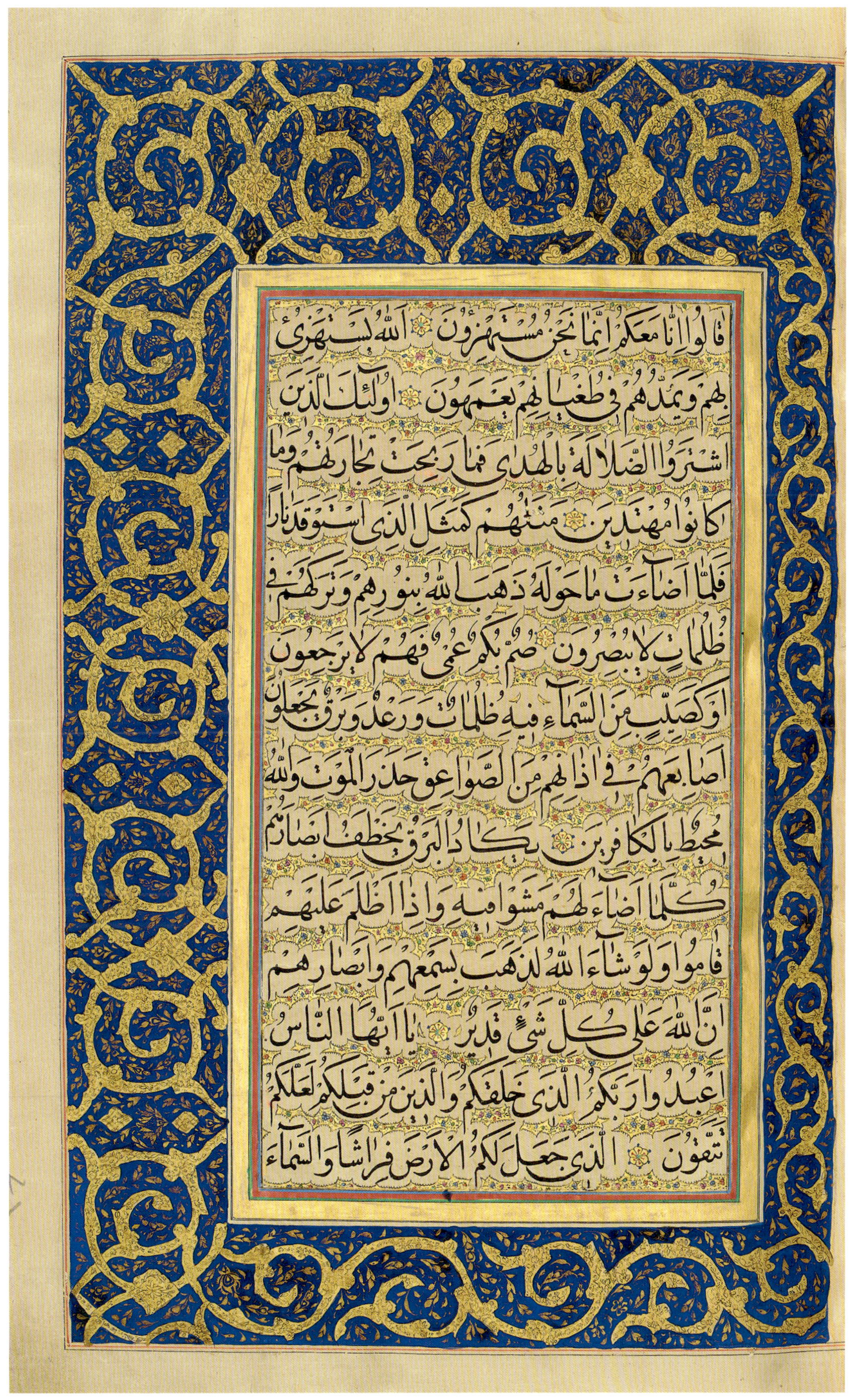

قالوا انا معكم انما نحن مستهزءون ۞ الله يستهزئ
بهم ويمدهم في طغيانهم يعمهون ۞ اولئك الذين
اشتروا الضلالة بالهدى فما ربحت تجارتهم وما
كانوا مهتدين ۞ مثلهم كمثل الذي استوقد نارا
فلما اضاءت ما حوله ذهب الله بنورهم وتركهم في
ظلمات لا يبصرون ۞ صم بكم عمي فهم لا يرجعون
او كصيب من السماء فيه ظلمات ورعد وبرق يجعلون
اصابعهم في اذانهم من الصواعق حذر الموت والله
محيط بالكافرين ۞ يكاد البرق يخطف ابصارهم
كلما اضاء لهم مشوا فيه واذا اظلم عليهم
قاموا ولو شاء الله لذهب بسمعهم وابصارهم
ان الله على كل شيء قدير ۞ يا ايها الناس
اعبدوا ربكم الذي خلقكم والذين من قبلكم لعلكم
تتقون ۞ الذي جعل لكم الارض فراشا والسماء

Above: Cat. 59: Folio 46, side A
Following pages: Cat. 59: Folio, colophon and folio, closing page

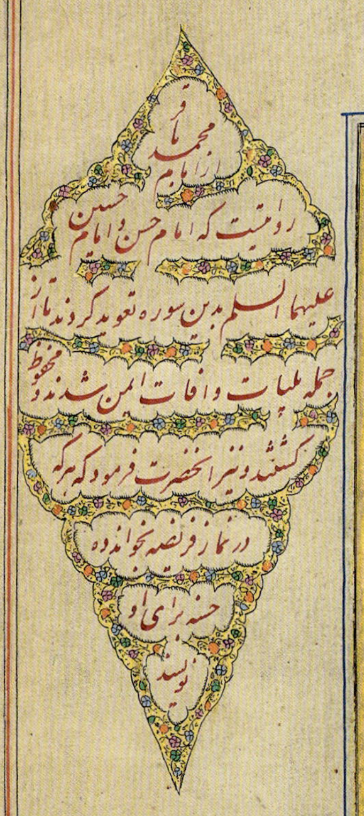

قُلْ أَعُوذُ بِرَبِّ النَّاسِ ۝ مَلِكِ النَّاسِ ۝ إِلَٰهِ
النَّاسِ ۝ مِن شَرِّ الْوَسْوَاسِ الْخَنَّاسِ ۝ الَّذِي
يُوَسْوِسُ فِي صُدُورِ النَّاسِ ۝ مِنَ الْجِنَّةِ وَالنَّاسِ

كتبه اقل عباد الله المحتاج لرحمة الله
الملك الغني ابن خير الحاج مير عبد الكريم
محمد صادق الحسيني اليزدي ١٢٦٠ في من الهجرة
المقدسة الشريفة النبوية عليه الف صلوة و تحية

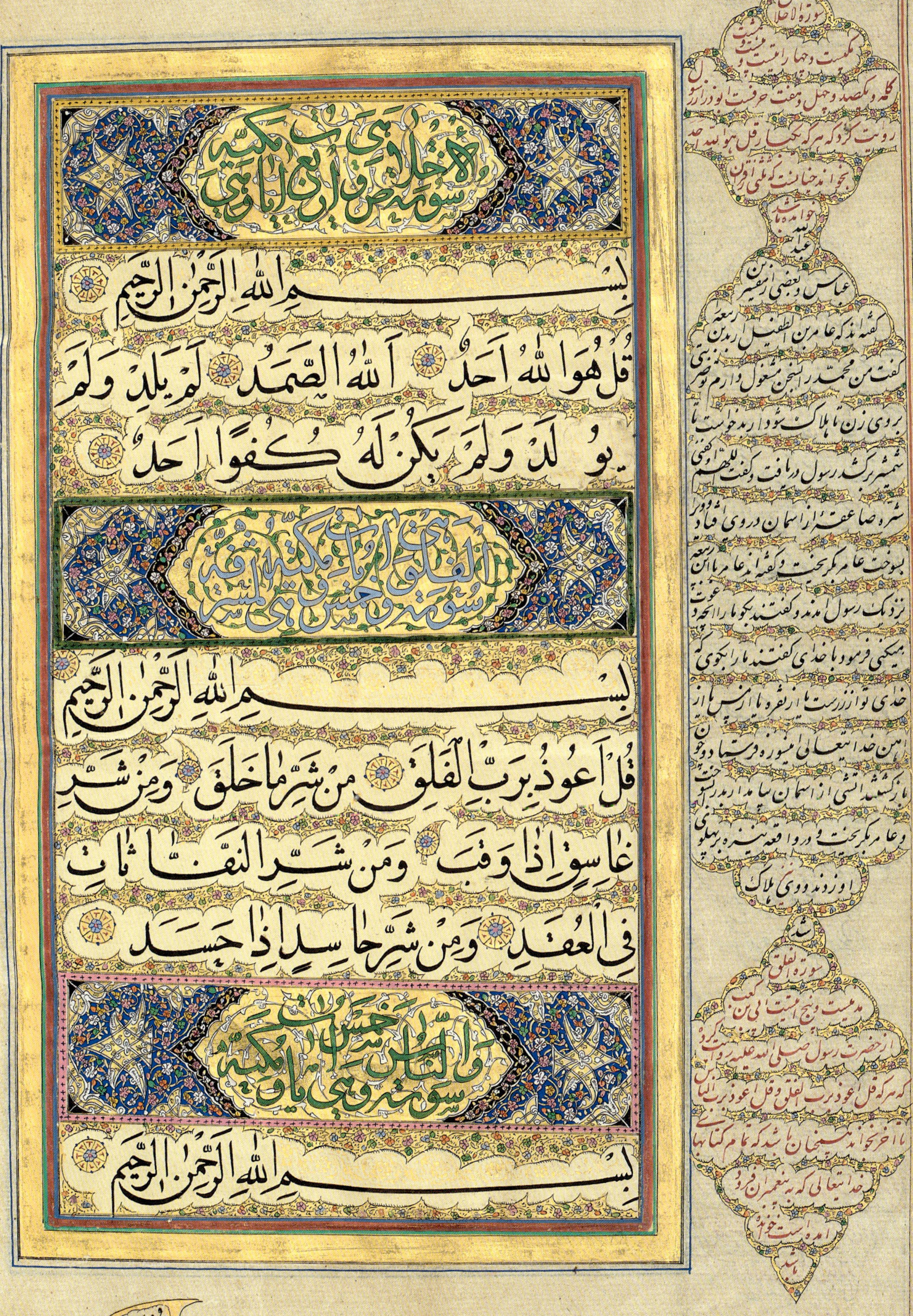

بسم الله الرحمن الرحيم
قل هو الله احد الله الصمد لم يلد ولم
يولد ولم يكن له كفوا احد
بسم الله الرحمن الرحيم
قل اعوذ برب الفلق من شر ما خلق ومن شر
غاسق اذا وقب ومن شر النفاثات
في العقد ومن شر حاسد اذا حسد
بسم الله الرحمن الرحيم
قل اعوذ

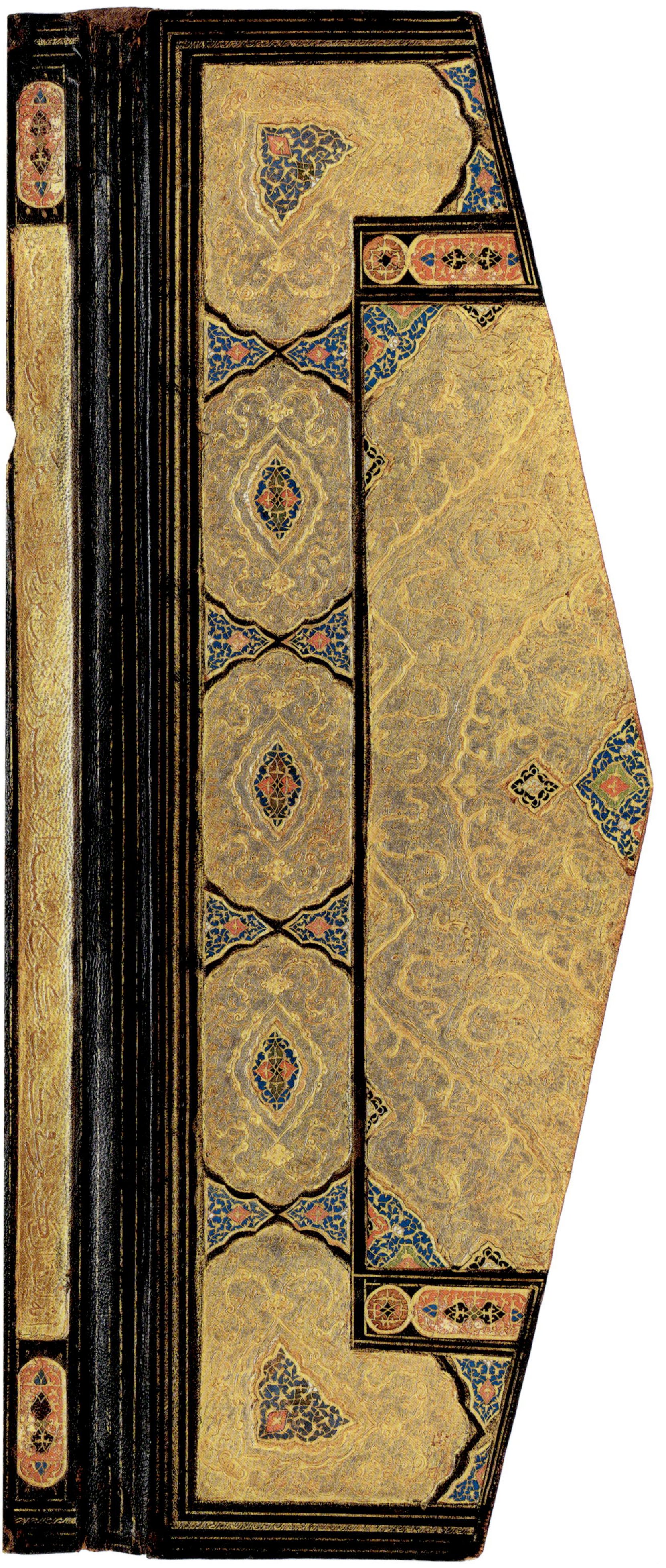

Outer side

Bookbinding Flap (Envelope Flap with Fore-Edge Flap)

Iran, c. 1550–1600
Leather binding over pasteboard, gilded, tooled, and stamped; overlaid with gilded and colored paper filigree; the outer and inner sides share features in design, composition, and motifs comprising a central panel (with floral scrolls and cloudband) set inside two borders composed of cartouches with stamped or filigree ornament; a greater quantity of filigree is found on the inner side.
Overall: 14 9/16 × 7 7/8 inches (37 × 20 cm)
Outer side of envelope flap: inscription in *thuluth* script, sura 56, *al-Waqiʿa* (The Inevitable), verses 77–80
Inner side of envelope flap: inscription in *thuluth* script, sura 33, *al-Ahzab* (The Allied Troops), verse 56 concluding with "the Most High and Almighty God speaks the truth" (*wa sadaqa Allah al-ʿali al-ʿazim*), a formula used to mark the end of a quotation from the Qurʾan
TR:882-2015.1

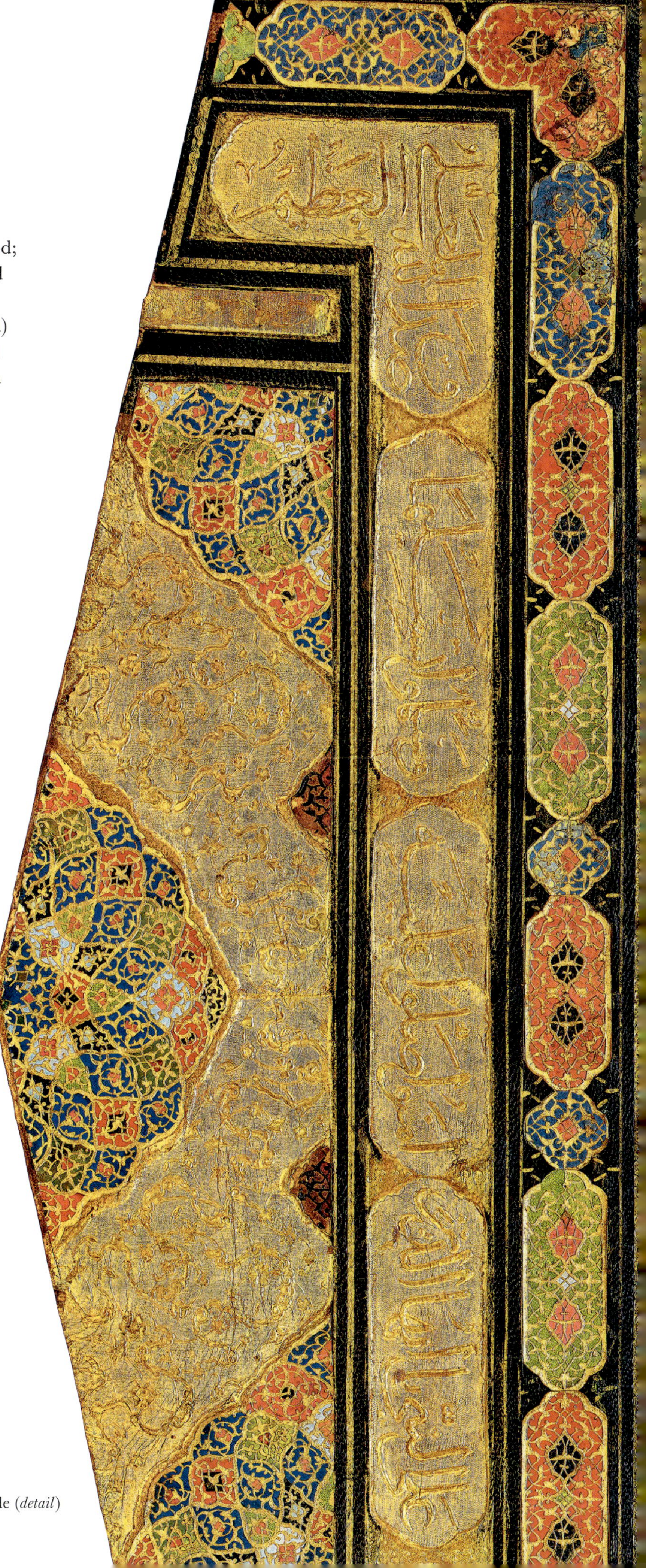

Inner side (*detail*)

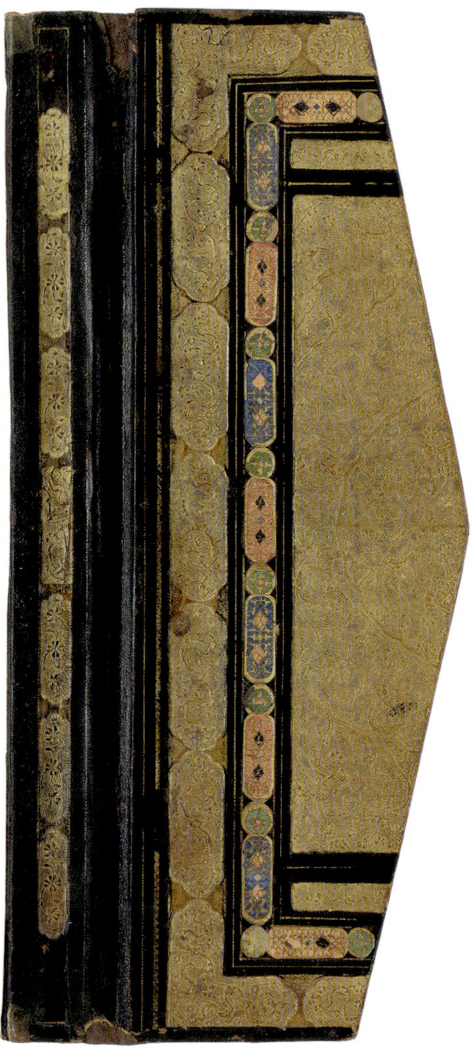

Outer side

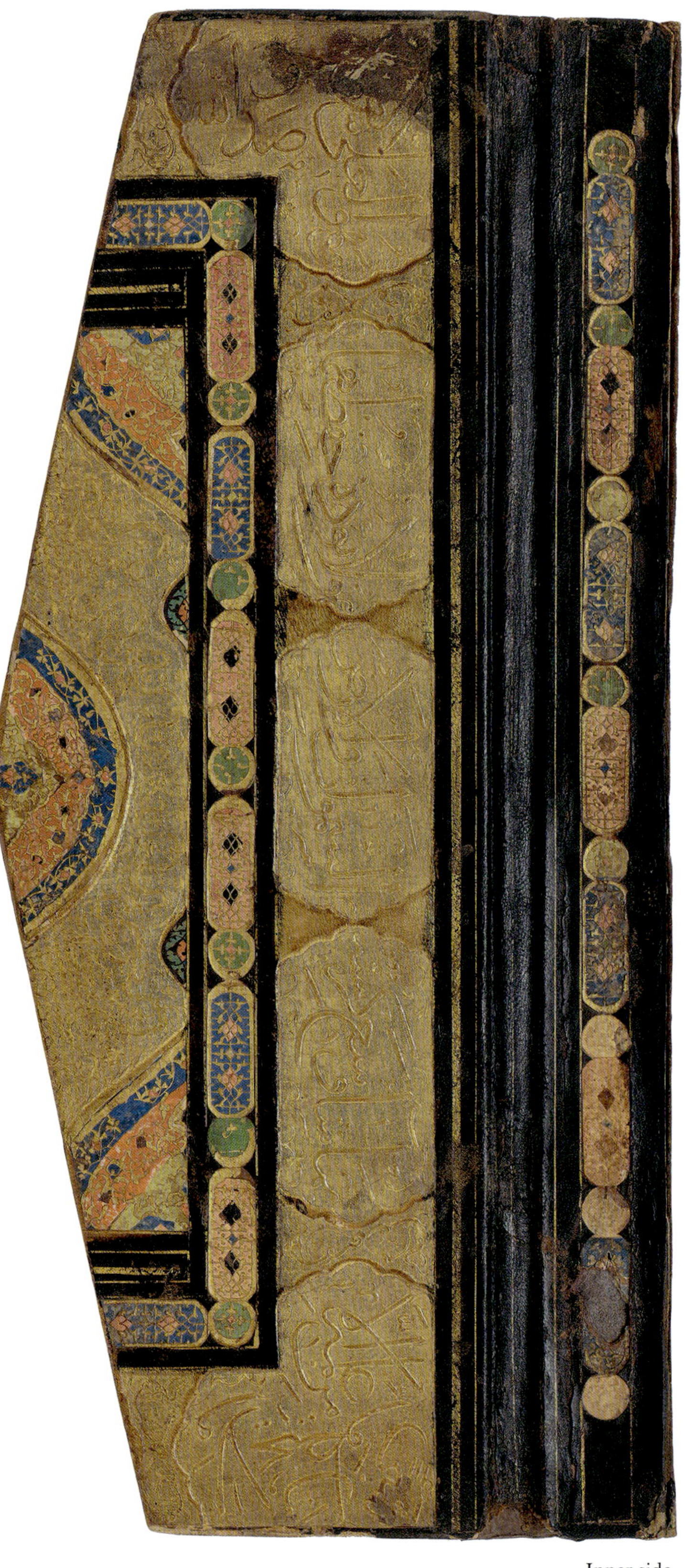

Inner side

61

Bookbinding Flap (Envelope Flap with Fore-Edge Flap)

Iran, c. 1550–1600
Leather binding over pasteboard, gilded, tooled, and stamped; overlaid with gilded and colored paper filigree; the outer and inner sides share features in design, composition, and motifs comprising a central panel (with floral scrolls and cloudband) set inside two borders composed of cartouches with stamped or filigree ornament; a greater quantity of filigree is found on the inner side.
Overall: 14 9/16 × 7 7/8 inches (37 × 20 cm)
Outer side on fore-edge flap: inscription in *thuluth* script, sura 56, *al-Waqi'a* (The Inevitable), verse 79
Inner side of envelope flap: inscription in *thuluth* script, sura 2, *al-Baqara* (The Cow), second half of verse 255 concluding with "God speaks the truth" (*wa sadaqa Allah*), a formula used to mark the end of a quotation from the Qur'an
TR:882-2015.2

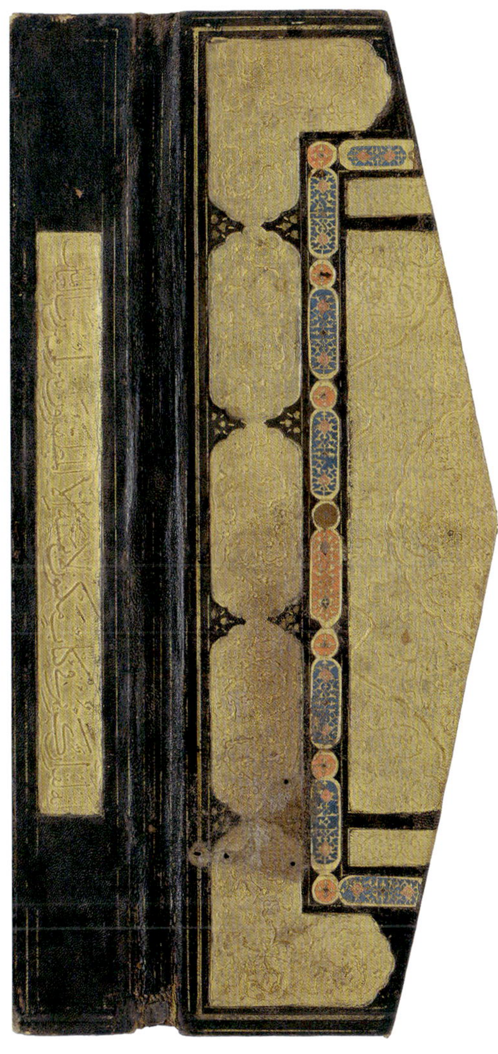

Outer side

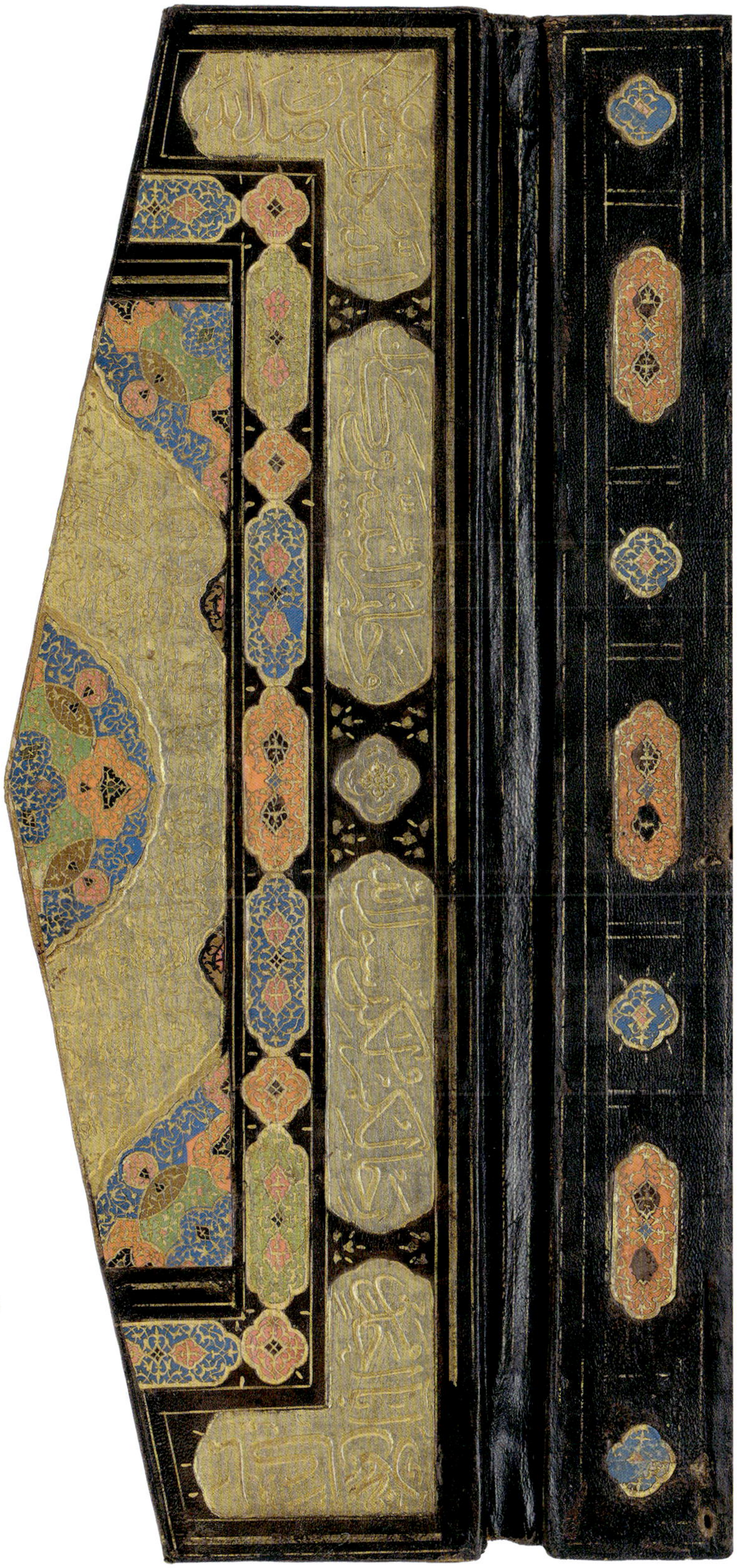

62

Bookbinding Flap (Envelope Flap with Fore-Edge Flap)

Iran, c. 1550–1600
Leather binding over pasteboard, gilded, tooled, and stamped; overlaid with gilded and colored paper filigree; the outer and inner sides share features in design, composition, and motifs comprising a central panel (with floral scrolls and cloudband) set inside two borders composed of cartouches with stamped or filigree ornament; a greater quantity of filigree is found on the inner side.
Overall: 14 9/16 × 7 7/8 inches (37 × 20 cm)
Outer side of envelope flap: inscription in *thuluth* script, Sura 56, *al-Waqiʿa* (the Inevitable), verses 77–80
Inner side of envelope flap: inscription in *thuluth* script, sura 33, *al-Ahzab* (the Allied Troops), verse 40 concluding with "God speaks the truth" (*wa sadaqa Allah*), a formula used to mark the end of a quotation from the Qurʾan
TR:882-2015.3

Inner side

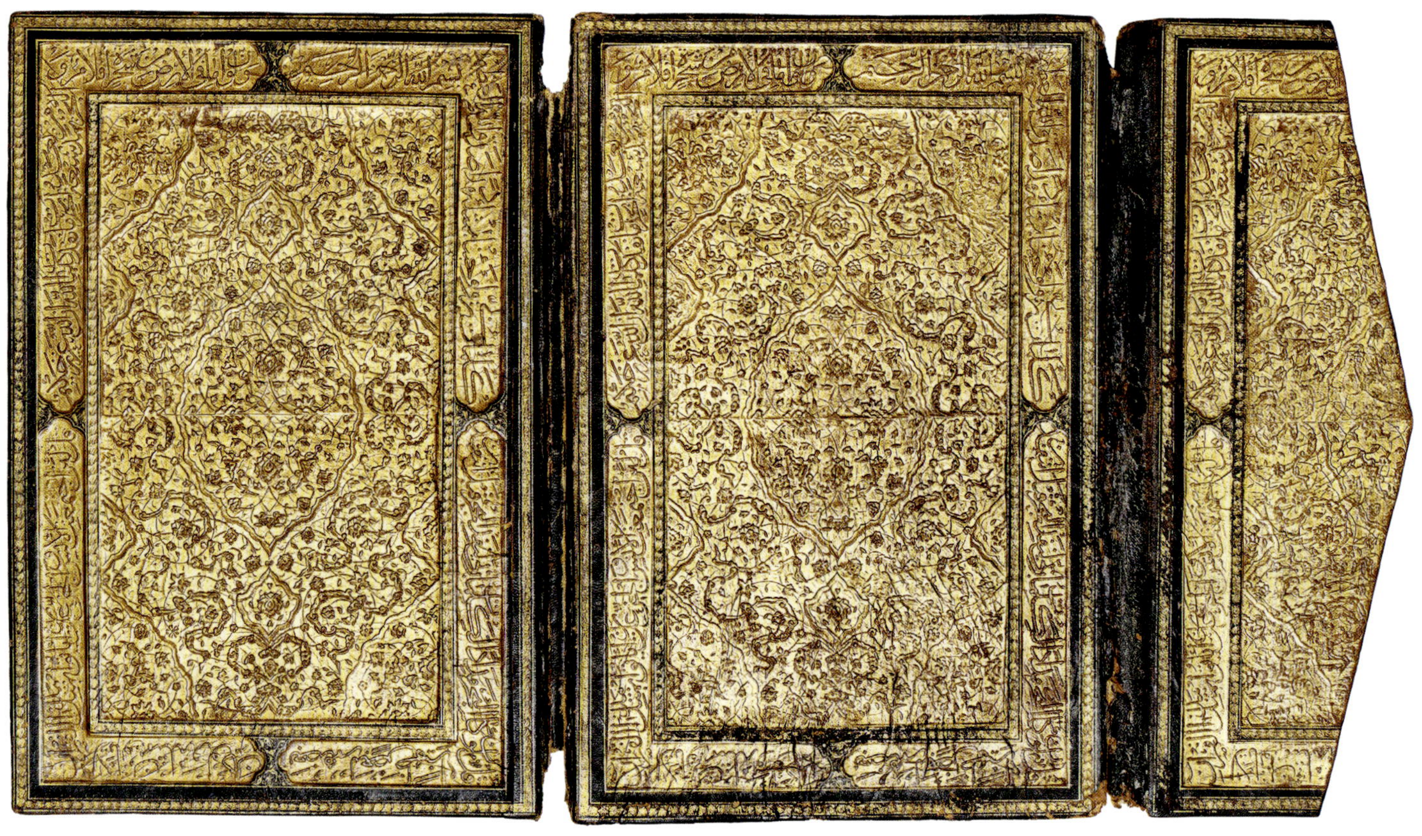

63

Bookbinding for a Qur'an

Iran, c. 1525–50
Leather binding over pasteboard: upper and lower covers block stamped and gilded (central field composed as cusped medallion with pendants and corner pieces containing floral scrolls and cloudbands; outer border composed of epigraphic cartouches); doublures brown leather with cusped medallion, pendants, and corner pieces of gilded leather filigree over colored paper ground (red, black, pale and dark blues); the envelope flap shares the same materials and designs as the outer covers and doublures.
Overall: 25 × 13 3/4 inches (63.5 × 34.9 cm)
Outer covers (upper and lower): inscription in *thuluth* script: *basmala*; sura 31, *Luqman* (Luqman) verse 27; sura 17, *al-Isra'* (The Night Journey), verse 88; sura 18, *al-Kahf* (The Cave), verse 109, concluding with "the Almighty God speaks the truth" (*sadaqa Allah al-'azim*), a formula used to mark the end of a quotation from the Qur'an
TR:869-2015

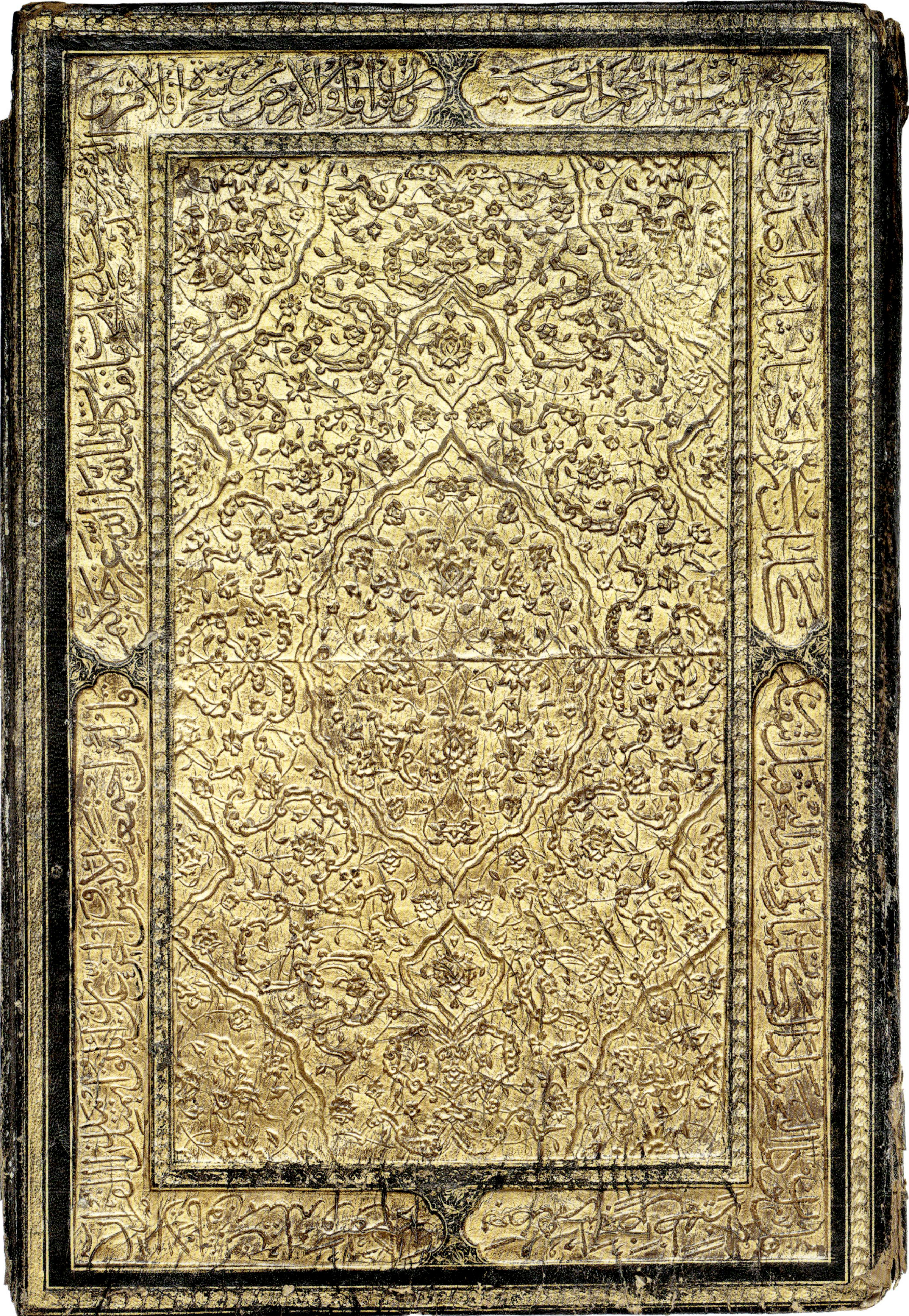

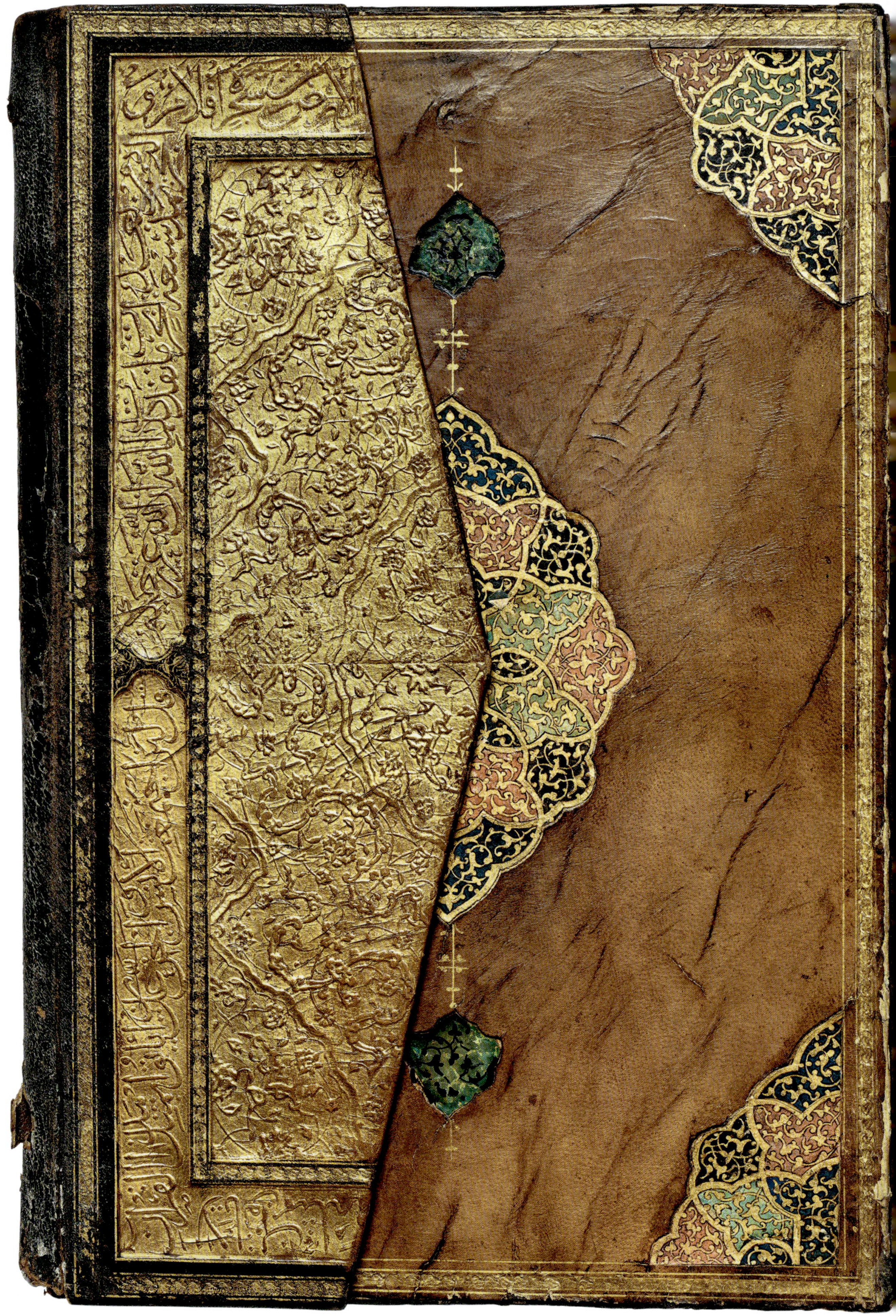

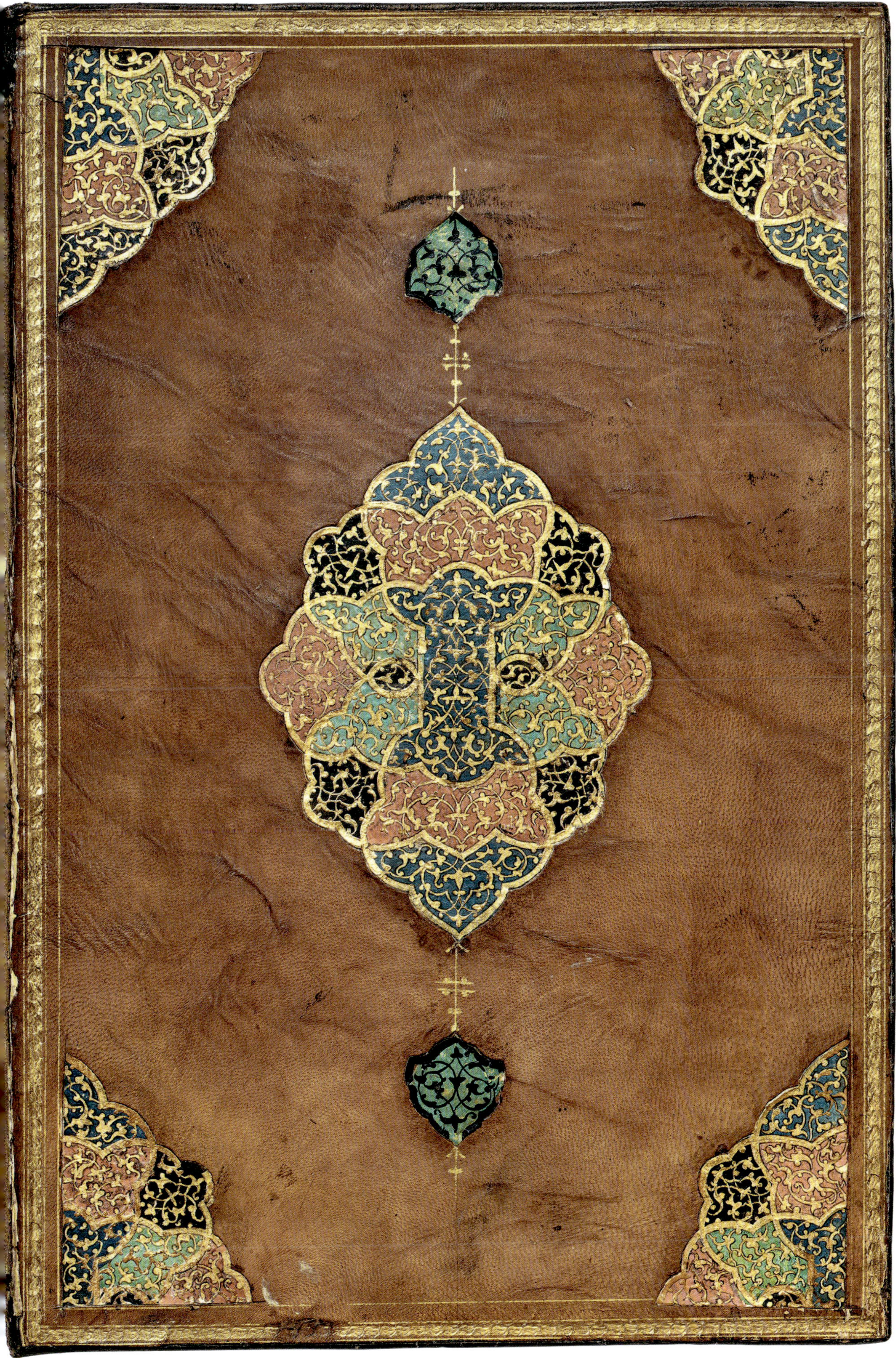

Doublures, upper and lower covers

NOTES

1 The early history of the Qur'an is described, with references to key secondary sources, in Roxburgh 2007, 1–4. A thorough review of textual sources and material remains can be found in the *EI3*, s.v. "Canon and Canonisation of the Qur'ān" (Aziz al-Azmeh). On the chronology of Qur'anic codification also see Whelan 1998 and Schoeler 2010a. For the autograph editions leading up to the ʿUthmanic recension, see Jeffery 1937, in his study of *Kitab al-masahif* (Book of the Qur'anic Codices) by Ibn Abi Da'ud al-Sijistani (d. 929 CE). Jeffery 1937 also provides a detailed narrative history of the Qur'an (esp. 1–10).

2 For the names of the "seven," see Jeffery 1937, 1–4.

3 See Déroche 1992, 27–33.

4 See George 2017, esp. 111–16. For other notable aspects of Hijazi folios, including their relation to earlier and non-Islamic scribal practice and sacred texts, see George 2010, 31–53.

5 These typologies are the work of modern art historians who have attempted to arrange the corpus of Qur'anic folios into a more refined chronological sequence, which might eventually be correlated to more precise geographical regions. See Déroche 1992, esp. 34–47, and George 2010, 55–114.

6 Déroche 1992, 17, suggests that the shift in orientation may have been a way to make the Qur'an distinct from other texts.

7 For practices of vocalization, see Dutton 1999 and Dutton 2000.

8 See George 2003, 3, and Blair 2008, 78.

9 The history of paper and its diffusion are discussed in Bloom 2001, esp. chaps. 1 and 2.

10 The nature of the reforms and their effects are discussed in Tabbaa 1992, esp. 121–43. Tabbaa suggests a link between Ibn Muqla's calligraphy reform and his enforcing the "caliphal order to establish a body of canonical Qur'ānic readings," efforts which coincided with a contemporary "emphasis on correct verse count" (ibid., 142). For a reappraisal and critical evaluation of the sources and Ibn Muqla's relationship to reform, see George 2010, 134–37.

11 On the naming of the script and other matters related to its features, see Déroche 1992, esp. 132–35, and George 2010, 115–25.

12 On the broad topic of art histories produced in the late medieval period, see Roxburgh 2001, passim.

13 Qadi Ahmad 1959, 53–55.

14 A well-studied example is the Qur'an commissioned by Mamluk ruler Baybars b. Jashnagir in 1305 for the *khanaqah* that he endowed. See James 1984.

15 For examples and synthetic overviews of key developments in the Qur'ans of this period, see James 1988, James 1992a, and James 1992b.

16 For a good overview of the types of illumination found in Qur'ans across the centuries, see Baker 2007, passim.

17 On the use of metals, in particular, see Porter 2021.

18 See Knipe et al. 2018, esp. 32–33 and 38.

19 For some of the primary sources and their analysis, see Bosch 1961, 1–13, Bosch, Carswell, Petherbridge 1981, Haldane 1983, and Levey 1962, 1–79.

20 The letter is discussed and translated in French in Richard 2001, 97.

21 Trans. Haldane 1983, 9.

22 According to some sources, ʿAli b. Abi Talib attributed the "collection" of the Qur'an "between two tablets" to the caliph Abu Bakr. The narrative is recorded in the *Kitab al-masahif* by Ibn Abi Da'ud al-Sijistani. Interpreters of the hadith varied in their opinion about the significance of "collection" whether it referred to Abu Bakr's memorization of the Qur'an or a complete physical copy in a binding. See Saleem 2010, 241–42.

23 For the technical development of the Islamic bookbinding, see Scheper 2019, passim.

Opposite: Cat. 63, detail

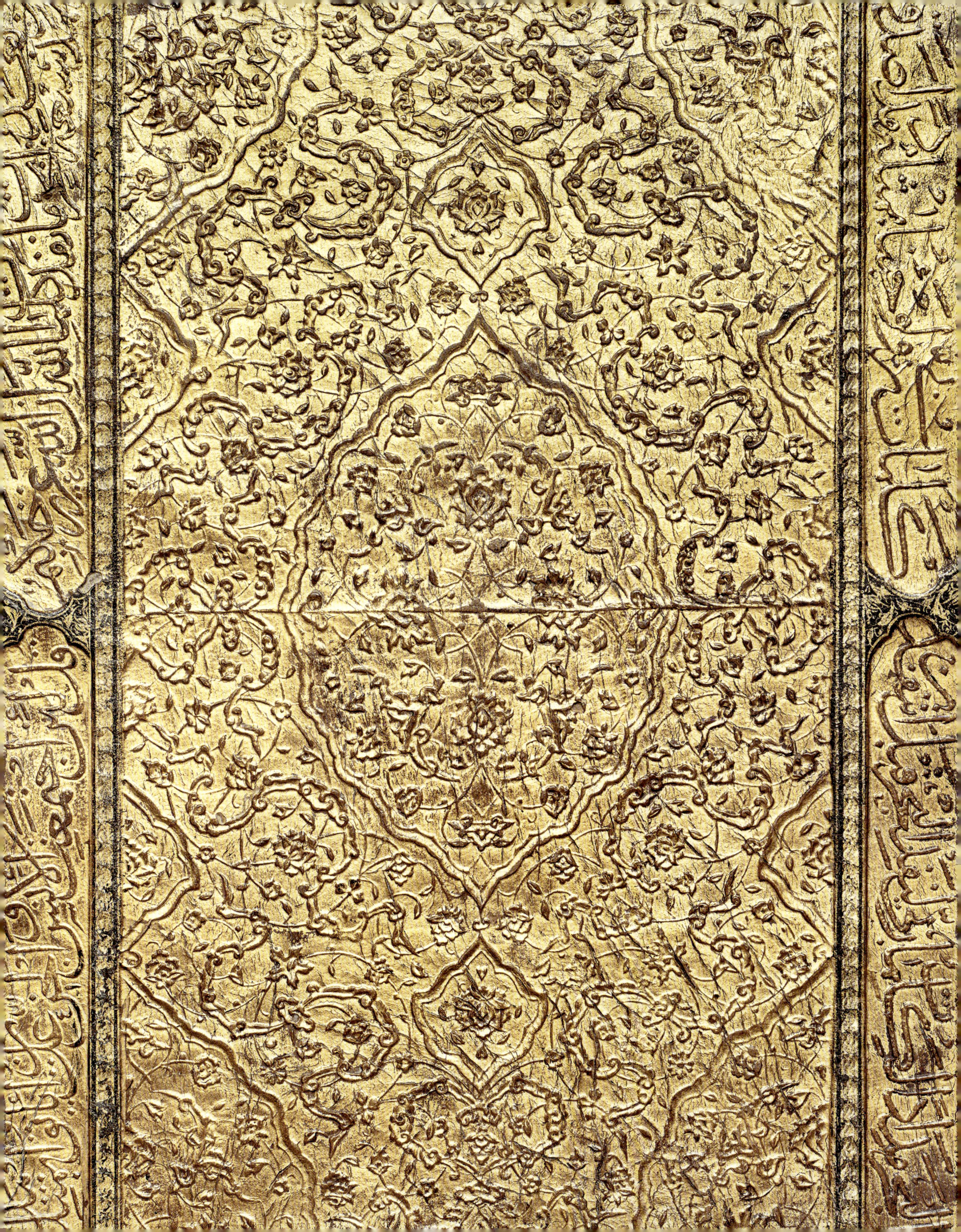

Illustrated Glossary

ANUSHKA HOSAIN

KEY TERMS

Aya (singular); ***Ayat*** (plural)
Verses. The Qur'an comprises more than 6,000 *ayat*.

Juz' (singular); ***Ajza'*** (plural)
Qur'ans may consist of sets of multiple parts, or *juz'*, such as seven parts for reading in one week or thirty for reading over one month. The beginnings and endings of the parts may be marked by illuminations.

Manzil
A seven-part division for reading the Qur'an in a week.

Sajda
Points in the Qur'an that require prostration.

Shamsa
Marking frontispieces, a *shamsa* is a medallion that resembles a burst of light.

Suras
Chapters. The Qur'an contains 114 suras.

Al-kitab, "The book"
A scripture, book, or writing. *Al-kitab* refers to the revelations sent down to the Prophet Muhammad in Mecca in 610 CE. The separate revelations to the "people of the book" (*ahl al-kitab*)—Jews, Christians and Muslims—are only a part of the divine prototype of the Qur'an.

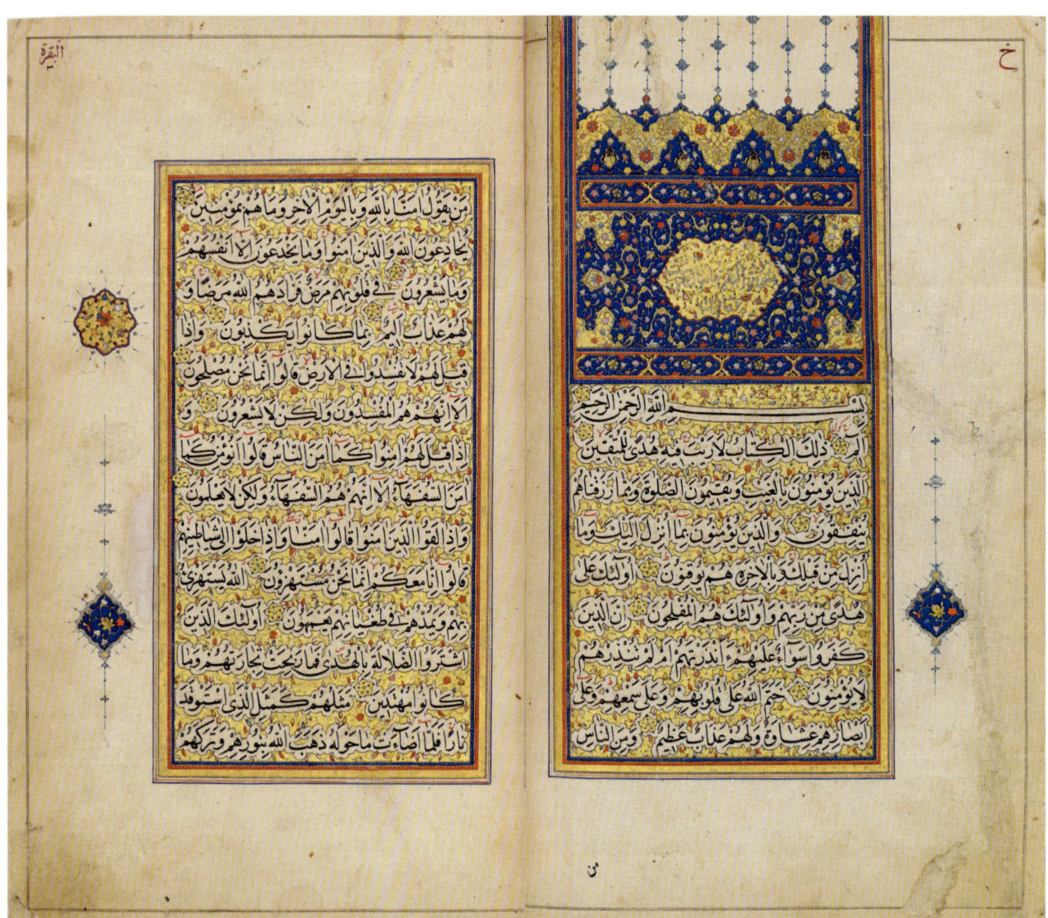

Qur'an Manuscript (*cat. 57*), signed by Husayn al-Shirazi al-Fakhkhar.

Abjad

The Arabic and Semitic writing systems are *abjad* rather than alphabets. Most or all of the letters in an *abjad* are consonants, with vowels represented occasionally. Arabic has twenty-eight letters using eighteen different graphic forms. Every letter has two forms, initial and final, and some of them a third, medial, for those letters that are connected in the middle. *Abjad* are written from right to left.

Abjad also refers to the use of letters as numbers, with numerical value assigned based on their position in the letter sequence. In cat. 6, counters of ten are represented as square boxes containing an Arabic letter corresponding to their *abjad* value.

ا	*alif*	ض	*ḍād*
ب	*bāʾ*	ط	*ṭāʾ*
ت	*tāʾ*	ظ	*ẓāʾ*
ث	*thāʾ*	ع	*ʿayn*
ج	*jīm*	غ	*ghayn*
ح	*ḥāʾ*	ف	*fāʾ*
خ	*khāʾ*	ق	*qāf*
د	*dāl*	ک	*kāf*
ذ	*dhāl*	ل	*lām*
ر	*rāʾ*	م	*mīm*
ز	*zāʾ*	ن	*nūn*
س	*sīn*	ه	*hāʾ*
ش	*shīn*	و	*waw*
ص	*ṣād*	ى	*yāʾ*

Khatt

Khatt may refer to a mark, a sign, a stroke, or anything delineated, as well as handwriting, calligraphy, and penmanship. The art of beautiful writing, *khatt* enhances the spiritual, philosophical, and semantic significance of language by enriching its graphic potential through ornamentation.

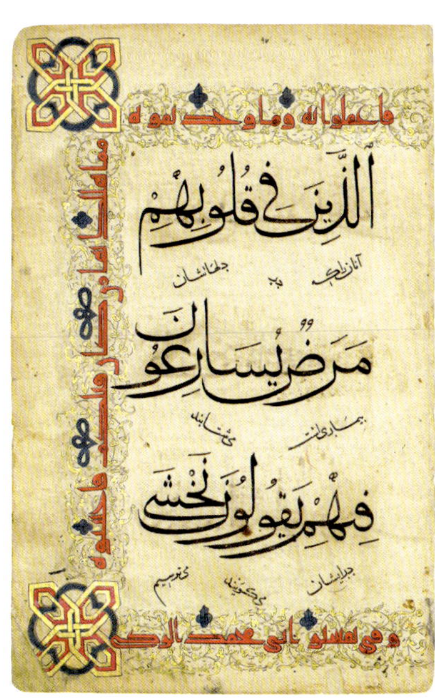

Folio from a Thirty-Part Qurʾan Manuscript (*cat. 37*), Anatolia, Iran, or Central Asia, early 14th century.

Mushaf

The physical Qurʾan, in its material forms of embodiment as a book. *Mushaf* refers to the earthly version of the heavenly, uncreated original. Calligraphic styles, illumination, embellishments, and the use of precious materials are employed to produce *mushaf* that are readily distinguishable from other manuscripts.

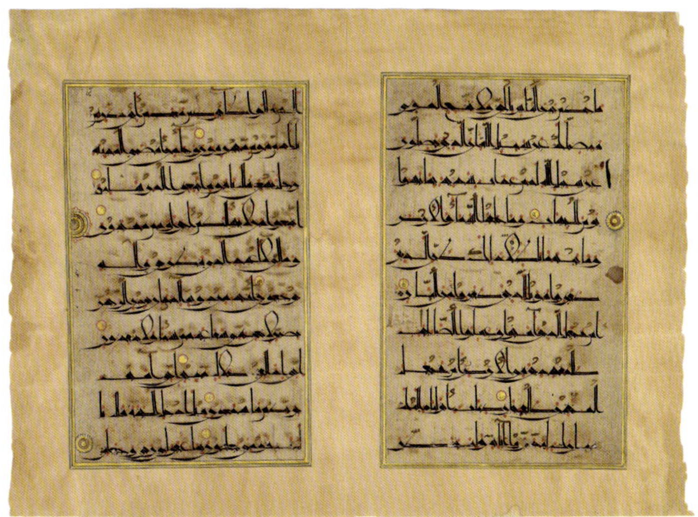

Two Folios from a Qurʾan Manuscript (*cat. 31*), Eastern Islamic Lands, 12th century.

Tafsir

Qurʾanic exegesis or commentary on aspects of interpretation, including grammar, meaning, and reading. Here, *tafsir* is seen as marginal notations in red, blue, and black ink.

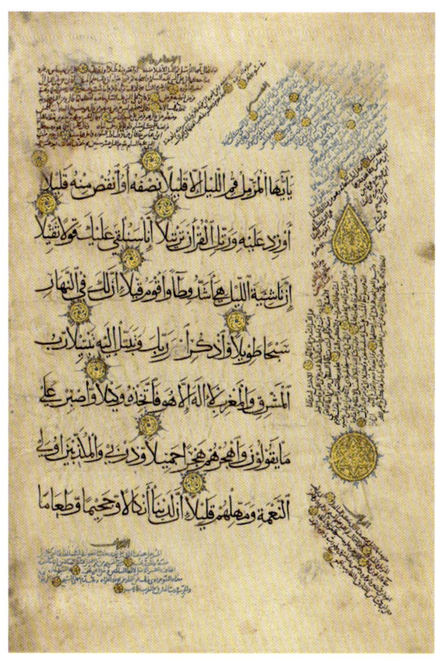

Folio from a Qurʾan Manuscript (*cat. 35*), Egypt, probably Cairo, late 13th–early 14th century.

TOOLS

Ink
Two types of black ink were used for historical Qur'ans: *midad*, carbon or soot-based inks, and *hibr*, tannate or gallnut inks. Colored inks could be used to additionally differentiate the various textual elements on the page, such as headings or vocalizations.

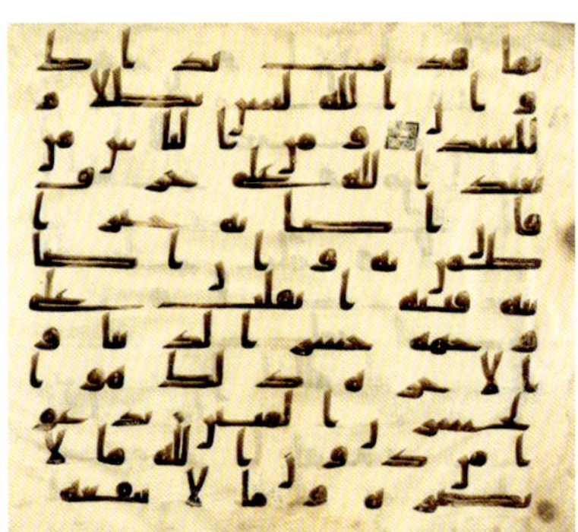

Folio from a Qur'an Manuscript *(detail, cat. 2)*, North Africa, early 8th century.

Chrysography
Writing in gold, suggestive of the transcendental nature of the word. May refer to the use of gold leaf or shell gold, a liquid suspension of pulverized gold particles used as ink.

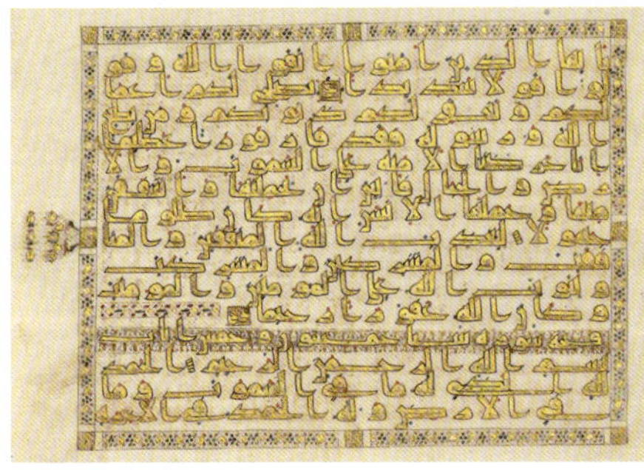

Bifolio from a Qur'an Manuscript *(detail, cat. 5)*, North Africa or Central Islamic Lands, 9th century.

Supports
Parchment (*jild*, *raqq/riqq*) and paper (*kaghad*) were the primary supports for manuscripts of the Qur'an with use of papyrus (*bardi*, *qirtas*) limited to North Africa. Supports could be colored with pigments.

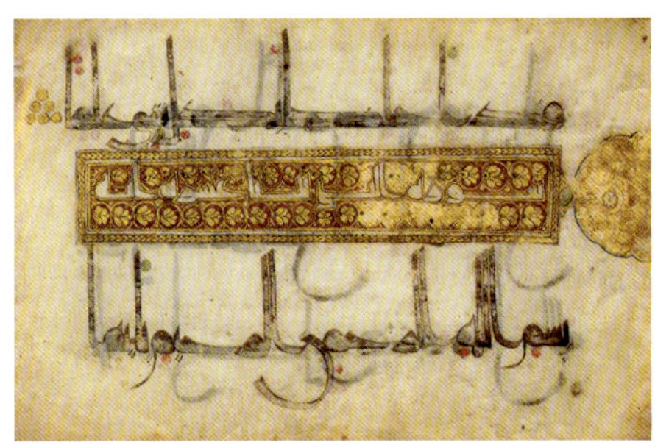

Folio from a Qur'an Manuscript *(detail, cat. 22)*, North Africa, 10th century.

Writing Instruments
Pens (sing. *qalam;* pl. *aqlam*) were most often made from reeds (*qasab*) but could also be made from quills (*rish*), wood (*khashab*), and bamboo (*khayzaran*). The latter two were used for large-scale calligraphy. Brush pens, made by affixing animal hair to a wooden, ivory, or ebony handle, were also used. Qur'anic references to the pen fostered a symbolism of the pen as the primordial agent of creation.

SCRIPTS

Hijazi
The script of the earliest extant physical copies of a Qur'an manuscript. Taking its name from the Hijaz region, where Mecca and Medina are located, this script is spare, with tall, backward-leaning, vertical strokes, and without embellishment. Hijazi script began to be supplanted by Kufic in the late seventh century.

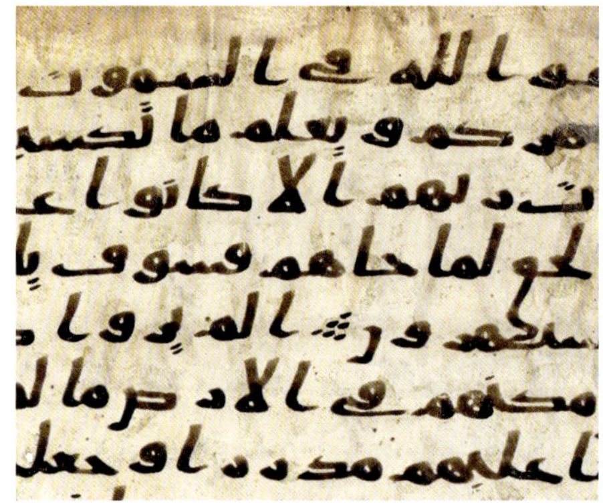

Folio from a Qur'an Manuscript *(detail, cat. 1)*, North Africa or Central Islamic Lands, 10th century.

Kufic

al-khatt al-Kufi
The preeminent script used for Qur'anic calligraphy from the seventh to the tenth centuries. A thick, angular script, with consistently defined letter forms, named after the city of Kufa in southern Iraq.

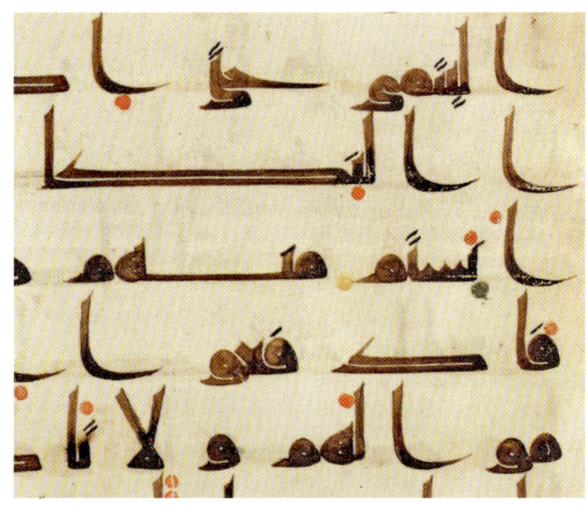

Folio from a Qur'an Manuscript *(detail, cat. 11)*, North Africa or Central Islamic Lands, 10th century.

New Style and "Eastern Kufic"
A cursive and rounded form of Kufic with thinner, more attenuated strokes, this script was in wide use from the early tenth to the early thirteenth centuries.

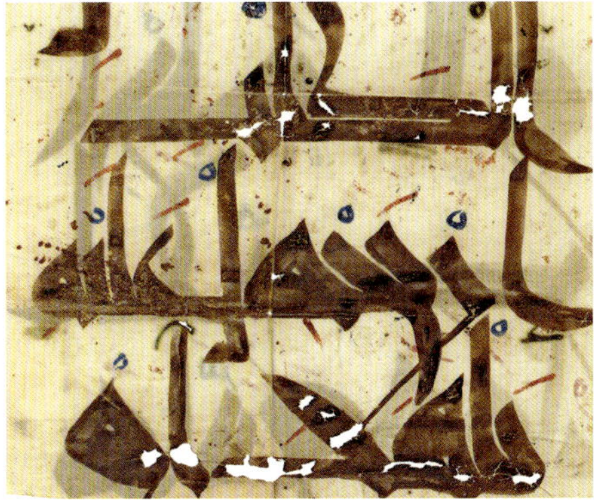

Folio from the Nurse's Qur'an (***Mushaf al-Hadina***) (*detail, cat. 23*), Tunisia, Kairouan, AH 410/ 1019–1020 CE.

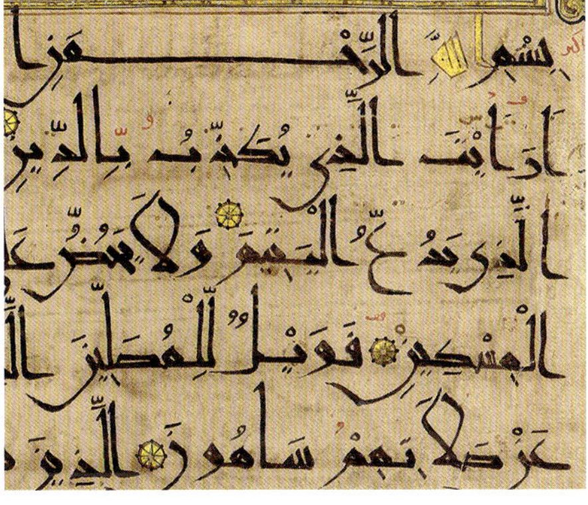

Bifolio from a Qur'an Manuscript (*detail, cat. 24*), Iran, 11th–12th century, ink, opaque watercolor, and gold on paper.

Six Scripts/Pens (*al-aqlam al-sitta*)
In the tenth century, there emerged a new canon of cursive scripts attributed to Ibn Muqla (d. 940 CE), an Abbasid vizier and noted calligrapher. Ibn Muqla selected six commonly used scripts (*naskh*, *thuluth*, *muhaqqaq*, *rayhani*, *riqa'*, and *tawqi'*) and systematized them geometrically and proportionally. These scripts replaced the New Style and "Eastern Kufic" by the thirteenth century.

Naskh
A highly legible cursive script with horizonal lines and well-proportioned letters. With the literal meaning of copying or transcription, *naskh* has been the most widely used Qur'anic script since the fifteenth century.

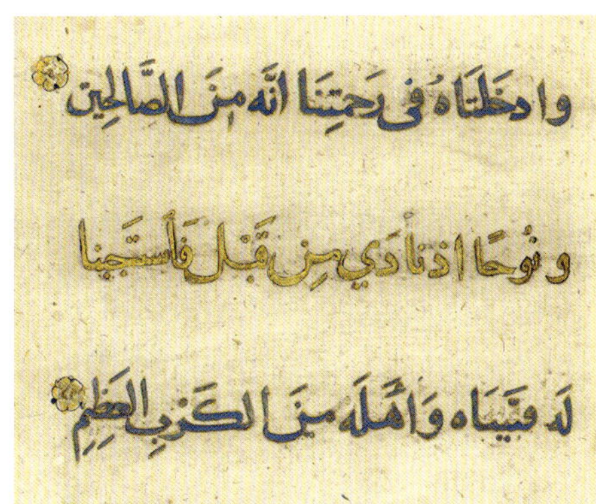

Folio from a Qur'an Manuscript (*detail, cat. 43*), Central Islamic Lands, 14th century.

Nasta'liq
Blending the features of *naskh* and *ta'liq,* this script emerged in the fourteenth century. *Nasta'liq* grew to become the most commonly used script for copying non-Qur'anic manuscripts throughout Iran, Central Asia, India, and Türkiye.

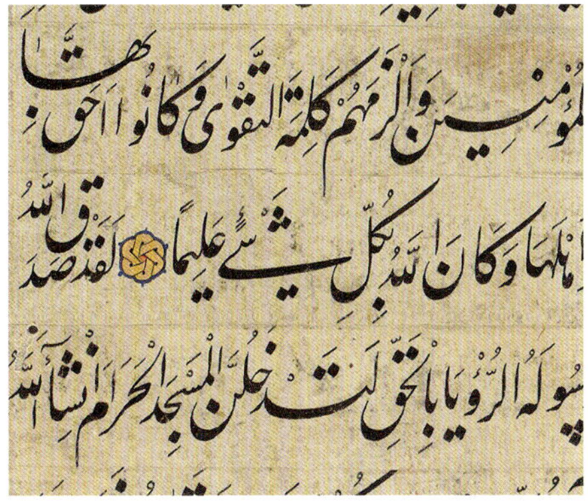

Calligraphic Specimen Composed of Selections from the Qur'an (*detail, cat. 46*), calligraphy attributed to Shah Mahmud Nishapuri (active 16th century), Iran, 16th century.

Thuluth
From the Arabic word for "one-third," because one-third of each letter slopes. A script largely reserved for Qur'anic headings, architectural epigraphy, religious inscriptions, and royal titles.

Folio from the Nineteenth Part (*Juz'*) of a Qur'an Manuscript (*detail, cat. 52*), Iran or Egypt, 14th century.

Muhaqqaq
Along with *naskh*, the most common script used for copying Qur'ans. Meaning "clear" or "strongly expressed," *muhaqqaq* is a precise, angular script used to write fine, large Qur'ans. The script has a strong horizontal emphasis with careful balance achieved between the vertical ascending letters and the shallow descending letters.

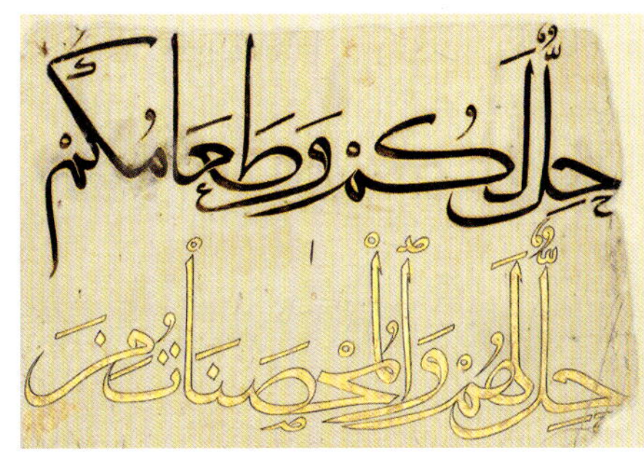

Lines from a Qur'an Manuscript (*detail, cat. 38*), calligraphy attributed to Ahmad b. al-Shaykh al-Suhrawardi al-Bakri (d. 1320/21), Iraq, probably AH 707/ 1307–8 CE.

ELEMENTS OF ILLUMINATION

Qur'anic illumination developed the particularized iconographies highlighted here over the centuries to mark the internal structure of the text and provide directions to the reader. These forms of illumination distinguish the Qur'an from other manuscripts.

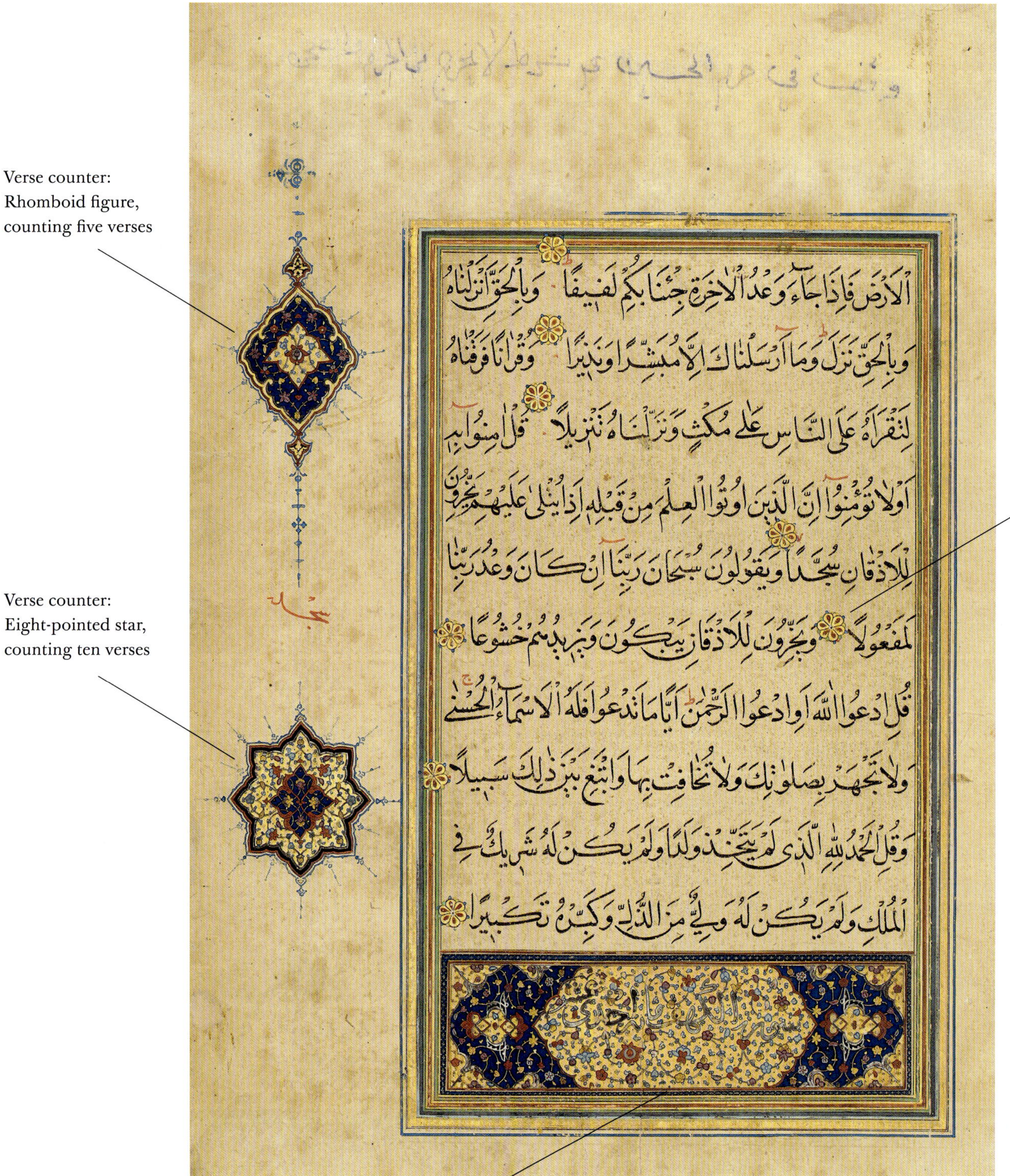

Verse counter: Rhomboid figure, counting five verses

Verse counter: Eight-pointed star, counting ten verses

Verse marker, gold rosette

Title of sura (chapter) and number of verses in white *thuluth*: *sura al-Kahf* (The Cave) 110 (verses)

Bifolio from a Qur'an Manuscript (*cat. 53*), Iran, late 16th century.

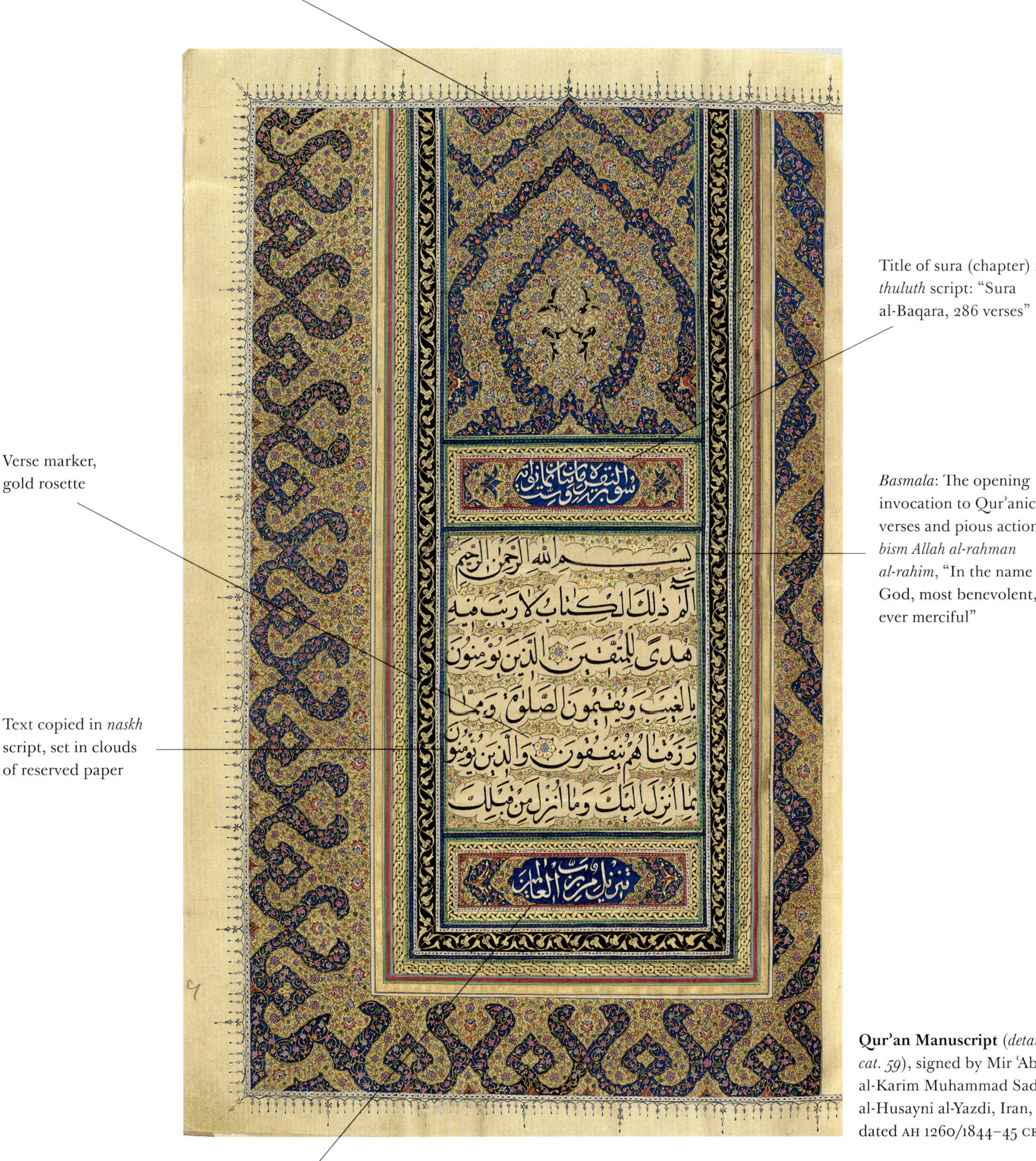

Qur’an Manuscript (*detail, cat. 59*), signed by Mir ʿAbd al-Karim Muhammad Sadiq al-Husayni al-Yazdi, Iran, dated AH 1260/1844–45 CE.

Works Cited

Ali 1990
Ali, Ahmed. *Al-Qur'ān: A Contemporary Translation*. Princeton: Princeton University Press, 3rd printing, 1990.

Atanasiu 2000
Atanasiu, Vlad. "Le retroencrage: déduction du ductus d'une écriture d'après l'intensité de l'encre." *Gazette du Livre Médiéval* 37 (2000): 34–42.

Baker 2007
Baker, Colin F. *Qur'an Manuscripts: Calligraphy, Illumination, Design*. London: British Library, 2007.

Bayani, Contadini, Stanley 1999
Bayani, Manijeh, Anna Contadini, and Tim Stanley. *The Decorated Word: Qur'ans of the 17th to 19th Centuries*. 2 parts. London and New York: Nour Foundation in Association with Azimuth Editions and Oxford University Press, 1999.

Behrens-Abouseif 1999
Behrens-Abouseif, Doris. *Beauty in Arabic Culture*. Princeton, NJ: Princeton University Press, 1999.

Berque 1995
Berque, Jacques. "The Koranic Text: From Revelation to Compilation." In *The Book in the Islamic World: The Written Word and Communication in the Middle East*, edited by George N. Atiyeh, 17–29. Albany: State University of New York Press, 1995.

Blair 2006
Blair, Sheila S. *Islamic Calligraphy*. Edinburgh: Edinburgh University Press, 2006.

Blair 2008
Blair, Sheila S. "Transcribing God's Word: Qur'an Codices in Context." *Journal of Qur'anic Studies* 10, 1 (2008): 71–97.

Blair 2023
Blair, Sheila S. "Sultan Öljeitü's Baghdad Qur'an: A Life History." In *The Word Illuminated: Form and Function of Qur'anic Manuscripts from the Seventh to Seventeenth Centuries*, edited by Simon Rettig and Sana Mirza, 97–122. Washington, D.C.: Smithsonian Scholarly Press, 2023.

Bloom 2001
Bloom, Jonathan M. *Paper Before Print: The History and Impact of Paper in the Islamic World*. New Haven and London: Yale University Press, 2001.

Bosch 1961
Bosch, Gulnar K. "The Staff of the Scribes and the Implements of the Discerning: An Excerpt." *Ars Orientalis* 4 (1961): 1–13.

Bosch, Carswell, Petherbridge 1981
Bosch, Gulnar, John Carswell, and Guy Petherbridge. *Islamic Bindings and Bookmaking*. Chicago: University of Chicago Press, 1981.

Bsees 2019
Bsees, Ursula. "Qur'ānic Quotations in Early Arabic Papyrus Amulets." In *In The Author's Hand: Holograph and Authorial Manuscripts in the Islamic Handwritten Tradition*, edited by Andreas Kaplony and Michael Marx, 112–38. Leiden: Brill, 2019.

Colini 2021
Colini, Claudia. "'I tried it and it is really good:' Replicating Recipes of Arabic Black Inks." In *Traces of Ink: Experiences of Philology and Replication*, edited by Lucia Raggetti, 131–153. Leiden: Brill, 2021.

Déroche 1990–91
Déroche, François. "The Qur'an of Amagur." *Manuscripts of the Middle East* 5 (1990–91): 59–67.

Déroche 1992
Déroche, François. *The Abbasid Tradition: Qur'ans of the 8th to 10th Centuries AD*. New York and Oxford: Nour Foundation in Association with Azimuth Editions, 1992.

Dutton 1999
Dutton, Yasin. "Red Dots, Green Dots, Yellow Dots and Blue: Some Reflections on the Vocalisation of Early Qur'anic Manuscripts—Part I." *Journal of Qur'anic Studies* 1, 1 (1999): 115–140.

Dutton 2000
Dutton, Yasin. "Red Dots, Green Dots, Yellow Dots and Blue: Some Reflections on the Vocalisation of Early Qur'anic Manuscripts—Part II." *Journal of Qur'anic Studies* 2, 1 (2000): 1–24.

EI2
Encyclopaedia of Islam, 2nd edition. Leiden: Brill, 1954–2005.

EI3
Encyclopaedia of Islam, Three. Leiden: Brill, 2007.

Fani 2021
Fani, Sara. "The Literary Dimension and Life of Arabic Treatises on Ink Making." In *Traces of Ink: Experiences of Philology and Replication*, edited by Lucia Raggetti, 105–130. Leiden: Brill, 2021.

Farhad and Rettig 2016
Farhad, Massumeh, and Simon Rettig, eds. *The Art of the Qur'an: Treasures from the Museum of Turkish and Islamic Art*. Washington, D.C.: Arthur M. Sackler Gallery, Smithsonian Institution, 2016.

Fendall 2003
Fendall, Ramsey. *Islamic Calligraphy*. London: Fogg, 2003.

Flood 2012
Flood, Finbarr B. "The Qur'an." In *Byzantium and Islam: Age of Transition, 7th–9th Century*, edited by Helen C. Evans with Brandie Ratliff, 265–269. New York: Metropolitan Museum of Art, 2012.

Flood 2019
Flood, Finbarr B. "Bodies, Books, and Buildings: Economies of Ornament in Juridical Islam." In *Sacred Scriptures: Book Art and Book Religion in Christian, Islamic, and Jewish Cultures*, *Manuscripta Biblica*, vol. 2, edited by David Ganz and Barbara Schellewald, 49–68. Berlin: De Gruyter, 2019.

Fraser 2017
Fraser, Marcus. "The Origins and Modifications of the Blue Qur'an." In *Manuscripts in the Making: Art & Science*, vol. 1, edited by Stella Panayotova and Paola Ricciardi, 198–213. London and Turnhout: Harvey Miller, 2017.

Fraser and Kwiatkowski 2006
Fraser, Marcus, and Will Kwiatkowski. *Ink and Gold: Islamic Calligraphy*. London: Published for Sam Fogg by Paul Holberton, 2006.

Froom 2019
Froom, Aimée. *Bestowing Beauty: Masterpieces from Persian Lands—Selections from the Hossein Afshar Collection*. Houston: Museum of Fine Arts, Houston, 2019.

Gacek 1989
Gacek, Adam. "Arabic Scripts and their Characteristics as Seen Through the Eyes of Mamluk Authors." *Manuscripts of the Middle East* 4 (1989): 144–49.

Gacek 2004
Gacek, Adam. "Scribes, Amanuenses, and Scholars, A Bibliographic Survey of Published Arabic Literature from the Manuscript Age on Various Aspects of Penmanship, Bookmaking, and the Transmission of Knowledge." *Manuscripta Orientalia* 10, 2 (2004): 3–29.

Gacek 2006
Gacek, Adam. "The Copying and Handling of Qur'āns: Some Observations on the *Kitāb al-Maṣāḥif* by Ibn Abī Dā'ūd al-Sijistānī." *Mélanges de l'Université Saint-Joseph* 59 (2006): 229–52.

Ganz 2019
Ganz, David. "Clothing Sacred Scriptures: Materiality and Aesthetics in Medieval Book Religions." In *Sacred Scriptures: Book Art and Book Religion in Christian, Islamic, and Jewish Cultures*, *Manuscripta Biblica*, vol. 2, edited by David Ganz and Barbara Schellewald, 1–46. Berlin: De Gruyter, 2019.

George 2003
George, Alain Fouad. "The Geometry of the Qur'an of Amajur: A Preliminary Study of Proportion in Early Arabic Calligraphy." *Muqarnas* 20 (2003): 1–15.

George 2009
George, Alain Fouad. "Calligraphy, Colour and Light in the Blue Qur'an." *Qur'anic Studies* 11, 1 (2009): 75–125.

George 2010
George, Alain Fouad. *The Rise of Islamic Calligraphy*. London: Saqi Books, 2010.

George 2017
George, Alain Fouad. "The Qur'an, Calligraphy, and the Early Civilization of Islam." In *A Companion to Islamic Art and Architecture*, 2 vols., edited by Finbarr Barry Flood and Gülru Necipoğlu, 1:109–129. Hoboken: Wiley Blackwell, 2017.

Graham 1984
Graham, William A. "The Earliest Meaning of 'Qur'an.'" *Die Welt des Islams* 23–24 (1984): 361–377.

Haldane 1983
Haldane, Duncan. *Islamic Bookbindings in the Victoria and Albert Museum*. London: World of Islam Festival Trust in association with the Victoria and Albert Museum, 1983.

Harvey 2021
Harvey, Ramon. *Transcendent God, Rational World*. Edinburgh: Edinburgh University Press, 2021.

Herzfeld 1915
Herzfeld, Ernst E. "Die Tabula ansata in der islamischen Epigraphik und Ornamentik." *Der Islam* 6, 2 (1915): 189–99.

Ibn al-Nadim 1970
Ibn al-Nadim. *The Fihrist of al-Nadim: A Tenth-Century Survey of Muslim Culture*. Translated and edited by Bayard Dodge, 2 vols. New York and London: Columbia University Press, 1970.

James 1980
James, David. *Qur'ans and Bindings from the Chester Beatty Library: A Facsimile Exhibition*. London: World of Islam Festival Trust, 1980.

James 1984
James, David. "Some Observations on the Calligrapher and Illuminators of the Koran of Rukn al-Din Baybars al-Jashnagir." *Muqarnas* 2 (1984): 147–57.

James 1988
James, David. *Qur'ans of the Mamluks*. London: Thames and Hudson, 1988.

James 1992a
James, David. *The Master Scribes: Qur'ans of the 10th to 14th Centuries AD*. London and Oxford: Nour Foundation in association with Azimuth Editions and Oxford University Press, 1992.

James 1992b
James, David. *After Timur: Qur'ans of the 15th and 16th Centuries*. London and Oxford: Nour Foundation in association with Azimuth Editions and Oxford University Press, 1992.

Jeffery 1937
Jeffery, Arthur. *Materials for the History of the Text of the Qur'ān: The Old Codices. The Kitāb al-maṣāḥif of Ibn Abī Dāwūd*. Leiden: Brill, 1937.

Juynboll 1986
Juynboll, G. H. A. "The Attitude Towards Gold and Silver in Early Islam." In *Pots and Pans: A Colloquium on Precious Metals and Ceramics in the Muslim, Chinese and Graeco-Roman Worlds. Oxford Studies in Islamic Art* 3, edited by M. J. Vickers, 107–116. Oxford: Oxford University Press, 1986.

Knipe et al. 2018
Knipe, Penley, Katherine Eremin, Marc Walton, Agnese Babini, and Georgina Rayner. "Materials and Techniques of Islamic Manuscripts." *Heritage Science* 6, 55 (2018): https://doi.org/10.1186/s40494-018-0217-y.

Leatherbury 2019
Leatherbury, Sean V. "Framing Late Antique Texts as Monuments: The *Tabula Ansata* between Sculpture and Mosaic." In *The Materiality of Text—Placement, Perception, and Presence of Inscribed Texts in Classical Antiquity*, edited by Andrej Petrovic, Ivana Petrovic, and Edmund Thomas, 380–404. Leiden: Brill, 2019.

Levey 1962
Levey, Martin. "Medieval Arabic Bookmaking and its Relation to Early Chemistry and Pharmacology." *Transactions of the American Philosophical Society* 52, 4 (1962): 1–79.

Levey, Krek, Haddad 1956
Levey, Martin, Miroslav Krek, and Husni Haddad. "Some Notes on the Chemical Technology in an Eleventh Century Arabic Work on Bookbinding." *Isis* 47, 3 (1956): 239–43.

Lings 1978
Lings, Martin. *The Qur'anic Art of Calligraphy and Illumination*. London: World of Islam Festival Trust, 1978.

Loveday 2001
Loveday, Helen. *Islamic Paper: A Study of the Ancient Craft*. London: Don Baker Memorial Fund, Archetype Publications, 2001.

McWilliams and Roxburgh 2007
McWilliams, Mary, and David J. Roxburgh. *Traces of the Calligrapher: Islamic Calligraphy in Practice, c. 1600–1900*. Houston and New Haven: Museum of Fine Arts, Houston, and Yale University Press, 2007.

Necipoğlu 1995
Necipoğlu, Gülru. *The Topkapi Scroll—Geometry and Ornament in Islamic Architecture*. Santa Monica: Getty Center for the History of Art and the Humanities, 1995.

Ory 2000
Ory, Solange. "Du Coran Récité au Coran Calligraphié." *Arabica* 47 (2000): 366–80.

Porter 2011
Porter, Cheryl. "The Science of Color: Color Analysis and the Roles of Economics, Geography, and Tradition in the Artist's Choice of Colors for Manuscript Painting." In *And Diverse Are Their Hues: Color in Islamic Art and Culture*, edited by Jonathan Bloom and Sheila Blair, 205–222. New Haven and London: Yale University Press, 2011.

Porter 2018
Porter, Cheryl. "The Materiality of the Blue Quran: A Physical and Technological Study." In *The Aghlabids and their Neighbors: Material Culture in Ninth-Century North Africa*, edited by Glaire D. Anderson, Corisande Fenwick, and Mariam Rosser-Owen, 575–86. Leiden: Brill, 2018.

Porter 2021
Porter, Cheryl. "The Use of Metals in Islamic Manuscripts." In *The Making of Islamic Art: Studies in Honour of Sheila Blair and Jonathan Bloom*, edited by Robert Hillenbrand, 260–279. Edinburgh: Edinburgh University Press, 2021.

Porter Y 1989
Porter, Yves. "Une traduction persane de traité d'Ibn Bādis: 'Umdat al-kuttāb (c. 1025)." In *Les Manuscrits du Moyen-Orient: Essais de codicologie et de paléographie, Actes du Colloque d'Istanbul (May 1986), Varia Turcica* 8, 61–68. Istanbul and Paris: Institut Français and CNRS, 1989.

Porter Y 2003
Porter, Yves. "La réglure (mastar): de la 'formule d'atelier' aux jeux d'esprit." *Studia Islamica* 96 (2004): 55–74.

Qadi Ahmad 1959
Qāḍī Aḥmad. *Calligraphers and Painters: A Treatise by Qāḍī Aḥmad, Son of Mīr Munshī (Circa A.H. 1015/ A.D. 1606)*. Translated by V. Minorsky. *Freer Gallery of Art Occasional Papers* 3, 2. Washington, D.C.: Smithsonian Institution, 1959.

Rettig and Mirza 2023
Rettig, Simon, and Sana Mirza, eds. *The Word Illuminated: Form and Function of Qur'anic Manuscripts from the Seventh to Seventeenth Centuries*. Washington, D.C.: Smithsonian Scholarly Press, 2023.

Richard 2001
Richard, Francis. "Naṣr al-Solṭāni, Naṣir al-Din Mozahheb et la Bibliothèque d'Ebrāhim Solṭān à Širāz." *Studia Iranica* 30 (2001): 87–104.

Rosenthal 1947
Rosenthal, Franz. "Abu Haiyan al-Tawhidi on Penmanship." *Ars Islamica* 13–14 (1947): 1–20.

Roxburgh 2001
Roxburgh, David J. *Prefacing the Image: The Writing of Art History in Sixteenth-Century Iran*. Leiden: Brill, 2001.

Roxburgh 2003
Roxburgh, David J. "On the Transmission and Reconstruction of Arabic Calligraphy: Ibn al-Bawwab and History." *Studia Islamica* 96 (2003): 39–53.

Roxburgh 2005
Roxburgh, David J. *The Persian Album, 1400–1600: From Dispersal to Collection*. New Haven: Yale University Press, 2005.

Roxburgh 2007
Roxburgh, David J. *Writing the Word of God: Calligraphy and the Qur'an*. Houston and New Haven: Museum of Fine Arts, Houston, and Yale University Press, 2007.

Roxburgh 2008
Roxburgh, David J. "'The eye is favored for seeing the writing's form:' On the Sensual and the Sensuous in Islamic Calligraphy." *Muqarnas* 25 (2008): 275–98.

Sadan 1986
Sadan, Joseph. "Genizah and Genizah-Like Practices in Islamic and Jewish Traditions: Customs Concerning the Disposal of Worn-Out Sacred Books in the Middle Ages, According to an Ottoman Source." *Bibliotheca Orientalis* 43 (1986): 36–58.

Saleem 2010
Saleem, Shehzad. "Collection of the Qur'an: A Critical and Historical Study of al-Farāhi's View." PhD diss., University of Wales, Lampeter, 2010.

Scheper 2019
Scheper, Karin. *The Technique of Islamic Bookbinding: Methods, Materials, and Regional Varieties*. Leiden: Brill, 2019.

Schoeler 1997
Schoeler, Gregor. "Writing and Publishing on the Use and Function of Writing in the First Centuries of Islam." *Arabica* 44, 3 (1997): 423–35.

Schoeler 2010a
Schoeler, Gregor. "The Constitution of the Koran as a Codified Work: Paradigm for Codifying *Hadīth* and the Islamic Sciences?" *Oral Tradition* 25, 1 (2010): 199–210.

Schoeler 2010b
Schoeler, Gregor. "The Relationship of Literacy and Memory in the Second/Eighth Century." *Proceedings of the Seminar for Arabian Studies* 40 (2010): 121–29.

Schopen 2006
Schopen, Armin. *Tinten und Tuschen des arabisch-islamischen Mittelaters: Doukmentation-Analyse-Rekonstruction; ein Beitrag zur materiellen Kultur des Vorderen Orients*. Göttingen: Vandenhoek & Ruprecht, 2006.

Tabbaa 1992
Tabbaa, Yasser. "The Transformation of Arabic Writing: Part 1, Qur'ānic Calligraphy." *Ars Orientalis* 21 (1992): 119–48.

Thackston 2001
Thackston, Wheeler M. *Album Prefaces and Other Documents on the History of Calligraphers and Painters*. Leiden: Brill, 2001.

Watt 1950
Watt, W. M. "Early Discussions about the Qur'an." *Muslim World* 40 (1950): 27–40, 96–105.

Whelan 1998
Whelan, Estelle. "Forgotten Witness: Evidence for the Early Codification of the Qur'an." *Journal of the American Oriental Society* 118, 1 (1998): 1–14.

Zadeh 2008
Zadeh, Travis. "'Fire Cannot Harm It': Mediation, Temptation, and the Charismatic Power of the Qur'an." *Journal of Qur'anic Studies* 10, 2 (2008): 50–72.

Zadeh 2009
Zadeh, Travis. "Touching and Ingesting: Early Debates over the Material Qur'an." *Journal of the American Oriental Society* 129, 3 (2009): 443–66.

Zahrani 2009
Abdulsalam al-Zahrani. "Sacred Voice, Profane Sight: The Senses, Cosmology, and Epistemology in Early Islamic History." *Numen* 56, 4 (2009): 417–458.

Index

Note: Italic page numbers refer to illustrations.

Library of Congress Control Number: 2024909269

ISBN 978-0-300-27882-8

Produced by the Publications Department of
the Museum of Fine Arts, Houston
Editor: Melina Kervandjian
Index: Kay Banning
Cover and book design: Rita Jules, Miko McGinty Inc.
Typeset in Baskerville by Tina Henderson
Printed by PuritanCapital, New Hampshire

Photography by Neil Greentree with
Will Michels (pp. 9, 12,18, 25, 28, 30, 38, 48–49, 51, 74–75, 90–91, 99, 100–102, 110–111, 120–21, 123, 145, 188, 189–91, and 193)
and Ramon Perez (pp. 86–87)

Distributed by Yale University Press
New Haven and London
yalebooks.com/art

Frontispieces and separators:
Frontispiece: **Twelfth Part (*Juz'*) of a Qur'an Manuscript** (*detail, cat. 45*), signed by Ahmad al-Isfahani, Cairo, dated 10 Dhu al-Hijja AH 789/December 22, 1387 CE.
Table of Contents: **Qur'an Manuscript** (*detail, cat. 59*), signed by Mir ʿAbd al-Karim Muhammad Sadiq al-Husayni al-Yazdi, Iran, dated AH 1260/1844–45 CE.
Page 8: **Folio from the Nineteenth Part (*Juz'*) of a Qur'an Manuscript** (*detail, cat. 52*), Egypt or Iraq, 14th century.
Foreword: **Folio from the Ninth Part (*Juz'*) of a Qur'an Manuscript** (*detail, cat. 48*), North Africa or Central Islamic Lands, 9th–10th century.
Acknowledgments: **Illuminated Panel, Folio from a Qur'an Manuscript** (*detail, cat. 49*), North Africa or Central Islamic Lands, 9th–10th century.
Note to the Reader: **Folio from a Thirty-Part Qur'an Manuscript**, (*detail, cat. 37*), Anatolia, Iran, or Central Asia, early 14th century.
Map: **Map of the Islamic World** by Anandaroop Roy. Courtesy of The Metropolitan Museum of Art, originally published by The Metropolitan Museum of Art, New York. Copyright © 2022. Modified and reprinted by permission.
Page 16: **Folio from a Qur'an Manuscript** (*detail, cat. 43*), Central Islamic Lands, 14th century.
Pages 46–47: **Folio from a Qur'an Manuscript** (*detail, cat. 35*), Egypt, probably Cairo, late 13th–early 14th century.
Pages 48–49: **Folio from a Qur'an Manuscript** (*detail, cat. 1*), Saudi Arabia, possibly Medina, mid-7th century.
Pages 52–53: **Bifolio from a Qur'an Manuscript** (*detail, cat. 7*), North Africa or Central Islamic Lands, 9th century.
Pages 90–91: **Folio from a Qur'an Manuscript** (*detail, cat. 27*), Eastern Islamic Lands, 12th century.
Pages 110–11: **Lines from a Qur'an Manuscript** (*detail, cat. 38*), calligraphy attributed to Ahmad b. al-Shaykh al-Suhrawardi al-Bakri (d. 1320/21 CE), Iraq, Baghdad, probably AH 707/1307–8 CE.
Pages 142–43: **Illuminated Panel, Folio from a Qur'an Manuscript** (*detail, cat. 50*), North Africa or Central Islamic Lands, 9th–10th century.
Pages 158–59: **Qur'an Manuscript** (*detail, cat. 59*), signed by Mir ʿAbd al-Karim Muhammad Sadiq al-Husayni al-Yazdi, Iran, dated AH 1260/1844–45 CE.
Unless otherwise noted, all artworks are from the Hossein Afshar Collection at the Museum of Fine Arts, Houston.